PRETEND YOU'RE IN A WAR

MARK BLAKE is a former assistant editor of *Q* magazine and a long-time contributor to *Mojo*. He is the author of the definitive Pink Floyd biography, *Pigs Might Fly: The Inside Story of Pink Floyd*, as well as *Is This the Real Life? The Untold Story of Queen*, and edited *Stone Me: The Wit & Wisdom of Keith Richards* (all published by Aurum). He is also the editor of *Dylan: Visions, Portraits & Back Pages* and *Punk: The Whole Story*. He lives in London with his wife and son.

'Blake gives new reasons to appreciate the angst and theory behind The Who's music.' *Sunday Telegraph*

'The quality of research and analysis here is unsurprisingly of the highest standard...a superb biography.' Louder Than War

'A compelling read...and a story told with unflinching care and infectious enthusiasm.' *Classic Rock*

PRETEND YOU'RE IN A WAR
THE WHO AND THE SIXTIES

BY MARK BLAKE

Aurum
Press

First published in Great Britain
2014 by Aurum Press Ltd
74–77 White Lion Street
Islington
London N1 9PF
www.aurumpress.co.uk

ISBN 978 1 78131 523 1
EBOOK ISBN 978 1 78131 318 3

1 3 5 7 9 10 8 6 4 2
2015 2017 2019 2018 2016

Typeset in Spectrum MT by SX Composing DTP, Rayleigh, Essex
Printed by CPI Group (UK) Ltd, Croydon, CR0 4YY

CONTENTS

FOREWORD

Visitors to Pete Townshend's office in Richmond, south-west London, will find a gleaming Vespa scooter parked against one wall and the remains of a shattered electric guitar on another. In between are framed pop-art images and, on the table between us, a couple of Carnaby Street-style souvenir mugs. Wherever you sit in the room, the eye is drawn towards these visual reminders of the 1960s.

It is 3 October 2012, and Pete Townshend is talking about his soon-to-be published autobiography. Despite the surrounding objects, The Who's guitarist and songwriter hasn't tried to cling on to his youth. There's no sign of the Union flag jacket he wore on the cover of the *Observer* colour supplement in March 1966. Instead, Townshend favours an elegant waistcoat over a raffish pale pink shirt. These days, the nose that once seemed so prominent in that famous *Observer* photograph suits the sixty-seven-year-old face surrounding it.

Today, Townshend can't stop talking. In fact, he talks for two and a half hours, only pausing to sip from his souvenir mug. He talks about discovering there was a local criminal ('an awful, awful man') hiding under Roger Daltrey's bed when he auditioned for what became The Who, and he talks about how much he adored his ex-manager Kit Lambert ('even when I was punching him in the face'). He also talks about first wanting to write a book about his life, when he was twenty years old in 1965. 'About art, music and the post-war scene,' he says, almost wistfully. Inevitably, our conversation turns to the abuse he suffered as a child, and which has, subconsciously or otherwise, informed so much of his songwriting. 'I don't remember what happened,' he states emphatically, 'but I don't want to know all the details.'

What Townshend has to say is always fascinating, sometimes indiscreet, often amusing and occasionally sad. Some of his stories are probably exaggerated ('I saw a policeman murdered in front of me,' he claims at one point), their veracity lost to repetition and the passage of time. But it doesn't matter, because everything he says today is worth hearing.

This isn't the first time I've met Townshend or a member of The Who. Fifteen years earlier, I'd been asked to interview him and bass guitarist John Entwistle at the music magazine _Q_'s annual awards ceremony. That day, Townshend slipped away before anyone had the chance to speak to him, leaving Entwistle to collect The Who's award, and apologise for his absent bandmates, remarking drolly that only dead drummer Keith Moon had a valid excuse for not turning up.

Hours later, Entwistle was ensconced at a table in the tiny London club that was hosting the post-awards party. It was 1997, arguably the last boom year for Oasis, Blur and Britpop, and there were plenty of Who acolytes in the room. A stream of musicians and industry folk, many in a highly refreshed state, stopped by the table to offer their appreciation or mutely shake Entwistle's hand. The contents of the now-empty bottles of red wine on the table had left most of us feeling rather fuzzy, but Entwistle, whose glass was never less than half full, seemed unaffected.

Unfortunately, four decades spent in front of an earthshakingly loud PA system had left The Who's bass player partially deaf, and he now spoke in a low, lugubrious drawl. Still, Entwistle served up anecdotes about The Who's wild years like a seasoned after-dinner speaker, giving his admirers, with their imitation Keith Moon haircuts and pretend drug habits, what they wanted to hear.

Nine years later, Entwistle had passed away, and I found myself waiting for what was left of The Who at another _Q_ awards bash. This time it was Townshend and lead vocalist Roger Daltrey. That afternoon, Townshend ignored my greeting, preferring to stare through me as if he'd glimpsed a ghost on the other side. I wasn't offended or surprised. One of The Who's confidantes had told me that he could ascertain within two seconds of Pete Townshend entering a room what kind of mood he was in, and that it wasn't always a good one. Today was one of those days.

Townshend had fought and won some well-publicised battles with drugs and alcohol, and in 2003 he had been arrested after admitting to using his credit card to try and access online child pornography. He told the police and the press that he'd been researching his auto-biography and attempting to work through his childhood traumas. A year earlier, though, Townshend had published an essay on his website in which he'd mentioned his childhood abuse, expressing his outrage at the ease with which illegal pornography was available online. When no incriminating evidence was found on any of his computers, Townshend was released without charge. But, at this meeting, his doleful expression and glum silence suggested he was carrying the weight of the world on his shoulders.

In contrast, Daltrey, with his wiry physique and drill sergeant's demeanour, resembled a man who'd spent the past forty years doing a hundred sit-ups before breakfast and strictly observing NHS guidelines on alcohol intake. In recent years Daltrey had started wearing tinted spectacles of the kind only worn by other members of the rock aristoc-racy. They offered a subtle barrier against the rest of the world, but Daltrey was as loud as Townshend was quiet. He shook hands, laughed easily and answered questions he'd been asked countless times before, always about the past.

I would meet and interview Daltrey again several times over the coming years. What emerged from these encounters, and from inter-views with Entwistle and Townshend, is how The Who carried the past around with them, almost like another member of the band. It had been this way forever. By the end of the 1960s, a mythology had grown up around The Who, fuelled by tall tales of violence and hedonism, all of which seemed to go hand in hand with 'My Generation' and 'I Can't Explain'; songs that defined both The Who and the era.

Townshend has never taken the approach favoured by his contem-porary Mick Jagger, who cuts short too much talk about the old days with the words: 'That was a *long* time ago.' A 'long time ago' is a subject Pete Townshend can never escape from, because it still has so much bearing on his music, even in the present day.

What Townshend and Jagger, like John Lennon, Paul McCartney, Ray Davies and every figurehead of British 1960s pop have in common is a childhood and adolescence lived in the shadow of the Second World

War. More so than the Rolling Stones, The Beatles or The Kinks, though, it is The Who whose music has been most shaped by this post-war landscape and its often-damaged inhabitants.

For The Who, growing up in the 1940s and 1950s, the past was somewhere to escape from – but it was inescapable. It was there every day in the faces of their relatives and neighbours. 'We felt deeply affected,' said Townshend, 'and our parents and our grandparents had been deeply affected.' It was there in *The Dambusters*, *The Cruel Sea* and every other flag-waving war film screened at their local fleapit cinemas. And it was there in the tales of wartime heroism splashed across the comics they read, and in the bloody battles they re-enacted on the bombed-out ruins that surrounded their homes.

The 1960s was an era of reinvention that saw a concerted attempt to right the wrongs of previous decades. The music The Who made in the 1960s aspired to this brave new world, while still being haunted by the smoking battles of the old one. It was a music that grew out of bomb sites, ration books and unspoken childhood secrets, but also the great social and artistic changes sweeping through the new decade.

As Townshend and Daltrey, the last surviving members of The Who, celebrate the band's fiftieth anniversary with a world tour, the world in which they grew up slips further away from living memory, but still exerts a gravitational pull on everything they do. The paraphernalia that surrounds Pete Townshend in his office is a permanent reminder of where they came from. 'I'm like a cracked vinyl record,' he tells me. 'Post-war, post-war, post-war.' But it's also a reminder of what they've achieved since.

The story of The Who in the 1960s is the story of rock music in its infancy, and of a youthful band creating a new order from the wreckage of the old. As Townshend, the tireless storyteller, once said: 'The past is a great romantic adventure. You're never as interesting as you were when you were young.'

CHAPTER ONE
COINS AND BONES

'All the old soldiers coming back from war and screwing until they were blue in the face – this was the result. Thousands and thousands of kids, not enough teachers, not enough parents, not enough pills to go around . . .'

Pete Townshend, 1968

'Dulled by such extensive drabness, monotony, ignorance and wretchedness that one is overcome by distress.'

C.B. Purdom's description of London, 1946
How Shall We Rebuild London?

He smuggled the shotgun into the club under his jacket. He was a petty criminal from Shepherd's Bush with a score to settle, and he'd followed the trail from west London to The Who's gig at the Marquee in Soho. The weapon's sawn-off barrel was pressed against his ribs; its vague tang of metal and grease masked by the overriding fug of stale sweat and cigarette smoke inside the venue.

He squinted at 'the faces' in the shadows, looking for his adversary. His plan was simple: to shoot the man he believed had wronged him. Eventually he blundered into the Marquee's tiny dressing room, and found his friend, the group's lead singer Roger Daltrey.

The gunman and the pop star shared the same tough upbringing. Daltrey knew how easy it was to get drawn into the criminal world; he knew too that his friend wasn't one to make idle threats. But he gently persuaded him to forget about taking his revenge, and to hand over the weapon. 'It was a sawn-off shotgun,' Daltrey recalled, fifty years later, 'and I took it away from him.' The rest of The Who watched the exchange, terrified that the would-be killer would lose his temper and turn the gun on them, but also impressed that their singer had the nerve to talk him down.

When they finally went onstage the band exhibited a violence all their own. At the climax of their set, the four young men began to systematically destroy their equipment with scant regard for their own safety or that of the audience. Pete Townshend, the beanpole skinny guitarist, plunged the head of his instrument into his amplifier, inducing a wail of piercing feedback much like an air-raid siren.

Beside him, the permanently scowling Daltrey added to the din by striking the head of his microphone against the drummer's cymbals. The drummer, Keith Moon, his cheeks flushed with exertion, kicked his bass drum across the stage before attacking the rest of his kit. Only John Entwistle, the bass guitarist with a shock of dyed black hair, failed to participate in the destruction, preferring to stand back and observe the chaos.

The noise was overwhelming and disorientating, and some of the audience had instinctively backed away from the stage. The girls had stopped dancing, and the boys, many of whom had taken amphetamines, stared boggle-eyed, jaws grinding, at the violent pageant unfolding in front of them. With their amps howling and their ruined instruments strewn across the stage, The Who turned their backs on the crowd and trooped back to the dressing room.

It was late 1964. Many years later, an inquisitive journalist would ask Pete Townshend how he'd prepared for such aggressive live performances. Townshend's answer would be simple and to the point: 'Pretend you're in a war.'

Turmoil, noise and chaos seemed to follow The Who from the very beginning. Pete Townshend and his future bandmates had all been born during or immediately after the Second World War, into a capital city whose buildings and people had been bombed out and brutalised by the recent conflict.

Lead singer, Roger Daltrey, was the first to appear. But his arrival was anything but easy. Roger's father, Harry Daltrey, was born in 1911 in Stowe Road, Shepherd's Bush, west London, and was the son of a bus conductor. Roger's mother, Grace Stone (but known to everyone by her middle name, Irene) came from Fulham. The couple married in 1936 and set up home in Shepherd's Bush.

'The Bush' was some five miles to the west of central London and had been a largely rural area until the mid-nineteenth century. Its name was derived from the fact that it was once a resting ground for shepherds driving their flocks east to Smithfield Market. The grand Shepherd's Bush Empire Theatre opened on Shepherd's Bush Green in 1903 and hosted the great music hall acts of the day, among them Fred Karno, whose troupe of comedians included a young Stan Laurel and Charlie Chaplin. Five years later came the 68,000-capacity White City Stadium in time for the Summer Olympics.

By the mid-1930s, commerce and jobs had brought more people into the area. Before long, London County Council had proposed the building of what would become the White City Estate, to house Shepherd's Bush's ever-expanding population.

A year after the Daltreys' marriage, Irene was diagnosed with kidney disease. After one of her kidneys was removed, her health deteriorated further and she was diagnosed with polyneuritis, an inflammation of the nerves, which led to polio. Barely able to move, she spent two months at the infectious diseases hospital in Fulham, confined to an 'iron lung', a body-length medical ventilator that enabled her to breathe. When Irene was released from hospital, she had limited movement in her legs and hands and was forced to use a wheelchair in which she would remain for the next few years.

The couple moved into rented rooms at 15 Percy Road, a three-storey house on a narrow avenue off Uxbridge Road, the main thoroughfare running through Shepherd's Bush. With the outbreak of the Second World War, Harry was drafted into the Royal Artillery, but granted regular compassionate leave to spend time with his sick wife. Against all expectation, Irene became pregnant in the summer of 1943 at the age of thirty-two. The start of the following year, however, saw the German Luftwaffe commence their second major bombing campaign over London, following on from the first, known as 'the Blitz', which claimed the lives of almost 20,000 Londoners between summer 1940 and spring 1941.

Irene spent many fitful nights during her pregnancy huddled in the over-crowded, subterranean air-raid shelter at Shepherd's Bush tube station. She was there, listening to the eerie rumbling of another raid overhead, when she first thought she was going into labour. Wardens helped her up to the street, where an ambulance braved the latest onslaught and raced her to nearby Hammersmith Hospital. It was a false alarm. Roger Harry Daltrey finally appeared a week later in the small hours of 1 March 1944.

Any hopes Irene had of bringing her son up in a safe environment were soon dashed. Two months after Daltrey was born, Germany launched its first V-1 flying bomb offensive over London. The V-1 was an airborne, jet-propelled device, nicknamed 'the Doodlebug' after the buzzing drone of its engine. Worse still was the deathly silence that followed as the engine cut out and the bomb began its descent.

On 16 June more than three hundred doodlebugs were launched on the south of England in what Germany called 'the day of vengeance'. By the end of the month, V-1 strikes had claimed the lives of hundreds of civilians and military personnel in explosions at Victoria railway station, the Wellington Barracks in London's Birdcage Walk, close to Buckingham Palace, and the Air Ministry in Aldwych, near the West End.

Shepherd's Bush wasn't spared either. It was now commonplace for Irene and her neighbours to emerge from the tube station after another raid to see charred towers of brick where houses had once stood, or buildings with their fronts torn away, revealing the rooms inside, eerily still intact. After flying bombs set the Pavilion Theatre near Shepherd's Bush Green ablaze and ripped through buildings in Percy Road, including the house next door to number 15, Irene refused to tempt fate any longer.

Harry Daltrey had been posted back overseas, and his wife decided to join the thousands voluntarily evacuated out of the cities and into the countryside. Mother and son moved to an isolated farmhouse in the Scottish coastal town of Stranraer. Living conditions were spartan and Irene was still struggling with poor health, but it proved to be a wise move.

In September, Germany began launching V-2 long-distance ballistic missiles on London. The V-2 was even more devastating than its prede-cessor. The first warhead landed just two miles away from Shepherd's

Bush in Chiswick, and its impact was felt almost ten miles north in Islington. Other warheads would follow, leaving a trail of devastation across the capital. Yet despite the carnage, allied forces were gradually closing in on Germany's rocket-launching sites. In June, allied troops landed on the beaches at Normandy and began the slow, but determined invasion of German-occupied Europe. The allies were winning the war. On Palm Sunday in March the following year, the last V-2 landed in London's Tottenham Court Road, decimating Whitefield's Tabernacle church; it was the beginning of the end.

By the time the Führer, Adolf Hitler, turned a gun on himself on 30 April 1945, hastening Germany's surrender, more than 62,000 British civilians, nearly half of them Londoners, had been killed. Irene Daltrey and her one-year-old boy returned to a city that been irrevocably changed by six years of warfare.

Lance Corporal Harry Daltrey was demobbed from the army and came home to a son who had no idea who he was. 'That was my very first memory – of my dad coming back from the war in his tin helmet,' recalled Daltrey, who was also surprised when he saw this stranger climbing into bed with his mother. After a spell working as an insurance clerk, Harry found a job at Shanks, a bathroom fittings company on an industrial estate in nearby Acton.

Daltrey once described his early childhood as 'a wonderful period'. But the streets around Shepherd's Bush that he and his friends would explore were still piled with debris from the German rocket strikes, and the conflict had taken a toll on its survivors. 'My parents never talked about the real things that had happened in the war,' he said. 'Our parents were repressed and had had the stuffing knocked out of them. They were shell-shocked.'

The infant Daltrey had escaped the doodlebugs, but a harmless game in peacetime would lead to a near-death experience when he was just four years old. 'My dad and I were playing a game called Hide the Nail,' he said, 'and I thought, "I'll get him" . . . So I ate the nail.' Daltrey was rushed to Hammersmith Hospital where the nail was removed from his intestine. But the surgery was problematic, and left him with a prominent scar. Rust from the nail would result in an ulcer and a further spell in hospital, followed by a lifetime of intermittent stomach problems, although the teenage Daltrey would wear his scar with pride.

Against Irene's doctors' expectations, the Daltrey family grew with the arrival of two daughters, Gillian in 1946 and Carol a year later. Irene's sister and her offspring occupied the other rooms at 15 Percy Road, and would join the rest of the clan on summer holidays to Clacton-on-Sea in Essex. 'We were a fabulous big working-class London family,' said Daltrey, who would often refer to his working-class roots when interviewed in The Who. 'It was post-war England. People say, "everyone was very poor", but I never felt we were poor. We had an incredible social structure that supported us.'

Britain's new Prime Minister Clement Attlee and his pioneering Labour government had begun the enormous task of both physically and emotionally rebuilding a damaged country. Coming to power in the summer of 1945, with the slogan 'Let Us Face the Future', they would implement some of the widest-reaching social reforms of the twentieth century, not least of which included creating a publicly funded national health system. But in the meantime, food and luxuries remained in scant supply.

Thirteen months living on a remote farm and surviving on a meagre wartime diet had left its mark on Daltrey. As a child he suffered from rickets and bow legs. '1944 and 1945 were the worst years of the war,' he said. 'There was no food in the parlour, and even the bread was half-chalk.' The Ministry of Food had devised this ruse to bulk out loaves and make them appear whiter. Daltrey was even convinced that his reduced stature, five foot, six inches, as an adult was a result of rationing: 'Look at anyone born in 1944 in the working class. We're all short.'

In 1967, Daltrey would be photographed in a bath filled with Heinz baked beans for the front cover of the album *The Who Sell Out*. It was an eye-catching image but one far removed from his early childhood, where bread, potatoes, sweets and clothes were rationed on and off until 1954. The singer later claimed that his 'war baby' upbringing also made him uneasy when the rest of The Who began destroying guitars and hotel rooms: 'I'd had to fight too hard for anything I had in my life.'

In 1950, Daltrey became a pupil at Victoria Junior Boys School on the corner of Beckton Road, barely a minute's walk from his family home. In 1994 Pete Townshend described the young Daltrey as 'a tough guy and a local hard nut', but there is little evidence of a thuggish reputation in his early schooldays. Instead, Daltrey was remembered as a conscientious pupil. His form teacher Mr Blake at Victoria Junior Boys recorded: 'A boy of wide interests – practical, intellectual, musical and athletic,' in his 1955 report, with only a mention of Daltrey's participation in the school choir and a recent boxing tournament giving any indication of where his future interests might lie.

At home, the only music Daltrey heard was what was playing on the radio. 'It was the era of the crooners on the BBC,' he said. 'That was it. We couldn't afford records. People couldn't in those days. We'd only just got the roofs and windows back in the houses after all the bombings.' Instead, Daltrey played cricket and football, collected stamps, built a train set, sang in church and played the trumpet for the Boys' Brigade, the popular Christian youth organisation, whose objectives when founded in the nineteenth century were to promote 'habits of obedience, reverence, discipline and self-respect'. He was also academically bright.

In the summer of 1955, Daltrey scored highly in his Eleven Plus, the examination sat by all eleven year olds in England and Wales to determine whether they qualified for a place at a grammar school, technical school or secondary modern. So coveted were grammar school places that the Eleven Plus was regarded less as a gauge of a child's natural ability and more as an intelligence test that would determine their path through life. Those who 'passed' were whisked away into the grammar school system and considered to have had a head start over those who supposedly 'failed' and were educated elsewhere.

Daltrey's exam result led to him being offered a place at Acton County Grammar School. It was a pivotal moment, but perhaps not in the way that his parents had hoped. After a promotion at Shanks, Harry Daltrey moved the family out of the cramped rooms at Percy Road and into a rented house at 135 Fielding Road in more upmarket Bedford Park, Acton.

The new house was barely two miles from Percy Road, but this upheaval combined with the move to a new school left Daltrey feeling displaced. 'It was as if everything had changed,' he said. 'And suddenly I found myself in a place where I didn't fit in. Nobody spoke the way I did. Nobody seemed to be like me.' This sense of displacement would only increase. As Daltrey bluntly explained: 'From then on, it all turned to shit.'

In later life, John Entwistle sometimes told interviewers that he was born during the Blitz, and to the sound of Hitler's bombs falling on the surrounding streets. In fact, The Who's bass guitarist missed the Blitz by almost three years. Nevertheless, Entwistle's childhood neighbourhood of Chiswick, close to Shepherd's Bush, felt the force of the V-1 and V-2 bombing campaigns throughout the summer and autumn of 1944.

John's father, Herbert, was born in 1915 in Wheelton, a small mill town near Chorley in Lancashire. Herbert's unmarried mother, Mary Ellen, had worked since childhood as a rag sorter in the local paper mill. There was no father listed on Herbert's birth certificate, so he was given Mary's family name, Entwistle. As soon as he was legally old enough, Herbert enlisted in the Royal Navy. 'He played the trumpet in the Navy band, and he played in brass bands,' said John later, 'and he ended up singing in a Welsh male voice choir.'

Herbert married eighteen-year-old Queenie Maude Lee in 1941 in Brentford, west London. John Alec Entwistle was born three years later on 9 October 1944 in Hammersmith Hospital, the same facility in which Roger Daltrey had made his arrival seven months previously. Herbert returned from wartime service, but the marriage wasn't to last. After eighteen months, Queenie took the infant John to live with her parents in their flat at 81 Southfield Road, three minutes' walk from where the Daltreys would later end up living, in Bedford Park.

Queenie played the piano, and had performed with a semi-professional band. By the time John was three, he was singing the world-famous vaudeville performer Al Jolson's hits 'Sonny Boy' and 'My Mammy' for friends and family. After being taken by Queenie to see a Jolson film at the cinema, John burst into spontaneous song as soon as the singer appeared on the screen. To his mother's surprise, the cinema's other patrons told her to let the little boy carry on singing. Later, John's grandfather would take him to a local working men's club, where the toddler would stand on a chair and perform while a cap was passed around for loose change.

These impromptu performances continued until John accidentally toppled off a bar-stool and gashed his face open. Piano lessons were considered a safer, if less financially rewarding, option – but Entwistle loathed them. Week after week, he would sit down with his piano teacher to try and learn his scales. The room in which she taught him reportedly 'stank of cats', and she 'had fingers like spoons', he said darkly.

From the age of five, John attended Southfield Primary School, a five-minute walk from his grandparents' maisonette, at the far end of Southfield Road. As well as his musical ability, it was here that his artistic talents were first noticed. Twenty-five years later Entwistle drew the artwork for the album *The Who by Numbers*, and his cartoons and sketches were exhibited in numerous exhibitions throughout his later life.

Aged seven, Entwistle and his classmates went on a day trip to the coastal town of Dartmouth, to sketch the annual regatta. Entwistle drew caricatures of his teachers instead. An over-zealous schoolfriend showed one to their teacher, expecting John to be punished. Instead, the headmaster asked Entwistle to finish the drawing and enter it in the school's art competition, where it won first prize.

Back in Acton, the bombed-out ruins and wasteground became a makeshift playground for Entwistle and his friends. Piles of rubble and bricks from war-torn buildings could be turned into anything the imagination conjured up: a medieval castle, a cowboy's ranch . . . 'It was like having toys everywhere,' said Entwistle. The war was still fresh in everyone's memory, especially the children born into it: 'I remember there was an old warehouse on the other side of the railway tracks that was full of German helmets. So we'd get a helmet each and play Nazis.'

When he turned eleven, Entwistle abandoned the hated piano lessons and his spoon-fingered teacher, and took up the trumpet. 'It was a more glamorous instrument, and I was better with it,' he said. 'My father taught me, and I played the trumpet until I was fourteen.' Like Daltrey before him, Entwistle joined the Boys' Brigade.

In 1953, the Entwistle family unit would be shaken up by a new arrival, Queenie's second husband, Charles Johns. 'John's stepfather was a good guy,' said Pete Townshend, who also added abstrusely, 'but John hated him, until he grew up.' In reality, Entwistle was simply confused by the appearance of this interloper, and feared that he would no longer be able to spend time with his biological father.

The new marriage prompted a move into a house at 17 Lexden Road, to the north of Acton and close to Ealing. One of their new neighbours was a drummer named Teddy Fullager, whom Queenie had known since her schooldays. Fullager was putting together a dance band and, impressed by the schoolboy Entwistle, invited him to play second trumpet with the group for their regular Saturday night bookings. There was just one caveat: the band was required to wear dress suits.

The only suitable clothes the twelve-year-old Entwistle owned were his school uniform and his Boys' Brigade cap and tunic. Fullager passed down one of his father's old moth-eaten suits, which Queenie's mother diligently repaired and altered. With the suit's holes patched up and the sleeves shortened, Entwistle made his debut with Fullager's dance band. He had performed in public with the Boys' Brigade, but this was different. This was an adult audience, fuelled by alcohol and nicotine, and buzzing with sexual tension. It was a portent of his life to come with The Who.

In one of his characteristically quixotic interviews, Pete Townshend recalled being four years old and playing with a friend in his garden, before climbing through a hole in the fence and wandering on to the playing fields at Acton County Grammar School. 'I remember dozens of blue-uniformed boys tumbling down the stairs and gathering around us,' he claimed. 'They were friendly, and I decided then that I would attend that school.'

Attending Acton County, though, was still several years away. In 1949, the four-year-old Townshend was living with his parents in their ground-floor flat, blissfully unaware of the emotional upheaval that was about to blight his life. That upheaval would later provide an essential emotional motor for The Who's music. But for Townshend, the trauma was a personal dividing line: there was his life before and then there was his life after.

Unlike Daltrey and Entwistle, Townshend's background was anything but conventional. His family had been involved in show business and entertainment for three generations going back to the mid-nineteenth century. His paternal grandfather Horace, known as Horry, had been a semi-professional musician and songwriter, who also played woodwind in the Jack Shepperd Concert Party, a troupe that later featured the famous music-hall comedian Max Miller.

In 1908 Horace married dancer and singer Dorothy 'Dot' Blandford, whose father had performed as a black-and-white minstrel. Dot worked as a soubrette, a comic singer and performer, in a cabaret act. The pair formed a partnership and busked, sang and acted in seaside venues every summer in the years leading up to the First World War.

After marrying, they settled in Hammersmith, west London. Their second son, Clifford, was born in 1916. By the time he turned sixteen, 'Cliff' was playing the clarinet for tips at house parties and in pubs, which led to his expulsion from school. Soon after, he joined one of the many dance bands playing around London's Soho, performing regularly at the Stork Club, a cabaret bar on Swallow Street through which numerous famous performers – including drag artist Danny La Rue – would pass in the 1950s and 1960s.

In his autobiography, *Who I Am,* Townshend revealed that his father had once been a 'blackshirt', the nickname given to supporters of the British Union of Fascists and their leader Oswald Mosley. In 1978, Townshend told the music magazine *Trouser Press* that 'Fascism had been quite an acceptable thing in this country under Oswald Mosley . . .' and how his father, 'as a kid, used to goosestep down the street. Then the war broke out and everybody knew that it was the thing to fight.'

When Britain and France declared war on Germany, Cliff enlisted in the RAF, eventually rising to the rank of lance corporal. In time, he became a clarinettist and saxophonist in the RAF Dance Orchestra, an ensemble led by his schoolfriend, pianist Ronnie Aldrich. Cliff landed the job after Vera Lynn's husband, fellow RAF saxophonist Harry Lewis, turned it down. By day, the musicians performed regular RAF duties; and in the evenings, they played morale-boosting concerts for the troops, mixing up everything from romantic ballads to swing and jazz.

A nation at war needed light relief, a distraction from the horrors raging around them. In 1941 the RAF Dance Orchestra's recording of the smooth foxtrot ballad *There's Something in the Air* became a radio hit. That same year, the musicians' bible *Melody Maker* declared a BBC broadcast of one of the orchestra's shows as 'the greatest dance band performance ever broadcast this side of the Atlantic'. Two years later, the band's blaring call-to-arms *Commando Patrol* would be heard in filmmakers Michael Powell and Emeric Pressburger's military comic drama *The Life and Death of Colonel Blimp*.

'My dad's band were up there with the Sid Phillips band, the Ted Heath band and the Joe Loss Orchestra,' explained Pete Townshend. 'They were like the pop stars of the day, and my dad looked a bit like Cary Grant.' Among the Orchestra's featured vocalists later on was Ruby Murray, described by Pete Townshend as 'the notoriously wild, red-haired singer'.

When another of their glamorous female singers cried off sick, the band recruited twenty-one-year-old Betty Dennis. She'd joined the RAF after lying about her age, while still a teenager, and had sung with another popular wartime ensemble, the Sidney Torch Orchestra. Cliff and Betty married after just seven weeks. In truth, they'd only spent seven days together – the seven consecutive Sundays that Betty was booked to sing with the orchestra – but at a time of war and such uncertainty, it seemed pointless to wait. The couple wed in Pontypool, South Wales, in the spring of 1944.

Like her husband, Betty also came from a musical family. Her parents, Maurice and Emma, had both been singers and performers, working in music hall and cabaret acts, but the couple split up when Betty was still a child. Emma moved out to live with a wealthy boyfriend, leaving Betty and her brother with their cuckolded father. Emma, later known as Grandma Denny, would return to cast a formidable shadow over The Who guitarist's childhood.

According to Pete Townshend, 'I was conceived in Wales,' but Peter Dennis Blandford Townshend made his entrance on 19 May 1945 in an annexe of the West Middlesex Hospital in Isleworth, a west London suburb close to Heathrow Airport. Unlike Daltrey's and Entwistle's births, there wasn't a German bombing raid to herald Townshend's arrival. Two weeks earlier, London had rejoiced at the news of victory in Europe.

As Townshend would often tell interviewers, he came into the world during the same hour that Hitler's Minister for Armaments, Albert Speer, was arrested. He later wrote in his autobiography, *Who I Am*: 'I am a war baby, though I have never known war. Yet war – and its syncopated echoes – the sirens, booms and blasts carouse, waltz and unsettle me while I am still in my mother's womb.'

Cliff Townshend missed his son's birth. Once the war was over, the RAF Dance Orchestra changed their name to The Squadronaires and carried on working. They were too popular to consider giving up. The band took a year's engagement at a British army barracks in Germany. On the night of Pete's arrival, a motorcycle messenger drove into the venue where the Squadronaires were playing, scooted up to the stage in front of Cliff and shouted 'It's a boy!' Those same three words would return as a song title on The Who's *Tommy* album.

On the surface, his parents' show-business lives might have suggested they had been spared the horrors of the previous six years, but it wasn't so. 'My mum told me that she went to see my dad in Bath and Bristol, and the place where he was playing was bombed,' said Townshend, 'and they pulled out bits of bodies from the rubble. This was happening on a daily basis.' Like Roger Daltrey's description of his 'shell-shocked' parents stoically getting on with their lives, reluctant to discuss what had happened, Townshend's family were also tight-lipped about what they'd survived. 'It's just bizarre,' he said, 'suddenly the war is over – and this idea that they go on living their lives after what they'd seen.'

Cliff's long absences soon impacted on his marriage, though. For a time Betty and the infant Pete moved into a bedsit with another musical couple and their young child. 'My mum was a post-war mum,' reflected Townshend. 'She'd driven trucks, got married too young to this handsome man and was worried that it wouldn't work.'

The presence of other adults meant that Betty had someone else to help look after her son. Her own musical career had stalled; a situation exacerbated by motherhood. But Betty was also barely twenty-three years old, and with her husband away, had no shortage of male admirers – her son among them.

'I used to see my mother as this fantastically glamorous figure who kind of shot in and out in a different outfit,' said Townshend. In later years, Townshend would refer to 'this fantastically glamorous figure . . . with long, dark hair, deep gypsy eyes and sinewy calves in seamed stockings.' Over time, his relationship with his mother would become fiery and unpredictable, and strafed with resentment on both sides. Later, the image of the beautiful but aloof female would reappear in his songwriting.

Eventually, Townshend's parents were reconciled after Cliff promised to spend more time with the family. Betty and Pete left the bedsit and moved with Cliff into a ground-floor maisonette at 22 Whitehall Gardens, close to Ealing Common. Now when Cliff went on the road, he took his wife and son with him. On weekday nights, The Squadronaires played provincial ballrooms; at the weekend they'd perform at variety shows where they shared the bill with comedians, magicians and that most glamorous of all performers, visiting American singers.

In Ealing, the four-year-old Townshend began attending the local fee-paying Silverdale Nursery School. A year later, he took up a place at another private establishment, Beacon House School. Cliff Townshend's dance band wages stretched to paying his son's school fees, but this was no guarantee of academic advancement. Townshend struggled in class. While others progressed, he remained a poor reader and writer. He would later talk of feeling isolated from the other pupils, in their expensive bright-red uniforms. Instead he gravitated towards a neighbour's son, Graham Beard – nicknamed 'Jimpy' after a cartoon character in the *Daily Mirror* – and his gang of friends.

'Jimpy and I went everywhere together,' he said. The pair re-enacted the cowboy films, cartoons and slapstick comedies they saw at the cinema, and roamed the neighbourhood's bomb sites. According to Townshend, 'twelve people had died' at 22 Whitehall Gardens during the war. It was a macabre fact that would cross his mind as he and Jimpy looked for treasure in the shells of countless bombed-out buildings. Like Entwistle and his booty of German soldiers' helmets, Townshend dug through the rubble and unearthed watches, coins, bones and 'sad things, like a teddy bear and other children's toys'. The war was still there, all around them.

Meanwhile, Betty had reluctantly given up her singing career, and now helped to run The Squadronaires' West End office. During the summer holidays, she and her son would join the band on their tour bus, heading off to seaside theatres, ballrooms and holiday camps. Touring with The Squadronaires plunged Townshend into what he called 'an extremely adult world, full of men drinking, beautiful women and wild behaviour'. It was a glimpse into the life he'd later live with The Who. 'What I remember the most was the celebration of alcohol,' he said. 'There were also a couple of guys on the bus in the latter years that smoked Jamaican weed. So you'd also have this funny smell coming down the aisle. But everything about it seemed glamorous to me as a small child.'

In the evenings, Townshend would be allowed to roam around the dance halls, collecting the musicians' empty beer bottles and eavesdropping on their grown-up conversations in the dressing rooms. When the show began, he would watch from the side of the stage or from the edges of the dance floor, the only child in an adult world, weaving unnoticed between the legs of dinner-suited men and enchanting women in huge petticoat dresses.

The Squadronaires' repertoire was wide ranging. They played the jazz of Gene Krupa, Count Basie and Duke Ellington and the swing hits of Glenn Miller, the superstar American bandleader whose plane had crashed over the English Channel in 1944, snuffing out a glittering career. They also performed tunes from morale-boosting wartime Hollywood musicals and the romantic ballads of Irving Berlin and Jerome Kern. 'They were songs about hope,' explained Townshend, 'and the restoration of romance.' They were songs designed to raise the spirits in an uncertain peacetime just as they'd done during the war.

Everyone and everything around The Squadronaires seemed steeped in an impossible glamour. 'Sometimes when we were away, my mum and dad would take me round to see one of their fabulous American officer mates,' he recalled. Visiting these US Air Force bases, Townshend glimpsed a world far removed from Britain's ration-book culture. 'We would sit in these officers' fabulous houses with their fabulous cars outside, and there would be loads of food about, and they'd have food we didn't have, like sugar.'

The innocent excitement of these early years, touring with his father's band, was short-lived. That turning point in Townshend's early life was imminent. After the summer of 1951 nothing would ever be quite the same.

News had reached Betty that her mother, Emma Dennis, was experiencing what Townshend described as 'some kind of breakdown', prompted by a combination of the menopause and the collapse of a relationship. 'She'd been the mistress of some industrialist who'd set her up down there in a love nest and then dumped her,' he said.

When Townshend was four he'd stayed with Grandma Denny for a time at her house in Kent. 'I enjoyed it,' he said, 'which, presumably, is why my mother thought it would be OK to send me to live with her later when she was going nuts.' It was an extraordinarily misguided idea. But Betty believed that her mother's state of mind might improve if she had the responsibility of looking after her grandson. Later, Townshend would discover that his mother's judgement was partly clouded by the fractious state of her relationship with Cliff and the fact that she was about to embark on an affair. In reality, history was repeating itself, and she was abandoning her son, albeit temporarily, in the same way that Denny had once abandoned her.

So it was that Pete Townshend was sent to live with his maternal grandmother, beginning what he later called 'the darkest part of my life'. When Denny was still with her lover, he'd paid for her to live in a luxurious bungalow. Now she was forced to rent a small flat above a shop in Westgate-on-Sea, a few miles from Margate on the Kent coast. Townshend moved into the second bedroom and was enrolled at the local St Saviour's Church of England Junior School.

He would remain with Denny until summer 1952, in an environment marred by neglect, cruelty and a hazy, unspecified, but possibly sexual, abuse. He struggled to fit in at St Saviour's, and later spoke of pupils being caned almost for the amusement of the other children. But life was even worse at his grandmother's flat.

Denny would frequently hit her grandson and deny him food as punishment for any minor misdemeanours. At bath time she would scrub his body until the skin was sore, and held his head under the water for so long he once feared he would drown. 'I was always being locked in the metaphorical cupboard under the stairs,' as Townshend put it. 'There was physical brutality and frequent punishment. But there was also this lascivious underlying sense of bizarre smutty eroticism around her life.'

Denny's estranged boyfriend's parting gift had been a fur coat that she now wore as a dressing gown. 'It was from some incredible London furrier and she kept wanting people to see the label,' said Townshend. 'She would open it and forget that she was naked underneath. It created this bizarre, embarrassing situation. On one occasion she was found walking down the street naked.'

Denny would also visit the bus garage opposite her flat, chatting and flirting with the drivers, always draped in the omnipresent fur coat. Sometimes Townshend would be sent over in his pyjamas, ferrying cups of teas to whichever employee had caught her eye. 'She was always pursuing these drivers or else the airmen at the US airbase,' he said. 'Sometimes we would do these unbelievable forced marches. She would wake up at four o'clock in the morning and then get me up, and at five we would walk all the way from Westgate to Manston Airport just to meet some fucking US officer. She would pursue these handsome US servicemen, giving them food and trying to get something from them. But I could never work out what we got.'

For many years Townshend could barely recall anything about his time in Westgate: 'One of the things that has been so strange is to have such extraordinarily vivid early memories of my childhood which stop within a few weeks of being sent to stay with Denny.'

These gaps in his memory would be one of the spurs behind his decision to have therapy in later life. During one therapy session in the 1980s, Townshend was disturbed to recall a visit to an American serviceman that ended with him getting into the man's car. What happened next remains a mystery. 'I began shaking uncontrollably,' he said, 'and couldn't remember anything else.'

Denny also had male visitors at the flat: there was, Townshend wrote later, a 'half-deaf' man whom he was instructed to call 'Uncle'. 'She had these weird blokes to stay who would bounce me on their knee,' he explained. 'I am not that much of a little boy at this point. I am six years old. You don't bounce a six year old on your knee if you are a distant uncle, in inverted commas.' Townshend has claimed not to recall the precise nature of his abuse, only 'that something happened'. When he reached adulthood, the events at Westgate-on-Sea would both consciously and sub-consciously find an outlet in The Who's music.

While staying with his grandmother, Townshend would have occasional fleeting visits from his mother. But Betty would often disappear as quickly as she'd arrived, in a cloud of perfume, wearing another new dress and radiating her usual glamour. Busy performing with The Squadronaires, Cliff rarely visited. Instead, he sent his son five shillings a week, with which Townshend would buy toys.

Jimpy was also allowed to visit, but noticed that something was amiss. 'You would go round to the house and there would be toys everywhere,' he said later. 'But as soon as the adults left, the toys were put away. It was as if the toys were only there for show, to pretend it was a normal home.' Month after month, the bizarre rituals continued: the nudity, the hazy night-time visits from 'Uncle', the 'forced marches', being sent to bed hungry . . . 'The whole thing was so strange,' said Townshend. 'I was terrified. I lived in constant fear.'

During one of his infrequent visits, Cliff Townshend was so troubled by Denny's eccentric behaviour, that he insisted Pete came home: 'My parents basically realised that they had left me with someone that was insane.' At various times, Townshend would tell journalists that he spent eighteen months or two years with Denny. In recent times, he has claimed it was less than twelve months.

Jimpy was there in July 1952 when Townshend came home from Westgate-on-Sea. 'Peter said that it was like getting out of prison,' he recalled. Back home, Townshend soon discovered that his parents' relationship was unravelling again, and that Betty had acquired a rich boyfriend. Townshend first encountered Dennis Bowman when he, rather than Cliff, arrived with Betty and Jimpy to bring him home from his grandmother's: 'I think he worked for BP and was the head of the oil division in Aden. He was wealthy. He had a car – it was a Volkswagen Beetle. Hardly anyone we knew had cars then.'

Dennis Bowman suggested that Betty divorce Cliff, and that she and Pete come and live in Aden. 'Years later, my mother explained it to me as, "Oh, your father was letting me down. He was away on the road so much,"' said Townshend. 'She didn't go as far as to say he was shagging chorus girls, but that could have been happening. I did know that he had a girlfriend when my parents had split up before. But I just think my mother was screwed up.'

Bowman went as far as to buy airline tickets for Betty and Pete, but Cliff eventually persuaded his wife to stay. He also suggested that Denny move in with them, where she could be better cared for. Denny arrived and took over the front bedroom at Whitehall Gardens. Her grandson, meanwhile, strove to blank out what had happened to him. Initially Townshend never told his parents about his experiences at Westgate, only broaching the abuse with his mother some thirty years later.

'Everybody has a different way of processing what happens to them,' he explained. 'But I think I'm damaged, and I think that goes back to being four and a half, to six and a half. Something happened . . . and I think it made me particularly receptive to the sensitivities of others who'd been damaged.'

Meanwhile, just as Townshend was suppressing his memories, his parents were struggling to keep a lid on their own discontent. Betty established an uneasy truce with her husband, but continued her affair with Denis Bowman, albeit in secret. There were frequent drink-fuelled rows and violent arguments, but they stayed together. Many years later, Betty told her son that she had become pregnant by Bowman and had paid for an illegal abortion, going on to confess that she had ended a further five pregnancies herself.

Townshend now began attending Berrymede Junior School, a run-of-the-mill state school in a poorer suburb of South Acton. At Berrymede, he discovered the one positive outcome of his time living under Denny's harsh regime: he'd become a proficient reader and writer. 'She read halfway through the book *Black Beauty*, and then stopped,' he explained. 'She told me if I wanted to hear the rest, I'd have to learn to read.'

At Berrymede, Townshend would entertain his teacher and the other pupils by telling wildly imaginative stories. At times, this tipped over into fantasy and he'd be admonished for passing off some of his fiction as fact. Townshend would bring his taste for exaggeration with him to The Who, where the make believe of his schooldays proved a good apprenticeship for giving interviews as a rock star.

Now, according to Townshend, he and Jimpy became 'inseparable, like brothers'. Aside from spending several months in Westgate, Townshend had attended three different schools by the time he was seven. Every summer he was away on the road with The Squadronaires. His life had been spent in the company of adults rather than other children, and he'd missed out on having stable friendships with boys his own age. Townshend's upbringing seemed far removed from Daltrey's 'fabulous big working-class London family', and although Entwistle grew up in what newspapers still haughtily called 'a broken home', in its way, Townshend's home was the most broken of them all.

Summer seasons on the road with The Squadronaires continued as before. Except now Townshend had Jimpy to keep him company on the tour bus. In 1952, the band began an annual residency at the regal-looking Palace Ballroom in Douglas, on the Isle of Man. Despite his father's profession, Townshend had so far showed little interest in playing music. That summer, however, he saw a one-man-band act playing elsewhere on the bill, and was fascinated to see the multitasking musician puffing away on a harmonica. Cliff promised to buy his son the same instrument. But, after tiring of waiting, Townshend shoplifted one for himself.

From now on, each passing summer at the Palace Ballroom gave the schoolboy another peek into a world he would later experience first hand with The Who. 'There was always sex and violence,' he said. 'And in those years from eight until ten I started to become more aware of it – of being in these romantic ballrooms where one minute the men would be saying to the women, 'Can I have the pleasure of this dance?' . . . and then the next pulling out a blade and trying to hack someone to death,' he added, melodramatically.

The Ballroom's summer season was given over to different themed weeks. 'There would be Scottish week, Northern Irish week, Welsh week, and it was when they intercepted that the trouble would start,' said Townshend. 'You'd get these Scotsmen coming in, going "We're taking over now Jimmy!" – and it would kick off. The girls would run away screaming, and the Palace Ballroom had this sprung dance floor, which would bounce as the fighting went on. But the band wouldn't stop. And later The Who wouldn't stop.'

Townshend claims to have witnessed the worst violence during one of these themed weeks. 'There was a policeman, a motorcycle rider, and a fight had broken out. He was murdered in front of me,' he said. 'He didn't die on the spot. He died subsequently after being practically kicked to death.' These troubling images would be mentally filed away, along with the abuse he had endured at Westgate; grist to the mill when he began writing songs for The Who.

Back at Whitehall Gardens life muddled on much as it had done before. Betty's affair with Dennis Bowman had finally ended, but she and Cliff still fought and drank too much. At weekends, they threw impromptu late-night parties, which woke up their son, who later wrote of 'the smell of cigarettes, beer and Scotch floating down the hall'.

So far, Townshend's interest in music hadn't progressed beyond the harmonica, and he received little encouragement from his distracted parents: 'There wasn't much music at home except for my dad practising his clarinet.' Cliff had also instructed his son never to touch his instruments: 'We didn't have a very good record player and we had a shitty radio. There was no piano in the house.'

Townshend would find the encouragement he needed elsewhere. On his rare days off, Cliff would sometimes take the family to visit his parents, Horry and Dot. 'My dad's mother was the good grandmother,' said Townshend, who celebrated the end of sugar rationing with a special treat at Dot's house. 'She made me a sugar sandwich. It was white bread with thick white butter and about half a pound of sugar. It was like eating cake mix.'

Dot's sister, Trilby, lived in the flat above. Aunt Trilby was artistic, read tarot cards and, most importantly, showed her great-nephew how to play the old, slightly out-of-tune piano in her living room. Trilby encouraged him as Townshend felt his way around the keyboard, shaping chords and slowly picking out melodies.

Townshend was now approaching his eleventh birthday. At home, he played his stolen harmonica or studied his growing collection of books, comics, drawings and model cars. In the evenings, when Cliff and Betty made one of their frequent trips to the pub, the family's newly acquired television set became Townshend's friend, babysitter and window on to a changing world. 'What I was doing,' he later said, 'were all the things post-war kids everywhere did before we all discovered rock 'n' roll.'

CHAPTER TWO

UNKEMPT HUMANITY

'It is the business of everybody to obey orders.'

Sir Cyril Norwood, *The English Tradition of Education,* **1929**

'Should We Surrender to the Teenagers?'

Melody Maker **headline, June 1956**

'I was a horrible little sod.'

Roger Daltrey remembers his schooldays, 2008

What was once Acton County Grammar School is now Acton High School, 'a centre for media arts and applied learning'. Most of the plain brick buildings on Gunnersbury Lane in which Roger Daltrey, John Entwistle and Pete Townshend were schooled over fifty years ago are long gone. The main school building now splays out from either side of a circular tower that has been constructed from clear polished glass and turquoise steel. In 1955 it might have resembled a pupil's drawing of what a school would look like in impossibly far-off 1999.

Acton County was a typical British post-war grammar school. Founded in 1906, it extolled the same principles as a public school, and placed equal emphasis on sporting and academic achievement. The masters shunned traditional mortarboards of the kind still worn at fee-paying Harrow, the famous public school six miles away, but nonethelesss wore gowns to morning assembly. Here, the navy-blue-uniformed boys lined up for prayers and hymns, honouring the Latin motto on the school's insignia: 'Pactum serva' – 'Keep the faith'.

Roger Daltrey's arrival at the school coincided with the appointment of a new headmaster, forty-year-old Desmond James Kibblewhite. Four years later, Kibblewhite would make a decision that would seriously impact on Daltrey's prospects and unwittingly lead him towards a career in music. But in 1955, Daltrey came with a glowing report from Victoria Junior Boys, where he'd been described him as 'eager, helpful and co-operative'. He had the intelligence and the acumen for a grammar school education, but he also felt self-conscious about coming from Shepherd's Bush. 'Everybody looked at me like I was a working-class twit,' he said. 'Nobody at this new school spoke the way I did. I was very cockney, and Acton felt like it was more upper class. Looking back now, maybe it was more in my head than it actually was. It was there that I had my first run-in with a different class of people.'

In fact, Acton County drew its pupils from a broader cross-section of society than Daltrey remembers. 'There was nothing unusual about Daltrey,' recalls one former Acton County pupil from the class of 1955. 'There were other boys there from Shepherd's Bush; there were boys from Wembley and Sudbury as well. There was a whole bunch of tough kids at Acton County, it's just that Daltrey ended up at the tough end of toughness.'

According to this ex-pupil, Daltrey's insecurities were unintentionally inflamed during one of the school's early end-of-year comedy revues. The same pupil recalls Daltrey being cast in a sketch set during wartime. Lights flashed on and off in the darkened school hall to signify explosions, as Daltrey appeared onstage dressed as a soldier. A 'gunshot' rang out and he fell to the ground. Another pupil dressed as an officer, knelt down to cradle the wounded soldier's head. 'Are you okay?' 'the officer' asked. 'No, sir,' replied Daltrey, 'I've been shot.' 'Don't speak,' he snapped back. 'Why, sir?' 'Because you're so common.'

'Roger and I weren't in bother for the first couple of years,' said another ex-pupil Reg Bowen, who joined the school in 1955 and would go on to play in Daltrey's first group. 'To start with, we really weren't bad kids at all.' Bowen's memory seems to match the image of Daltrey in the 1956 school photograph. Sat cross-legged among his peers, this boy, with his blonde hair neatly combed into a side parting, looks younger than his twelve years.

Feeling uncomfortable about his accent, Daltrey has since said that he retreated into himself. His insecurity was exacerbated by the fact that he was small and, as a younger child, had broken his jaw after falling on to a manhole cover: 'So my face was lopsided. My chin stuck out. So I was treated different and got ribbed about it. I shut off, and I started to get bullied.' According to Daltrey, everything changed when he decided to stand up to his tormentors, and threatened one of them with a chair.

Alan Pittaway was in Daltrey's class and later joined his first musical group. 'The first contact Roger and I had was because we both had train sets,' he says now. 'He and his father built all these tiny cottages and bridges to go with the trains. They were both very good with their hands.'

Pittaway soon witnessed just how good Daltrey could be with his hands: 'Roger was great, but he could be quite an aggressive character,' he laughs. 'We used to have these play fights, but they'd get to the stage where he had his hands around my neck, and I'd be thinking, Roger that's enough now, but you could see the red mist in his eyes.'

Any hope that the school's music lessons would provide a distraction for Daltrey were quashed early on. Roger could play the trumpet and had previously sung in church ('I was told I had perfect pitch. I didn't know what perfect pitch was but I had it.') But taking violin lessons proved disastrous. 'The music teacher Mrs Holman actually told him, "Roger, you will *never* make a living in music,"' recalls Reg Bowen. 'She probably said that to anyone that couldn't hold two notes. But it always stuck in my mind that she said it to him.'

In 1955 the music that Daltrey would later make his living from had yet to make its mark in Britain. For the most part, popular music was still defined by the BBC's strict programming policy. It was the preserve of the Ted Heath Orchestra's former crooner Dickie Valentine or the American singer Frankie Laine, whose speciality was light jazz, show tunes and the themes to many of the cowboy movies shown at the Acton Gaumont.

That year's big hits included Dickie Valentine's 'The Finger of Suspicion', Frankie Laine's 'Strange Lady in Town', Ruby Murray's tender ballad 'Softly Softly' and Kentucky-born Rosemary Clooney's sugar-sweet 'Where Will the Dimple Be?', in which a mother-to-be pondered the cuteness of her unborn child. In many ways, these were still the songs about hope and the restoration of romance with which The Squadronaires had soothed their wartime audience.

But at some point that year Daltrey stumbled across an alternative. 'I was listening to some crackly American services radio station, or maybe Radio Luxembourg,' he said. 'Whichever station it was, that's where I first heard Bill Haley — and that changed everything.'

Singing guitarist Bill Haley and his band had been playing their home state of Pennsylvania since the late 1940s. Around 1951, they'd ditched the yodelling cowboy ballads and jaunty western swing tunes for a sped-up fusion of country and black rhythm and blues that critics would soon start calling 'rock 'n' roll'.

To reflect the change, Haley scrapped the group's original name The Saddlemen and rebranded them The Comets. Their next US hit, 'Crazy Man Crazy', married a revved-up tempo with American hip-ster-speak ('Oh man, that music's gone gone . . .'). In truth, The Comets had removed much of the sex, saltiness and swing of black rhythm and blues, but, in the context of the times, even their sanitised version sounded new and, more importantly, young.

The Comets' 'Shake, Rattle and Roll', had become a US rhythm and blues chart hit in April 1954. Within six months it was being played on Radio Luxembourg, the pioneering station that inspired the first wave of pirate radio broadcasters. Crucially, Radio Luxembourg had none of the BBC's musical constraints. A year later, the station launched *Jamboree*, a two-hour Saturday night show, where British teenagers could hear these exotic American rock 'n' roll artists.

'Shake, Rattle and Roll's frantic syncopated rhythms couldn't have been further away from 'Where Will the Dimple Be?' 'It was ground-breaking,' said Daltrey. 'I'd honestly never heard anything like it.' In November 1955, The Comets' 'Rock Around the Clock' had topped both the American and British charts. The song's seesawing rhythm had also been heard in the opening credits to the movie *Blackboard Jungle*, a graphic tale of teacher-versus-pupil conflict in a US high school. The film was immediately given an X certificate in the UK, making it even more enticing for a young audience.

As tame as the film might seem today, *Blackboard Jungle* exposed British teenagers to the hairstyles, clothes, language and music of their American peers. War babies that had grown up with US culture, via the cartoons and Westerns they'd watched in regional cinemas, were now exposed to another grittier side of American life. It was a colourful, even dangerous antidote to the drab uniformity of 1950s Britain, where boys still dressed like their fathers and the BBC shunned presenters with any hint of a regional accent.

Rock 'n' roll polarised opinion among established home-grown performers such as Cliff Townshend. Musically, Haley's 'Rock Around the Clock' wasn't so distant from the rowdier swing numbers The Squadronaires played. But it was considered by many musicians and critics to be nothing more than the latest fad; albeit one popular enough to cause many dance hall orchestras to reassess their repertoire.

In 1955, The Squadronaires' big-band contemporaries Jack Parnell and His Orchestra released a buttoned-up and terribly English version of 'Shake, Rattle and Roll'. The Squadronaires, though, would go even further. For a time between March and July, bandleader Ronnie Aldrich changed the orchestra's name to Ronnie Aldrich and The Squads. In March they released 'Ko Ko Mo (I Love You So)' with the B-side 'Rock Love'. Over the coming months, they followed it up with other songs, including 'Rock Candy', that used the phrasing of American rock 'n' roll, but were still rooted in big-band jazz. Nobody was fooled.

The Squads failed to take off, and by August they were back as The Squadronaires, once again charming holidaymakers with their version of 'Somewhere Over the Rainbow' at the Douglas Palace Ballroom. But a seed of doubt had been planted. In November, *Melody Maker* published an article under the prescient headline, 'ARE WE HEADING FOR A DANCE BAND SLUMP?'

The arrival of rock 'n' roll also marked a transitional time for Cliff Townshend. In 1955, while still a member of The Squadronaires, he signed a solo deal with Columbia Records. A year later he released his version of 'Unchained Melody'. 'Norrie Paramor [Parlophone Records' recording director], the guy who later discovered Cliff Richard, decided that my dad was sexy enough to flog dance records to teenage girls,' Townshend later told *Melody Maker*.

The single sold modestly, but Cliff's fleeting brush with pop stardom made a lasting impression on his son. 'I remember watching him play in some ballroom, and these two women came and sat next to me. They smelled of a perfume I later came to recognise as sex. One of them said, "Oh, I like the drummer", and the other said, "Oh, I want to fuck that one, he's gorgeous", and I realised to my horror that she was pointing to my father. I said, "That's my dad!" and she went bright red. I remember thinking, "That's it. I'm gonna be in a band."'

But in 1955, Pete Townshend was still ten years old, and was, he claimed, preoccupied by other, more spiritual matters. Cliff and Betty had recently started sending him to Sunday school, a decision that coincided with an improvement in the couple's relationship. 'It was probably so they could go to the pub or have sex,' he speculated. 'I became religious, but my parents weren't. Later I graduated from Sunday school to singing in a church choir.'

It was around this time that Townshend experienced what he would later call 'hearing angels'. 'It doesn't happen so much now,' he told the author in 2012. 'But I am able to go to a place where I can hear sound – not so much music, just sound.' (He then suggested that this 'might be an admission of some kind of aspect of bipolar [affective disorder]'.) In other interviews, Townshend has compared the sound with 'violins, cellos, horns, harps and voices . . . countless threads of an angelic choir.'

'I had this sense that maybe because I'd heard this stuff, that I would hear it again when I sang in church,' he said, 'because in church the echo of our voices would go on for four or five seconds.' It wasn't to be. Instead, Townshend experienced the mystical sound outside of church. At a school friend's suggestion, he joined the Sea Scouts, the nautical wing of the scouting movement, another Christian organisation that aimed to promote similar 'habits of obedience, reverence, discipline and self-respect' to those espoused by the Boys' Brigade.

Townshend accompanied the troop on their weekend camp beside the River Thames. Late one Saturday afternoon, they took to the water near Isleworth, in west London, where Townshend claimed to hear 'the angelic choir' merging with the sound of the boat's outboard motor. 'By the time we had gone up the river and back again, I had to be carried off. I was in a trance of ecstasy,' he said. 'When they turned the outboard motor off, I actually physically broke down.'

In his memoir Townshend enlarged on the story: how the scout leaders had been concerned for him; how the other boys in the troop had refused to answer when he asked if they, too, had heard the 'angels singing'. But in this version of events, the evening ended with Townshend stripped naked and sprayed with cold water by two senior scouts. It was, they told him, his 'initiation ceremony' into the troop. Townshend noticed that they were both masturbating at the time. 'I felt disgusted,' he wrote. 'But also annoyed because I knew I could never go back.'

Townshend later said that throughout his fractured childhood and beyond, he was 'looking for a gang to join'. The insular world of The Squadronaires and their tour bus had offered an early version of that gang. Then came Jimpy and his friends, Sunday school and the choir. Any hope that the Sea Scouts might bring him the fraternity he so desperately sought were dashed. But he would keep on looking.

That summer, Townsend and Jimpy again spent the summer holidays on the Isle of Man. This year, though, there was another distraction, far more exciting than last year's one-man-band and his wheezing harmonica. A new movie, *Rock Around the Clock*, was being shown at Douglas' Palace Cinema. *Rock Around the Clock* was a clunky, fictionalised account of the birth of rock 'n' roll, starring Bill Haley and His Comets. It didn't matter that Haley was pudgy and looked closer to fifty than thirty (a state that may have owed something to his alcoholism), the film-makers were eager to exploit rock 'n' roll – presumably before it faded and became last year's craze. Despite its shortcomings, *Rock Around the Clock*, the movie, was a hit.

Townshend was smitten. Later, Betty would recount how her son and Jimpy saw the film almost every day of the holiday. While The Squadronaires charmed their now ageing fanbase at the Palace Ballroom with their familiar set-list of wartime and post-war hits, Haley and His Comets were enthralling their offspring at the nearby Palace Cinema. One encapsulated the past, the other the future.

Back in Ealing, Jimpy persuaded his father to make him a guitar, mainly so that he could pose with it in front of the bedroom mirror. The finished instrument was pieced together from a wooden box and discarded piano wire. But it did the job.

'The first guitar I ever played was Jimpy's,' said Townshend. 'It was barely functional, but I got a tune out of it.' Perhaps more significantly, it was symbolic of a transition. 'I remember thinking, "My dad is hand-some, well-dressed, he wakes up in the morning and plays Prokofiev, he's sophisticated, he drinks and all the women love him. But his time is up." I could point that guitar at my dad and say, "Bang! You're dead!" The guitar had replaced the saxophone as the sexy instrument of the late twentieth century.'

Before long, the religious fervour Townshend felt when he sang in the choir began to wane. 'As much as I loved, "Oh Jesus Christ our Lord, he came to save our souls" and much as I loved being part of the flock, it soon felt to me like it was all over. There was something about all this ritual that made me think I was looking at the end of the show. Instead, my time had come.'

If 1956 was the year Pete Townshend discovered rock 'n' roll, it was also the year that, despite his later insistence that he was 'profoundly unacademic', he passed his Eleven Plus exam. That summer Townshend took up his place at Acton County, the school he'd first explored as an inquisitive four-year-old. Among the other new pupils that year was John Entwistle. But with the two boys placed in different classes it would be months before they made contact.

In February 1957, Bill Haley and His Comets disembarked from the *Queen Elizabeth* at Southampton Dock amid much fanfare to begin their first UK tour. Townshend and his father caught one of the Comets' shows in London: 'We had seats in the gallery at the very back, and the walls rumbled and the floor moved.' Reportedly, Cliff's verdict on the music that was now usurping his own was gracious, if nothing else: 'Not bad.'

What Pete Townshend, and every would-be 1960s pop star who saw one of those shows, didn't yet know was that Haley's career was already fading. In America the hits had dried up, and even his latest UK releases, 'Don't Knock the Rock' and 'Rock the Joint', were failing to match the sales of 'Rock Around the Clock'. Just like the dance bands they'd started overshadowing a year earlier, Haley and His Comets were about to be eclipsed themselves. The threat had been there all along.

Elvis Aaron Presley was a Tupelo, Mississippi-born singer, whose first single 'Heartbreak Hotel' had been a UK Number 2 hit in May 1956. 'There was this slot on the BBC on Sunday between midday and one o'clock, where they handed over to the Armed Forces Network,' said Roger Daltrey. 'Down the pipe came the sound of Elvis singing "Heartbreak Hotel".' As he had been with Bill Haley, Daltrey was smitten once again. Before long, Presley was back in the charts with 'Hound Dog' and 'Blue Suede Shoes'; songs that sounded like a sexualised hybrid of black rhythm and blues, hillbilly country and gospel, and which easily outdid 'Rock Around the Clock' for swagger and energy.

Better still, unlike the prematurely aged Haley, with his kiss curl and outmoded bow tie, Elvis was a handsome twenty-one year old with a magnificent haircut. The Rolling Stones' future guitarist Keith Richards, at the time a schoolboy in Dartford, Kent, and listening to the same 'crackly American service radio stations' as Daltrey, would characterise Elvis' impact more succinctly than anyone. 'It was,' said Richards, 'as if the world had gone from black and white to Technicolor.'

Pete Townshend has expressed conflicted opinions about Presley, claiming at different times that Elvis made him 'want to vomit', but also that he went cold the first time he heard 'Heartbreak Hotel': 'I remember thinking, "What the fuck is that?"' What Townshend already knew, though, was that Elvis was a role model in a way that Haley had never been, not least to a boy brandishing a home-made guitar in front of a bedroom mirror. In July 1957, Elvis landed his first British Number 1 with the stuttering, sexually charged 'All Shook Up'. Suddenly, Bill Haley already seemed like a distant memory.

Presley's effect on Roger Daltrey was immediate and overwhelming. After catching his first glimpse of Elvis on a TV show, he returned to school enthusing about what he'd just seen: 'I said to my teacher, "Did you see Elvis Presley on the TV at the weekend?" – and he went through the roof saying it was bloody disgusting! It was anathema to the teachers. Their attitude was, "What is this stuff? It's rubbish." In fact, they thought it was worse than rubbish. It was as if they put a blindfold on and didn't want to know anything about it at all.'

As the months passed, Daltrey and his peers would discover more American rock 'n' roll, via Radio Luxembourg's crackly transmissions. There was rhythm-and-blues veteran-turned-rock 'n' roll poet Chuck Berry, whose 'Sweet Sixteen' and 'Never Can Tell' captured the frustration and exuberance of adolescence in just three minutes; Buddy Holly, the bespectacled Texan with the exotic Fender Stratocaster guitar, whose 'Peggy Sue' and 'Rave On' would inspire the first wave of British rock 'n' roll guitar heroes; and Little Richard, the preening, pompadoured showman who described his hits 'Tutti Frutti' and 'Long Tall Sally' as 'music to make your liver quiver, your bladder splatter and your knees freeze'. This was music that sounded as if it came from another galaxy. It was essential listening.

The class-conscious Daltrey also sensed a division emerging. Some, it seemed, regarded rock 'n' roll as the music of the secondary moderns and technical schools: 'It did feel in those days that it was the few working-class kids at my school that were really on the button with what was going on, especially with music.'

There was also another attraction. As rock 'n' roll began challenging the status quo of Dickie Valentine and Frankie Laine, the newspapers began running stories about delinquent male rock 'n' roll fans. In reality, the so-called 'Teddy Boys' made up a tiny fraction of the rock 'n' roll audience, but they made for great headlines. They wore their hair long and sculpted into voluminous quiffs, and dressed in garish Edwardian drape jackets. Their look was in complete defiance of austere plain-suited post-war fashions. 'The general effect was aggressively masculine,' observed the jazz singer and music critic George Melly, 'a return to the dangerous male dash of the Regency Buck or the Western desperado.' The press gleefully reported how Teddy Boys were so transported by the music in the film *Rock Around the Clock* that they slashed cinema seats with their flick knives and danced, claimed one eyewitness, 'like monkeys' in the aisles.

In September 1956, the *Daily Express* had run a two-page investigation into what it called 'THIS CRAZY SUMMER'S WEIRDEST CRAZE', illustrated with a photograph of four Teddy Boys smoking outside a south London courthouse. These Teds had each been fined £1 for 'insulting behaviour', namely dancing during a screening of *Rock Around the Clock* at the Peckham Gaumont. 'I've never felt so excited in my life. The rhythm makes me feel like nothing else mattered,' said eighteen-year-old Kenneth Gear, who preferred the nickname 'Rat Killer'. Elsewhere in the article, the newspaper's 'psychiatrist' declared rock 'n' roll to be 'excessively stimulating only to the maladjusted or people of a primitive type'.

The newspapers echoed the sentiments of Acton County's teaching staff; all of which made Daltrey love the music even more. Now, though, he had an image to aspire to as well: 'I got myself pink socks, green trousers and a Teddy Boy jacket with about five pockets going up the side.' Daltrey, in his own words, 'just wanted to be Elvis Presley'. No small ambition for an ordinary boy from Shepherd's Bush.

In February 1957, the BBC broadcast the first edition of *Six-Five Special*, a magazine show unlike any before in that it was aimed squarely at rock 'n' roll-loving teenagers. The show went out live early on Saturday evenings. At producer Jack Good's insistence, the studio was filled with dancing, grinning teens, while its co-presenter, thirty-two-year-old BBC disc jockey Pete Murray, gamely tried to pass himself off as one of them. But the main problem Jack Good's team faced was finding any genuine rock 'n' roll acts to board the *Six-Five Special*. Bill Haley had gone home to Pennsylvania, and Elvis Presley had yet to perform in the UK, and never would.

In the absence of rock 'n' roll stars, *Six-Five Special* signed up the leading lights of the British jazz scene, Humphrey Lyttelton and Chris Barber. Despite the fanfare surrounding rock 'n' roll, jazz had been enjoying a quiet renaissance in Britain, and Barber's band would later help spearhead a revival of pre-war New Orleans jazz. In February 1959, their hit single 'Petite Fleur' would become one of the defining records of the 'trad jazz' boom; a trend that would inspire Pete Townshend and John Entwistle.

In contrast to the TV-friendly Barber and Lyttelton was Barber's former bandmate, trumpeter and cornettist Ken Colyer. Colyer was a New Orleans jazz buff, born in the less exotic locale of Great Yarmouth, who had moved to London and played with the Crane River Jazz Band. Colyer joined the merchant navy in 1952, and jumped ship in Mobile, Alabama, with the intention of seeking out his New Orleans jazz heroes, the George Lewis Band. Once he had made contact, Colyer defied the 'colour ban' in place throughout the American South, and played with his black idols.

His behaviour attracted the attention of the local police who denounced him as 'a nigger lover'. As soon as Colyer's visa expired, he was arrested. His letters from a New Orleans jail to *Melody Maker*, cast him as a jazz hero; a martyr suffering for his art. When Colyer returned to England in early 1953, Chris Barber was waiting. Together, they formed Ken Colyer's Jazzmen.

There would be no appearance on *Six-Five Special* for Ken Colyer, though. Colyer was a jazz purist who would never compromise his beloved New Orleans sound, and was once overheard telling a disrespectful club owner, 'While we've been playing music torn from the souls of oppressed people, all you've done is fucking cook fish and chips.' Perversely, it was from his band that a musical fad emerged that would galvanise the next generation of British pop stars, including Roger Daltrey.

One of Colyer's Jazzmen was twenty-two-year-old banjo player Anthony Donegan, better known as Lonnie, a moniker he'd borrowed from the black American guitarist Lonnie Johnson. Donegan was highly ambitious, and leapt at the chance to play in the break during the Jazzmen's set. As a contrast to the steady flow of New Orleans jazz, Donegan would join Colyer and Barber for an interlude of black American folk music, which soon acquired the name 'skiffle', and was described by one early critic as 'folk song with a jazz beat'. Before long, Donegan was performing these interludes on his own.

Most jazz clubs at the time didn't have a licence to sell alcohol, and Donegan's 'skiffle break' was a shrewd way of dissuading the audience from dashing off between sets to the nearest pub. Before long, though, the skiffle breaks were attracting as much attention as the Jazzmen's main sets and Donegan's recording of the 1930s folk-blues standard 'Rock Island Line' was heading for the charts.

The song had first been made popular by Huddie William Ledbetter, better known as Lead Belly, a black American bluesman who'd grown up dirt-poor in Texas and had served time in prison for attempted murder. Lead Belly's background couldn't have been more different from Donegan's, the Glasgow-born son of a professional violinist. But it didn't matter. Lead Belly's song immediately found an audience among the teenagers avidly watching *Six-Five Special*, and Donegan became a regular on the show.

In skiffle, guitars and banjos were simply strummed, and the rhythm supplied by equally simple drumming, the scrape of fingernails on a washboard and the single-note twang provided by a piece of string tied between the top of a broom handle and a tea chest. The music had its roots in the American jug bands of the 1920s and 1930s, where plantation workers used makeshift instruments out of financial necessity. Now suburban teenagers across Britain would do the same.

As Bill Haley and His Comets were finishing up their UK tour in March 1957, Donegan's version of an Appalachian folk song called 'Cumberland Gap' was heading for the top of the British charts. Donegan wasn't alone. Within weeks, he'd been joined by The Chas

McDevitt Skiffle Group, whose cover of another arcane folk song, 'Freight Train', reached Number 5, and The Vipers, with their top-ten hit 'Don't You Rock Me Daddy-O'. Out of the same pool of players as The Vipers came south London teenager Tommy Steele. A goofily grinning, blond-haired ex-merchant seaman, Steele was pitched as Bermondsey's answer to Elvis. His first single, 'Rock With the Caveman', raced to Number 1 and became a favourite for Daltrey and his friends. 'Skiffle had that DIY quality that punk later had,' said Pete Townshend. 'Even if it didn't have the drive and the message.'

'Everybody wanted to be Elvis,' said Daltrey. 'But nobody could be Elvis. But even if you couldn't be Lonnie Donegan, everybody could do a pretty good imitation. That was the great thing about skiffle. It had a vibrancy and energy, but it was touchable. It was possible. Every street in Shepherd's Bush had a skiffle group.'

Daltrey's next step was to acquire a guitar: 'We couldn't afford to buy one so I bought some wood and some guitar strings and made one. It wasn't very good. But it made the noise of a guitar and I could play, relatively in tune, the first three chords that anyone needed for most skiffle songs.'

On a summer holiday trip to Brighton, Daltrey busked for loose change on the seafront and talked his way into playing in one of the local pubs. His parents were outraged. 'I did my first pub gig in Brighton at fourteen,' he said. 'I wasn't even old enough to drink in there.' He was already determined to play music. 'I didn't care. It was what I wanted to do.'

The London skiffle scene had germinated in a network of Soho dives: the 44 Skiffle Club in a basement in Gerrard Street, Wardour Street's Blues and Barrelhouse Club and, most famously, the 2i's Coffee Bar on Old Compton Street. Daltrey and his friends rode the Central Line into the West End to make their pilgrimage to the 2i's, only to be disappointed. 'We kept reading about this place,' he said. 'But when we got there it was just full of prossies [prostitutes].'

It was at the 2i's, though, that one of Daltrey's later musical collaborators had recently been discovered, and was now being groomed as a rock 'n' roll star. Daltrey's first solo album, released in 1973, would be co-produced by Adam Faith, and the pair would star together in the prison drama *McVicar* (1980). In 1958, though, Faith was one of a new breed of British singers, like Tommy Steele, being pitched as the nation's answer to Elvis Presley.

Faith had grown up in a council flat in Acton Vale, where he was known by his birth name Terry Nelhams. In 1957, he was spotted at the 2i's playing with a skiffle group called the Worried Men. After dumping the band he was signed as a solo artist. Later, when the Worried Men's guitar player quit, Roger Daltrey tried out with the group.

Vic Gibbons, now Chris Barber's manager, but, in the late 1950s the Worried Men's drummer, dimly remembered Daltrey from Victoria Junior Boys. 'Roger was two years behind me at school,' he says now. 'But I later became aware of him because I had a summer job at Shanks where his father was the general manager. What we didn't know was that Roger played the guitar, until he came down to the house.'

Daltrey turned up with his makeshift guitar, but the Worried Men were unimpressed. 'Basically, he couldn't play,' insists Gibbons. 'That was the trouble with skiffle groups. A lot of them couldn't even strum one chord.' Gibbons was also discouraged by Daltrey's manner. 'He was very surly. I remember that from the way in which he used to address his father when he came to see him at work. He was a typical teenager. There didn't seem to be any shape or substance to his conversation. But he seemed utterly obsessed by one thing – playing.'

Whatever misgivings the Worried Men had about Daltrey's musical ability, his ambition was never in question. When he heard about a forthcoming Spirit of Skiffle talent competition, Daltrey put together a group of his own. His bandmates were fellow Acton County boys, Reg Bowen, Alan Pittaway, Mike McAvoy and Derek 'Del' Shannon (not to be confused with the rock 'n' roll singer Del Shannon of later 'Runaway' fame).

'Roger was the first one to get into skiffle,' says Alan Pittaway. 'I started strumming my dad's old guitar. But Roger was always ahead of me. He knew more chords.' With Bowen and Shannon also playing guitars, McAvoy ended up on bass. 'They said, "You can play bass Mike",' he recalls. 'I said, "What's that?" They said, "Just a piece of string and a tea chest . . ."'

In the summer of 1958, the group, calling themselves the Sulgrave Rebels after the Sulgrave Boys' Club, of which Daltrey and Bowen were members, entered the competition, which was held at Wormholt

Park School in Shepherd's Bush. In the playground beforehand, Daltrey took Alan Pittaway aside and told him he wasn't able to sing *and* play the little guitar licks in their chosen Lonnie Donegan songs, 'Ham and Eggs' and 'Grand Coulee Dam'.

'So he showed me these licks, and I had to learn them before I went on, so he could just concentrate on singing,' says Pittaway. 'We still had the classic skiffle set-up and I thought we'd get blown offstage, because the best band there had two electric guitars and these cornflake-box-sized amps. But the contest was all about the spirit of skiffle. So we were perfect for it. We won.'

The Sulgrave Rebels were awarded record vouchers and a photograph appeared in the *Acton Gazette & Post* which showed five grinning schoolboys, four of them cradling guitars almost as big as they are. They never played together again.

Around the same time that *Six-Five Special* first appeared on television screens across the country, Betty Townshend gave birth to her second son, Paul. His older brother welcomed the new addition to the family, and even more so the extra pocket money his parents now gave him for babysitting. A third son, Simon, would join the family in October 1960.

Paul's arrival in the spring of 1957 coincided with the Townshends leaving their flat in Whitehall Gardens and moving to a terraced house at 20 Woodgrange Avenue. The new home was also closer to Ealing Common, where Betty had taken over the running of an antique-cum-junk shop called Miscellanea.

The Squadronaires were still touring, but Cliff was now forty and no longer harboured any ambitions for a pop career. At weekends, his musician friends would fill the living room at his new house, and the drinking that had begun at lunchtime in the pubs around the Common would carry on into the evening, often accompanied by the blare of saxophones and trumpets.

But Pete Townshend was still hesitant about whether he wanted to make music of his own. 'Although he was in the choir, I never thought he was talented musically,' said Betty. Townshend saw the absence of a piano in the family home as further evidence of his parents' lack of encouragement: 'My father didn't see any point in having a piano in the house because I showed no musical aptitude.' Later, Cliff tried to teach his son how to play music, but gave up when he saw how much he struggled with it. When Pete started to excel in his English classes, Cliff suggested a career in journalism.

In the summer of 1957, Cliff helped his son with what would become Pete Townshend's first published work: a poem called 'The Museum', which appeared in the summer issue of the school magazine, *The Actonian*. The twelve-line verse was squeezed in between a report on current developments in the world of rocket building ('This leads one to think that the day when an unmanned instrumental satellite encircles the Earth is not so far distant . . .') and a rundown on the athletic team's fair performance at an intra-school championship ('The outstanding performance was Carter's 10.7 seconds in the under 15s . . .').

In 'The Museum', the twelve-year-old Townshend wrote of 'dug-up fossils and ships of old, that makes one's dreams of deeds so bold . . .', 'plays by Shakespeare . . . verse by Brooks', before arriving at the conclusion, 'I realise I have much to learn.'

It was during that same summer that Townshend took up the guitar. Encouraged by his ability to coax a tune out of Jimpy's homemade instrument, Pete had asked his parents for a guitar of his own. Cliff had offered to buy him one for Christmas in 1956, but didn't fulfil his promise. 'But what happened is *she* bought it,' said Townshend.

The 'she' in question was Grandma Denny. Unfortunately, Denny acquired what Townshend described as 'a cheap guitar of the kind you'd see hanging on the wall of a Spanish restaurant'. Cliff showed him the basic chords, but Townshend found it a struggle. He claimed to have spent a year battling with the instrument before putting it aside in frustration. Instead, he acquired a banjo from a friend of his father's, and bought himself a chord book.

Before long, Townshend was attending Sunday evening sessions at the Chiswick Jazz Club, held in a nearby pub, where Ken Colyer was among the regular performers. The attraction lay in what he described as 'the vital, bright sound' of the British banjo players, who had a more attacking style than their American counterparts. Townshend didn't know it yet but this same attacking style would manifest itself later in his idiosyncratic guitar playing with The Who.

Trad jazz might have seemed picturesque after the dynamism of American rock 'n' roll. But, like skiffle for Daltrey, Townshend found it 'touchable and possible'. It was the music of the left-wing, duffel-coated, art-school 'ravers' that Humphrey Lyttelton had nicknamed 'the 'Ooblies'. It was the music played on the Campaign For Nuclear Disarmament Easter 1958 protest march from London to the atomic weapons research establishment at Aldermaston. Better still, it was another pot shot at what Townshend called 'the kind of serene, dance hall music my father played'.

By 1958, Townshend and John Entwistle had become aware of each other. What Townshend's hastily learned chords on the banjo gave him was potential entry into his next gang, of which Entwistle was already a member. 'John was this big guy, very funny, very sharply dressed,' recalled Townshend. Both boys were just coming up to their teens, but Entwistle was already nearly six feet tall and towered over his future bandmate. At first, though, it wasn't music that drew them together. 'I just remember Pete having a good sense of humour,' said Entwistle. 'So he joined the comedy clique that we had.' That clique comprised of boys who would meet in the playground at Acton County to, as Entwistle put it, 'stand around making up jokes'.

Among their topics of conversation were the BBC's surreal comedy radio programme *The Goon Show*, which Townshend considered 'youthful and rebellious', and *Mad*, the American satirical magazine. *Mad* had launched six years earlier and poked fun at the establishment with its witty cartoons and razor-sharp parodies of popular culture.

'They were all very keen on *Mad*,' remembers fellow pupil Michael Wheeler. 'Some lunchtimes I used to join them as they sat there flicking through the latest issue. *Mad* was American, and anything American in the 1950s was jumped on at school.' But what Wheeler also remembers now is the contrast between the two pupils: 'Pete always had a bit of mystique, because his father was in show business, so we were impressed by that. John was very arty and creative and musical.'

John Entwistle now played the French horn in the school orchestra, and would also spend two years playing in the Middlesex Youth Orchestra. At the same time, he was still performing with 1st South Middlesex Boys' Brigade, where he would remain until 1962. As Roger

Daltrey later stressed: 'John was the only one of The Who that had any kind of serious musical background.'

In the late 1950s, Dave Lambert, who would go on to become guitarist/vocalist with the folk-rock group The Strawbs, encountered the teenage Entwistle at the Boys' Brigades' annual camp in Woolacombe, North Devon. 'I'll never forget my first sighting of John,' says Lambert now. 'He was wearing winkle-picker boots, drainpipe trousers and an American ice-hockey jacket that we used to call a 'Richmond jacket', because people wore them at Richmond ice rink. He struck me as a very hip young teenager.'

Lambert was similarly impressed by Entwistle's casual approach to leadership. 'We were all split up into tents. Each tent had different duties, called 'fatigues'. On the first morning, John's tent were doing their fatigues, which involved washing up after breakfast. John was in charge, but he was stood there, watching, arms folded, whistling, and tapping his foot in that L-shaped stance he always had, while everyone else did the work. I remember thinking, "How the hell does he get away with that?"'

On Sunday, the Brigade marched from their camp down into Woolacombe for a church service and then back again. Sounding the drumbeat as they marched, Lambert quickly realised that the nonchalant teenager was also a gifted musician. It was Entwistle's job to play the Brigade's bugle calls. At the end of each day, he would perform the final call, known as 'Sunset'. 'It's a beautiful tune anyway,' says Lambert. 'But when John played it . . . I had never heard anybody play a brass instrument as well as that before.'

'John once gave our fourth-form teacher, Mr Marks, a trumpet fanfare when he entered the class,' recalls fellow Acton County pupil Brian Adams. He also remembers Entwistle's artistic ability from the art classes they attended together: 'He had a particular style. He was a great cartoonist but nearly all his works were knights in armour.' This fascination would manifest itself later when the pop star Entwistle bought suits of armour for his first house in Ealing and, later, his rock star's mansion in the Cotswolds.

As a brass player, trad jazz was unlikely to pass Entwistle by. 'I never really liked trad, but it is the only thing you can play with a trumpet,' he said. So, in the spring of 1958, he joined a group of pupils for a weekly trad session. His bandmates included drummer Chris Sherwin, and a fellow school orchestra musician, clarinettist Phil Rhodes. They called themselves The Confederates. It didn't take long for Entwistle to suggest that Townshend join as their banjo player.

'We used to rehearse in my parents' front room in Ealing,' says Chris Sherwin now. 'There was John, Pete, Phil Rhodes and I. There was also another guy from school called Rod Griffiths who played half a trombone like a bugle. Pete was pretty accomplished, even back then. But I do remember that one time he was having trouble tuning the banjo as the rest of us were making such a noise, so he went to the outside loo in my garden for a little peace and quiet.'

The outside lavatory was still common in British houses through the 1950s and beyond, and provided a similar retreat/rehearsal room for John Entwistle. 'He used to practise in the loo as it was best for the echo,' remembered Queenie. 'But the neighbours would complain.'

The Confederates played Dixieland jazz such as 'Maryland', 'Marching Through Georgia', 'Willie the Weeper' and 'When the Saints Go Marching In'. Townshend had finally found his gang – but he knew his place in it. 'What you have to do is find a good bloke,' he explained. 'A strong bloke. Find the top man and become his lieutenant. It worked tremendously well for me as a young kid. My memory of that time was, "Hey, I'm a little boy, but I'm happy with that because the gang like me."'

The only published photograph of The Confederates shows Entwistle and Rhodes dressed in Edwardian-style waistcoats and bowler hats. Their outfits were in honour of trad jazz figurehead, Acker Bilk, who was enjoying his first chart hits. Entwistle and Rhodes look every one of their thirteen years. Townshend, sat next to Chris Sherwin's drums and playing a banjo that looks almost as big as he is, still resembles a primary school boy.

In 2013, Sherwin's memories of the now famous rock star he knew as a kid are far less nuanced than Pete's memories of him. Over the years, Townshend has portrayed Sherwin in interviews as the gang's 'top man', who took him under his wing and apparently took him to see his first X-certificate film, the voyeuristic thriller *Peeping Tom*. Although they were both in the same school year, this was a reprisal of the surrogate older-brother relationship Townshend had enjoyed with

Jimpy. 'I always looked for older boys to hang around,' he said, 'or certainly boys more emotionally equipped than I was.'

But if there was such a hierarchy in their friendship, Chris Sherwin seems unaware of it. 'Pete and I were great mates as well as being in this band together,' he stresses now. 'I spent a lot of time with him doing all sorts of other things as well. I remember us building a bike together. We went to the dump and stole the bits – wheels, a frame and handlebars – and messed about building it in my backyard. It was just the usual boys' stuff. So we also had that kind of friendship on top of playing music.'

Chris Sherwin became a regular visitor to Woodgrange Avenue. On one occasion he was asked to help out with one of Betty Townshend's business ventures: 'Pete's mum used to go to this company who made carpets for cars, and I went with her and Pete once to this little factory in North Acton. She picked up all these off-cuts of carpet, took them home, and had me cut them into squares.' The squares were then taken to Miscellanea, 'where she used to sell them as carpet tiles. Betty was a bit of a wheeler-dealer.'

The weekly rehearsals in Sherwin's front room paid off the following year when The Confederates were asked to play at the Congo Club, a youth club held in the hall of the Congregational Church on Churchfield Road, Acton. It was one of the band's regular rehearsal spaces, but now they were playing to an audience, although Townshend has since stated that as few as five or ten people turned up.

Performing in the same church's choir as an eleven year old, Townshend wished he could hear 'the angels singing', on the night of The Confederates' debut gig, though, the only sound he heard was the band clattering noisily through 'When the Saints Go Marching In'. The blood rushed to his head. 'I really blushed,' he said. 'It was the only time in my whole life that I've been really nervous.'

When Townshend returned to Ealing after another summer holiday on the Isle of Man, he discovered that the rest of the group had been lured away. 'There was another guy from school called Barry Smith who played trombone,' explain Sherwin. 'Barry lived opposite Alan Maynard, who called himself 'Alf'.'

The banjo-playing Alf Maynard was a former Acton County pupil, who quickly co-opted Barry Smith, Griffiths, Sherwin, Rhodes and

Entwistle into a trad band he modestly christened Alf Maynard's New Orleans Jazzmen. Townshend sat in with them for a time. 'But Alf played banjo,' says Sherwin, 'so there was really nowhere for Pete.' Alf Maynard's Jazzmen played one of their few gigs at the Corgi Books Factory's Christmas dinner and dance in Acton. 'Everybody came with instruments in cases,' recalls Sherwin, 'and everybody left with instruments out of cases, but the cases filled up with books, which we'd nicked.'

By the end of the year though, Townshend was also becoming drawn to the same skiffle sound that had so enthralled Roger Daltrey. Rather than Lonnie Donegan's prevalent hits, though, it had been the Chas McDevitt Skiffle Group's 'Freight Train' that had seized his attention. The band featured four guitars backing the song's guest vocalist, Scottish folk singer Nancy Whiskey. 'I just loved the sound of those guitars rattling along together,' he said. 'That's when I decided to focus on playing guitar.'

Townshend took the cash he'd made from a newspaper round and purchased an acoustic guitar he'd seen in his parents' shop. He had his banjo and his guitar and he was a part of the gang, but Townshend was still desperately insecure. Sex and violence seemed to have been part of the problem. The onset of adolescence had made Townshend acutely aware of what he thought was his greatest physical shortcoming: the size of his nose. 'The geezers that were snappy dressers and got chicks years before I even thought they existed would always like to talk about my nose,' he told *Rolling Stone* in 1968.

Townshend's self-consciousness was worsened by the fact that he felt he'd let his good-looking parents down: 'My mother seemed to think that anyone who wasn't beautiful wasn't any good.' Cliff was more sympathetic to his son's plight, but awkwardly reminded Pete of how well his friend, the bandleader Ronnie Aldrich, had done in life, despite having a large nose, or how the unprepossessing American playwright Arthur Miller had ended up marrying blonde pin-up Marilyn Monroe: 'Whenever my dad got drunk, he'd come up to me and say, "Look, son, you know looks aren't everything" – and shit like that.'

It didn't help that some of Townshend's surrogate older brothers seemed to be more sexually active than he was. In Townshend's mind, at least, 'fifteen-year-old girls were getting their brains fucked out on the pool table' in the darkened back room of the Congo Club, while other teenagers innocently listened to pop records outside. He also believed that some of his peers had lost their virginity while trying to Ban the Bomb: 'Everybody and their brother seemed to have had his first fuck on the Aldermaston march.' Even allowing for exaggeration, some of Townshend's friends were clearly more daring around the opposite sex than he was.

'Me and a mate would go to Hyde Park on a Saturday afternoon,' Townshend told the author. 'It's nice and sunny, and he pulls a couple of girls, rolls over and starts snogging the really good-looking one. The other one's left, and he's looking over at me, waving his hand and saying, "Move in, move in." But there's all these people about walking their dogs, and this girl's looking at me with a look on her face as if to say, "You move in and I will fucking kill you."'

On the train home, Townshend challenged his school friend about what had happened: 'I said, "We were in the middle of Hyde Park and you're trying to fuck this girl, while we're surrounded by all these people . . . and spaniels! Explain it to me." And he goes, "Oh, you'll understand one day." And he was the same age as me, and he was always very kind to me, but he *got* it – and I just didn't. I didn't even kiss a girl until I was eighteen.'

In 1957, the all-male establishment at Acton County had begun admitting female pupils. 'That certainly improved things,' remembers Alan Pittaway. (Among the new arrivals were the Wise twins, one of whom, Alison, would later become John Entwistle's girlfriend and first wife. Their first date was a Boys' Brigade concert at the Royal Albert Hall.)

Over the fifty-odd years since he left school, Townshend has frequently portrayed Acton County as a harsh environment where violence and humiliation were rife. The arrival of female pupils only made it worse. 'It wasn't so bad until they brought in the girls,' he said. 'But the old guard were still doing all the stuff they did before – caning boys on the spot if they were caught running in the corridor, and giving you a thick ear that made you cry out of shock, with tears all over your face. Except now there was a group of girls looking at you while it happened.' Like teachers at every other post-war school in Britain, many of Acton County's staff were also trying to rationalise their own grim wartime experiences. 'That post-war period was ghastly for all of them,' said Townshend. 'They were traumatised.'

'It was strict,' concurs Michael Wheeler. 'I was in fear of the teachers and remember being scared a lot of the time.' Among the strictest teachers, and still remembered by some ex-pupils even now, was the house master Leonard Hurse, known by some of his victims as 'Basher' Hurse and 'Hitler'.

'Oh, he was a nasty man,' says Chris Sherwin. 'We used to call him Hitler because he had the same little moustache and side parting.' The nickname seemed even more apt as Hurse taught German. On one occasion a foolhardy pupil shouted the Führer's name as he walked past: 'So he asked whoever did it to own up. When they didn't, he lined us all up outside the science lab – there were about twenty of us – and with his knuckles went down the line and nutted every one of us.'

According to Sherwin, his teachers were mostly 'nasty bastards' with the exception of his English, art and metalwork tutors. Townshend also recalled a teacher hurling a blackboard rubber – 'this bloody great big piece of wood' – at one impudent pupil, who was then carried, in a semi-conscious state, out of the classroom. Like the murky abuse he'd suffered in Westgate-on-Sea, Townshend's memories of this violence and humiliation would later find an outlet in the us-versus-them sentiment of 'My Generation' and the brutal treatment meted out on the main character of *Tommy*.

One pupil guaranteed to upset 'Basher' Hurse and every other 'nasty bastard' at Acton County was Roger Daltrey, whose Teddy Boy image coincided with an increasingly confrontational attitude and a sharp decline in his schoolwork. During one of Hurse's classes, Daltrey's disinterested attitude drove Basher to a violent outburst. 'The classroom we were in had this highly glossed wooden floor, so the desks and chairs slid very easily,' remembers one ex-pupil, who witnessed the altercation. 'Daltrey was messing around. I think he was making fun of Hitler. Suddenly, the teacher shoved this empty desk. It slid so hard across the floor, it hit Daltrey's desk, driving it back hard into his stomach. It must have hurt. And I'll never forget, he [Hurse] uttered the wonderful words – "Daltrey, you'll never amount to anything in this world!"'

Acton County's school photograph from April 1958 depicts Daltrey as a junior Elvis-in-the-making. He stares sulkily into the camera with his once neatly combed hair coaxed up into a quiff. It was a rare sighting of him wearing the school uniform. 'We all had to wear blazers,' says Alan Pittaway. 'But Roger was the first guy at school to get away with wearing a drape jacket. He opened the drape one day to show me and there were these little loops sewn inside, and inside one was this miniature axe.'

'Roger got us all into it,' adds Mike McAvoy. 'I remember my mum actually saying to me, "You cannot go out like that!" I had my hair slicked back like Elvis, the tightest black jeans you could find, black brothel creepers and bright yellow fluorescent socks.' McAvoy and Daltrey had also begun excusing themselves from lessons: 'We'd be there for registration, then slip out through the orchard behind the school, and go to the cinema to try and see one of the X-certificate films. The teachers eventually realised what we were doing, and I think we both got caned.'

Headmaster Desmond Kibblewhite summoned Daltrey's parents to complain about their son's appearance, behaviour and frequent absences. But Daltrey had made up his mind. 'I just wasn't interested in learning,' he said. 'And I wasn't interested in wearing their silly uniform.'

Pupils in the years below were also wary of the scowling apprentice Teddy Boy. Pete Townshend maintains that his first exchange of words with The Who's future lead singer came after seeing him setting about another pupil in the playground. 'I shouted that he was a dirty fighter, because he kicked the guy when he was on the ground. Roger came over to me and said, "Who called me a dirty fighter?"' before forcing Townshend to apologise.

'I probably shouldn't talk about this,' Townshend told *Playboy* in 1994. 'But I'm on a good enough ground now with Roger to address it. He used to be the worst bully, terrorising other kids.' Unsurprisingly, Daltrey doesn't agree: 'I got a reputation as a tearaway but I don't think I knowingly picked on anyone. I just loved to fight, that's what boys did.'

'Roger didn't mind using his fists when he wasn't winning an argument but he never bore a grudge,' confirms Reg Bowen. 'He could have a fight with you one day and the next day be your best mate. The trouble is, we were in a grammar school, and you weren't supposed to behave like that in a grammar school.'

In spring 1959 Kibblewhite's patience finally ran out and Daltrey was expelled. In a 1967 interview, Daltrey claimed that 'I got slung out of school' and cited the reason: 'Someone got shot . . . It was an accident. Someone aimed an air gun at the door . . . it bounced off the door and hit someone in the eye.' In later interviews, however, Daltrey has said that his expulsion was as a result of being caught smoking.

'Roger and I both got caught smoking,' says Bowen, who maintains that Daltrey's reputation as a hard man at school has been overstated. 'I got suspended for a week, and was allowed back to do my exams. Roger was out on his earhole. I think they wanted an excuse to get rid of him. But he was fifteen and, at that time, many kids left school at fifteen to start work.'

The way Daltrey tells it, he was expelled the day before his fifteenth birthday, which he then spent roaming the building sites of Acton looking for work: 'My parents were devastated. But in a lot of ways it was the best day of my bloody life.' For a time, Daltrey took a job earning a shilling an hour as an electrician's mate. But he quit after being offered an apprenticeship at Chase Products, a sheet-metal factory in Packington Road, South Acton, that specialised in making storage racks and specialist equipment boxes.

'I had no choice. I had to get a proper job. Mum still needed to be paid,' he said. To begin with, the work involved making tea for his workmates rather than learning a trade. But despite clashing with Desmond Kibblewhite, 'Hitler' and every other teacher at Acton County, Daltrey settled down and even came to enjoy the routine and camaraderie of life inside 'this big tin shed'.

'I hated getting up in the mornings, but I actually enjoyed going to work,' he said. 'You turned up, you knew what you had to do, and then you went home.' In years to come he would talk almost fondly of the ordered life he'd had at the factory and how it compared to the chaos of life with The Who: 'I had some very good times there. Never mind your cotton fields, we were in Acton, banging out bits of metal and getting a rhythm going. There was no radio, but we'd all start singing. We sang from ten in the morning until five at night. We drove the guv'nor mad. But that's where I learned to sing.'

Better still, after his mother had taken her share from his weekly pay packet, Daltrey still had money left over to spend on the most important thing in his life. But that wasn't music. Despite the Sulgrave Rebels' victory at Wormholt Park School, Daltrey had given up singing and playing guitar. 'We tried to persuade him to carry on,' says Alan Pittaway. 'But he'd completely lost interest. He'd fallen head over heels for this girl. He was mad about her, and he told us he was packing in music.' It couldn't last.

In 1958, the British rock 'n' roll star Marty Wilde announced, 'Kids these days would rather listen to a jukebox than the prime minister.' He wasn't wrong. Nevertheless, the recently elected Conservative government of Prime Minister Harold Macmillan had passed a bill that would change the lives of Wilde and every other pop star of the 1960s.

The 1948 National Service Act had been introduced to determine how and when young men should serve in the armed forces now that the war was over. It decreed that all eighteen-year-old males were required to serve for eighteen months, unless excused on medical grounds. In 1957, though, Macmillan's government announced the gradual abolition of national service.

Being 'called up' had proven disastrous for several of Britain's earliest rock 'n' rollers; eighteen months was the equivalent of several lifetimes in pop music. Terry Dene, once billed as 'Britain's first rock 'n' roll rebel', had deferred his national service, but conscription into the army could only be delayed for so long, and as soon as he set foot on the parade ground his musical career was over. He broke down in tears in his barracks' mess hall and was later threatened with violence by some of his fellow conscripts. Two months later, Dene was discharged on medical grounds. He never had another hit record, rejected pop music and found religion instead.

Others were more fortunate. Tommy Steele failed his medical on account of his fallen arches and corns. (Although his manager insisted it was better for his image to tell the press that he had been diagnosed with a heart condition.) Adam Faith, meanwhile, was so desperate to avoid the call-up that he offered a Harley Street doctor money to amputate one of his toes. They refused. Faith turned eighteen just after the bill was passed: 'It was as if I'd been on death row, and somebody suddenly came along and said, "It's OK, you can go home now."' National Service continued until the end of 1960, with the last conscripts serving until 1963. But Acton County's junior Lonnie Donegans and Elvis Presleys were all spared.

For Pete Townshend the reprieve was bittersweet. 'Those of us born after the war were never called up,' he told the author. 'But we were the ones who were also told, "You're never going to have to kill anyone, you're no use to this country or to anyone, just go out there and enjoy the sugar, you're lucky to have it."'

Those who opposed the end of national service and considered it far better to have thousands of hormonal teenage boys off the street, had their prejudices reinforced in the summer of 1960. On 31 July, a strange incident of youth-cult violence took place at the Beaulieu Jazz festival, a three-day event held in the grounds of jazz buff Lord Montagu's bucolic stately home in Hampshire. Members of the 9,000-strong audience, condemned in the *Observer* at the time as 'unkempt humanity', clambered on to a lighting scaffold, causing it to topple over while Acker Bilk and his band were playing below.

A piano was damaged, Humphrey Lyttelton's trumpet went missing, in what were described as 'mysterious circumstances', and, most shockingly, the BBC's coverage was interrupted by the fracas. A drunken beatnik grabbed a BBC microphone and demanded 'More beer for the workers!' on air. The police and the ambulance services were called, several arrests were made and the press were outraged.

After the uproar that had attended Teddy Boy violence in 1956, this latest incident was seen as another example of how pop music was expediting the decline of civilisation. 'A tribal dance to the sound of a tom-tom has a more civilised air than this modern wreck and roll to the beat of a jazz drum,' wrote the *Bradford Telegraph & Argus*, the day after the so-called 'Battle of Beaulieu'.

Where once the soundtrack had been Bill Haley, it was now Acker Bilk. Where once the protagonists had worn drape coats and brothel-creeper shoes, there was what the *Observer* called 'a standard uniform of rumpled jeans, T-shirts, sandals and haircuts that must have wrung the hearts of the two former Irish guard sergeants running the campsite behind the car park'.

Yet Pete Townshend shared some of the *Observer*'s disdain for those unkempt jazz fans. Trad had inspired him to learn the banjo, and skiffle had been the spur to him picking up the guitar. But he was growing weary of both. 'I remember going to see Ken Colyer and being disgusted by the state of the audience,' he said. 'It was all chaps in duffel coats, and instead of a handkerchief they'd have a toilet roll in their pocket.' Townshend insisted he'd seen a group of Colyer fans casually urinate down themselves as they stood at the bar of the Hammersmith Odeon, too drunk or lazy to use the lavatory.

Despite these misgivings, trad and skiffle's legacy would endure in what Townshend called 'the weird shit you can hear in The Who's music' (try the banjo-style guitar playing and marching-band brass on 1966's 'Cobwebs and Strange'). Yet the principal reason Townshend had moved away from the music was that rock 'n' roll had become something he could completely identify with. 'It was now the Everly Brothers, Buddy Holly, Ricky Nelson,' he explained, 'and then there was Cliff Richard aping Elvis Presley on TV.'

Cliff Richard and his backing band, The Shadows, dressed in decent suits and were unlikely to walk around with toilet rolls stuffed in their pockets or piss themselves while stood at the bar. Despite his Elvis-style sneer and greasy quiff, the nineteen-year-old Richard (birth name: Harry Webb) came from a middle-class family and lived in suburban Hertfordshire. He'd had his Eureka moment watching Bill Haley and His Comets at the Edmonton Regal. Like Adam Faith, Cliff had been 'discovered' at the 2i's. His first single, 'Move It', became a hit in August 1958. It was a riposte to the *Melody Maker* critic Steve Race, who'd recently condemned rock 'n' roll as 'a monstrous threat to popular music' and it was a defining record. After so many awkward attempts at the genre, 'Move It' proved that the Brits could play rock 'n' roll without sounding hopelessly tame.

Cliff Richard had also appeared on the first edition of ITV's new teen-orientated music show, *Oh Boy!*. Within months, *Oh Boy!* had become a shop window for other home-grown rock 'n' rollers, including Marty Wilde and Billy Fury, and Americans such as Gene Vincent and Eddie Cochran, who, unlike Elvis (recently conscripted into the US army), were willing to come to Britain.

Eddie Cochran played chunky chords on a low-slung guitar, in a style that Townshend would later co-opt for The Who. His signature song, 'Summertime Blues', would become a mainstay of The Who's set. But Cochran was doomed to the same lost hero status as Buddy Holly, dying after a car accident in the English countryside in April 1960.

In truth, Cochran was too hip and too American for an English schoolboy to impersonate. But Cliff Richard's guitarists weren't. Cliff had hired several former skiffle players for his backing group The Shadows, including Bruce Welch and Hank Marvin, both former grammar schoolboys, only a few years older than Pete Townshend. They were believable role models. Townshend's cheap guitar had a pick-up on it. It could be made 'electric'. The next step, then, was for him to buy an amplifier.

Townshend wasn't alone in his enthusiasm for adding electricity. John Entwistle had now discovered the American guitarist Duane Eddy, whose resonant, twanging instrument sounded impossibly futuristic. Moreover, the weekend dance band in which he played trumpet had just added an electric guitarist. But Entwistle was self-conscious about his big hands and the fact that his best friend was already a capable guitarist. Instead he chose the electric bass; an instrument that had only been in circulation for a few years, but had quickly overtaken the upright bass as the preferred choice of the aspiring rock 'n' roller. What nobody knew yet was that Entwistle had no intention of playing it like a conventional bass. Inside him was a lead guitarist, who would spend the whole of his career with The Who trying to get out.

The Shadows' Jet Harris owned the first Fender electric bass in Britain. But that was beyond Entwistle's budget. Instead, he started to make one of his own. 'He bought the wood, carved it out, made the neck and got someone to put the frets on,' remembered Queenie Entwistle. 'Then he painted it mauve. I never thought it would play. But it did.'

The only downside, other than ruining the finish on his grandparents' dining table, which he'd used as a workbench, was that Entwistle had built an unusually long neck to resemble the coveted Fender. Fenton-Weill, the Chiswick guitar-makers tasked with fretting the instrument, used the standard Höfner bass as a guide, which meant several spare inches at the top of the neck without any frets. 'It was diabolical,' said Entwistle, but it was a start.

Townshend and Entwistle began practising together at Woodgrange Avenue. But the noise became too much for Denny. On one occasion, after being told by his grandmother to 'turn it down', all his repressed anger spilled over. Townshend screamed 'Fuck off!', picked up his new amplifier, bought with money saved from his paper round, and hurled it across the room. Entwistle, stoic as ever, lightened the mood by asking, 'What now? Another paper round?'

Townshend managed to get the amp repaired. But his outburst was a forewarning of the destructive behaviour for which The Who's live performances would become notorious. As he later admitted: 'Every time I smashed a guitar I saw my grandmother's face.'

Back at Acton County, not everyone was impressed by Entwistle's and Townshend's musical volte-face. 'When those guys started messing around with rock 'n' roll we thought they'd sold out,' says Chris Sherwin. 'The rest of us were traddies, wearing donkey jackets and sandals, thinking we were beatniks. To us, rock 'n' roll was disgusting.'

Townshend's musical defection would coincide with a dramatic end to his friendship with Sherwin. According to Townshend, the two boys had an argument on the way home from school after Sherwin had been 'harping on about my failings with girls'. In Townshend's version, he swung his schoolbag at Sherwin's head and almost knocked him out. Townshend thought the other boy was feigning injury, but Sherwin was still recovering from a concussion he'd sustained playing rugby. In 2011, Townshend told the BBC that Sherwin retaliated by hitting him with a brick: 'He smashed me on the back of the head with it.' By the time *Who I Am* was published, the brick had disappeared and Townshend wrote that Sherwin had punched him on the side of the head.

In every retelling of the story, though, Townshend has insisted that the brawl led to him being ostracised by his school friends, with the exception of Entwistle: 'Everybody said, "It's terrible what you did to poor old Chris." Apparently he had just been to hospital with concussion, and I had retriggered it. I am sure he could have killed me if he had wanted to. But what he did was arrange to send me to Coventry.'

Sherwin, of course, remembers the incident differently: 'It was the end of term and we all had to take our books home. Pete and I had an argument, and he smacked me round the head with his heavy bag of books. I went down, he did a runner and I got up and chased him down the road and punched him in the ear. I heard an interview he did on Radio 2 where he talked about how the whole school sent him to Coventry. I knew nothing about this.' Whatever the exact circumstances, the fight signalled the end of their relationship. 'We were absolute best mates until this massive falling out,' sighs Sherwin. 'We were talking about me and him going to the Isle of Man where his dad did his summer season . . .'

By now, Sherwin was playing weekend gigs and taking lessons from the local jazz drummer Jim Marshall. In 1960 Marshall opened his first musical instrument shop in Ealing, and would go on to supply instruments and amplifiers for the biggest rock bands of the 1960s and 1970s, including The Who. After leaving school, Sherwin would take a full-time job at Marshall's. 'The Who were big customers, so that made things difficult,' he admits. 'Because Pete and I never spoke to one another again.'

Believing that his school friends had turned against him, Townshend brooded about his predicament, while obsessively practising the electric guitar. 'Maybe I did him a favour then,' offers Sherwin. 'Because I heard on the radio that he became introspective and practised the guitar like mad.'

When Townshend re-emerged, it was the reliably faithful Entwistle who invited him to join his next band. Entwistle was now playing his home-made bass in a group that included two boys from the *Mad* magazine-reading 'comedy clique', guitarist Pete Wilson and drummer Mick Brown. 'Mick's great ambition at that time was to see a hundred X-certificate films before he was actually eligible,' remembers Michael Wheeler.

The group rehearsed at Brown's house. As well as being a proficient drummer, he owned a tape recorder. 'So we did a lot of taped gags — like *The Goon Show* — sped-up sound effects, silly voices, stupid nonsense, but incredibly funny,' said Townshend. While creating their own take on the Goons, Brown also taped his school friend playing The Shadows' hit 'Man of Mystery' on the guitar. Later, Mick took Pete aside and told him that his playing was 'magical'.

'I said, "Oh good". And he said, "No Pete, it's magical,"' recalled Townshend. 'So I went up to see him and his mother, who was a very glamorous, extremely sexy redhead — all the boys were crazy about her — and she sat and listened and said, "Yes, it's magical."' After the uncertainty of the past few months, it was the endorsement Townshend needed: 'Mick Brown and his glamorous mother liked me.' After the paranoia that had dogged him since the fight with Sherwin, Townshend was again part of the gang.

Mick Brown believes that their new group still used the name The Confederates, and that they rehearsed far more than they ever played live. Others, though, including Entwistle, have said they called themselves The Aristocrats and, later, The Scorpions, and that they once played their Shadows covers at that hotbed of sexual activity, the Congo Club. 'We were terrible,' Entwistle said.

Regardless, Townshend felt empowered. Playing guitar to an audience, however small, helped compensate for his lingering anxieties: his large nose, his parents' disinterest, his grandmother's complicity in his abuse, his lack of sexual experience. 'It gave me confidence,' he said.

Unlike Roger Daltrey, though, Townshend still found it hard to imagine making a career out of music. His earlier hopes of becoming a journalist had been usurped by his growing interest in art. Townshend was now taking Saturday morning classes at the local Ealing Technical College & School of Art. His plan was to leave school and take up a place there. The prospect of a factory job, like Daltrey's, with its steady income and camaraderie, held little allure. A life of drawing nude models, listening to pop music and dressing, as he put it, 'in a Bohemian manner' seemed much more appealing.

By 1960, Roger Daltrey's smoking partner and ex-schoolmate Reg Bowen had started playing guitar with a new group. Reflecting the popularity of The Shadows at the time, this new ensemble contained no fewer than four guitarists. Everybody, it seemed, wanted to be Hank Marvin or Bruce Welch.

It was at the Fuller, Smith & Turner brewery's social club in Chiswick that the group acquired one of those guitarists, Vic Arnold. 'I joined them after meeting a guitar player called Bill,' says Arnold now. 'I can't remember Bill's surname, and every time I asked him what it was, he seemed to change it. I did wonder if he was on the run . . .' But 'Bill', who also sang with the band, was well connected. 'His mate's sister was married to Gene Vincent,' remembers Bowen. 'So he had contacts, which helped us get gigs.'

When another of their guitarists left to join an Irish show band, Bowen recommended Roger Daltrey. The girlfriend that had so preoccupied him during his final months at school hadn't been enough to turn him off music for good. Vic Arnold remembers Daltrey auditioning with a gutsy performance of Elvis' 'Heartbreak Hotel'. The band wanted him to join, but Daltrey didn't even own a guitar. To start with, he borrowed Bill's. Then, resourceful as ever, he spent weeks building a new one, based on a photo of a Fender Stratocaster, the hallowed instrument of Hank Marvin and Buddy Holly. 'He came back with this bright-red thing,' marvels Arnold, 'but it worked.'

It didn't take long for Daltrey to make his presence felt and graduate to playing lead guitar. So far, the band had played under several names (none of which anybody can recall now). At Daltrey's suggestion, they started using the name The Detours, lifted from the song 'Detour' by Duane Eddy. 'What stood out for me about Roger Daltrey was that he knew what he wanted,' says Vic Arnold. 'Blinkers on, straight ahead, very confident.' Before long, they all agreed that having four guitarists was a little excessive: 'So it was suggested that someone should learn bass instead, and all eyes seemed to be looking at me.'

Arnold bought a bass on hire purchase, hoping The Detours would make enough money for him to pay off the instalments. Over the coming months, various players, including the enigmatic 'Bill', came and went, lured away by rival groups, parental disapproval or the need to concentrate on a day job. The lead singer's role was soon filled by another ex-Acton County pupil, eighteen-year-old Colin Dawson, whose ability to mimic Cliff Richard made him the ideal candidate for the job.

'My mother always used to say, "Colin is a good singer, but he's very much a Cliff Richard clone,"' says Reg Bowen. 'Whereas she always pointed out that Roger was a proper singer, but he wasn't one for putting himself forward at that time.' When The Detours performed live, Vic Arnold remembers playing songs by Elvis, Cliff Richard, Duane Eddy, Little Richard and poor Buddy Holly, who had now acquired a tragic-hero status, after the plane he was travelling in crashed, killing Holly and all on board in February 1959.

Thanks to Daltrey, The Detours secured an out-of-town booking at Chislehurst Caves in Kent, where Arnold lost his plectrum and 'splattered everyone with blood from the broken blisters on my thumb'. He also fixed them up with the Chase Products' annual work dinner and dance: 'It was at this hotel out of town, and we travelled down there on a coach with all the revellers, and everyone passing bottles of brown ale down the aisle.'

However, after several months, Arnold still wasn't earning enough. When he was asked to join a group booked to open for Chubby Checker, the Philadelphian rock 'n' roller of 'Let's Twist Again' fame, on his UK tour, Arnold didn't hesitate. 'We were at Reg Bowen's house when I told The Detours I was leaving,' he says. 'I went to catch the bus, and Roger ran down the road after me to try and persuade me to change my mind. He kept saying, "Things are looking up, there'll be more gigs . . ." But I kept saying, "No, no . . . I've got this tour support-ing Chubby Checker . . ."'

Vic Arnold caught the bus from Acton, after walking out on the group that was about to become The Who: 'Looking back, it was the probably the silliest mistake anybody's ever made.' Arnold made it into the charts in 1964 with the folk-pop three-piece the Lorne Gibson Trio. He now writes and performs country music. 'The Who wasn't for me,' he insists. 'I have no regrets.'

Daltrey wouldn't have to look far to find a new bass guitarist. It was one of those strange, serendipitous moments: one evening Acton County's most feared hooligan and the 1st South Middlesex Boys' Brigade's star bugler crossed paths in Acton. 'I'd just finished work and I was in hobnail boots and jeans covered in grease,' Daltrey recalled, 'when I see this guy walking towards me with what looked like the biggest guitar I had ever seen in my life.'

It was John Entwistle. Daltrey recognised him from school and also on account of his odd gait. 'John walked a bit like John Wayne,' he recalled. 'He had a swagger.' But he'd never seen the peculiar looking instrument Entwistle was carrying over his shoulder before: 'I said to John, "What is that?" He said, "It's a bass, innit." This thing looked like a football boot, but with a neck on it that was about five feet long.' Being an experienced guitar-maker, Daltrey wasted no time in point-ing out its shortcomings: 'I told him, "That neck's going to fold up on you soon . . ."'

An undeterred Daltrey gave Entwistle a similar speech to the one he'd given Vic Arnold: that The Detours had bookings, that they were earning money, that things were looking up . . . Entwistle listened. Although he was wary of Daltrey's reputation, The Detours played regularly, whereas his school group rehearsed more than they gigged. Entwistle agreed to an audition at The Detours' drummer's house the following week. 'Our drummer at the time was called Harry Wilson,' remembers Reg Bowen. 'A lovely bloke, Harry, but not the greatest of drummers.' Entwistle brought along his 'football boot'-shaped bass, played a couple of songs in the front room and was invited to join the group.

This casual jam session would alter the course of Daltrey and Entwistle's lives. Not that either of them could have imagined it at the time. Fame, it seemed, was something that happened to other people, and even then there was always someone to remind you of where you'd come from.

Adam Faith was, by then, the local Acton boy made good. He had already enjoyed ten top-twenty hits, including the recent 'Someone Else's Baby', a maddeningly catchy song that paired his hiccupping London accent with pizzicato strings, à la Buddy Holly's 'Raining In My Heart'. Faith had left skiffle and rock 'n' roll behind and was about to appear at the Royal Variety Performance.

Bowen and Daltrey had a school friend who lived in the same block of flats in Acton Vale as Faith's mother. 'We'd go over to this guy's place to listen to records,' says Bowen. 'And you'd see Terry Nelhams, as we all still knew him, driving around in a Ford Consul. Later, after he'd made a bit of money, he started turning up this big, flash Yankee job, and all the kids in the flats threw rubbish and old fruit at it.'

Daltrey was ambitious, but nobody truly believed that he was going to become the next Adam Faith or that The Detours would ever rival The Shadows. When they first rehearsed at Bowen's house, Entwistle remembered plugging into Reg's parents' radiogram, as he didn't yet have an amp of his own. When the group did get a booking, they'd arrive at the youth club or church hall in a van driven by Harry Wilson's father. 'None of us took it that seriously,' insists Bowen. 'The whole music scene at that time was a bit "bash it and run".'

Over more than fifty years, the memories have become hazy and half-remembered anecdotes accepted as facts. In some accounts, The Detours' ever-changing line-up included a guitarist named Roy Ellis who accidentally drowned in the Thames, but left behind an expensive

Vox amplifier, which was used to lure Pete Townshend into the band. In fact, the Vox amp was Reg Bowen's, and Ellis died in the summer of 1962, by which time Townshend was already a member.

Whatever the reason, Daltrey made his initial approach to Townshend during his final term at Acton County in the spring of 1961. Entwistle had mentioned Townshend's name to his bandmates on several occasions, but Daltrey was well aware of the Acton County pupil whom he thought resembled 'a nose on a stick' and who'd also dared to challenge his fighting etiquette. He decided to pay Townshend a visit.

After having Daltrey expelled, Desmond Kibblewhite had insisted that he never set foot in the school again. But since his departure, Townshend had occasionally spotted Daltrey in the playground, visiting what he called 'his various cronies'. In his eye-wateringly tight drainpipe trousers and with a quiff so large it now resembled the prow of a ship, Daltrey was difficult to miss. But his school visits went unchallenged by the staff. As Townshend remarked, not without exaggeration though: 'Roger was quite capable of beating to death any teacher that threw a blackboard rubber at him.'

Townshend was in his final term at Acton County and remembers being outside his classroom talking to his form teacher, when he saw Daltrey marching down the corridor towards him. Like Entwistle, Townshend was cautious: he hadn't forgotten their first exchange of words. Communicating via the sort of barked questions and monosyllabic grunts that had so irked the Worried Men's Vic Gibbons, Daltrey told Townshend that he'd heard he was a good guitarist and asked if he wanted to try out for The Detours. 'As calmly as I could,' said Townshend. 'I told Roger I was interested.'

It would be several months before Townshend heard from Daltrey again, but the connection had been made. Townshend had been invited to join his next gang. 'We always try to fill in the missing pieces, don't we?' he said. 'Maybe Roger Daltrey was the thug of an older brother I never had.' Either way, for Townshend, 'It was the greatest bloody triumph of my life.'

CHAPTER THREE

THE DEVIL'S REPERTOIRE

'Oh Lord, don't let them drop that atomic bomb on me.'

Charles Mingus, from the 1962 album, *Oh Yeah!*

'I'd have been much happier as an artist than playing in a rock band.'

Pete Townshend, 2012

Pete Townshend once described The Who as 'four people who shouldn't be in a band together.' Anyone looking for evidence of this might consider how very different Townshend's and Roger Daltrey's lives were at the beginning of 1962. By now, Daltrey was in the third year of his steelworker's apprenticeship. It was a tough job that sometimes left his hands covered with lacerations, making it difficult and even painful to play the guitar.

Meanwhile, Pete Townshend was beginning his second term at Ealing Technical College & School of Art. As part of his study of colour and semiotics, he helped construct an art installation out of Perspex and polythene sheeting. Known as *The Experience Shed*, it stood in one of the classrooms, and became a talking point for students and staff, most of whom had no idea what it was or what it was meant to represent.

That Daltrey and Townshend ended up playing in the same group still seems implausible. Indeed, for a time it looked as if it might not happen at all. Several months lapsed between the singer asking Townshend if he was interested in joining The Detours, and actually inviting him to audition. In the meantime, Townshend and John Entwistle had passed their O Level exams and left Acton County.

Townshend had enrolled as a full-time student at Ealing. It was a seamless transition. But Entwistle who, with his drawings of knights in armour and years of performing in the Middlesex Youth Orchestra, would have made an ideal art or music student, succumbed to family pressure and found a job instead.

He started working as a trainee tax officer. Over the next three years Entwistle worked for the Inland Revenue, at several of its offices, including its main headquarters in Bromyard Avenue, Acton, where his mother Queenie was also employed. Reg Bowen remembers seeing Entwistle emerging from the office looking very much the junior civil servant: 'Pinstripe trousers, a black jacket, detachable shirt collars, a tie, a waistcoat and always carrying a hook-handled umbrella . . .' It was, after all, a career for life.

After Entwistle joined The Detours, Townshend played a couple of local gigs with The Mustangs, a group that included former Sulgrave Rebels Mike McAvoy and Alan Pittaway. They played Shepherd's Bush Cricket Club, and a dinner and dance for the Middlesex BP Scout Guild at the White Hart, in Acton, in September 1961. 'We didn't get paid,' says Mike McAvoy now. 'But when we'd finished the audience all threw money on the floor for us, and we had to scrabble around picking it up.' It was Townshend's first taste of playing a pub that would later become one of The Who's strongholds.

Townshend finally received the call he'd been waiting for in January 1962, after The Detours' wavering line-up changed yet again. John Entwistle later said that Reg Bowen was squeezed out of the group because 'he only knew five chords'. Asked about it now, Bowen says he left willingly: 'I decided that I would sooner play bass than rhythm guitar to Roger's lead.' There were, he insists, no hard feelings, and Bowen was soon playing bass with other groups and working as a roadie for the band: 'They carried on practising at my place for quite a bit longer. My mother always said, "Better here than roaming the streets."'

With Bowen gone, Daltrey finally asked Townshend to audition. As Townshend approached the Daltrey family home in Fielding Road, he witnessed a scene that now sounds like something from a TV movie. A beautiful blonde emerged from Daltrey's house in floods of tears. When she spotted Townshend's guitar case, she asked him to relay a message to the singer. Between sobs, 'She told me to tell Roger that it's either me or that guitar of his.'

In interviews, Townshend has always stressed how sexually precocious the teenage Daltrey was, once telling *Q* magazine: 'Roger was shagging everything that moved, when I was still wanking four or five times a day.' By the time he reached the house, Townshend was convinced Daltrey would postpone the audition: 'But he said, "Get in here. Let's play." I remember she was one of the most beautiful girls I had ever seen in my life. And he was going to dump her because he wanted to play guitar. I was awestruck.'

Daltrey ushered Townshend upstairs to his bedroom. Once inside, he barked out his orders: 'He said, "Can you play [Buddy Holly's] 'Peggy Sue'?" Then, "Can you play [The Shadows'] 'Apache'?" So I sat there and did my Bruce Welch bit and played the rhythm . . . Then he said, "Can you do the steps?"'

Whenever The Shadows played live or appeared on TV, Welch, Hank Marvin and bass guitarist Jet Harris would do a choreographed walk in time to the music. When The Detours played a Shadows number, the audience expected the same. 'So I stood up and did the footwork. After that, Roger said, "OK, see you Tuesday." And that was it.' 'Pete could *really* do the Bruce Welch rhythm,' said Daltrey. 'He could out-rhythm Bruce Welch. I'd never heard guitar playing like it.'

What Townshend didn't know was that while he was doing his Welch impersonation, one of Daltrey's acquaintances was hiding under the bed. The silent witness to the audition was one of two brothers who were then notorious around Shepherd's Bush. One brother, said Townshend, 'was totally crooked, but always very good to me.' The other 'was an awful, awful man.' It was the latter that was hiding in Daltrey's bedroom. 'He was my mate,' confirmed Daltrey. 'He came from a family of villains, he was on the hop, so he stayed under my bed for a few days.'

'All my mates were doing terrible things,' he added. In later interviews, Daltrey would define these as anything from 'larking about' to 'petty villainy'; to 'robbing banks' to 'my mate taking a chopper to someone on the common'. Roger's parents were aware of the company he was keeping, so were all the more happy to let him play music: 'I was a bit of a tearaway. So when I was doing music I wasn't tearing away.' Their approval was tested, though, when Daltrey started holding Detours rehearsals in the house while his parents were out playing cards. The sessions were quickly curtailed after the neighbours complained about the terrible noise.

Pete Townshend remembers making his Detours debut at a hall in Chiswick some time in early 1962. Daltrey was unable to play for long, as he'd cut his hands so badly at work and a nervous Townshend was forced to play lead guitar instead. Soon after, Harry Wilson's father wrote to the BBC's Light Entertainment Department requesting an audition for the group. But they were turned down for not having enough experience.

With each booking, though, The Detours' experience was increasing. In Townshend's case, another Ealing Jewish Youth Club gig or social function at CAV, the engineering firm where Entwistle's girlfriend Alison Wise worked as a secretary, meant another few hours of valuable guitar practice. Playing in the group also reacquainted him with the world he'd glimpsed with The Squadronaires. While The Detours performed their rag-tag collection of Shadows tunes, country and western and trad jazz numbers, Townshend would watch the courtship rituals unfolding among the audience. For him, playing onstage was still infinitely preferable to having to negotiate the battle of the sexes on the dance floor. Daltrey, Dawson and Entwistle all had girlfriends. Townshend didn't.

In July, a year after leaving Acton County, Townshend and Entwistle reunited with drummer Mick Brown and guitarist Pete Wilson to play the annual school leavers' dance. 'Being a big Buddy Holly fan, I shouted out for "Peggy Sue,"' recalls Michael Wheeler. 'Pete Townshend said, "Well, I'll play it, if you come and sing it."' Wheeler obliged, albeit badly. But the gig was a success, and Entwistle and Townshend were invited back to play the following year's school leavers' dance. This time, they came with The Detours. When Desmond Kibblewhite spotted Roger Daltrey, he stormed out of the hall. Acton County's former Teddy Boy rebel had not yet been forgiven.

No sooner had Townshend settled into the band than The Detours' line-up changed again. Drummer Harry Wilson was going on holiday. The group had bookings to fulfil while Wilson was away, and started looking for a temporary replacement. That replacement was

Doug Sandom, who would become The Who's first official drummer. It was a job that would leave him with very mixed feelings, even five decades later.

Harrow Cricket Club in Sudbury, north-west London, has occupied the same quiet spot off Wood End Road since 1958. It's a short drive down from the famous public school and eye-watering property prices of Harrow on the Hill, and a short, if less scenic stroll from Sudbury Hill Underground station, where the air hangs heavy with fumes from the buses snaking along Greenford Road, past rows of drab convenience stores and fast-food outlets.

Most Sunday afternoons, Doug Sandom can be found socialising in the bar of Harrow CC. He is now in his eighties, but in his jeans and Harrington-style jacket looks younger. On the wall beside the bar are framed photographs of Sandom playing drums with The Who. After leaving the group in spring 1964, he could only watch as the band he'd once been a part of became rich and famous without him. 'Leaving The Who wrecked me,' he once said. 'I became a nightmare to live with.' When he did begin drumming again, the pressure of work and family life intervened, and by the late 1970s he had stopped playing altogether.

Local newspaper articles such as the one in 1985 headlined 'DOUG WHO? . . . THE MIGHT HAVE BEEN MAN' only compounded the impression that Sandom had missed out. What the articles didn't acknowledge was that The Who might not have been as successful had they stayed with Sandom and not recruited Keith Moon. Though as Sandom points out, any regrets about leaving The Who are tempered by the fact that 'I'm still alive and Moonie isn't.'

Born in Brentford, Middlesex, nine years before the outbreak of the Second World War, Douglas Sandom started drumming as a child. Fired up by the 'Teddy Boy records' he bought at Shepherd's Bush market, Doug played drums with numerous local bands: 'Anyone that would have me. When one finished I'd move on to the next.' By the time he joined The Detours, he was thirty-two, had been married for almost ten years, and had a young son and a steady job as a bricklayer.

Sandom's entry into The Detours was the result of a strange coincidence. He had heard via an acquaintance that there was a local band looking to hire a drummer. Doug was told he'd be met by one of the band at the playing fields behind Priory Girls' School in Acton Green: 'When I got there, though, the place was locked up. So I'm standing there, thinking I've wasted my time, when I see this little bloke bouncing towards me.'

It was Roger Daltrey. 'He said, "Hello mate, what are you doing?" And at first, I thought, "What the fuck's it got to do with you?"' When Doug relaxed and explained why he was there, Roger told him he played in a band and that he'd been due to meet a drummer for an audition. 'He wasn't waiting for me, though,' insists Sandom. 'He was waiting for somebody else. But they hadn't turned up. At first I thought I'd been set up. But I said I'd have a go with his group anyway.'

The Detours were playing the Paradise Club in Peckham, south London, the following Friday. It was Harry Wilson's final gig before going on holiday, and Sandom agreed to try out by taking over for the second set. That evening, he turned up to meet the band outside Acton Town Hall. 'Remember, I'd only met Roger before then,' he says. 'Walking up, I saw these two blokes standing in the doorway. I thought, I hope that's not them. There was Peter, with his great big nose, and there was John, who was really tall and had this fuzzy hair. Then Colin Dawson came along, and he looked really posh. I thought, "God, it's getting worse . . ." When they turned up with the van, and said, "Jump in, mate", I didn't know whether I wanted to or not.'

That night, it quickly became apparent that Sandom was a better player than Harry Wilson. The Detours were just out of school; Sandom had been playing drums for more than a decade: 'So poor Wilson got sacked.' What Doug Sandom brought to The Detours was focus and experience. What Sandom hadn't told them, though, was his age: 'They thought I was about twenty-four.' He was in no hurry to correct them.

Sandom's first impression of The Detours was only reinforced the more time he spent with them. 'They were so different,' he says. 'Colin was a pop singer, like Cliff Richard. Pete . . .' He hesitates. 'I didn't hate Pete, but I didn't understand him and he didn't understand me. He was an art student; I was a bricklayer. He and I were so different; but when he got onstage, I loved what he did. John was the one I became closest to. I had a lot in common with Roger too. But Roger thought he was the leader of the band and nobody except me would speak up against him.'

Townshend and Daltrey have denied they ever came to blows, and it's also difficult to imagine the gangly, introverted art student squaring up to the school hard-man-turned-steelworker. However, Sandom says they came close on several occasions: 'Always while we were rehearsing. Pete used to say, "Oh, you shouldn't do it like that . . ." Then Roger would say, "I'll do it how I want!" And then it would start.' Townshend would never have dared to hit Daltrey, but he wasn't afraid to voice his opinions. 'I used to jump in between them sometimes. Roger had a temper on him. Poor John was always stood at the back with his arms folded.'

At this point, Sandom was exactly what this group of disorganised ex-schoolboys needed. He was a seasoned pub musician, whose bluff personality helped keep them in line. As a husband and father, Sandom found The Detours a source of valuable extra income, but the band also offered a little glamour after another day on the building site. 'I loved it,' he says. 'I used to rush home from work, get clean, put the suit on. My kid would be watching from the window, and he'd shout out, "Dad! The van's here." I'd think, "Fuck it, I've had no dinner." It didn't matter. I'd been working hard all day but all I wanted to do was get out and play.'

Sandom's age and experience also proved useful when trouble started on the dance floor: 'The thing is, I wasn't afraid to say, "Don't be a cunt."' During his Peckham Paradise audition, a group of blood-stained youths had turned up straight from a fight in a neighbouring club. A week later when The Detours played again, the rival club's gang came seeking revenge.

'The Paradise was a rough, rough place,' confirms Reg Bowen. 'One evening there was a real Wild West fight, with tables and chairs going everywhere. Somebody came flying backwards at the stage and Rog clouted him with his spare guitar.' The soundtrack was now The Shadows instead of Glenn Miller, but the bloodshed and macho posturing weren't so different from what the young Pete Townshend had seen with The Squadronaires at the Palace Ballroom.

The year before, Alan Pittaway had witnessed Betty Townshend's temper during a visit to Woodgrange Avenue: 'As soon as she heard us playing guitars, she'd come down the hall and you knew it was time to leave. I think Pete was terrified of his mother.'

Cliff and Betty were now showing an interest in The Detours. Betty argued that the group needed an agent if they wanted to play anywhere other than birthday and wedding parties. She was also tired of the noise they made when they rehearsed at home: 'I told Cliff, I was going to try and help them because the only way of getting rid of them was to help them.' In September, Cliff called in a favour from a music-biz contact and helped get The Detours on to the bill at Acton Town Hall's Gala Night.

Betty persuaded local promoter Bob Druce to attend the performance. Druce and his business partner ran their agency, Commercial Entertainments, from his house in Wembley. A week later, the *Acton Gazette & Post* reported on the show ('TOWN HALL DANCE GALA SWINGS WITH A NEW LOOK!') and ran a photograph of the 'Acton jazz and jive group The Detours' in their matching suits and ties. John Entwistle was captioned as 'John Johns', and Doug Sandom's age was given as eighteen.

Despite the publicity, Bob Druce had been unimpressed by The Detours' gala performance. But, with Betty to contend with, agreed to give them a second chance at an audition at the Oldfield Hotel in Greenford. The Oldfield once stood at 1089 Greenford Road, a short drive west from Harrow Cricket Club, but was bulldozed around the turn of the millennium. Doug Sandom scavenged a brick from the pub's remains before the site was flattened to make way for a block of flats. The brick was a memento of the drab, west London pub that became The Detours' second home.

Sandom remembers the night of The Detours' audition, mainly because of how nervous his bandmates were: 'Roger was as white as a sheet.' Nonetheless, Druce was impressed enough to take the band on. His first booking was a gig in the coastal town of Broadstairs, Kent. When The Detours arrived at the stately looking Grand Ballroom, a coach pulled up alongside, discharging scores of pensioners. It was their audience for the night.

'Bob Druce struck me as very streetwise and shrewd,' says Alan Pittaway, whose group The Mustangs were also signed to Druce's agency. 'His thing was – find a pub with a hall, offer to put a band in there and tell the manager that it would be good for profits.' Druce's circuit of venues included the Oldfield, the Railway Hotel in Greenford and the White Hart in Acton, whose proximity to the police station was fortunate. Sandom: 'They were some terrible fights in there. Absolutely terrible.' But Druce's territory also extended into the West End to Leicester Square's Notre Dame Hall and further out to dance halls in south London.

Under the terms of their deal, Druce pocketed ten per cent of The Detours' earnings, and a further ten for his role as de facto manager. Since Harry Wilson's departure, Betty Townshend had taken to bussing the group around in the small van she used for her antiques business. 'Betty was a handful,' says Doug Sandom. 'I wouldn't like to argue with her, but she did us a lot of favours.' Roger Daltrey was less impressed: 'It was a bloody nightmare in the back of a five-hundred weight van with the roof three inches from our heads.' Before long, the singer had talked Bob Druce into paying for some new transport. He agreed, but the cost of The Detours' new van meant their agent taking a further cut of the band's modest earnings.

Daltrey took it upon himself to drive the new vehicle, despite not having passed his test. In time, he'd crash it into the side of a bridge and dent the passenger door so badly it never opened again. While his bandmates accepted having to clamber over the driver's seat to get into the van, Daltrey's numerous girlfriends found it less appealing. Later on, several inventive paint jobs would fail to conceal the van's numerous dents and blemishes.

The final months of 1962 marked the beginning of a period when, as Townshend put it, 'we went a bit nuts'. The Detours' well-groomed lead singer Colin Dawson had gone through a period of calling himself 'Del Angelo', in homage to the American rock 'n' roll star Del Shannon, of hit-single 'Runaway' fame. Entwistle would also adopt several different stage names: John Allison (after girlfriend Alison Wise), John Johns (his stepfather's surname) and, for a time, John Browne. There was also a brief attempt to play with another ex-Acton County pupil, guitarist Peter Vernon-Kell.

'Irish' Jack Lyons, co-author of *The Who Concert File* and one of The Who's earliest fans, caught his first glimpse of the band at a Saturday night 'record hop' at Boseley's dance hall in Shepherd's Bush in 1962.

'The Detours were dressed in funeral suits and did special formation steps just like The Shadows,' he wrote. 'Roger on lead guitar and trombone, not even singing. Pete was playing rhythm guitar, still just about learning to play then. John was on bass guitar and trumpet. The singer was a guy called Colin Dawson who did Cliff Richard impressions.'

As Christmas 1962 approached, though, Dawson's days as a Detour were numbered. John Entwistle later said that Dawson, with his yachting blazer and slacks, was 'a bit too dapper for us', and that the rest of the band, especially Daltrey, wanted a tougher image. 'They used to take the piss out of Colin,' says Doug Sandom, 'always standing there in the front with his little arse wiggling.'

'The guys were determined to go professional,' Dawson explained. 'But I had a decent job with a company car, selling bacon, and I decided to quit.' Colin Dawson's days as a rep for Danish Bacon wouldn't last. He went on to run several British theme parks, and in 2010 was awarded with an OBE for his services to the tourist industry, prompting a congratulatory text message from Daltrey.

Dawson's departure prompted The Detours to bring in a new vocalist, as Daltrey still didn't feel confident enough to sing a whole set. Gabby Connolly had previously sung and played bass with another popular Commercial Entertainments act, The Bel-Airs. His vocals were to prove a winning addition to one of the group's latest bookings. Betty Townshend had called an old contact from her wartime singing days and secured the group a regular Sunday afternoon gig at the American Officers' Club in Douglas House, Bayswater.

'We did Douglas House, but we also did every American base camp from the Wash [on the East Anglian coast] down – Lakenheath, Mildenhall, Brize Norton,' says Gabby Connolly now. 'They paid so well, but their lifestyle was so different to what I was used to.'

As a child, Townshend had accompanied his parents to many US Air Force camps and marvelled at the rich food and smart cars. Now history was repeating itself. 'I was living in a dirty old block of flats in Latimer Road, Notting Hill,' says Connolly. 'But once you drove through the gates of those camps it was like being in America. There were flash cars everywhere, the money was all dollars, and you could even buy Levi's. It was like entering another world.'

Connolly was especially adept at singing country and western, and his version of gravel-voiced country star Johnny Cash's 'I Walk the Line' went down particularly well with dewy-eyed US servicemen, thousands of miles from home: 'I'm not sure if the others in the group liked it so much. But I didn't care – the audience bought me drinks all night.'

Connolly now compares The Detours gigs to 'huge jamming sessions with everyone swapping instruments'. He sang but also played bass when Entwistle switched to trumpet for the Dixieland jazz numbers. Nothing if not versatile, on an average night The Detours would flit from trad jazz to country, to Del Shannon's 'Swiss Maid' and The Ventures' 'Walk Don't Run'.

There was just one problem: their rhythm guitarist was leading a double life. 'None of the people in or around The Detours had much idea what I was up to at art school,' Townshend later wrote. 'And I found it difficult to say much about the band to my art school friends.' It would be some time yet before he would reconcile the two worlds.

On reflection, Pete Townshend was both a typical and atypical art student. In his 1970 pop culture study, *Revolt into Style*, George Melly famously wrote that British art schools in the 1950s and 1960s were the 'refuge of the bright but unacademic, the talented, the non-conformist, the lazy, the inventive and the indecisive: all those who didn't know what they wanted but knew it wasn't a nine-til-five job'.

Art schools had provided a refuge for several of Melly's jazz-musician peers, including Humphrey Lyttelton. And they would do the same for a younger generation that included The Kinks' Ray Davies, The Faces' Ronnie Wood, John Lennon and early Beatle Stuart Sutcliffe, Eric Clapton, Jimmy Page, Keith Richards and Freddie Mercury. 'It was the place where everybody went who didn't fit in anywhere else,' said ex-Harrow and Croydon School of Art student and future Sex Pistols' manager Malcolm McLaren.

Rolling Stone Keith Richards was a perfect example of the kind of student Melly had been writing about. Richards arrived at Sidcup Art College in the summer of 1959 only because he'd been expelled and couldn't face the prospect of getting a job. 'It was a pretty lax routine,' he recalled in his 2010 autobiography, *Life*. 'You did your classes, finished your projects and there was a little hang-out classroom, where we sat around and played guitar. There was a lot more music than art going on at Sidcup.' Richards was being steered towards a career in graphic design and advertising. But he was part of what he described as 'the dilapidated tail-end of a noble art-teaching tradition from a pre-war period.'

Ealing Technical College & School of Art on St Mary's Road housed departments for graphic and fine arts, fashion, photography, science and mathematics. In 1961, the British artist and theorist Roy Ascott was appointed its head of foundation studies, and introduced a revolutionary two-year groundcourse that aimed to challenge the pre-war 'noble art-teaching tradition' Keith Richards had experienced at Sidcup.

Ascott had studied fine art in the mid-1950s under the influential painter Richard Hamilton and the abstract artist Victor Pasmore, and arrived full of ideas. In 1961, Sir William Coldstream, the chairman of the National Advisory Council on Art Education, introduced a new diploma in art and design (known as the DipAD) into the country's art schools. Its purpose was to give students the chance to explore fine art, three-dimensional design, graphics, fashion and textiles. Coldstream's reforms empowered Ascott, whose groundcourse included these subjects but also, unusually, semiotics, computer thinking and cybernetics – 'a word that wasn't even in the dictionary,' said Townshend.

To help achieve his aims, Ascott appointed a group of like-minded tutors. These included the British abstract artists Anthony Benjamin, Robert Brownjohn, and Bernard and Harold Cohen, and the American collage artist Ronald 'R.B.' Kitaj. Townshend's planned three-year graphic design course was preceded by two years of what he called 'being disabused of our preconceptions about art, art schools, art teaching and all forms of design'.

Before long, though, Townshend and his fellow students were embracing their newly acquired freedom. Richard Barnes, nicknamed 'Barney', and author of the first Who biography, *Maximum R&B*, joined Ealing in 1961, and later became Townshend's closest friend. Barnes was a Willesden County Grammar School boy who'd joined the Young Communist League and 'gone all left wing and rebellious'. Attending art school was his latest act of dissent: 'My school wanted its pupils to go to Oxford or Cambridge. When I said I wanted to go to art school, it was as if I'd said I wanted to work in a brothel.'

Ascott and his staff introduced exercises intended to challenge their students' inherited ways of seeing. One art class were told to re-imagine the world from the perspective of a sponge. Another was given wildly varying timeframes in which to draw different parts of a life-model's body: two days to sketch one ankle; six seconds to draw both legs.

'We had one exercise that involved forming into groups and going up to Ealing Broadway with the instructions to "make something happen",' says former student John Bonehill. 'My group stole an apple from the greengrocer's. Then we had to write an essay about this, do a series of drawings explaining peripheral public reactions, then build a machine which would express the essence of this experience.' On another occasion, Bonehill's group were arrested for leaving a fake bomb on an Underground train, which resulted in the closure of Mansion House tube station: 'We were suspended from college until we'd written up the reaction to what we'd done. But I think Roy Ascott was secretly pleased.'

Other students, including Townshend, were told to imagine they'd been deprived of some physical or emotional sense. One student spent a day standing stock still in a display case in the college hallway. 'We sneaked downstairs to spy on him to see if he kept up his pose even when nobody was watching him, and he did,' says Richard Barnes.

Townshend, meanwhile, pushed himself around in a trolley cart to experience life as an amputee. He was also told he could only communicate in a phonetic alphabet devised by his fellow students; a portent of the sensory-deprived character Tommy in The Who's 1969 rock opera. Townshend would later credit Ascott with inspiring his notion of a global computer network, essentially a prototype internet, in *Lifehouse*, the planned follow-up to *Tommy*.

Barney found Roy Ascott's counter-intuitive approach to teaching both inspiring and confusing: 'Some of what Ascott wanted to do was very laudable and some of it was laughable. He used to say, "I'm going to break down all your preconceptions about art," but you could say he left us with nothing. Most of the time we didn't know what was going on. I walked into a classroom once and the students had stuck all the furniture to the walls. Everything – tables, chairs, the lot. It was like looking at the room from the ceiling. But the feeling was, "Don't say anything," because we were having such a good time.'

To begin with, few of Townshend's fellow students knew that he played in a band. In 1961 and 1962, jazz was the preferred music of many art students, be they sandal-wearing "Ooblies' still flying the flag for trad, or modernists enthusing about Miles Davis. In the late 1950s, John Lennon had railed against the jazz lovers that ran Liverpool School of Art's music club: 'What a lot of fucking shit you play,' he protested. 'Why don't you play something proper, like Little Richard, Chuck Berry or Elvis Presley?' In contrast, Pete Townshend joined the college jazz club and worried that playing in a rock 'n' roll group wasn't terribly hip.

It was a strange existence. By day Townshend was constructing art installations and pondering Canadian philosopher Marshall McLuhan's communication theory. At night, he was playing 'Walk Don't Run' to pubs full of drunks. 'I've been at art school, hearing about the way media and electronics have changed the semiotics of society,' he said, 'and the guys in the band are going, "Great-looking blonde down there. Let's see if we can get her in the van."'

In October 1962, Townshend's anxieties about The Detours and the true nature of art were briefly forgotten. He was now convinced he was going to die. That summer, the US government had discovered Russian-sponsored nuclear missile sites in Cuba. The missiles were part of a plan to deter the US from attempting to overthrow Cuban president Fidel Castro's Communist regime. America demanded that the sites be dismantled, and imposed a military blockade. Castro refused. When a US surveillance plane was shot down over the Caribbean island, the world braced itself for the possibility of nuclear war.

'Like every other kid my age, I'd grown up afraid that Russia was going to drop a bomb on us. And it shaped my life,' said Townshend. 'I remember going into college during the Cuban Missile Crisis and thinking, That's it, my life is finished. Why am I even doing this?' After a tense, fifteen-day standoff, US president John F. Kennedy and the Soviet Premier Nikita Khrushchev reached an agreement. The missile sites were dismantled. The world collectively breathed a sigh of relief, and The Detours went off to play their regular gig at the Grand Ballroom in Broadstairs.

Townshend couldn't help feeling disappointed. In 1960, he'd listened to a radio broadcast of the Labour MP Michael Foot and the socialist historian Bertrand Russell speaking in Trafalgar Square at the outset of the Aldermaston March. Both men had warned of the horrors that lay ahead unless the world agreed on nuclear disarmament. Russell's speech had quoted from the author and left-wing publisher Victor Gollancz's book *The Devil's Repertoire*. 'I remember hearing Bertrand Russell repeating the words of Victor Gollancz – "Unless you young people end this horror, this abhorrence, sooner or later you will be walking into the sea, with pus running from your eyes." I was absolutely fucking terrified.' The fear, relief and disappointment he experienced during and after the Cuban Missile Crisis would later colour his songwriting: 'The threat passed, but when it passed, there was also this sense of, oh, we've been fooled again' – a feeling that would colour one of The Who's most famous songs, 'Won't Get Fooled Again', in 1971.

In the aftermath of this near-death experience, Townshend claimed to have made a life-changing decision: that being introverted would get him nowhere with his classmates and, especially, with women. He asked Roger Daltrey's sister, Carol, on a date, and, soon after, had his first taste of alcohol at the Oldfield. 'I said, "Have a drink, one pint won't hurt you," ' recalls Doug Sandom, 'and the next thing he was pissed out of his head.' Years later, when Townshend discussed his alcoholism, The Detours' drummer felt a twinge of guilt and wondered whether he'd set the wheels of addiction in motion.

As Townshend emerged from his shell, his social circle at Ealing widened. By late 1962, Townshend had become part of a clique that included, among others, American photography student Tom Wright, and other groundcourse pupils Richard 'Barney' Barnes and John Challis. 'To this day I don't know how I got together with Pete,' says Barnes. 'He was shy, at first, very shy, and I had a feeling that perhaps he'd suffered as a child because of his looks. I know he had a problem with other people, but our relationship was always easy. Pete and I always got on.' However, it was some time before Barnes discovered that his new friend played in a band.

Tom Wright met Townshend after his flatmate and fellow student Tim Bartlett had seen him in the common room playing guitar. 'He said, "You've got to see this guy,"' recalled Wright, who wandered over to find a crowd gathered around 'a big-nosed kid', wearing jeans and a scarf. He was strumming an acoustic guitar and casually demonstrating chord changes and intricate licks far beyond than anything they'd seen before.

Wright also played guitar and was so impressed he asked Townshend back to his flat in the hope that he'd teach him how to play. Tom Wright had been living in Florida before his stepfather re-enlisted in the US Air Force and was posted to the American airbase in Ruislip, west London. After leaving school, Tom and a fellow American pupil, Cam McLester, enrolled at Ealing. Joined by Tim Bartlett, they took over a flat at 35 Sunnyside Road, barely a three-minute walk from the college.

McLester's father worked in the oil business, and both he and Wright enjoyed a higher standard of living than most of their impoverished peers. 'Compared to the rest of us they were rich kids,' says ex-Ealing student, now illustrator and musician John Challis. 'I remember them picking us up from Ealing Broadway in Cam's dad's car, and it was this huge Cadillac with fins. It was so big, once you were in it, you had to shout to be heard.'

Between them, rich kids Wright and McLester had built up a collection of over two-hundred LPs. 'We had every record that Jimmy Reed, Chuck Berry, Ray Charles, Elvis, Buddy Holly and Booker T and the MGs ever made,' said Wright, who went on to become a music photographer and, for a brief time, The Who's tour manager. The collection also included jazz LPs by John Coltrane, Charles Mingus and Dave Brubeck, and dozens of blues records by the likes of Howlin' Wolf, Little Walter, Big Bill Broonzy, Muddy Waters and Lightnin' Hopkins. Stacked together, spine to spine, the collection snaked around the walls of the flat, their sleeves as colourful and inviting as the music inside.

Townshend already knew the country-blues players Broonzy, McGee and Lead Belly, the last of whom had recorded 'Rock Island Line' long before Lonnie Donegan. But the Sunnyside Road collection was a revelation. During visits to the flat, he'd plug his guitar into the record player and play along to whatever was spinning on the turntable. The rest of the time was spent rifling through the collection, discovering unheard gems by soul singers Ray Charles and James Brown, the folk songwriter Joan Baez and Mississippi blues guitarist Jimmy Reed.

However, Townshend's introduction to American blues was accompanied by another significant discovery. The Sunnyside Road flatmates regularly ventured into Soho, to clubs frequented by black American GIs and Jamaicans, where marijuana was readily available. By the time they met Townshend, the Americans had access to a regular supply and were smoking on a daily basis. The ritual was always the same: draw the curtains, light a candle, drop a record on to the turntable and roll a joint. Townshend smoked dope for the first time in Sunnyside Road, and immediately noticed the effect it had on the music. 'You put a record on and it was like, aaaaah,' he told the author. 'Remember, we had shitty little mono record players at the time, but on dope you were already hearing everything in stereo.'

'Tom Wright said to me a few years ago, "Remember all that research we did flat on our backs?"' says Richard Barnes. 'And he was right. We used to lie there smoking and really going deep into the jazz and the blues. Booker T and the MGs' 'Green Onions' was played all the time, but the main one was Jimmy Reed. We didn't stop listening to Jimmy Reed.' The Mississippi bluesman with the drawling voice and mesmerising guitar had a stoned-sounding insouciance that made him the ideal accompaniment to an afternoon smoke.

When they weren't researching the music through clouds of pot smoke, the party would drift over to Sid's Caff ('not café,' cautions John Challis), a 'greasy spoon' opposite the art school. Sid's was a refuge from lectures and tutorials, where friendships and love affairs could be cultivated over endless cups of tea, and hangovers cured by what Challis calls '*spécialité de la maison*': 'Baked beans on a fried slice with a smear of Marmite, and if you wanted to push the boat out you could have a fried egg on top for an extra fourpence.'

To improve the ambience at Sid's, Tom Wright persuaded the owner to let him put some of his records on the jukebox. Figuring that his student clientele would spend more money, he readily agreed. From now on, Little Eva's exuberant 'The Loco-Motion' would be followed by 'Green Onions', Charlie Parker's 'Cosmic Rays' or the Jimmy Giuffre

Trio's exquisitely laid-back 'The Train and the River'. Not all of Sid's clientele were impressed. 'You used to get a lot of lorry drivers in there,' says Barnes. 'We'd have Roland Kirk's "Three for the Festival", where Roland's playing nose flute, blasting away, and the lorry drivers were going, "Fuck this, I want to hear [Frank Ifield's] 'I Remember You'."'

In 1962, Roger Ruskin Spear, who would go on to join the satirical pop group the Bonzo Dog Doo-Dah Band, was studying applied maths and physics at Ealing. There was just one problem: he was constantly distracted by the female students from the fashion college who floated past his classroom on their way to Sid's. 'The fashion department at Ealing was full of all these lovely, fizzy girls,' recalls John Challis, 'any number of which seemed to be called Sue or Jenny.'

Roger's father, the painter Ruskin Spear, lectured at the Royal College of Art, but advised his son that 'art schools were full of drop-outs, and that I'd be better off doing something else'. This paternal advice went ignored: 'By Christmas, I realised I was in the wrong place and I just *had* to go to the art school.' Spear transferred onto the ground-course, but didn't completely sever his ties with reality by continuing to study applied maths. 'It was a schizophrenic life. Halfway through line-drawing class, I had to pop off to a maths class. Then, when I went to Sid's, the stoned art students would ask me what I'd been doing and I'd try and teach them about partial integration.'

Spear first encountered Pete Townshend in Sid's. The introverted, beatnik-looking student Tom Wright had met a few months earlier was gone. 'My main recollection is of Pete wearing a yellow shirt, a blue felt jacket and a red bow tie,' says Spear. 'That and, of course, this enormous conk. When I saw him I remember thinking, there's a guy who's really enjoying being an art student. Before that, art students were all duffel coats and scruffy hair, with paint rags hanging out of their pockets, like a hangover from the trad jazz era. Everything about Pete said, "I am a sophisticated graphics student."'

Spear had seen Townshend playing his guitar in the college, but hadn't realised he was anything to do with The Detours. He also lived in Acton and had spotted the band's van parked outside Roger Daltrey's house in Fielding Road. As well as having 'The Detours' and a large arrow painted on the side, the van also had 'a rather dodgy-looking witch's smokestack' that Daltrey had welded to its roof: 'I sometimes followed the van into Ealing, but it was a while before I saw Pete get out of it and twigged what was going on.'

As his confidence grew Townshend started to let his guard down about the group. By the spring of 1963, the band's audience had begun to include a smattering of curious art students. Tom Wright ventured out to see The Detours at the Fox and Goose Hotel in nearby Hanger Lane. He thought Townshend's guitar playing sounded better at Sunnyside Road, and was unsure about Doug Sandom: 'They had a drummer who looked like somebody's dad or older brother, and didn't seem to be having as much fun,' recalled Wright in his 2007 memoir, *Raising Hell on the Rock 'n' Roll Highway*.

Things were changing. When Townshend looked out from the stage at Hanwell's Park Hotel one night, he was delighted to spot some of the Ealing's fashion department's 'lovely fizzy girls' in the audience. Women were showing an interest in him, but he was still unsure of himself. 'At Ealing there were two girls at the college that I can only describe as quantum nymphomaniacs,' he said. 'They shagged *everybody*. There were occasions I would go round to Tom's and listen to records, and at the end of the night, Tom would say, "Can you see 'Sue' home?" We'd be walking along the road and she'd say, "I only went to see Tom so I could have a fuck." I'd go, "Oh really, you must be very disappointed." And she'd say, "Yes, because I really wanted to have . . . a *fuck*." We'd be outside her house, and I'd say, "You're here now, in you go." And the next day Tom would come up to me and say, "Pete, she fucking spelt it out for you."' Townshend said he lost his virginity a few months later: 'It happened when it was meant to happen – when I was eighteen. Late for some, but fine for me.'

Not all of The Detours shared Townshend's reticence. After the group played a wedding reception in Perivale, Bob Druce received a note complaining about their behaviour towards one of the married women at the event. 'Pete was shy, and John had Alison at the gigs so he couldn't get up to much,' says Doug Sandom. 'That left it open for Roger . . . and me.' Vic Arnold, who'd left The Detours almost two years earlier, saw his old band playing in a west London pub, and was shocked: 'They were drinking cheap sherry onstage and acting like they would when they became The Who. They were all pissed and wild. I remember thinking, my god, what a change.'

In June, The Detours played the first of what would turn into a regular Friday night gig at the Shepherd's Bush Club, a working men's bar at 20 Goldhawk Road. Commercial Entertainments were now hosting groups in the club's downstairs function room, a small space down a few steps from the main bar and accessible through a curtain of brightly coloured plastic strips. The Shepherd's Bush Club soon acquired a new name, 'the Goldhawk Club', at weekends. It became a regular haunt for The Detours/Who, and was a place where the band and Roger Daltrey's so-called 'terrible tearaway' friends would meet head on. 'It was packed with guys that were just coming out of the nick,' recalled one old regular.

In the meantime, the Goldhawk became the venue where Doug Sandom first encountered his number-one fan. 'She was a big girl called Sue,' he says fondly. 'Massive, really tall.' But the diminutive drummer's lack of height clearly appealed: 'Every time we turned up she would be waiting on the pavement outside, and she would pick me up and walk me in like I was a toy, and put me on the stage.'

The power struggles within The Detours were soon matched by those taking place at Ealing art school. Roy Ascott and his hip new teaching staff were still meeting resistance from some of the college's more traditionally minded lecturers and pupils. 'Despite the groundcourse, we still had to have the odd lesson with the old guard, because the college couldn't afford to employ all new teachers,' says Roger Spear. 'This meant that one moment you'd be with all these lovely old art-school types, and the next it was all morphism and abstract modern art with Ascott and his buddies.'

'The groundcourse wasn't great for me, because I wanted to be an animator,' says John Challis, who later worked on The Beatles' 1968 film *Yellow Submarine*. 'What you needed for that is lots of drawing practice. I used to have to go to life-drawing classes with the old ladies in the evening because it wasn't being taught on the course, which seemed ridiculous. I realised then how much of art school teaching is founded on bullshit.'

Townshend, however, found all the bullshit, conflict and left-field ideas inspiring. Before long, they would start to influence his approach to music and what he was doing with The Detours. He was excited to see Anthony Benjamin cutting his thumb, smearing blood across a piece of paper and declaring 'That's a line' in front of a baffled line-drawing class. On another occasion, Townshend attended a lecture by the American artist Ronald Kitaj, who spent three minutes standing in front of the class silently weeping, before declaring: 'This is what being an artist is about – pain!' Kitaj had such an effect on Townshend that he, like English pop artist Peter Blake, was later hired to contribute to the cover art for The Who's 1981 album *Face Dances*.

Through late 1962 and into 1963, Townshend attended several lectures by visiting artists and playwrights; many of which would have a significant impact on his thinking. The English dramatist David Mercer's trilogy of plays, *Where the Difference Begins*, *A Climate of Fear* and *The Birth of a Private Man*, all explored issues of socialism and class loyalty, and had recently been broadcast on the BBC. Mercer gave a lunchtime lecture at Ealing in which he railed against the suburban mentality of the British middle classes; albeit to an audience comprising a fair number of middle-class students.

'He was an incredibly impressive speaker,' said Townshend. 'He said, "Once you're on the Left, you have to stay there whatever happens. I don't care if you become a fucking billionaire, stay there." And I've always kept that in mind.' A year later, Mercer's trilogy was published in book form as *The Generations*, inspiring the title of The Who's single 'My Generation'.

The New York-born musician, poet and artist Larry Rivers was another visiting lecturer. Rivers had played saxophone with Miles Davis and Charlie Parker, and been discharged from the US Army on bogus medical grounds to become a painter and sculptor. By the early 1960s, he was regarded as a founding father of the pop art movement, where art was created out of ordinary, kitsch and supposedly lowbrow influences lifted from popular culture.

To Townshend, Rivers' Ealing lecture was a revelation: 'He was the first gay, American junkie sax-playing painter I'd ever met.' Four years later, you could trace a line between Rivers' images of mundane consumer goods and flashy American cars and the spoof ads for acne cream, baked beans and deodorant on the cover of *The Who Sell Out* LP. But it was his wisecracking New York humour that most, if not all, of those who attended his lecture appreciated.

'Larry Rivers was one of the tipping points, where the trad teaching faculty gave up hope,' says Roger Spear. 'There was a teacher called Miss Ockenden who taught us lettering, and she was there when Rivers came in. He just started beating two rocks together, and the tone of his lecture was, "Art is crap, you are all wasting your time, go out and do something else." And, of course, this upset poor Miss Ockenden. At the end of the lecture, he asked if anyone had any questions, and she put her hand up and said, "How dare you come here?" Rivers just laughed and said, "I thought that would have been the first question."'

'The question that was *always* being asked at Ealing, was: "How can we subvert art?"' adds Spear. 'And that often meant doing anything but painting a picture.' This approach was endemic in the work of the German artist Gustav Metzger. As a young Jew growing up in Nuremberg in the 1930s, Metzger witnessed the rise of Nazism before fleeing to England. Having survived the Second World War, he became a committed Marxist in favour of unilateral nuclear disarmament.

In 1959, Metzger created a work of art as a protest against nuclear weapons by spraying hydrochloric acid on to sheets of nylon. Two years later, he gave a demonstration at London's South Bank of 'acid action painting'. This involved flinging acid at three canvases, and observing the results; a technique he would call 'auto-destructive art'. Elsewhere, Metzger made art out of newspapers, discarded packaging and other everyday objects. In late 1962, during his first Ealing lecture, he showed slides of 'acid action paintings', and Super 8 film of art students smashing up a piano in the street, and of a Japanese youth slashing through a canvas with a Samurai sword.

The slides showed Metzger, his bald head framed by wild tufts of hair and squeezed into a protective helmet and goggles, attacking vast hanging canvases with corrosive substances. In The Who's story, Gustav Metzger is often reductively described as 'the man who inspired Pete Townshend to smash his guitar'. In fact, his influence went further still. Metzger's philosophy was essentially: 'We are destroying our planet and art should reflect that destruction,' according to Townshend. 'He was the first person that I ever heard use the word "environment".' From listening to Metzger, Townshend came to believe that 'art should reflect accurately on what society was doing to its habitat". He was also taken with Metzger's idea that an artist should not only destroy his art but should also destroy the tools he uses to make that art.

In 1967 Townshend touched on environmentalism by writing about an over-populated world on *The Who Sell Out* track 'Rael'. Three years later, Metzger's ideas would feed into the aborted *Lifehouse* project, where Townshend imagined a world ruined by pollution, and a population forced to live in an artificial environment. *Lifehouse* was scrapped, but many of its ideas were explored on 1971's *Who's Next* album with its anthems, 'Baba O'Riley' and 'Won't Get Fooled Again'.

But what Townshend also took away from Metzger's lecture was a very specific image. During the lecture, he was struck by the footage of a Japanese youth painting a canvas before cutting through it with a sword: 'As he comes through, he's holding his arm in the air, and it's very characteristic of loads of photos that you see now of me as a young man with my arm in the air [playing guitar]. I've still got that picture in my head.'

Townshend thought that the youth wielding the sword was a colleague of Yoko Ono's (although in a 2007 interview he suggested it was Ono herself). At the time, Ono was part of Fluxus, a network of devoutly anti-commercial artists. In 1965, she would appear onstage at New York's Carnegie Hall and demonstrate her own destructive art by inviting the audience to cut off her clothes.

However, while Metzger was a huge influence on Townshend's thinking, he never destroyed a musical instrument. In Townshend's mind, that accolade went to jazz musician and visiting lecturer Malcolm Cecil. 'Malcolm came out and talked about being a musician and what a musician does,' said Townshend. 'A student challenged him and said, "What does a bass do? It just goes boom boom boom."' And Malcolm got quite angry.' In Townshend's memory, Cecil started demonstrating increasingly aggressive ways of playing the double bass, which included hitting the strings with the bow. Then, after spotting a wood saw in the room, he proceeded to hack through the strings, much to the class's delight. In some interviews, Townshend has said that Cecil went further still by sawing through the body of the bass, but Cecil denied this. 'I didn't saw through the bass,' he told a BBC interviewer. 'Just through the strings. But Pete was most impressed apparently.'

Fellow musicians Roger Spear and John Challis had mixed feelings about it all. 'I couldn't quite make out what Gustav Metzger was saying because his accent was so thick,' admits Challis. 'And I was worried if he started chucking acid about I'd get hurt.' But Spear, who would soon join the Bonzo Dog Doo-Dah Band, a group who mixed jazz and rock with Dadaist humour, found inspiration in this anti-establishment approach: 'It went along with our philosophy in the Bonzos to break down barriers.'

While Townshend would use the destructive elements in The Who, Spear would borrow some of the more absurdist ideas for the Bonzo Dog Doo-Dah Band. Where their tastes met was in a shared appreciation of an unusual local musician, bearded, bespectacled jazz aficionado and GPO engineer Andy Newman. Together with Roger Spear's college friend Dick Seaman, Newman had recorded an album called *Ice and Essence*, of which only two copies existed. The music used tape effects and echoes. It was deeply atmospheric, deeply odd and far removed from conventional pop. Seaman booked Newman to play a Friday lunchtime gig at the college.

That afternoon, Newman placed a metronome on top of his piano before proceeding to perform for over an hour without once addressing the audience. He sang in a high falsetto, occasionally breaking off to blow into a kazoo. 'Pete thought this was marvellous,' says Richard Barnes. 'He really did become obsessed with Andy Newman. We saw him walking around Ealing one day. He looked so odd, like a professor, or something out of a *Rupert Bear* annual. Pete and I were ducking behind cars, so he wouldn't see us.' Five years later, Townshend would steer Andy Newman into the pop charts with the group Thunderclap Newman and the hit single 'Something in the Air'. In 1963, though, this GPO engineer with his kazoo, metronome and strange tape effects became one of many disparate influences that Townshend would later channel into The Who .

Metzger's and Cecil's destructive art, Rivers' wisecracking humour and Mercer preaching class war, all left their mark on the eighteen-year-old Townshend. After sex, marijuana and blues had been added into the mix, the result was a dramatic new manifesto: 'That the band would last a year and then we would destroy ourselves, and then I planned to go off and become a serious artist.'

Naturally, it was impossible to describe this destructive thesis to his bandmates: 'I wanted to do art. They wanted something more straight-forward.' It was hardly surprising. The Detours were now playing three or four nights a week to a crowd that expected straight copies of chart hits. In time, Townshend would sneak an obscure blues or jazz number such as Jimmy Smith's 'Plum Nellie' into the set and feel momentarily triumphant, before it was back to playing Del Shannon's 'Swiss Maid'.

Yet over the summer of 1963, everything started to change again. Gabby Connolly's fiancée was complaining about how much time he spent with the band: 'So I told her I'd pack it in.' But there were other factors besides the workload: 'I know the rest of them weren't happy with the sort of music we were doing. Also I was drinking too much. I did some silly things. I had a terrible temper and couldn't always curtail it.' Connolly maintains that he got on well with all of the band, but admits that he and Daltrey might have come to blows if he'd stayed: 'I was a tearaway, and always thought me and him might end up in a bust-up once day.'

Connolly sold his Fender Precision bass to John Entwistle, gave up music and later took a job for life delivering bread. Three years after his exit, Gabby and his fiancée were eating their evening meal when The Who appeared on television: 'I looked up and thought, "You've missed the boat again, Connolly. Jesus! That could have been you." Of course I have regrets. But, in all honesty, I don't think I'd have lasted five minutes in The Who.'

With The Detours now a four-piece, Townshend's confidence grew – just as Roger Daltrey's diminished. Factory work was taking its toll on Daltrey's hands. 'It just became impossible to play in the end,' he said. 'And it made sense for Pete to play lead guitar. He was so much better than I was.' At the time, nobody could have predicted how significant Daltrey's decision would turn out to be.

'That change really threw Pete in at the deep end,' says Doug Sandom. But Townshend rose to the challenge. His head was now full of colliding influences: from country picker Chet Atkins to dead rock 'n' roll hero Eddie Cochran; from Stax Records' session king and Booker T and the MGs guitarist Steve Cropper to the rumbling sounds of bluesmen Howlin' Wolf and Jimmy Reed. And in the autumn of 1963, he'd add another influence to the mix; one that would also convince Daltrey it was time to let Townshend play lead guitar.

Bob Druce was now routinely booking The Detours as an opening act to more established groups. Over the coming months, they'd share the bill with Shane Fenton and the Fentones (Fenton would go on to chart success in the 1970s as leather-clad glam-rocker Alvin Stardust), the Swinging Blue Jeans and Cliff Bennett and the Rebel Rousers. Also among these headline acts were Johnny Kidd and the Pirates, a north London quartet whose lead singer wore an eye patch and leather boots, and whose real name was the less swashbuckling Fred Heath. The band had released two exhilarating rock 'n' roll singles, 'Please Don't Touch' in 1959 and the following year's 'Shakin' All Over'.

Unusually, The Pirates had just one guitarist, Mick Green, whose punchy, staccato style was a respite from the timid string-picking heard on most pop records. The Detours opened for The Pirates at St Mary's Church Hall in Putney that autumn. 'After that,' said Townshend, 'Mick Green became my idol.' The Pirates' bare-boned sound became the template for the new four-piece Detours. With Gabby Connolly gone, Daltrey concentrated on being the lead singer: 'I thought, get out front and do what they say you're good at doing.'

For Daltrey, The Detours' date supporting The Pirates was also memorable for non-musical reasons. It was the night he met Putney teenager Jacqueline Rickman. A year later, he wed a pregnant Jackie at Wandsworth Registry Office. The marriage started as it meant to go on, with Daltrey leaving his bride at home the day after the ceremony to play a gig in Brighton.

However inspirational and exciting their guitarist may have been, Johnny Kidd and the Pirates were already relics from another era. Their generation of late-1950s British rock 'n' roll groups had been eclipsed. In October 1962, previously unknown Liverpudlian four-piece The Beatles had released their debut single, 'Love Me Do'. By the following summer, they'd enjoyed three top-five hits with 'Please Please Me', 'From Me to You' and 'She Loves You'.

Like every other group in Britain in 1963, The Beatles had been inspired by Elvis, Bill Haley, Buddy Holly, The Shadows and skiffle. But they were fundamentally different. They didn't have a designated leader or a conventional lead vocalist, they could play their instruments, performed on their own records and wrote their own songs.

These songs had captured their teenage audience, who, in turn, responded to how The Beatles dressed, talked, wore their hair and presented themselves onstage. 'All of a sudden, Bang! Wack! Zap! Swock! Out of nowhere, there it is – The Beatles,' said Townshend.

From now on, where The Beatles led, everyone, including all the bands on the Bob Druce circuit, followed. The Mustangs' bassist Mike McAvoy was now working for a jukebox company in Soho. 'I used to get all the demonstration discs sent to the company,' he says. 'As soon as a new Beatles single came in, I'd borrow it and we'd learn all the chords and words. It was a way of staying one step ahead.' The Beatles' influence on every one of those acts would only increase.

But there were other musical developments at work in early-1960s Britain. London was now the crucible for a flourishing rhythm and blues scene. Barely fifteen minutes' walk from the art school was the Ealing Club on Ealing Broadway, a tiny, subterranean room where the condensation pooled on the floor and the District Line trains rumbled overhead. The Ealing Club had hosted Wembley panel-beater turned harmonica player Cyril Davies and the so-called 'father of British blues', ex-Chris Barber's Jazz Band guitarist Alexis Korner. (Davies and Korner's bands would become finishing schools for John Mayall, Jimmy Page and future members of the Rolling Stones.) Further south on the River Thames was Twickenham's Eel Pie Island Hotel, once home to the art school ravers and now hosting gigs by the Stones, Mayall and fellow young blues aficionado Long John Baldry. Elsewhere, in Richmond, you could catch Kingston Art College students The Yardbirds at the Crawdaddy Club. The Detours, however, were missing it all.

'They didn't have the chance to see other bands unless they were playing on the same bill with them,' explains Richard Barnes. Instead, Barney and his girlfriend Jan would visit the clubs and report back. 'Pete would listen to me and Jan saying "Manfred Mann are doing this, The Yardbirds are doing that . . ." It was their business but they never saw any of this.'

It was through Barney and Jan that Townshend first became aware of the Rolling Stones: 'Jan had been Keith Richards' girlfriend, and she'd first seen the Stones at the Crawdaddy and Eel Pie Island. I remember her telling stories from Eel Pie, how girls were climbing on to guys' shoulders, until there were three people on top of each other swaying along when the Stones played. Later on, we saw them in the street in Ealing. People were up in arms about The Beatles' hair, but The Beatles still looked neat. The Stones were scruffy, and we thought they looked spectacular.'

Not for the last time, Townshend fretted that something was happening in pop music, and he was in danger of being left behind. Onstage, he gave a physical performance. He would strike a ringing chord, and sometimes swing the guitar above his head or stick his arms out horizontally, like a swooping aeroplane. Over the coming months, whenever the guitar started feeding back, he turned the noise into part of the show, even sticking his speaker on top of a chair so that it was closer to his guitar and more likely to feed back. It was, he told himself, 'a creative use of sonics', and a noisy artistic statement worthy of Roy Ascott or Gustav Metzger.

Except he wasn't the only one doing it. Roger Daltrey had seen another west London band, The Tridents, whose guitarist Jeff Beck did the same: 'Roger said, "There's a shit-hot guitar player down the road and he's making sounds like you."' Beck was now playing in The Yardbirds, and had brought his love of feedback with him. He was a showy musician, a proper guitar hero; everything Townshend wasn't. 'I could hear the notes in my head,' said Townshend, 'but I couldn't get them out on the guitar.'

If he couldn't challenge Beck's virtuosity, then Townshend had to find another way to make his mark. Back at Sunnyside Road, Barney had acquired the New York folk singer Bob Dylan's first album and played it to his flatmate. 'There was something extraordinary there,' Townshend later wrote, 'but I wasn't sure what it was.'

Dylan, like The Beatles, wrote his own songs. Townshend had often heard his father telling him that the real money was in songwriting. That summer Townshend presented The Detours with two songs he'd written: 'Please Don't Send Me Home' and 'It Was You'. Both sounded like the sort of easy-going beat-pop that was all the rage at the height of Beatlemania. Doug Sandom recalls that it was through Cliff Townshend that The Detours were introduced to Barry Gray, the musical director to the children's TV puppet show *Fireball XL5*. Gray offered them use of his home studio in north London. The band recorded the two

Townshend compositions, and a cover of Chuck Berry's 'Come On', a song the Rolling Stones had just released as a single.

With his father's help, 'It Was You' and 'Please Don't Send Me Home' were enough for Townshend to attract a songwriting deal from The Beatles' co-publisher Dick James. Townshend had now become The Detours' lead guitarist *and* their songwriter: 'I remember showing up at art college having visited the publisher, full of talk of "advances" and "really big money".'

The 'really big money' failed to materialise, but the balance of power within the group had subtly shifted. Daltrey's perceived leadership faced another challenge. 'Pete had written a song,' says Doug Sandom. 'None of us had done that. It was obvious he had a talent.'

Sadly The Detours' interpretation of 'Come On' has gone unheard for five decades, and Sandom can't recall how it compared with the Rolling Stones' version. Just before Christmas 1963, though, the band opened for the Stones at Putney's St Mary's Church Hall. (A photograph of Doug playing drums that night now hangs in the bar of Harrow Cricket Club.) Townshend had gone to Putney wanting to hate the Stones. Instead, he was both impressed by and envious of their singer Mick Jagger's raw sex appeal, Keith Richards' ice-cool demeanour and fellow guitarist Brian Jones' haircut. The Stones were hooked on Muddy Waters, Little Walter and Jimmy Reed. But they'd twisted these black American sounds into something white and English, but still strangely convincing.

'I was blown away by everything about them,' said Townshend. 'How wild they looked and how erotically charged everything around them was.' When the Stones tottered on to the stage, girls in the audience started screaming: 'I was thinking, "How the fuck did they do that?"'

Aspiring guitarist Max Ker-Seymer would play in a band that supported The Who in 1966. But he had his first sighting of The Detours in December 1963 at the St Mary's Church Hall gig. 'The Detours were onstage when I arrived, and I can remember John Entwistle's fingers reminded me of spiders' legs the way they were running up and down the neck of bass – they were so fluid. Pete Townshend had a tab collar on his shirt that was up to his ears. Roger was so small, he looked like a dwarf, and he barely spoke, just "'Ere's another one . . ." Before the

Stones even came on, you could hear this incredible noise behind the stage curtain.'

It was at this point, with the stage curtain still in place, that The Detours spotted the Stones' guitarist Keith Richards warming up. 'He was stretching his right arm high above his head,' remembered Daltrey. 'And we were all standing there watching him do it.' As the curtain came up, Richards' arm came down, and the Stones launched into their first song. Townshend made a mental note, filing the image of that outstretched arm next to that of the Samurai sword-wielding youth in Gustav Metzger's film.

A few weeks later The Detours supported the Stones again, this time at Forest Hill's Glenlyn Ballroom. Townshend waited for Richards to perform the move. When he didn't, Townshend sidled up to him and asked why. Richards stared back at him, confused. 'He said, "Whaaaaat?"' recalled Townshend. 'He didn't have a clue what I was talking about it. That was the moment I thought, "Right, I'm having that."'

Sometime towards the end of his first year at Ealing, John Challis contracted scurvy. 'I got it from living on a diet of fried slices, chips, beer and weed,' he explains. 'I was too busy experiencing everything in any direction I could find. We all were.' Unfortunately, the ongoing blues and dope experience at Tom Wright and Cam McLester's flat was about to come to a temporary halt.

One evening Challis was strolling towards 35 Sunnyside Road, when he spotted police cars parked outside: 'There were Ford Zephyrs everywhere, outside a house that was full of dope. I thought, "Oh shit!" But I was close enough that if I turned around and walked away, it would look suspicious.' Challis carried on walking. As he came closer, he spotted television cameras and realised that the street was being used to film an episode of the new TV police drama *Z-Cars*.

What came as a relief that night, proved to be a bad omen. Not long after, Wright and McLester were arrested and charged with drug possession. The pair had recently befriended a new Californian student and invited him back to the flat. It transpired that the 'Californian' was actually an East German who'd mugged an American GI for his money and passport in Berlin, and fled to England. After being arrested for drunk and disorderly behaviour, he'd told the police about 'the local dope den' in return for a reduced charge.

Marijuana had made the newspaper headlines that summer in connection with the Profumo affair. Harold Macmillan's Conservative government had been shaken by the discovery that its Secretary of State For War John Profumo had been sharing a lover, Christine Keeler, with a Soviet naval attaché. There were fears that the nation's security had been compromised by careless pillow talk. But it was also revealed that Keeler had West Indian lovers and frequented what the newspapers called 'the dope dens of Notting Hill'.

The drug culture was growing, but the police were still playing catch-up. 'It wasn't unusual for us to go up to a policeman for a dare and ask for directions while smoking a joint,' says Richard Barnes. After the tip-off, McLester and Wright came home late from college to find a group of plain-clothes officers searching the flat. In a panic, Wright handed over a jar containing a couple of ounces of pot. The police were delighted, unaware that there were actually pounds of marijuana still hidden throughout the flat. After spending a fortnight in prison, Wright and McLester were told they had twelve days to leave England or be deported. McLester went home to the US. Wright bought a ticket for Paris.

Barney moved into Sunnyside Road with Townshend as soon as the Americans moved out. 'We took the flat,' he says. 'We inherited their record collection, and everything carried on as before. Listening to blues, smoking dope with the curtains shut and with one of those red lights glowing in the corner of the room that we'd nicked from a building site.'

Before long, both the blues and the marijuana would begin to impact on The Detours. Townshend's average day at art school might begin any time between ten and eleven in the morning. On occasion, he'd skip college all together to spend the day exploring Soho with Barney. However, while you could smoke pot and still attend lectures about kinetic sculpture and morphism, you couldn't smoke it and spend eight hours a day toiling on a building site or in a factory.

Doug Sandom maintains that he's never taken a drug in his life and was bemused by Townshend's love of dope. Daltrey, meanwhile, hated the effect marijuana had on his bandmate. 'Someone had to be in charge,' he told the author. 'Someone had to get Pete up and out of bed; and that someone turned out to be me.'

'It was hard for Roger,' admitted Townshend. 'There were times when he arrived at the flat and Barney and I had spent the day with a couple of beautiful girls, smoking dope and listening to Jimmy Reed, and then at half-past six I'd hear the knock on the door. And I'd think, "Oh shit, now I've got to play the Peckham whatever . . ." And in walks Roger: "Alright then, come on!" I would be lying there, going, "Urrrgh . . ." But Roger would be saying, "Come on, get your suit, come on."'

'Roger thought we were lazy fuckers, a couple of art school woofters,' says Barnes. 'At the flat we had women, we had pot and we had music. What more do you want? Roger's life must have been awful, working in that shithole factory. So of course he wanted more and Pete must have seemed so blasé to him.'

Yet as time went on, Barney slowly realised that his flatmate was less blasé than he thought: 'Pete would play gigs three, sometimes four, nights a week. We'd carry on smoking and playing records, while he went off to the White Hart or wherever. When he came back, we'd still be where he left us. The Detours never missed a gig. It was a running joke – how John Entwistle would turn up one day and say, "I think I'm coming down with the flu," and Roger would go mad: "You can't get the flu now! We've got too many gigs!" And somehow John would hold off getting ill until the band were less busy. It took me a long time to realise how dedicated they were.'

Although Daltrey loathed their drug taking, Townshend and Barney's newly inherited record collection was more to his liking. At first, he'd denied the guitarist's request to shoehorn blues songs into The Detours' set. Ever the pragmatist, Daltrey didn't want to alienate those people who turned up week after week to hear 'Twist and Shout'. But the more he listened, the more he understood.

One evening, Bob Druce asked The Detours to play the Oldfield, after the scheduled act had cancelled. 'We said, "Okay, as long as we can do it without wearing our pretty little mohair suits",' said John Entwistle. 'And we told the promoter we were going to play exactly what we wanted to play.' In the outside world, Gerry and the Pacemakers' 'You'll Never Walk Alone' and Freddie and the Dreamers'

'You Were Made For Me' were the big hits of the day. But The Detours played a set of hard rhythm and blues that went down well enough for them to play it all again the following week.

The Sunnyside Road record collection gradually became the mother lode of The Detours' set. Bo Diddley, Mose Allison (whose 'Young Man Blues' would become a staple of The Who's live act) and lots of Howlin' Wolf quickly found its way into the show. 'That's where The Who's sound came from,' explained Daltrey. 'We knew we were up against the other London groups, like the Stones and Yardbirds. But the Stones were doing all those Chuck Berry-ish things. We went heavier with Howlin' Wolf's "Smokestack Lightning".'

Standing over six-and-a-half feet tall, Chicago bluesman Wolf, né Chester Burnett, sounded as imposing as he looked. In June 1964, after the Stones had started selling American blues to record-buying Brits, Wolf's version of 'Smokestack Lightning' scraped into the top fifty. Until then, he had been unknown to most pop fans, although he was idolised among the Ealing blues clique. The Yardbirds' interpretation of 'Smokestack Lightning' had a wonderful groove, but The Detours and, later, The Who would transform the song completely. 'They did a stunning version,' says John Challis. 'I heard it, and it felt like someone had driven an iron bar through my ears and lifted me up so I was hanging from it.'

'Howlin' Wolf's voice sounded like it travelled across the universe,' said Townshend. 'It was manly, powerful.' Its manly quality appealed to Daltrey, but it was a challenge for a white nineteen-year-old from Shepherd's Bush to recreate the sound of a black fifty-something bluesman. Still, he tried. Daltrey took to slugging whisky to give his voice the necessary rasping quality: 'It sounded fucking terrifying, frightening the women to death. But I did quite a good impression.'

For Townshend, American blues had the authenticity and emotion he thought was missing in most English pop. It was music that challenged and provoked, just like the free-thinking artists lecturing at his college. But among those it challenged and provoked was The Detours' drummer. Doug Sandom disliked the blues, and by this point he was struggling with Townshend too. Onstage, he admired the guitarist's creativity and musicianship: 'Offstage, I never knew what Pete was thinking. We were just too different.'

Despite these differences, Sandom was still committed to keeping the band together. Some months earlier, a pair of aspiring agents/ managers had approached The Detours. They agreed to an audition in the back room of a pub in Willesden, north London. 'Afterwards, they got me, John and Roger in the bar while Pete was loading up his gear,' says Sandom. 'This bloke turns round to us and goes, "I'll sign you up but you've got to get rid of that tall bloke." Roger and John were all for it. But I said, "No. We're a four-piece and that's how we stay." The other two were looking at me, as if to say, "Are you sure Dougie?"' It would be several years before Townshend discovered that Sandom had defended his position. 'Nobody told Pete,' says Doug. 'Because nobody wanted to hurt Pete's feelings.'

The pair's relationship was further tested on the night Sandom persuaded his reluctant wife, Lily, to watch the band at the Oldfield. It was all going well until the interval, when Townshend sidled over and asked Lily to take off her wedding ring: 'He said he didn't want people to know that I was married. She hated him from that moment on.' It was a sign that Doug's age and family situation might count against him now the band were getting serious about their future. When The Detours landed another mention in the *Acton Gazette & Post* ('Are you fed up with The Beatles? Then try screaming for a home-grown group!') Sandom gave another fictitious age: twenty-five. Unfortunately, his days were numbered.

Johnny Devlin and The Detours were a Sussex beat group who had been working the pub and ballroom circuit on the south coast since 1961. Unlike west London's Detours, they'd bagged themselves a record deal. In February 1964 they released their debut single, 'Sometimes', and were invited to appear on Granada TV's music variety show *Thank Your Lucky Stars*. It was an important night for the group. They'd be sharing the bill with Ealing Club regulars Manfred Mann and Acton Vale's king of pop Adam Faith.

It was John Entwistle who saw *Thank Your Lucky Stars* and raised the alarm. Just the fact that these Detours had appeared on TV meant the other Detours would have to change their name. Townshend was already having doubts and thought that their current name sounded old-fashioned; too much of a throwback to the early-1960s.

Nevertheless, it was a brave move for an established band. Once again, blind optimism and arrogance played its part.

For the next few days they suggested alternatives to each other as they travelled between gigs at the Oldfield, St Mary's Church Hall and the Goldhawk Club. After one gig, the whole group piled into the Sunnyside Road flat for coffee and a brainstorming session, supplemented in Townshend and Barney's case with marijuana. 'Pete and I smoked a joint and put forward the most surreal names we could think of,' says Barnes. 'I suggested "The No One". Pete suggested "The Hair".'

These suggestions were conceived to deliberately confuse and antagonise the old-school, bow-tied compéres in the pubs they played. Doug Sandom remembers lying half-asleep on the settee when Barney suggested 'The Who', and everyone laughing at how ridiculous it sounded. Reg Bowen also recalls various Detours lounging around at Sunnyside Road studying Commercial Entertainments' gig sheet and saying, "'Oo's on here then? 'Oo's on there? 'Oo's on at Southall?"'

'The name "The Who" was daring and assertive,' says Barnes. 'It was a pop-art idea, straight out of the art school. I wanted people to do a double take when they heard it. It also meant that if you had a name like that, you'd better be good.' The band lived with the idea for a few days, wavering between The Hair and The Who and even 'The Hair and the Who' ('but it sounded too much like a pub') until Roger Daltrey turned around and said, 'It's The Who, innit?' 'I was always surprised that Roger went along with it,' says Barnes.

When the newly named The Who played the Oldfield on 20 February, the pub's compére Lou Hunt struggled to communicate the change of name to the crowd. To Townshend's satisfaction, the audience looked completely bemused. Lying on their backs doing further research, Townshend and Barney also realised that a short name would have far more of an impact on a poster. Even if The Who were playing bottom of the bill, the three letters would have to be rendered in a larger typeface to fill the space. 'So even though they were playing under some band like the Mark Leeman Five, The Who's name would be just as big,' says Barnes. 'It was a bold statement.'

To go with the new name, Barney and Townshend devised what marketing gurus would later call a 'mission statement' for the band.

The pair were at a party thrown by fellow Ealing student Michael English, who would later become one half of the avant-garde graphic design partnership Hapshash and the Coloured Coat. 'We were at Michael's flat in Princedale Road, and we were off our heads,' says Barnes. 'We worked out our strategy while standing on Michael's narrow staircase for about an hour while people brushed past us. But we knew what we wanted. Everybody was now doing the blues. It was all about being different and mainly being different from the Stones. We thought The Who could be more ambitious and attempt the more sophisticated stuff we were also listening to, soul, jazz and Motown. We wanted The Who to be like Miles Davis meets Johnny Kidd and the Pirates.'

Townshend turned the garbled conversation into reality and typed it up on three sheets of paper. 'I assume he showed it to the others,' says Barnes. 'But maybe he just kept it to himself and used it strategically to influence the course of the band.' Nearly forty years later Townshend contacted Barney to see if he still had a copy. 'He thought he had it but he couldn't find his. It was long gone.' Townshend called the document 'a proclamation'.

CHAPTER FOUR

SAWDUST CAESARS

'Retarded artistically . . . idiotic in other respects.'

Keith Moon's school report, autumn 1959

'The unhappy faces of mods and rockers reveal profound, pitiful and precocious dramas of sorrow, of distrust, of vice, of nastiness and of delinquency.'

Pope Paul VI, August 1964

On a rainy Thursday afternoon in March 1964, the Labour Party leader Harold Wilson met The Beatles. The Variety Club of Great Britain had voted the group Showbusiness Personalities of the Year. As MP for Huyton in Merseyside, Wilson was asked to present the Liverpudlians with their Silver Heart awards. The guest list for the ceremony at London's Dorchester Hotel included The Beatles, Dirk Bogarde, Julie Christie, *The Avengers* actors Honor Blackman and Patrick Macnee, and James Bond star Sean Connery.

In his introductory speech, Wilson gently chided Prime Minister Alec Douglas-Home's Conservative government, and jokingly quoted from a recent *Times* review that had praised The Beatles for their 'pandiatonic clusters'. Wilson, with his snowy hair and three-piece suit, was clearly part of the old guard, but it would have been difficult to imagine the aristocratic Douglas-Home or his predecessor Harold Macmillan cracking jokes and appearing so relaxed in a similar situation.

'One at a time,' Wilson ordered The Beatles as they crowded around him to collect their awards. Paul McCartney, George Harrison and Ringo Starr held their plaques up and said a polite 'thanks' into the microphone, but John Lennon, the last of the four to collect his award, had other ideas. 'Thanks for the purple hearts,' he said, to a ripple of knowing laughter. 'Ooh, sorry Harold.'

A 'purple heart' was the common name for the US military decoration awarded to servicemen killed or wounded in action. But Lennon's reference was more subversive. He was referring to the nickname for the heart-shaped antidepressant pill Drinamyl. These 'purple hearts' contained dexamphetamine sulphate, which provided an exhilarating rush and a barbiturate to ease the comedown. They were completely legal and prescribed by doctors to exhausted and anxious patients, including, it later transpired, several MPs

There was nothing new about musicians, writers or artists taking drugs. The Rolling Stones were about to be turned on to speed by the blues bands they travelled with on their first US tour. 'I felt like I'd been let into a secret society,' said Keith Richards, who was soon scoring speed at truckstops across America. However, the musician that gave Keith Richards his first speed pill also told him to 'Keep it dark, and keep it among yourselves.' By late 1964, though, the word was out, and the British press had discovered that pop groups and many of their teenage followers were popping 'purple hearts' and similar amphetamines for fun. Before the year was over, most of The Who and many of their fans had joined the not-so-secret society.

In the meantime, the sight of an MP glad-handing The Beatles demonstrated pop music's growing importance to politicians wooing a potentially powerful young electorate. Shortly before meeting The Beatles, Harold Wilson had given a speech at Birmingham Town Hall in which he assiduously courted the youth vote. 'Our young men and women have in their hands the power to change the world,' he told the 2,000-strong audience. Seven months later, Labour were voted into power at the general election on the back of Wilson's promise of a 'New Britain'. The man who'd given The Beatles their Silver Heart awards became Britain's new Prime Minister.

Also at the Dorchester that afternoon was another man caught up in Wilson's youthful revolution: The Beatles' manager, a thirty-year-old former furniture salesman named Brian Epstein. For anyone who wanted to make money out of pop music but lacked the necessary hairstyle or musical nous, Epstein was the perfect role model.

Helmut Gorden had Brian Epstein's success in mind when he began managing The Who in early spring 1964. Born in Germany during the First World War, Gorden was a Jewish refugee who now lived with his mother in Golders Green, north London, and was already forty-nine years old when he encountered the former Detours. 'He was,' said Pete Townshend, 'a single man who wanted some excitement in his life.'

Gorden ran a brass foundry, making door handles in Wendell Road, Shepherd's Bush. Just the mention of his name now prompts an instinctual negative response from Doug Sandom: 'I hated the bastard.' But although their relationship would turn sour, it started well enough. Sandom's sister-in-law Rose Kume worked at the foundry, and Helmut and Rose were frequent visitors to the Sandom household. Before long, the subject of Doug's band came up: 'So, in the end, he got curious and came to see us.'

Gorden showed up at The Who's regular Sunday night gig at the White Hart, and was impressed by the sound of the band but also the noise coming from the audience. He'd seen The Beatles on TV being mobbed by screaming girls. 'And,' says Sandom, 'he thought he could have some of that with us.'

Helmut Gorden didn't have any music industry experience, but he offered The Who money and promises. 'He was this short, balding guy who spoke in this incredibly thick guttural German accent,' recalls Richard Barnes. 'But he was a successful businessman, who worked hard to build up this strange niche business, and he had money to spend.'

Gorden told The Who that he could get them a record deal, and more gigs, and produced a list of music business contacts, most of whom came from the pre-Beatles era. It was a less than compelling pitch. But when the band told him that their van had just broken down on the way home from a gig in the Midlands, Gorden immediately offered to buy a new one. 'He decided he wanted to waste some money on a pop group, so we thought, well, we'll waste your money for you,' said Roger Daltrey, Before long, Daltrey had taken to referring to Gorden as 'the cash register'.

On their frequent trips to Wendell Road, Townshend and Barney were both fascinated and appalled by their benefactor's squalid workplace and strange demeanour. 'The foundry was like something out of

Dickens: dark and filthy, with this big black bloke melting metal in one corner,' says Barnes. 'Pete and I were in Gorden's office once, stoned out of our heads, when the phone rang. It was someone ordering door handles. Helmut was confirming the order and shouting, "Yah, a gross! A gross gross!" He really sounded like an actor doing a bad Shylock.' Outside the foundry, the stoned pair collapsed in fits of giggles.

Yet Gorden was as good as his word. Over the coming months, 'the cash register' would keep paying out. Roger Daltrey had previously built the band oversized wooden cabinets in which to conceal their modest-sized amps. It was, he said, a way to psychologically intimidate other bands on the circuit. With Gorden's help, The Who now had money to spend on the real thing.

Jim Marshall had started playing drums in the 1940s, before becoming a drum teacher and opening his first music shop in Ealing in 1960. Among his pupils was Pete Townshend's estranged school friend Chris Sherwin, who was soon managing the shop. Marshall's soon expanded and began producing its own amps, starting with the JTM 45, in 1962.

From the mid-1960s onwards, Marshall's was supplying amplification to The Who and every other band in west London. It was John Entwistle who first purchased a Marshall 4x12-inch cabinet. It doubled his volume, so Townshend, determined not to be left behind, bought one for himself. For Townshend, bigger speakers were another way of keeping The Who's audience in line. 'We made loud music because we were playing in pubs that were full of yobbos,' he said. 'If you tried to play "The Tennessee Waltz", the yobbo would get up in the middle of the song and get hold of Roger by the scruff of the neck and say, "It's Lucy's birthday, play Cliff's latest or I'll chin ya!" At which point Roger would chin him and a fight would break out. After that John and I would go over to Jim Marshall's store and say, "We need a really big set of amplifiers, so we don't get heckled."'

Jim Marshall came from the jazz and big band era. His son Terry worked in the family business, was the same age as The Who and played saxophone in a group called The Flintstones. He understood what the band needed. 'We opened a factory in Hayes in 1964,' says Terry now, 'which is when Pete and I discussed the first eight-by-twelve cabinet. Pete was frustrated with what was around. No one had considered a cab that big before. But Pete's enthusiasm was what sparked me. We sketched out what was wanted, and I took the sketch down to my dad. Two eight-by-twelves either side of a stage looked and sounded fantastic. It also gave the audience something to look at that wasn't the pub wallpaper.'

From the mid-1960s onwards, few serious rock groups would go onstage without a backline of Marshall cabs. But it was the fledgling Who that pioneered the concept of the Marshall stack. They led where Marshall's other customers, the Stones and Eric Clapton, would soon follow.

One morning, Townshend and Barney opened the door of their flat to a woman they'd never seen before holding a letter from Tom Wright. Their American friend was now living in Ibiza and wanted his record collection back. Soon after, the landlords at 35 Sunnyside Road asked the pair to vacate the premises. 'I think they kicked us out,' says Barnes. 'There was a family living beneath us and, looking back, I don't know how they put up with it.'

For a short time, they rented what Barney calls 'a glorified bedsit' in nearby Disraeli Road, but hated it there. On a whim, the pair bought a Morris Commercial ambulance from a girlfriend's father, and decided to live in it. 'There were beds in the back, and it was quite comfortable,' says Barnes. 'It was the sort of vehicle they used to carry old people around. So policemen would stop the traffic and wave us through.'

One night, Barnes drove to the Crawdaddy R&B club in Richmond, parked outside, and returned to find 'The Yardbirds' scrawled across the back of the ambulance in lipstick: 'And because we never cleaned the thing, it stayed there.' Barnes did all the driving, as Townshend couldn't master the vehicle's double de-clutching. 'We used to say we could give our address as Knightsbridge or Mayfair by parking up and sleeping there for the night. However, I think we spent one night parked on Ealing Common and the rest in Warwick Road outside Sid's.' After a couple of weeks, the novelty had worn off: 'We had no sounds, and Pete complained that it was getting too cold and he couldn't sleep.'

After three weeks in the ambulance, Barney and Townshend moved into the flat above Cliff and Betty Townshend's, in Woodgrange Avenue. The rent was £8 a week, and they had more space than they knew what to do with. The ambulance, the mattresses, the dope and the omnipresent red light from Sunnyside Road moved with them. The party carried on.

While The Who were soon too loud to be ignored, their image was still non-existent. They'd dumped The Shadows-style suits, but hadn't replaced them with a unified look. In February 1964, The Detours had supported a north London group called The Kinks at the Goldhawk Club. The headliners wore foppish frock coats onstage. There might have been something incongruous about men dressed like Regency dandies in a working men's club where the night rarely passed without a brawl. But the coats had the desired effect: they made The Kinks look like a gang.

The Kinks' lead singer/songwriter Ray Davies was fresh out of Hornsey College of Art. 'I wanted to be an artist,' he said. 'I just changed my palette, if you like, left the drawing board and went to music.' Townshend was already measuring The Kinks' powerful sound against that of The Who's. The band's managers, another pair of would-be Epsteins, stockbroker Grenville Collins and society man-about-town Robert Wace, had recently signed up a third partner, Larry Page, a rock 'n' roll singer-turned-producer and image consultant. It was Page who'd changed the group's name from The Ravens to The Kinks and styled them as a more sexually ambiguous version of the Rolling Stones.

Believing that The Who needed to look more like a gang, Townshend designed a set of stage clothes. 'Pete and I didn't have a TV, so we'd just sit around, getting stoned, writing, drawing and scribbling,' says Barnes. 'Pete designed these leather apron things, and got Helmut Gorden to pay for them.' The sleeveless leather garments reached down almost to the knees, and were reminiscent of something Robin Hood's merry men might have worn. John Entwistle immediately complained that they made the band look like 'poof dustmen'. The aprons didn't last long, but were Townshend's first serious attempt to give The Who a look.

Any hope that Helmut Gorden might contribute some constructive ideas were quickly dashed. 'Helmut was spending all this money, but he didn't have a clue,' says Barnes. 'I was sat in the car with him once, when The Who were visiting an agent, and Gorden suddenly said, "What I want to do with the band is shave their heads and dress them in kilts." It could have worked twenty years later in the era of the new romantics, but not in the 1960s. I thought he was joking, but he wasn't, he was completely serious.'

In the end it was Gorden's contacts, rather than Gorden himself, that would facilitate The Who's transformation. Helmut was a regular customer of Jack Marks, aka 'Jack The Barber', a hairdresser in London's Marble Arch. Marks had several music business clients, among them Chris Parmenter, a big-band leader turned A&R man for Fontana Records. Parmenter had just overseen the comic actress Dora Bryan's novelty Number 1, 'All I Want for Christmas is a Beatle'. After Marks told him about The Who, Parmenter was persuaded to go and see them at the Oldfield. Parmenter liked what he saw, but had one reservation: the drummer.

Doug Sandom was due to celebrate another birthday in April. When Helmut Gorden asked Rose how old her brother-in-law was going to be, she let slip that he was about to turn thirty-four. Sandom is convinced that Gorden had wanted to fire him ever since he started managing the band: 'He knew I was older, and he kept saying it was "bad for ze image" – those were his exact words – "You are bad for ze image."' When Gorden found out Doug's true age, the drummer's days were numbered.

In reality, ever since Townshend had told Lily Sandom to take off her wedding ring at the Oldfield, Doug had been under pressure to give up the band: 'My missus hated Pete, and we were having arguments all the time, because I was out playing sometimes seven nights a week.'

Despite Parmenter's reservations, he agreed to audition The Who for a possible record deal. On 9 April, Gorden hired the Zanzibar restaurant on Edgware Road. By now, the band knew that Parmenter had criticised Sandom's playing, and had discovered that their drummer was almost fifteen years their senior. Daltrey and Entwistle felt a sense of loyalty towards Doug but Townshend had no intention of letting the drummer stand in the way of a record deal. 'John and I were close, and he told me they wanted me out,' claims Sandom now. 'He told me before we got in the van. He said "Dougie, you're being set up."'

In the past, Doug Sandom has described 9 April 1964 as 'the worst day of my life'. He now insists that after Entwistle's tip-off he'd already made the decision to leave the band by the time they reached the Zanzibar. As soon as The Who arrived at the restaurant, Chris Parmenter told Sandom that he shouldn't unpack his gear. He was to use a drum kit already set up onstage. Within minutes of Doug playing the unfamiliar kit, the problems started. 'It was all very theatrical and dramatic,' recalls Richard Barnes, who witnessed the audition. 'Chris Parmenter said, "It's not sounding right," and Pete suddenly jumped up, pointed at Dougie and shouted, "You fucking get it together!" I was shocked. Pete got very aggressive and I'd never seen that side to him before.'

When it was over, Parmenter explained that he wanted to make a record with The Who but that the drummer would have to go: 'It was all very strange,' adds Barnes, 'because Chris Parmenter was also the first person to say anything good about Pete. He turned round to him and said, "You're tall and skinny. You look great onstage." That didn't happen very often.' Feeling empowered, Townshend took the lead and decided to tell Sandom the bad news: 'At that moment my heart turned to stone, and I went out and said, "He said, he'd give us a record deal, but not if you're in the group, so you're out."'

Years later, Townshend would admit to feeling guilty about Sandom's dismissal, and would describe the ex-drummer as 'my friend and mentor'. Sandom's behaviour in the immediate aftermath of the decision certainly merits Townshend's contrition. Straight after the incident at the Zanzibar, he joined the rest of The Who for a BBC audition at Broadcasting House. He also agreed to stay until the band found a replacement, allowing them to honour any existing bookings. It was a ridiculously big-hearted gesture, but one that failed to soften the blow of being ousted from the group he'd spent almost two years of his life with.

Four days after the audition, Sandom played his final gig with The Who at the 100 Club in London's West End. 'And when it was over,' he says, 'I put my stuff in the van and had to go home by train.' He was standing on Oxford Street when he heard someone sobbing behind him. It was Sue, 'the big girl' who used to carry him on to the stage at the Goldhawk: 'She must have come out to see us because she knew it was my last gig. She threw her arms around me and she was in tears.' The morning after, Sandom went back to the building site.

Before the month was over, another drummer had entered The Who's orbit. Doug Sandom had seen his replacement before in the audience at the Oldfield. He was a teenage boy, who looked far too young to be in a pub: 'He used to say, "Hello Doug, hello Doug" . . . Really enthusiastic. But he was just this boy hanging around.' Nobody could have imagined this boy playing in The Who, until they saw what he could do on a drum kit.

One Saturday afternoon in 1961, an unidentified male telephoned the emergency services, claiming Wembley Empire Pool was on fire. Within minutes, several fire engines with their sirens screaming pulled up outside the building. It was a hoax. Nobody can be one hundred per cent certain that it was Keith Moon who made the call. But then again . . .

Ken Flegg, who would go on to make amplifiers for The Who at Marshall's, was one of a group of Wembley teenagers that who went ice-skating with Moon at the Empire Pool. He was there on the day of the 'fire'. 'What happened is *somebody* pulled out all the toilet paper in the gents' and set it alight,' says Flegg now. The small blaze burnt itself out in a matter of minutes. Nevertheless, that same 'somebody' called the fire brigade. 'Whoever rang up said, "The Empire Pool's burning! Send everything you've got!" Fifteen fire engines turned up outside – all for nothing. Now, Keith always swore blind he didn't ring them, but everybody there knew it was him.'

Over time, Moon drifted away from the ice-skating crowd. 'Then one day I got a call from one of my friends, saying "Are you watching *Ready Steady Go!*? Moonie's on it."' Ken Flegg tuned in to the ITV pop show to see Wembley's failed arsonist playing drums with The Who.

The Empire Pool prank may or may not be another example of the amusing, strange, sad and sometimes tragic behaviour that character- ised the late Keith Moon. But, like so many stories about his life, it's shrouded in hearsay and rumour. The myth of Keith Moon started to overshadow the reality almost as soon as The Who became famous. As Roger Daltrey later said: 'Keith lived his entire life as a fantasy.'

Nothing with Moon was ever quite what it seemed, including his date of birth. Although he was the youngest member of The Who, he still felt the need to lose a year from his show-business age. Keith John

Moon was born in Central Middlesex Hospital in Park Royal, west London, on 23 August 1946, not 1947 as reported for many years in the press. Keith's father, Alfred Charles Moon, was the youngest of five children and had grown up on a farm in north Kent. He met Kathleen Winifred Hopley, known by all as Kitty, from Harlesden, north-west London, when she was on holiday on the Kent coast.

The couple married in summer 1941, and moved into 224 Tokyngton Avenue, Wembley, just off the Harrow Road, the long, wide thorough-fare that cuts north from Paddington into Harrow. No sooner were they married than Alfred went off to serve overseas, and Kitty and her family spent the next four years braving the best efforts of the German Luftwaffe. With its railway network and industrial estates, Wembley was a target for German air raids. Almost a thousand bombs wreaked widespread damage and loss of life upon the area.

After being demobbed, Alfred took several jobs, before becoming a motor mechanic. The couple's first child, Keith, was followed three years later by a sister, Linda. Soon after, the family moved to a council-owned house at 134 Chaplin Road, Wembley, where a second daughter, Lesley, was born in 1958. Aged four, Keith became a pupil at nearby Barham Primary School. A class photograph shows him with his face turned away from the camera and his mouth wide open in an expression of cartoon-like shock. It's the same look he'd often have when playing drums. Moon is remembered by his peers at primary school as 'a mischievous child with very little interest in learning'.

Peter 'Dougal' Butler, who became Moon's driver and close friend in the 1960s, is adamant that in the twenty-first century, a young Keith 'would have been diagnosed with ADHD [attention deficit hyperactivity disorder]. They would have spotted that he needed help, that some-thing wasn't right.' In the less enlightened 1950s, though, Moon's poor concentration was chalked up to stupidity. There was nothing malicious or violent about his behaviour. He was just inattentive and prone to showing off. Even his ever-forgiving mother conceded that her son 'got bored easily'. Nothing seemed to engage him.

In the summer of 1957, Moon failed his Eleven Plus exam, and was packed off to the newly built all-boys wing of Alperton Secondary Modern School. Headmaster Thomas Hostler had lost a leg serving his country in the Second World War, and is now remembered by a former colleague as 'a gentleman and a scholar [who] brought humour and distinction to the role of headmaster'. Hostler was determined not to let his school become a dumping ground for Eleven Plus 'failures'. Unfortunately, Moon spent most of the next four years resisting all his good efforts.

Despite scraping through in English language and literature, most of Moon's autumn 1959 school report, with its proliferation of C and D grades, made for grim reading. His music tutor unwittingly predicted the future: 'Must guard against a tendency to show off.' However, Moon's physical education teacher's comments were the most revealing: 'Keen at times, but 'goonery' seems to come before everything.'

Like Pete Townshend, Moon had fallen under the spell of *The Goon Show*. The BBC's comedy programme exuded a streak of very English eccentricity, which Moon would later share. His eerily accurate impersonations of the Goons' characters amused his classmates but frustrated his teachers. 'Keith was a savant,' said Roger Daltrey. 'The most amazing mimic. He could vacuum a character off someone in ten minutes and he would then become them. Not just a caricature, he'd get inside.'

Moon joined the local branch of the sea cadets, where, like John Entwistle in the Boys' Brigade, he learned to play the bugle and the trumpet. However, his first public performance was disastrous. According to author Tony Fletcher's definitive Keith Moon biography *Dear Boy*, Moon was asked to play the trumpet at morning assembly. He arrived onstage and started 'When the Saints Go Marching In', but, said an eyewitness, 'murdered the first few bars and left [the stage] to cheers from his contemporaries'. It's an amusing anecdote, but it invites the question: could Moon really not play or was it another example of that infamous goonery?

According to Kitty Moon, it was in the sea cadets that her son first started playing the drums. Like his future bandmates in The Who, Moon had discovered Elvis and Bill Haley, and had nagged his parents into buying him a copy of the 'Bermondsey Elvis' Tommy Steele's hit 'Singing the Blues'. In one of the rare moments when he gave an interviewer a straight answer, Moon would name The Shadows' Tony Meehan and Presley's drummer DJ Fontana as his early heroes. But most drummers just sat there with their head tilted to one side, tapping the kit. And that, Moon decided, was boring.

For showmanship and flair, he first looked to the American jazz drummer Gene Krupa for inspiration. Krupa was a bandleader, whose offstage life was as tempestuous as his playing. *The Gene Krupa Story*, starring Sal Mineo in the title role, was sold to cinema audiences in 1959 with the blurb: 'He hammered out the savage tempo of the jazz era!' Moon saw the film and was fascinated as Mineo's Krupa twirled his sticks, mugged to the audience and played as if his drums were a lead instrument. The parallels between Krupa's playing and Moon's remain striking, as is the fact that Krupa also liked his whisky and drugs.

Not long afterwards, Moon started telling other pupils at school that he was a drummer and that he had a band. He wasn't and he didn't. Not yet. By the spring of 1961, his schoolwork had deteriorated to such an extent that he was allowed to leave Alperton Secondary without taking any O Levels. The only subject in which he'd gained any qualification was science. Moon enjoyed tinkering with transistor radios and crystal sets, signed up for electronics classes at Harrow Technical School and managed to get a first-rung-of-the-ladder job at an electronics company in nearby Park Royal. His electronics expertise later came in useful when he showed his future bandmates how to 'hotwire' a public telephone and make calls for free. But in his mind the job was a means to an end: to get him enough money to buy his own drum kit.

It was while trawling the music shops in Soho one Saturday afternoon that Moon met Gerry Evans, a teenage employee of Paramount Music on Shaftesbury Avenue, who also played drums in a north London group called The Escorts. Over the coming months, Moon would watch The Escorts rehearsing in the back room of a Kingsbury pub. When Evans took a break, Moon jumped behind the kit. What he lacked in ability he made up for in enthusiasm. Before the year was over, he'd talked his father into counter-signing a hire purchase agreement for a pearl-blue Premier kit. Moon could barely play, but he was determined to learn.

Like Doug Sandom, other musicians started to notice the impossibly young-looking Moon in the audience. Gabby Connolly remembers seeing Moon in the crowd when he played with his pre-Detours group The Bel-Airs: 'Keith was this tiny kid and he used to come all the way out to the Boathouse in Kew to watch our drummer Ray Cleary. In the interval, he'd plead with Ray to let him have a go on the kit – "Can I have a go, Ray? Can I? Can I?"'

Among Moon's early heroes was Screaming Lord Sutch and the Savages' drummer Carlo Little. The Screaming Lord was singer David Sutch, whose stage show pre-dated shock-rocker Alice Cooper and featured him climbing out of a coffin and terrorising his audience with an axe. Carlo Little was a formidable-looking character, who'd spent his national service overseas with the Royal Fusiliers and was not a man to be trifled with. His party piece was a feverish solo during 'Good Golly Miss Molly'. After the Savages played Wembley Town Hall, Moon marched up to the drummer and asked if he'd give him lessons. Little was so shocked by the teenager's audacity he couldn't refuse.

For possibly the first time in his life, Keith Moon began to engage with something. At his weekly thirty-minute lessons, Little taught him the rudiments of drumming but also his own personal style. 'When I hit something I didn't just tap it. I walloped it,' Little said. 'It was impressive. Especially in those days, because I took it hard as it could go.' At a time when most rock 'n' roll drumming was positively polite, this was a revolutionary approach.

When his friend Gerry Evans left for a fortnight's holiday, Moon sat in with The Escorts. When Evans returned, the band didn't have the heart to fire him, so they carried on as before, but slipped away to play extra gigs with Moon. His drumming was often sloppy and he hit the cymbals too hard for their repertoire of sedate Shadows covers, but he brought excitement to their act.

Moon, it seems, had turned his fantasy into reality. To celebrate, he bought a gold lamé suit on hire purchase from the fashionable clothes shop Cecil Gee, and wore it most days of the week around Wembley. 'He looked ridiculous,' The Savages ex-bass guitarist Tony Dangerfield told the author in 2004. 'I bumped into him on Wembley High Road and he had the suit on, in the middle of the day. It was the first time I'd seen it. You couldn't help but love him, but he was chattering away at me, and I couldn't hear a word he was saying. The suit was too fucking loud.'

Moon's bandmates were just as baffled as Dangerfield. But as they'd quickly discovered, Moon was a baffling character. Onstage, his extrovert drumming made the group stand out. Offstage, his extrovert behaviour was sometimes less appealing. Wearing the suit was harmless fun; his tendency towards casual vandalism and petty shoplifting less so. On late-night train journeys from the West End back to Wembley, Moon would wreak havoc in the deserted carriages, tearing up the seat covers and pulling down the advertising placards. When Evans caught Moon smuggling a snare drum out of the shop in which he worked, their friendship soured.

None of The Escorts were that surprised then when Moon drifted out of their lives as casually as he'd drifted in. By the summer of 1962, he'd talked his way into a new south London group, Mark Twain and the Strangers. With the help of their lead singer, Moon found a new job in the printing room of the National Council of Social Service in Bedford Square, just a few minutes from the Soho music shops. The job lasted almost as long as his time in the band.

The split came after The Strangers were offered a tour of US army bases in Germany. 'Keith turned up to go ice-skating and told us he'd been asked to go to Germany with a band, but didn't know whether to or not,' recalls Ken Flegg. 'Until then, we didn't even know he played in a band. All we knew was that he was a nutcase. After that, though, he seemed to fade away from our group.' Moon never made the trip. He was only sixteen and his parents refused to give permission. Mark Twain and the Strangers faded away soon afterwards.

Keith Moon joined the band that led him to The Who in April 1963. Clyde Burns and the Beachcombers were a five-piece ensemble whose members lived around Wembley and Harrow. Like The Detours, they were signed to Commercial Entertainments, but the comparisons didn't stop there. The Beachcombers had developed out of the skiffle craze, and were known for their perfect versions of Shadows hits, and their ability to do the requisite Shadows 'walk'.

When The Beachcombers' drummer left, Moon answered their advert for a replacement in the *Harrow & Wembley Observer*. He arrived with his father for an audition in the Conservative Hall behind Harrow-on-The-Hill station. Keith was one of several drummers to arrive that day, and it was only Alf Moon's persuasiveness that secured him an audition. 'Keith was like this little kid,' says the Beachcombers' former rhythm guitarist John Schollar. 'We were all twenty-two, three or four.

Our singer, Ron Chenery [aka Clyde Burns], was even older. Keith kept saying, 'Can I have a go?' But we had to say to his dad, Alf, "Look, come on, we're going to be playing pubs. He's too young."' However, as the afternoon wore on, none of the other drummers passed muster. 'We went through them all, and there wasn't one we wanted. So Alf came up to us again and said, "Come on, let him have a go, please."'

Whereas the earlier candidates had all set their kits up facing The Beachcombers, which was common practice at auditions, Moon set his up behind the group, as if he was already in the band and they were playing a gig. 'We said, "Right, let's do [Bo Diddley's] 'Road Runnner'",' says Schollar, 'and as soon as Keith started we all looked at each other and went, "Bloody Hell!"' In an effort to catch him out, the band next suggested The Shadows' 'Foot Tapper'. 'It was all off-beat and none of the other drummers could do it. But Keith nailed it straight away. In the end, we said to Alf, "We might have a problem in some of the clubs because he's underage, but he's in."'

That evening, Moon joined Schollar, Chenery, bass guitarist Tony Brind and lead guitarist Norman Mitchener at Mitchener's family home in Stanmore. As soon as they arrived, recalls Schollar, 'Keith was picking up Norman's mum's ornaments, opening all the cupboards, fiddling with everything he could find . . . Ron said, "Look at him, he's like a bloody weasel."' The nickname stuck.

The Beachcombers wore suits onstage, but their previous drummer had walked off with his. 'Our suits were this goldish brown in colour,' says Schollar, 'so Keith straight away said, "I've got one I can wear already." So he turned up with the gold suit on, looking like Liberace. By then, I think he only had the jacket left. Later, when we had matching suits made, within four gigs, he'd torn the arse out of his trousers, because of the way he played.'

Not long after joining the band, Schollar took Moon to see the English jazz drummer Eric Delaney in concert. Delaney had played tuned timpani drums on his 1956 hit 'Oranges and Lemons'. He was a highly animated drummer and a flamboyant showman. Moon had never heard of Delaney before. But Schollar quickly spotted his ability to, as Roger Daltrey said, 'vacuum up a character'. 'Keith was blown away, and picked up some stuff from Delaney. The same thing happened when we went to see Wayne Fontana and the Mindbenders.

He said, 'See the drummer John, he's playing that double beat. I'm gonna do that.' And the next gig we played, he was doing it as well.'

Schollar now sums up Moon's style as one of 'power and noise'. Ex-Beachcomber Tony Brind recalls that, 'Keith had twice as many cymbals as any other drummer on the circuit.' Later, he'd drill holes into his cymbals into which he'd insert rivets, making them noisier still. He also played with such force that it became necessary to drive nails into the stage floor to which he'd then tie his drums. 'What you have to remember is that drummers with The Shadows or The Crickets were dance-band drummers trying to play rock . . . except it wasn't even called "rock" back then,' says Schollar. 'So what Keith did was so much more powerful than what we'd been used to.'

Even offstage, Moon's drumming style could be problematic. Chris Sherwin was managing Jim Marshall's drum shop, where Keith had become a regular customer. 'If there was a kit set up, he'd get his hands on it and I'd have to change all the drum heads after,' says Sherwin. 'He was an awful drummer. His innovation and his free-flowing technique were wonderful, but instead of lifting off when you hit the drum, which is what you're supposed to do, he dug the sticks in.' When Moon 'beat the shit' out of an expensive Leedy kit just imported from America, Marshall banned him from playing on any of the shop's kits again.

Moon's musical tastes were as baffling to his bandmates as some of his behaviour. Despite his boisterous playing, Moon had little interest in the kind of R&B The Detours were playing, and was ambivalent about The Beatles and The Stones. Instead, he was fanatical about surf music, especially the Beach Boys and Californian duo Jan and Dean. This was music that evoked a picture-postcard image of America, where it was summer all year round and everyone had perfect hair and teeth. To Moon, in drab, post-war London, a world of bomb sites, bad weather, outside lavatories and stand-up strip washes, it made America seem like the promised land.

'He loved that surfing stuff,' says John Schollar. 'So he wanted us to play it as well. We did Jan and Dean's "Surf City" and we might have played the Beach Boys' "Surfin' USA". But the trouble was the voices were so high. Keith wanted to sing, but he was an awful singer. The trick was never to turn his mic on.' It was a trick The Who would later learn. Yet Moon's love of the music never diminished. 'Keith *only* seemed to like surf music,' said Townshend. 'Which is why those early Who records, like '[I] Can't Explain', have those silly high vocals on them.'

The Beachcombers resisted Moon's attempts to shoehorn more Beach Boys numbers into their set, but he was making his presence felt in other ways. When The Beachcombers played The Coasters' 'Little Egypt', Moon started introducing the song wearing comedy robes and a fez. Even when he was behind his drum kit, he performed as if he was the band's frontman. 'He improved us immensely, and he also improved the appeal of the band,' says Tony Brind. 'And after a while, people were turning up to see Keith. If you walked into a room, Keith was the one you'd notice. It may sound corny now, but I think even then he was destined to be a star.'

In February 1964, the American boxer Cassius Clay won the World Heavyweight title. Celebrating his victory, the outspoken Clay, who soon joined the Nation of Islam and changed his name to Muhammad Ali, coined his famous catchphrase: 'I am the greatest'. Shortly after, Moon turned up at The Beachcombers rehearsals with the same words spelt out in transfer letters on his bass drum case. 'And I think he genuinely believed it,' says Brind. 'He'd walk through a hall full of people with that case on show, and not feel embarrassed if anybody saw it.'

There were times, though, when Moon's over-confidence became an issue. The sheer force of his drumming made it impossible for the Beachcombers to perform the Shadows' 'walk' anymore. Schollar: 'Although by 1963 or 1964, the "walk" was getting corny anyway.' But for some in the group, sticking to a formula of The Shadows, Johnny Kidd and the Pirates and Billy Fury was keeping The Beachcombers in work. So why change? This attitude was evident in the Elvis and Marty Wilde ballads that singer Ron Chenery loved to perform, but which Moon disliked. 'There was friction between Keith and Ron,' says Schollar. 'Because Ron would make a point of telling Keith to play quietly and then halfway through the ballad, Keith would hit that bass drum and it was as if someone had fired a shot.'

One night, Moon took the prank further. After Chenery had reprimanded him for playing too loud again, Moon produced a pistol and pointed it at him. The band and the audience watched in disbelief as he pulled the trigger. It was only a starting pistol. But no one, other than Moon, knew that. After a few moments of stunned silence, the audience saw that Chenery was still standing and realised it was a prank. The gig carried on as before.

Offstage, Moon's ability to inhabit a character came into full effect when John Schollar obtained a pantomime horse costume that had been liberated from the Empire Wembley Pool after an ice-skating show. For months, the 'horse', with Moon inside it, went everywhere.

'The first time, Keith got in the front end and Tony got in the back, and they tried to get on a bus,' says Schollar. 'The conductor actually said, "You can't come on here with a horse", and Keith said, "What if we go upstairs?" When he was in the horse, Keith became the horse.' Military personnel at the Air Force bases The Beachcombers played would be amused to see a pantomime nag cantering around the hall during the interval. Elsewhere, Moon would put on the horse's head and walk into shops, pubs and public lavatories, 'where he'd stand next to some poor bloke who was trying to have a pee'.

Inevitably, the pranks extended, just as they'd done before, to vandalism and petty theft. A reel-to-reel tape recorder, an amplifier and cushions ripped from the seats in a seaside theatre were some of the items that ended up in Moon's possession during The Beachcombers' travels. By now, Moon had also bought himself a moped, which he rode as erratically as he played the drums, once attempting to ride it up a flight of steps and into the bowling alley at Wembley.

For a time at least, though, he stuck to the promise he gave club managers not to drink on their premises. When Moon did drink, the practical jokes became more elaborate. 'My girlfriend at the time had a birthday party,' says Schollar. 'Her father had this beautiful garden with tulips and daffodils, so she warned Keith, "Don't you touch my dad's flowers, I know what you're like."' The following morning, her father discovered that his prized flowers were still closed from the night before. A presumably drunken Moon had sprayed them with hair lacquer, which had effectively glued the petals shut.

In some accounts, Moon was already taking pills by this point, procuring his purple hearts from a coffee shop on Ealing Road. But it wasn't a habit his bandmates shared. Despite John Schollar's memories of Moon's drunken prank, Tony Brind insists Keith barely touched alcohol when he was with the band: 'We used to rehearse at my parents' house. One day, we were all talking about a party we'd been to. My mum told me years later that Keith had told her, "I make out I'm drinking, but when they're not looking I tip it into one of the flower vases." He was a youngster then, and people change. But later on, I sometimes think he played up to the image. It's as if it was almost expected of him.'

Despite the age difference between him and his bandmates, Moon felt part of their gang. But unlike the rest of The Beachcombers, he struggled to apply himself in his day job. Ron Chenery was a service engineer. Schollar, Brind and Mitchener were draughtsmen. Moon, meanwhile, was now working in the sales office of British Gypsum; a building supplies company, where his poor timekeeping and inattentiveness were quickly noted. 'He was supposed to be taking orders on the telephone,' says John Schollar, 'but I think he spent more time fixing up gigs.'

'He kept sending the wrong concrete to the wrong building sites,' claimed Townshend years later, mischievously adding to Moon mythology, 'so that in a few years' time the buildings would fall down.' Nevertheless, despite claiming to have been fired from every job he ever had, Moon stayed at British Gypsum until joining The Who.

By early 1964, The Beachcombers' resistance to change was coming to a head. Moon, Schollar and Brind could see that pop music was evolving, and thought the Beachcombers should evolve with it. Mitchener and, especially, Chenery, wanted to stick to what they knew. The Beachcombers faced the same dilemma as many bands on the circuit: play safe but risk becoming obsolete, or try something different and risk alienating your existing audience?

On rare nights off, Moon and Schollar would sometimes visit the Oldfield, which had become an unofficial drinking club for off-duty Commercial Entertainments bands. It was here that Moon first saw The Detours. 'They were outrageous,' he later told *Melody Maker*. 'All the groups at that time were smart, but onstage The Detours had stage things made of leather. Pete looked very sullen. They were a bit frightening...'

The Detours/Who, with their hard R&B covers and sullen guitarist, were doing something different. Moon and Schollar's group weren't.

When The Beachcombers were offered a residency in Hamburg, where The Beatles had served their apprenticeship in a haze of booze, pills and sexual misadventure, they turned it down. 'I'm sure if we'd said, "Let's pack in the jobs and go", Keith would have gone,' says Tony Brind. 'If we had, maybe things would have been a lot different. But I don't think we ever seriously considered going professional. Looking back, I dare say Keith was looking for other bands to join for a lot longer than we thought he was.'

When word spread that Doug Sandom had left The Who, The Beachcombers knew what was coming. The exact circumstances of how Keith Moon joined the other band are inevitably blurred by conflicting memories. In Moon's account, he turned up at the Oldfield, downed a few drinks, and told The Who that he was better than the stand-in drummer they were using. When The Who asked him to prove it, he climbed behind the kit, launched into 'Road Runner', and played with such ferocity that he wrecked the bass drum pedal and split two skins.

Moon thought he'd blown his chances, but said that Roger Daltrey took him aside afterwards and told him they'd pick him up in the van next week: 'Nobody ever said, "You're in." They just said, "What're you doing next Monday?"' Given The Who's reputation for poor communication, this non-job offer doesn't seem far-fetched. Both Entwistle and Townshend have told variations on the same story, with Entwistle describing Moon as 'a little gingerbread man' on account of his newly dyed ginger hair and the brown suit he was wearing that first night at the pub.

John Schollar says he accompanied Moon to the Oldfield that evening, and that the ginger hair was an accident: 'Keith had put some highlights in to try and look like [the Beach Boys' blonde drummer] Dennis Wilson. But it had gone a funny colour. It was in the interval when Keith asked if he could have a go. He did two or three numbers and broke the guy's drums.'

Reg Bowen says he was on roadie duties that night, and also adds to the story: 'Keith Moon's mum bought him down, and I remember that he was very self-conscious.' Meanwhile, Lou Hunt, the Oldfield's compére, told Moon biographer Tony Fletcher that the story is complete fiction. Hunt said that Moon came into the Oldfield looking for

The Who, on a night when they were rehearsing in Acton. Hunt had been watching Moon's progress with interest and urged him to offer his services to the band. But he insisted that the public audition at the Oldfield never happened.

'It *did* happen and I can remember it exactly,' says Dave Golding, who was drumming with The Who that night. With Doug Sandom gone, The Who were in a state of flux. The band placed an ad in Marshall's music shop looking for a drummer. The temporary post went to twenty-seven-year-old session musician Dave Golding, one of Jim Marshall's ex-pupils, and a protégé of the pioneering producer Joe Meek. If Golding could survive working with the disturbed Meek, who later murdered his landlady before turning a shotgun on himself, he could cope with the fledgling Who.

Golding was newly married and on the verge of giving up playing when Marshall urged him to get in touch with The Who. Golding had once deputised for Cliff Townshend's drummer: 'Jim said, "Cliff's son needs someone. Get yourself over there." But it was only ever a temporary thing.'

According to Golding, that night at the Oldfield had seen Townshend unveil his biggest amp yet: 'Pete didn't give us any warning and this thing was so loud. I liked playing with them, but by the time we got to the interval I just wanted to have a drink. Next thing, a guy comes up to Pete and asks if his mate can play. His mate was Keith Moon.'

That said, Moon's account of damaging Golding's kit is exaggerated: 'While I was having a drink in the long bar at the back of the pub, I heard a voice come over the Tannoy – "Can Dave Golding please come to the ballroom." When I got there, Moonie was playing away, and he'd broken the bass pedal. I clambered underneath and fixed it for him. It could have happened to anyone.' Golding watched the teenager play a couple of numbers with The Who, but remembers being unimpressed: 'He was erratic and mad and it was all very new . . . but, to be honest, it wasn't very good.'

Fifty years on, such conflicting memories only enhance the Keith Moon mythology. And as Pete Townshend would soon discover, blurring fact and fiction was a key ingredient to selling The Who. Having a possibly inebriated seventeen-year-old Moon jumping onstage, and trashing another drummer's kit made for a great story. 'Out of nothing legends have been built,' says Golding. 'At the end of that night, Pete came up to me and said, "We've got a recording session next week. Could you do it?" I said, "If you're looking for someone, what's wrong with the guy you've just got?" And Pete went, "Hmmm . . . Well . . . Mmmm . . ." I said, "Let him do it."'

This recording, for which there is no documentary evidence, took place, presumably with Moon. Dave Golding, meanwhile, returned to playing sessions and took a job at Drum City on Shaftesbury Avenue, where the schoolboy Keith had spent his Saturday afternoons. Golding is now in his mid-seventies and still playing the drums. 'I'm a working musician,' he says. 'I was never looking to become a pop star.'

Despite the band's initial misgivings, Moon soon made his mark on The Who. 'The most amazing thing is that we could actually hear him,' said John Entwistle, 'because most of the drummers we'd worked with weren't very loud.' Doug Sandom was a solid player. But the teenage Moon, zigzagging around the kit, playing multiple drum rolls and hitting everything twice as hard, was more exciting.

'Doug Sandom was like those drummers you see in a wedding band, tapping away with a fag in his mouth,' says Richard Barnes. 'I never thought there was anything wrong with that. But straight away, even I could see and hear that Keith was exceptional.'

Over time, Moon challenged his bandmates to work harder. He played the drums as a lead instrument. Entwistle adapted his style to mimic what Moon was doing, and turned his bass into another lead instrument. This, in turn, gave Townshend the space to strike those huge chords and not have to fill in the sound the way a conventional lead guitarist would do. The Who played upside down and back to front. It didn't make sense. But it worked.

Keith Moon supposedly made his Who live debut at a birthday party or wedding reception in early May 1964, in a pub on the North Circular, the name of which nobody can now remember. Unable to nail his drums to the stage, Moon secured his kit with a length of rope to a pillar. When he took a drum solo, the force of his playing caused the kit to lurch from side to side, like a ship listing in a storm. The rope was there to stop everything collapsing. 'Roger used to say, when Moon starts up behind you, it's like standing in front of a jet engine,' says Barnes. 'And that's exactly how it looked.'

On 29 July 1978, The Who's former publicist, Pete Meaden, died of a barbiturate overdose. Even before his death, Meaden had become one of those almost mythical characters that could only have been produced by the music business; a 1960s tastemaker, revered by those in the know, but denied the money and recognition heaped on his most famous discovery.

Roger Daltrey once described Meaden as 'The man who told us, "You can't be one of the flock, you have to the black sheep, or, better still, the blue or the red one."' Meaden entered The Who's lives around the same time as Keith Moon. His time with The Who lasted less than a year, passing in what seems to have been a Drinamyl-fuelled blur, but his impact on the band was longer lasting.

Born in Edmonton, north London, Meaden had gravitated towards the Soho jazz clubs as a teenager in the late 1950s. After working as a graphic designer for the fashion mogul John Michael Ingram, he formed a short-lived PR company with the future Rolling Stones manager Andrew Loog Oldham and was soon searching for a Rolling Stones of his own.

In the spring of 1964, Meaden heard about The Who from Jack the Barber. Helmut Gorden and Bob Druce knew they needed some fresh input if they were to take The Who any further. A meeting with Meaden was arranged. He then proceeded to dazzle the pair with stories about sharing a flat with Mick Jagger and how he'd handled publicity for Chuck Berry. Meaden was now looking after the English jazz/R&B singer Georgie Fame, who'd have a hit before the year was over with 'Yeh Yeh'. To enable his twenty-four-hour-a-day lifestyle and impress potential clients, he rented a bolthole in Monmouth Street, London W1. That it was just a single room containing a sleeping bag, a filing cabinet, a record player and an ironing board didn't matter. London W1 was one of the capital's smartest postcodes.

Crucially, Meaden was twenty-two years old and on first-name terms with every club manager, DJ, pop critic and, it transpired, drug dealer in London. Meaden later recalled in *New Musical Express* that

Druce asked him if he could 'make a supergroup out of The Who?' and promised him '£50 to start with'.

Neither man knew about Meaden's drug problems, or that these had contributed to a split with Andrew Loog Oldham. Meaden had been Oldham's mentor on the Soho club scene, but by 1963 he was losing his way. Meaden's doctor had prescribed him Drinamyl for anxiety the previous year. He started by taking thirty legally prescribed pills a month, but had soon increased his consumption, procuring the drugs by any means necessary. 'Pete was pill-drunk,' wrote the Stones' ex-manager in his autobiography *Stoned*, 'getting soft and emotional around the edges.'

'Pete Meaden was a proper Soho boy,' recalls DJ and promoter Jeff Dexter. 'He had a mad energy, but he was a bit fly, and he made most of his dough from flogging pills. And that's the thing – if you're a good dealer you don't take your own dope.'

The photographer Philip Townsend, who took some of the earliest pictures of the Rolling Stones, worked with Meaden directly after his split from Oldham in 1963. 'I didn't realise at the time that Andrew wanted rid of him,' he says. 'Meaden started hanging around my studio in Brompton Road, and telling everyone he was my assistant. He wasn't, but he'd do anything for me. I'd bang him a meal now and again because I felt sorry for him. I don't even think he was that ambitious. He just wanted to hang around. He was awful, but he was also great . . . if that makes any sense at all.' Meaden worked his charm, and the pair set up the Townsend-Meaden Agency, hiring out groups to play debutante balls. 'The trouble is, I did all the work. Pete also ended up nicking the money on two or three occasions, telling me he'd left it at home or it was lost. But it was so hard to get annoyed with him.'

The ability to talk his way out of trouble was part of Meaden's appeal. But Philip Townsend was perturbed by his drug use and noted how wounded he seemed to be by Oldham's rejection. Out of spite, Meaden had Oldham's number printed on cards for a fictitious prostitute named Madame Loogy, which he then distributed through phone boxes in Soho.

When Townsend-Meaden took on a male and female vocal duo called the Easy Riders (not to be confused with the American group of the same name), Meaden told Townsend 'he was not going to let

Andrew beat him, and he was going to make this group big'. One after-noon, Meaden showed up at the Brompton Road studio where the Easy Riders rehearsed, and found the couple having sex. 'He got very shocked when he saw they were having it away,' explains Townsend. 'He started stuttering – he was often stuttering – about how they couldn't do that if they were . . . w . . . w . . . working together on the road, and he actually threw them out. He was funny about sex. I don't think he liked it.'

The stuttering and the reduced libido were both side effects of taking too many amphetamines. Meaden's partnership with Philip Townsend dissolved: 'And the next time I saw him he was in a restau-rant with this group that I suppose was The Who, and he was babbling away about how they were going to be the biggest thing in the world.'

What appealed to Pete Meaden about The Who was that they were young and malleable enough to be moulded. Meaden wanted to turn them into mods, just like him. In 2014, 'mod' has become a catch-all phrase haphazardly applied to any music and fashion with a British 1960s influence. 'Mod' began as 'modernist', a description used by *Melody Maker* in 1959 to describe a group of sharply dressed modern jazz fans in Soho's Flamingo Club. Richard Barnes, in his 1979 pop-culture study *Mods!*, broadened the term to include 'various committed teenage free spirits . . . Kids who were passionately into fashion and style, and an appreciation for Italian styling' – kids exactly like Pete Meaden.

In contrast to the garish Teddy Boys of the mid-1950s and the unkempt trad jazz fans of the late 1950s, the modernist look was about sophistication. The inspiration came from wildly different sources. Andrew Oldham wrote about 'bonding with Pete Meaden over the look of American jazz style from the back of album covers'. Others quoted influences as diverse as American actor John Cassavetes in the American TV drama *Johnny Staccato*; French actor Jean-Paul Belmondo, and the Italian cinema star Marcello Mastroianni, zipping around Rome on a Vespa scooter in Fellini's *La Dolce Vita*. As Richard Barnes points out: 'Mod was the British wanting to be all things not British.' But what these men all had in common was style.

Barnes believes the mod look found its way to Soho in the late 1950s via visiting Italian and French students. Pete Townshend believes that a direct line can be drawn from Soho to Paris. 'It could have been the summer of 1959 or 1960, when a whole bunch of boys came to Paris from Milan for a concert, maybe Miles Davis,' he said. 'They wore soft shirts, no tie, a well-made suit, and these scooters that they had ridden all the way from Milan. This was the image that made its way to Soho in the early 1960s.' Over time, the scooter would become the mods' preferred mode of transport. These gleaming Vespas and Lambrettas, often decorated with extraneous wing mirrors and headlamps, suggested a stylish new world, and were as lovingly cared for as the clothes worn by their riders.

Mod fashion drew from a melting pot of European, American and English influences. But God was always in the details. 'It was a fanatical and dress-obsessed scene, where things would be considered "out" within a few weeks,' says Jeff Dexter, one of the self-confessed 'flash little fuckers' that gravitated towards the early mod scene. Italian short box jackets, winkle-picker shoes, narrow trousers varying over time between fourteen- and seventeen-inch bottoms, and button-down collar shirts became must-have items. But only a small number of shops stocked the 'in' clothes, among them Austin's in Piccadilly, John Michael Ingram's Sportique near Old Compton Street and John Stephen in Carnaby Street, all of which added to the mods' sense of exclusivity.

It was a cult in a way that the Teddy Boys had never been. Unlike Teddy Boys, mods could pass unnoticed in regular society. The finicky dress code meant that they could hold down regular office jobs. More often that not, the same smart young desk clerk earmarked by his boss for promotion was necking purple hearts and dancing all night in a Soho basement before returning to work, dazed, on a Monday morning.

Jeff Dexter's friend, Mark Feld, who later became the 1970s pop star Marc Bolan, was one of three north London mods interviewed in *Town* magazine in October 1962. His comments summarised that sense of exclusivity: 'You've got to be different from the other kids. You've got to be two steps ahead. The stuff that half the haddocks you see around are wearing, I was wearing years ago.'

In the article, Feld and his friends discussed the abuse they'd received from Teddy Boys for their individualist style. But the two tribes had more in common than they realised. Both adhered to a fastidious dress code, and both were embraced by working-class youths now enjoying a spell of relative affluence, without clothing rations or eighteen months' national service to spoil the party. Also, with the growing popularity of hire purchase payment schemes, they could put that Italian 'bum-freezer' jacket or those Prince of Wales check trousers on 'the never-never' and pay them off in instalments.

Naturally, articles such as the one in *Town* magazine attracted more so-called 'haddocks' to the scene, and Fred Perry shirts, razor-cut hair-styles, Harrington jackets and Levi's jeans, gradually moved into the mainstream. Jeff Dexter recalls Mark Feld walking into the Lyceum Ballroom in 1962 and declaring, 'Too many mods here, man, it's all over.' Of course it wasn't.

But the mods, like the Teddy Boys, and every other youth cult that followed, faced the same dilemma: how to remain unique while belonging to what was now a defined sub-culture. Moreover, as mod style went overground tribalism crept in, and the press picked up on and amplified the animosity between the snappily dressed mods and their less sartorially elegant counterparts. These 'rockers' were a rival youth cult and the early-1960s successors to the Teddy Boys. They favoured Gene Vincent, long hair, leather and motorcycles over Muddy Waters, French razor-cuts, Italian tailoring and polished Vespas.

The Who first became aware of the mods through Roger Daltrey's sister Gillian in 1963: 'Her first boyfriend had a scooter,' recalled the singer. 'He and his mates came from Lewisham and they were the first mods I'd ever seen. They wore herringbone bell-bottom tweed trousers and Dutch peaked caps.' Townshend was very impressed by the same boyfriend's PVC coat, and Gillian's newly acquired mod style: 'Gillian wore very tight pencil skirts below the knee, flat black shoes, and she was doing these dances that I believe evolved from 'The Twist' – tiny moves with her knees together. It was incredibly sexy, incredibly elegant.'

However frequently the fashions changed, they had to remain, as Pete Meaden put it 'neat, sharp and cool'. That same requirement applied to the music. By 1964, the mod soundtrack embraced R&B, soul, Jamaican ska and bluebeat and what Jeff Dexter calls 'good pop'. In London, the music could be heard booming out of a different venue on any given night of the week. The Locarno, Streatham, on Mondays; The Lyceum on the Strand on Tuesdays . . .

As the night wore on, the more nocturnal members of the tribe headed to the West End, and to Wardour Street's La Discotheque, or the Flamingo, where Georgie Fame and the Blue Flames were the resident band and Christine Keeler's lover, 'Lucky' Gordon had his face slashed by a rival a year before. At weekends, the Flamingo stayed open until 6 a.m., with many of its patrons fuelled by the purple hearts dealt in the doorway of the nearby Ravel shoe shop.

A two-minute march from the Flamingo was one of Pete Meaden's favourite haunts, the Scene, in Ham Yard, a cul-de-sac off of Great Windmill Street. The basement space, which was used as a dance academy during the day, had previously hosted Cy Laurie's Jazz Club. On Scene club nights, the concrete walls reverberated to Motown and R&B records played by the house DJ Guy Stevens, a soul music obsessive who kept his precious records in a trunk that he sat on while DJ-ing.

The Scene was also the place to purchase and take drugs. A 1964 World Health Organisation survey on drug dependency in the UK discovered that the source of most drugs in London came from thirteen doctors, one of whom had legally prescribed over 500,000 tablets in a single year. These surplus drugs found their way into Soho. Alarmed by the illicit trade in Drinamyl, the then home secretary, Henry Brooke, introduced heavy fines and prison sentences to anyone caught dealing.

When the supply of purple hearts slowed down, the market was flooded with new and more potent amphetamines, including 'French blues', 'dexies' and the especially lethal 'black bombers'. The music journalist and early Who advocate Penny Valentine visited the Scene in 1964 and described seeing 'kids standing spaced-out, glazed . . . on handfuls of uppers – red pills, bombers.' The Who's über-fan 'Irish' Jack Lyons would later describe these late-night drug binges as 'chewing-gum weekends', after the gum mods chewed while high on pills, and which left them with aching jaws come Monday morning.

By 1964, the British R&B boom was attracting a mod audience, even if Muddy Waters and Howlin' Wolf were considered superior to the English white boys. The mods didn't have a band they could call their own. The Beatles wore suits but their music was considered too poppy for hardcore mods. Drummer Ringo Starr would later poke fun at the mod-vs-rocker rivalry by describing The Beatles as 'mockers'. The Rolling Stones borrowed elements of mod style, but were too unkempt to be wholly convincing, and although The Yardbirds' guitarist Eric Clapton's two-button Italian suit and chi-chi loafers passed muster, the rest of the group's clothes didn't.

Shortly before Pete Meaden's arrival, The Who had played Brighton's Florida Ballroom. 'We partnered an older band, like a Georgie Fame clone [the Mark Leeman Five], and it was an entirely mod audience,' Townshend told *Mojo* magazine's Jon Savage. From the stage, Townshend peered down at gangs of impeccably dressed boys and what he called 'boyish mod girls'. The two groups danced separately with the girls moving the way he'd seen Gillian Daltrey dance a year earlier. For Townshend, it was the audience, not The Who, that were the stars of the show: 'We felt we were entering into their world, that we were being tolerated and given permission to stand on the stage.'

After the gig, Townshend turned down a lift home with the band. Instead, he stayed behind with a girlfriend from the art school: 'We missed the last train, so we decided to walk along the pier, and what we discovered were all these boys jabbering away at each other on purple hearts.' The couple stayed underneath the pier until 5 a.m., fascinated by these mod boys, their clothes, their hairstyles and their jabbering, before catching the milk train back to London. Townshend was infatuated.

At later Brighton gigs, he started to notice a clique of male mods offering sex in exchange for money or pills. Among them was one especially handsome youth, always dressed in a perfect Fred Perry shirt and a seersucker jacket, who would become one of the inspirations for Townshend's later songwriting. What Townshend glimpsed that night, he said, 'were the people I was supposed to be writing songs for'.

However, changes were needed before Townshend could become a fully realised songwriter and The Who a mod band. Pete Meaden first saw his future charges supporting 1950s rock 'n' roller Wee Willie Harris at the Goldhawk. It was the day after the Zanzibar audition, and Doug Sandom was still working his notice. Meaden approved of The Who's R&B set-list and Daltrey's wailing harmonica, but not Townshend's noisy guitar playing, and definitely not their image. 'They were all wearing Pierre Cardin leather jackets,' he told *New Musical Express*. 'They had cropped hair at the back and Beatle cuts at the front.' As ever, God was in the details.

'Pete Meaden came with a henchman of his, a very cool, dangerous-looking mod called Phil the Greek,' said Townshend. Andrew Oldham had hired a driver and bodyguard, Reg 'the Butcher' King, from London's East End. Meaden, therefore, had acquired a minder of his own. It was all part of the image. For Pete Meaden, image was everything.

That night at the Goldhawk, Sandom heard Meaden gabbling away about all things mod and was immediately suspicious: 'John Entwistle whispered to me, "I'm a rocker, not a mod."' And so was I.' But with Sandom soon gone, there was one less dissenting voice in the band. Like Larry Page with The Kinks, Meaden wanted to give The Who an identifiable image: 'I wanted to make them a group that would be a focus for the mods, a group that would actually be the same people onstage as the guys in the audience.'

Meaden's ideas complemented the art school theories whizzing around Pete Townshend's head. 'Pete and I used to sit around at Sunnyside Road dreaming up ways to sell a pop group as if it were a product,' says Richard Barnes. 'What Meaden did with The Who was put what we'd learned into practice.'

Townshend and Barnes were soon smitten by The Who's new publicist. Meaden educated them in mod culture, including the jargon, a mix of hipster speak and esoteric slang. It struck a chord with Townshend who was already fascinated by semiotics and language. 'Meaden called everyone "baby",' says Barnes. 'It was all, "Yeah, Barney, baby" walking around Soho clicking his fingers like something out of *West Side Story*. But he was also chattering about Smokey Robinson and Tamla Motown, which is the music we were interested in. It might seem ridiculous now, but at the time it was very persuasive. Meaden was always on pills, but there was this strange dark glamour about him.'

According to Meaden, the best-dressed mods were called 'faces', their underlings 'tickets' or 'numbers', the latter after the mod trend for T-shirts with numerals printed on them. '"Tickets" would wear whatever they could afford, maybe one cool item like a pair of Levi's,' said Townshend. But as Barnes points out: 'No one ever defined the terms. I think they were made up on the spot, in the streets, by no one in particular and spread by word of mouth.'

Meaden's ability to sell himself as an 'ace face' worked on Barney and The Who, but not everyone was convinced. 'Pete Meaden and I would often go out together looking for clothes,' says Jeff Dexter. 'But despite what everyone says about Pete being the "face", it's a bit of bollocks, to tell you the truth. He could buy a tab collar shirt or two when he'd sold enough pills, but he would never have been pulled out by the majority of folk around at that time as a tasty geezer.'

Pete Meaden's first step towards transforming The Who was to take them shopping and spend Helmut Gorden's £50 clothes budget. At a time when most groups wanted to look like the Rolling Stones, The Who did the opposite. 'Every band in those days were Stones lookalikes, especially on the London scene,' Daltrey told the author. 'Pete Meaden said no to that, and turned The Who around. He understood marketing, branding and the hype of rock 'n' roll.' Daltrey was soon dressed in a white seersucker jacket from Austin's, a button-down collared shirt and tie, and a pair of black-and-white two-tone shoes, which Meaden later revealed were Daltrey's Hush Puppies hand-painted navy and white.

In fact, most of the £50 budget went on Daltrey's jacket, meaning that Meaden and Townshend had to pay for the rest of the band's uniform. Townshend, Entwistle and Moon become 'tickets' to Daltrey's 'face' by wearing cycling jackets, boxing boots and Levi's jeans, the latter carefully turned up one inch to reveal the red stitching on the inside seam. In Townshend and Entwistle's case, it was a return to the playground hierarchy of Acton County.

Once The Who had acquired their new wardrobe, Meaden took them to Jack the Barber. Again, every other wannabe pop star was growing their hair to resemble Mick Jagger's carefully dishevelled mane. But, sticking with his 'red sheep in the flock' theory, Meaden demanded The Who cut theirs. They emerged from Jack's, newly shorn, and in Entwistle's case distraught. 'I'd spent about a year growing my Beatle fringe,' he protested. Disgusted, he messed up his new boxing boots by wading through a puddle, went home and smashed his bedroom mirror.

Although Daltrey was now the 'ace face', he was similarly unconvinced by their transformation. 'If they had told me I had to stick my head up a donkey's arse and I would have been a successful pop star, I would have done it,' he later told The Who fanzine *Naked Eye*. 'So being a mod was far less painful, and it was nice being a wolf in sheep's clothing.' But the clothes best suited effeminate, elfin youths such as Mark Feld, the future Marc Bolan, who was a regular at the Scene, and whom Townshend originally mistook for a rent boy.

Daltrey, with his scarred steelworker's hands and barrel chest, was anything but effeminate and his curly hair didn't lend itself to those precise mod cuts. 'For a mod, having curly hair was worse than the clap. It was a scourge. You could not be cool with curly hair.' Of all Daltrey's mod accessories, the most important was soon Dippity-Do, an American brand of hair gel that he discovered was powerful enough to keep his curls straight for long enough to make it through a gig. Before the year was over, he'd gained a new nickname: 'Dip'.

In his role as The Who's newest 'ticket', Keith Moon wore the clothes he was told to wear, and played the songs he was told to play. But his first few weeks in the band weren't easy. He faced some animosity from fans at the Goldhawk who remained loyal to local lad Doug Sandom, and he was also worried about letting The Beachcombers down. Indeed, he continued to play with both groups, until John Schollar forced him to choose: 'I was disappointed when he chose The Who, but not surprised.'

In May, Moon joined his new band for a second Fontana Records audition, only to discover that Helmut Gorden had booked another drummer, Brian Redman of the Merseybeat group The Fourmost. But as Pete Meaden and the rest of The Who pointed out, Redman looked far too much like a rocker.

The Who passed the audition and were offered a tentative record deal by Fontana. Moon was now officially their drummer, but it took him a while to work out his place in the group. Although he was wary of Townshend's acid wit and sullen moods, Moon's biggest problem was with Daltrey. 'Roger tried to befriend Keith, but Keith kept his distance,' was Townshend's tactful explanation of the relationship in *Who I Am*. 'Those two hated each other,' says another band confidante.

Part of the problem was that Daltrey, understandably, considered himself to be The Who's frontman, but Moon was used to being the focus of attention in The Beachcombers. 'Moon always thought the drums should be at the front of the stage,' Daltrey told *Mojo* magazine. 'I was the poor sod that had to stand in front of him.' Unlike Townshend and Entwistle, Moon hadn't grown up with Daltrey the feared, older boy at Acton County. Keith was two years younger than the singer but refused to defer to him, especially onstage. 'He'd always be doing things behind my back,' said Daltrey, 'and I never knew what was going on. I was blissfully ignorant of the fact that he was taking the piss out of me all night.'

Daltrey often drove himself to gigs, as he hated being a passenger and preferred to make his own getaway after the show. Townshend also often travelled alone. This left Moon and Entwistle to travel together. They soon found they shared a sense of humour and a love of the absurd, and quickly became inseparable. 'When Keith and John got together they could be very funny,' says Richard Barnes. 'Now, when Pete and Roger started arguing, John had someone else in his corner. So it was now him *and* Keith standing at the back with their arms folded saying, "Oh God, here they go again."'

Whatever their doubts and internal struggles, The Who agreed to follow Pete Meaden's game plan. Having dressed them and cut their hair, he now suggested they change their name to the High Numbers. Most promoters had only just become used to The Who. Changing the group's name for the second time in a year was potentially disastrous, but Meaden was adamant. 'He said The Who was a tacky, gimmicky name and it sounded uncool,' said Townshend. 'The [High Numbers] name was perfect,' explained Meaden. 'I dreamt of it one night. High – being a little high – and numbers was the name for the general crowd.' Reluctantly, the band agreed, and The Who transformed themselves again.

As a sign of his commitment, Helmut Gorden offered the group a weekly wage of £20 each. Moon had left British Gypsum as soon as The Who offered him a job and had been scraping by on gig money and his parents' generosity. Daltrey and Entwistle were in secure jobs, but were bored and exhausted by the never-ending cycle of late nights and early mornings. Meanwhile, Townshend had been neglecting his college work, and the combination of nightly gigs and endless dope smoking was taking its toll. When the head of his graphics course heard he was being offered £20 a week – 'a police sergeant's salary at the time', says Richard Barnes – he urged him to leave. Townshend walked out of Ealing, but believed that the band would be but a temporary diversion on his way to becoming an artist. 'I always thought that The Who would be very brief,' he said, 'and that I would shut it down after a while, and sit in my apartment making kinetic sculptures.'

Gorden prepared contracts for the band, but with four members still under twenty-one their parents had to act as co-signatories. Moon's, Daltrey's and Entwistle's agreed, but Cliff and Betty Townshend refused. Cliff, who'd signed his share of music business contracts, read every clause and decided the deal wasn't good enough. Their refusal was no obstacle for their son, but Gorden would later pay a high price for the missing signatures.

Now a professional musician, Townshend threw himself into the mod lifestyle as if it were another art project. 'The others didn't really care about it, but for Pete, it was like a new religion,' says Barnes. The guitarist felt like part of the world's most exclusive gang – 'A powerful, aggressive little army' – with its mysterious dress code, music, dances and semiotics. He learnt how to walk like a mod: 'Shoulders swaying, small steps,' according to Barnes, and mastered the spare, economic dance moves he saw at the Scene (where the High Numbers would soon have a residency); a significant development for someone who preferred the security of the stage to the sexually charged environment of the dance floor.

'There were never more than thirty or forty people at the Scene,' said Townshend. 'So the people that were there were very important. You would hear Charlie and Inez Foxx alongside a Memphis song by Snooks Eaglin, and it would all be about dancing. You have to remember that Elvis had turned into a complete prat by then, while other people simply, conveniently, died before they made idiots of themselves. Buddy Holly, Gene Vincent, Eddie Cochran, all gone. This felt new.'

The High Numbers had become the mod group Pete Meaden wanted. But, as Townshend admits, they were following their fans, not leading by example: 'We became "faces" by default. I felt that I had been given this incredible gift to be able to look down from the stage at these people and see exactly what was going on. You could see who was going to be next week's fashion.' Townshend would identify the top 'face' in the audience, and note what he was wearing, then go out and buy the same shirt or tie, wear it onstage and watch as the rest of the audience bought the same item a week later. 'And it looks like it's my idea, but I stole it from the poor bugger down the front.'

Townshend also followed his fanbase's drug habits, and added amphetamines to his menu of stimulants. Marijuana was a slow drug. Whereas the energy and heady buzz of purple hearts was perfect for late nights flitting between La Discotheque, the Scene and the Flamingo. Taking amphetamines bonded him with Moon and, before long, Entwistle. When Daltrey tried pills, though, he decided he didn't like them. His abstinence would soon create yet another division within the band.

No sooner had the High Numbers gained their new haircuts, clothes and name, than mod violence became front-page news. On the Easter bank holiday weekend, a group of mods travelled to the Essex seaside town of Clacton. It was a typically cold, wet English spring day. When the pubs closed after lunch, a few bored youths began misbehaving on the pier. The misbehaviour escalated, the police were called, and ninety-seven people were eventually arrested for offences ranging from vandalism and disorderly conduct to stealing an ice cream. The *Daily Mirror*'s subsequent headline 'WILD ONES INVADE SEASIDE' posited the mods as violent juvenile delinquents.

Three weeks later, during the Whitsun bank holiday, the High Numbers played Brighton's Florida Ballroom, and had a ringside seat for the next bout. 'I saw about two thousand mod kids, and there were three rockers up against a wall,' said an imaginative Townshend. 'The people who were kicking rockers out in front would then come and listen to our music.' There were similar clashes in Margate that same weekend resulting in broken deckchairs, smashed shop windows and more mod-on-rocker violence. Forty-five youths were arrested and sent before magistrate Dr George Simpson, who condemned each tribe alike as 'long-haired, mentally unstable, petty little hoodlums . . . Sawdust Caesars who can only find courage, like rats, in hunting packs.'

Simpson handed out fines totalling almost £2,000. But it didn't stop further skirmishes later that summer in Hastings. Even allowing for the media's exaggeration, it was as if Townshend's 'aggressive little army' had gone to war. However, the original mod ethics of style and individuality had been replaced by a simple gang mentality. As Mark Feld might have said 'the haddocks' had taken over. These mods weren't the elegant jazz fans Townshend had imagined gliding around Paris on their Vespas, and had admired for what he called their 'poetry of lifestyle'. These mods wanted something else: 'We need someone to take notice of us,' one thrill-seeker told the *Daily Mirror*, 'and fighting is a way of attracting attention.'

Nevertheless, all those 'sawdust Caesars' and all those broken deck-chairs meant that when the High Numbers recorded their first single in June in Fontana's own Marble Arch studio, every teenager in the country – and their parents – knew what a mod was.

Despite Pete Townshend's earlier songwriting efforts, it was Pete Meaden who came up with both sides of the band's one and only single. The A-side 'I'm the Face' featured Meaden's mod-conscious lyrics about 'faces' and 'tickets' laid over what was essentially the rhythm track from Louisiana bluesman Slim Harpo's 'Got Love if You Want It'. The B-side, 'Zoot Suit', was another Meaden-composed mod anthem, based on the song 'Country Fool' by the New Orleans doo-wop group The Showmen. A surviving acetate from the session, or possibly an earlier attempt, was later discovered with the words 'Andrew Oldham is a bum' scrawled across the label, presumably by Meaden. But the High Numbers had some way to go before they could challenge the Rolling Stones.

The trouble was, The Who's speciality was bellicose R&B songs 'about sex and women and feeling down and frustration', said Daltrey. At the same session, they'd cut a version of Bo Diddley's 'Here 'Tis' with Daltrey doing his best whisky-sozzled bluesman impersonation. Neither 'I'm the Face' nor 'Zoot Suit' could measure up to that. Moon's brisk drumming lifted both songs, but the rest of the group sounded tame. On 'Zoot Suit', Daltrey bragged about his two-tone brogues and his 'zoot suit jacket with side vents five inches long'. But this was a look the mod on the street already knew, and how long before Daltrey's clothes were out of date?

Fontana pressed just 1,000 copies, released the single in July, but did little to promote it. Instead, Meaden's pill-driven enthusiasm took over. He had flyers printed lauding the High Numbers as 'Four Hip

Men From London', raced around Soho with boxes of records under his arm, trying to get them into the shops, and pestered the pop magazines *Record Mirror* and *Fabulous* into writing about what he called 'the first authentic mod record'. The press obliged. Pete Meaden's wild ideas and the band's tense dynamic were interesting even if the record wasn't. *Fabulous* writer June Southworth turned up to watch the High Numbers in Tottenham, north London. After seeing the club's doorman attempting to strangle Roger Daltrey, she figured they must be worth writing about.

By now, mod fashions had infiltrated the group's west London fanbase. Dedicated Who watcher 'Irish' Jack had spotted his first mod in Hammersmith in the summer of 1963, and had soon adopted the clothes, the haircut, the purple hearts – everything, in fact, but the scooter. When Meaden asked him to take a dozen copies of 'I'm the Face' to sell in Shepherd's Bush market, Jack readily agreed. Unfortunately, he managed to shift just four copies. Meaden, despite trawling every record shop in London, was equally unsuccessful. In a later interview, he claimed to have bought 250 copies himself in an effort to get the single into the charts. But it wasn't enough. 'I'm the Face' sank without a trace. The image was in place, but it seemed the music was lagging behind.

'I remember them being stunned when it failed,' says Richard Barnes. 'We didn't think it would get to Number 1, but we thought it would get noticed. We didn't expect the High Numbers to be such a spectacular flop.'

CHAPTER FIVE

THE PEER AND THE GANGSTER

'Not for the first time, the East End wide boy and the public school ponce rubbed elbows or other body parts in the cellars of Soho.'

Ex-Rolling Stones manager Andrew Loog Oldham
remembers the early 1960s

'Kit Lambert and Chris Stamp were the pop equivalent of the Kray Twins.'

Roger Daltrey, 1994

What was once the Railway Hotel in Harrow burned down on a Sunday evening in February 2002. By midnight, the roof had caved in, the mock-Tudor frontage was charred black and the boarded-up windows ran with water where firefighters had tried to douse the flames. In 1964, this three-storey Victorian pub was the scene of some of The Who's most dramatic performances. Seven years later, the pub would be pictured on the back cover of the group's hits collection, *Meaty Beaty Big and Bouncy*. However, by the time the Railway caught fire, it had been empty for years, an abandoned wreck towering over the bridge where the traffic idled, bumper to bumper, en route to Harrow and Wealdstone train station.

Outside, the Railway's walls were daubed with graffiti. Inside, some of the stairs leading from the public bar down to the basement where The Who used to play had perished. But in the late 1960s, the basement had been filled with long-haired students in army greatcoats nodding along to blues guitarist Rory Gallagher or folk-rockers Jethro Tull. Later, the Railway's 60p Sunday-night reggae club brought in the skinheads from nearby Headstone Lane estate. By the early 1980s, the Railway was hosting Irish folk singers howling republican anthems, and frantic rockabilly groups praying for some of The Who's lingering magic to rub off on them.

Soon after, the Railway's reputation for beery violence outweighed its musical legacy. The singers and bands moved on, and while the seasoned drinkers stayed put, there was an air of decay, as if someone had already called time. Finally, even the landlord quit, and by the middle of the decade the Railway stood empty. The fire made headlines in the local press, but it was an ignoble end to what had once been an historic venue. In the days following the blaze, rumours circulated around the area about arsonists and alleged insurance scams. But if anyone was able to provide damning evidence they were reluctant to come forward. While local musicians swapped stories about the pub's illustrious past, the Railway's most famous alumnus, Roger Daltrey, gave a pithy statement to the press: 'It's like when the house you were born in is no longer there.'

For a few months, even after the bulldozers had done their worst, there was a chunk of the Railway's wall that stayed upright. It stood there as if in some futile gesture of defiance; a final reminder of what one regular visitor from The Who's era remembers as 'the horrible, black vomit-proof bricks' that had once walled the basement. By September 2004, two blocks of utilitarian-looking flats had risen up in the Railway's place. In what was a gesture that would have amused and shocked The Who's 1960s followers, the flats were named Daltrey House and Moon House. In December 2009, the council unveiled a blue plaque on the wall of Daltrey House, honouring the site 'where The Who made rock history by smashing a guitar in 1964'.

The Who's journey to the Railway Hotel began in December 1963, when the Wembley branch of the Young Communist League held its Christmas party in the pub's function room. Local R&B group the Bo Street Runners provided the music, and the party was such a success that by the following spring, the YCL was hosting a weekly blues club at the Railway.

Richard Barnes had seen Cyril Davies at the pub in 1962. 'It was an epiphany,' he says, even though Davies passed out drunk onstage prompting his singer Long John Baldry to start kicking him in disgust. By June 1964, Barney was co-promoting a Tuesday R&B night at the Railway, called the Bluesday Club, with the High Numbers headlining. His co-promoter, a fellow blues fan named Lionel Gibbins, dealt with the pub's management, while Barney took care of advertising. Flyposting all over Harrow and as far north as Watford paid off, and, before long, the gig was attracting large groups of suburban mods that lived too far out to travel to the Goldhawk or into the West End. The High Numbers' debut single had been a disaster, but that hadn't affected their ability to pull a crowd whenever they played live.

Barnes and Gibbins worked hard to create an atmosphere. The basement's radiators were turned on even though it was summer, the lights stayed off except for two coloured bulbs and the windows were blacked out as if anticipating a German air raid. 'We wanted to make it like a nightclub-cum-bordello,' says Barnes. When the show was over, Barney and Gibbins would jump into Lionel's Jaguar and grab a late meal in Harrow, paying for the food out of the night's takings. 'I lived on half crowns that year,' he says.

The High Numbers' Tuesday 14 July gig at the Railway was just like any other. There were the usual scooters lined up outside and the usual youths jostling for space on the dance floor. Barney was at the front desk when he first saw Kit Lambert, the man who would go on to become The Who's co-manager. 'I was taking money and sorting out membership cards when I spotted this rather aristocratic looking gentleman in a dark suit loitering outside,' he says. Presuming he was a representative from the local council, sent to investigate the noise, Barnes panicked, and asked the bouncers not to let him in: 'I was terrified he'd come to close us down.'

It was then that Lambert explained that he was looking for a pop group to star in a film he wanted to make. His Savile Row suit, cut-glass accent and the fact that he was almost ten years older than anyone else in the room suggested a cultured background and, more importantly, money. Barnes let him in. Lambert negotiated the steps down into the dank cellar. 'The Who were playing there in this room with just one red bulb glowing and an extraordinary audience that they had collected,' he later told the *Observer*'s Tony Palmer. 'They were the loudest group I'd ever heard.' How this former Oxford graduate and jungle explorer found his way to The Who in the first place is a story as strange as anything Pete Townshend could have dreamed up.

Born on 11 May 1935, Christopher Sebastian Lambert was the third generation of a musical and artistic dynasty. His grandfather, George, was a painter, his uncle Maurice a sculptor, and his father Constant a composer and conductor. Constant Lambert had been a star pupil of the Royal Academy of Music. At the age of twenty, he'd been commissioned to write a score for the Russian ballet impresario, Sergei Diaghilev. In 1928, Constant's work *The Rio Grande* set the writer Sacheverell Sitwell's poem of the same name to a score unusually influenced by jazz and classical music. A year later, he was appointed musical director of what would later become the Royal Ballet, and went on to write *Music Ho! A Study of Music in Decline*, in which he pioneered the idea of bridging European classical and black American music, leading to an irresolvable rift with many traditionally minded critics.

Constant had married Kit's mother Florence Kaye when she was still a teenager. Their only child was named after the English painter, and Constant's former lover, Christopher 'Kit' Wood and the composer Johann Sebastian Bach. Kit's godfather was Constant's friend, the esteemed composer William Walton; his godmother the Royal Ballet's star dancer, Margot Fonteyn, who'd begun a long-running affair with Constant at the age of seventeen.

The Lamberts' marriage ended soon after Kit's birth, and Constant left the family home in Knightsbridge. Kit spent his early years being raised largely by his maternal grandmother, Amy, while Florence established a property business and tried in vain to become a model. Aged two, Kit was admitted to hospital for the removal of a tubercular gland in his neck. The subsequent operation left him with a prominent scar, of which he was always self-conscious and which others later mistook to be the result of a skirmish when serving in the army.

Constant Lambert spent the war years touring with the Royal Ballet. After which he flitted in and out of his son's life, while also trying to balance his career and his second marriage to the painter Isabel Rawsthorne. Kit was an introverted child brought up in a female-dominated environment. It seems he was starved of affection or attention; factors he later blamed for the homosexuality to which he was never quite able to reconcile himself. Like Pete Townshend, an only child until he was fifteen, Lambert seemed to have spent his early childhood surrounded by, but sometimes ignored by, brilliant creative adults.

In the spring of 1949, Kit became a boarder at Lancing College near Shoreham, Sussex. He muddled through in most subjects, but his keen wit and insouciance are still remembered over sixty years later. 'Kit had a certain air of intellectual superiority,' says former Lancing pupil Richard Newton Price, who, like Lambert, was a member of the school's Field House. 'He was always very jokey, amusing and bright, but I don't think he was extraordinary. His schoolwork wasn't terribly good because of his laziness.'

Kit's chaotic approach to school life changed dramatically after the summer of 1951. On 21 August, his father died from bronchopneumonia and previously undiagnosed diabetes. He was just forty-five years old. Prior to his death, Constant's heavy drinking had accelerated into full-blown alcoholism and had started to impinge on his work; he was said to have passed out halfway through conducting a performance of Tchaikovsky's *Sleeping Beauty*. In his final months, Constant had focused all his remaining energy on composing a new ballet, *Tiresias*. It was an ambitious work based on the Greek legend of the blind prophet, who is transformed from a male into a female and back again, and then asked to decide which gender gains the most enjoyment from sexual intercourse. Lambert's score, the choreography, the design and the ballet's sexual themes were widely condemned: 'Did you ever see such a thing?' wrote the *Observer*. 'Idiotic and boring.'

Constant was deeply hurt by the response to the ballet and reportedly began drinking more than ever. In his wilder moments Kit blamed the speed of his father's death on the critical drubbing *Tiresias* had received. While this was an overstatement, Constant's desire to experiment and to introduce jazz and black American influences into his music had been viciously condemned by the critical elite. 'They couldn't understand,' said Kit, 'how someone of [Constant's] talents could hang around with Louis Armstrong rather than classical musicians.' In his later role as Pete Townshend's mentor and a champion of The Who's provocative rock opera *Tommy*, Kit would relish the opportunity to provoke the musical establishment just as his father had done.

Constant's death seemed to spur his son into focusing on his studies and widening his social circle. His school work improved, he started acting in several dramatic productions, and became a key member of two societies: the literary discussion group the Elizabethans, and, later, a dining club called the Library, where he struck up a friendship with the future Amazon explorer Richard Mason.

'It was an extraordinary thing, as one couldn't imagine anyone less Amazonian than Kit,' says Newton Price. 'Whereas Richard Mason was a games-playing prefect. Athletics and cross-country running were his forté. No way would Kit be seen on any games field.' Mason was athletic, rugged and a stickler for the rules. Newton Price remembers him beating a boy severely for talking in chapel, after which several pupils staged a singing strike as a protest. Nonetheless, Lambert and Mason's odd friendship endured.

Homosexuality was rife at Lancing, but it was strictly covert. 'There was a picture of [the conductor] Benjamin Britten and [his partner, the tenor] Peter Pears in the school magazine once,' says Newton Price, 'and I remember someone saying if we did what they did we'd get expelled. Everybody recognised it was a normal way of behaving if you put several hundred teenage boys in a monastery. But if the authorities became aware of it, they would have rejected it.' Newton Price recalls being politely propositioned by Lambert, 'but he was fine when rejected.'

In 1953, Kit's renewed commitment to his studies paid off. He was awarded with an open scholarship to read French at Trinity College, Oxford, which was deferred until he had completed his national service. Later, Lambert would brag that he had been the 'worst officer in the British army'. Nevertheless, he still showed enough commitment during basic training to be considered officer material, albeit of the lower-ranking variety.

Just before Christmas 1954, Junior Field Officer Christopher 'Kit' Lambert of the 14th Field regiment of the Royal Artillery was posted to Hong Kong. Here, he met fellow officer and lifelong friend Robert Fearnley-Whittingstall. 'I could see he was unusual then, compared to the young national service officers we had around us,' Fearnley-Whittingstall told Kit Lambert screenplay author Pat Gilbert. 'He was cultured and intelligent and we struck up an immediate accord, particularly after we found we were both going up to Trinity.'

The nature of officer life meant that the pair enjoyed what Fearnley-Whittingstall calls 'long periods of boredom broken up by long periods of leisure time'. At every available opportunity, Lambert travelled from his remote barracks to the coastal town of Kowloon, where his friend was stationed, and where there was a thriving nightlife. Both men loved the cinema and theatre, and began acting in amateur productions and reporting on the latest films for a Radio Hong Kong programme called *Going to the Pictures*.

By his own admission, Fearnley-Whittingstall was a reluctant soldier, but Lambert was even more disaffected and struggled to fit in: 'I don't think he cared for the army much. Superficially he appeared to have tremendous confidence. But underneath I think he was insecure. He was also very quick and very witty, and I don't think that appealed to some of his fellow officers.' Lambert's homosexuality while still discreet manifested itself in his fascination with a rather camp captain whom he'd spotted wearing a pink suit when off-duty: 'Nothing was ever said but he was obsessed with this chap,' says Fearnley-Whittingstall.

With their undistinguished spell of national service complete, both men took up their places at Trinity in October. Despite Kit's gift for languages, he switched to English history almost as soon as he arrived. At Trinity, Fearnley-Whittingstall had rooms two floors above Kit's, and watched, amused, as his friend challenged his strait-laced peers. Lambert's habit of wearing an exotically patterned dressing gown from Hong Kong drew disapproving comments, which, in turn, prompted him to wear the offending gown more often. Like Keith Moon, Lambert also showed great powers of mimicry, and impersonated one of his lecturers with pinpoint accuracy: 'He had a tutor called John Cooper, who was a famous history don. Cooper was incredibly learned, and much imitated. Kit used to invent these legends about Cooper – "At the end of a tutorial the topic will be the influence of metal ink on military thinking, 1831 to 1832. There is quite a good paper in the library . . ."'

But Lambert also showed a more decadent side, as if mimicking his late father. He started drinking heavily and, unusually for Oxford in the 1950s, experimented with marijuana and the hallucinogenic mescaline. The manager, producer and writer Simon Napier-Bell became a close friend of Kit's in the 1960s, and suggests that Constant's cycle of success and failure became a blueprint for his son. 'Constant was a prototype for Kit – emotionally volatile, easily bored, sexually ambivalent and irresistibly drawn to self-destruction.'

Nevertheless, in his lucid moments, Kit contributed articles to the university magazine *Isis* and was active in the film and theatre societies. The latter asked him to help promote their upcoming production of the Jacobean tragedy *The Changeling*. Lambert failed to do anything until two days before opening night. However, within twenty-four hours, he'd arranged to have hundreds of flyers printed, which were then dropped over Oxford from a hired aeroplane. 'Kit had a force of personality which was enough to let him overcome most adverse circumstances,' adds Fearnley-Whittingstall.

That force of personality helped see him through most tricky situations. Yet those that knew him suggested Kit relied on alcohol as a prop to boost his confidence and to blot out his insecurity. Moreover, he was still terrified that his mother would discover his homosexuality, although he was 'out' among his friends at Oxford.

After moving out of the college halls and into a succession of shared houses and flats, Lambert had several short-lived affairs and a more serious relationship with a brilliant fellow student named Jeremy Wolfenden. Later, Wolfenden would be recruited to the British intelligence services, where his lifestyle led to him being blackmailed by the KGB. Wolfenden featured in *The Fatal Englishman*, author Sebastian Faulks' study of three English lives, in which Lambert and his group of friends are described as 'dissolute . . . and given to displays of solid camp of a rare vintage.'

In 1959, as his time at Trinity drew to a close, Lambert had what Fearnley-Whittingstall called 'a disaster with his degree'. After taking the amphetamine Benzedrine and staying up for several nights revising, Kit stormed out of the examination room before completing his English history paper. Lambert later told the examining staff that he'd been hallucinating. Incredibly, he was still awarded a fourth; a decision that might have had more to do with preserving the college's reputation than accurately reflecting Kit's efforts.

After Trinity, Robert Fearnley-Whittingstall started training to become a stockbroker, and Lambert signed up to study film at the University of Paris. Although one of his cinematic idols, the director and screenwriter Jean-Luc Godard was lecturing at the university, Lambert couldn't settle. He thought the course was old-fashioned and found his fellow students less worldly than he'd expected. Before long, he was making frequent trips back to London. By early 1960, he'd quit Paris, moved into a flat in Earls Court, and taken a junior position at a documentary film-making company, supplementing his earnings with the modest royalties from his father's estate. Then, early in 1961, Lambert bumped into Richard Mason at a party in London.

After leaving Oxford, Mason had travelled extensively through South America and the Middle East, and had just secured funding for an expedition to Brazil to chart the source of the Iriri River, one of the longest unmapped rivers in the Amazon basin. It was a journey that would take the expedition through miles of uncharted jungle. When Mason learned that Lambert had been studying at film school, he suggested he join them to make a documentary about the trip. Lambert accepted.

Before embarking on the expedition, Mason and fellow explorer and Oxford graduate John Hemming spoke with the Villas-Bôas brothers, recognised as the foremost authority on South America's indigenous people, who told them they believed the area close to the Iriri to be uninhabited. Fearnley-Whittingstall remembers Lambert reassuring him that the trip wouldn't be dangerous before producing a book with pictures of a tribe of South American Indians 'who'd only been seen twice, spoke no known language and were terribly fierce'. It was an unwitting preview of the terrible events that lay ahead.

In April 1961, while a supposedly ostracised Pete Townshend was preparing for his O levels at Acton County, Kit Lambert joined Mason and Hemming for the voyage to Brazil. After arriving in Rio de Janeiro, the party was flown to Cachimbo, a sparse airstrip surrounded by over 900 miles of dense jungle, but as close as it was possible to get to the source of the Iriri.

Now one of the world's foremost authorities on the Amazon and a former director and secretary of the Royal Geographical Society, Dr John Hemming is the only surviving member of the expedition. 'In 1961 this was unmapped territory,' he says now. 'There was nothing, no aerial or satellite photography. All we had was a compass to try and stay on a northerly bearing.' The national mapping agency sent three surveyors to join the expedition, and Hemming and his team were granted permission to name any new features they discovered in the jungle.

The party was completed by five Brazilian woodsmen who helped carry supplies and built dugout canoes from the surrounding trees. 'These men were illiterate,' says Hemming, 'but they hollowed out trees with their axes and built these beautiful canoes using biblical hand measurements – the length of a thumb, a handspan or a forearm.' However, the arduous task of cutting a path through the jungle fell to the three Englishmen, working in shifts. For five months, they hacked a trail north-eastwards from the airstrip towards what they thought was the source of the river. Every three weeks the party would move their base camp further north along the cleared path. It was a painstaking process. Between fulfilling his role as a cameraman and shooting footage of the trip, Lambert also worked shifts cutting the path – a task in which he showed the same tenacity as his more experienced companions.

'Kit was different from us in a lot of ways,' says Hemming. 'But he was also a tough little chap. Richard Mason was about to become a doctor so he made sure we had enough vitamins. But we were always hungry, so one could get rather bad tempered.' On one occasion, Hemming and Lambert made the eighteen-mile trip from Cachimbo to camp together. The path they'd cut was so narrow that both men, heavily weighed down with backpacks, had to walk in single file: 'Kit had started just ahead of me. We were each carrying a revolver for signalling purposes, and Kit later told me that he'd got so angry having me walking right on his heels for several hours that he nearly took out his gun and shot my foot off.'

The team experienced a major setback when they discovered they'd wasted weeks making canoes for a river that turned out not to be the Iriri, but another tributary some five miles away. 'Richard and I spent three days doing some reconnaissance to explore the lie of the land,' says Hemming. 'Kit cut a trail on his own and then realised the river was curving in the wrong direction. So there was a moment of depression when we discovered that this river was not the one we wanted.'

After realising their error and how much time they'd wasted, Hemming returned to Rio in August to arrange for fresh supplies to be parachuted into the jungle. He then flew from Rio to a smaller Brazilian airbase, and persuaded the national radio station to broadcast a message to camp, telling them the time of the scheduled drop and instructing the team to light a fire as a guide for the pilot. However, technical problems with the plane delayed take-off for twenty-four hours. A day later, the Brazilian president, Jânio Quadros, resigned unexpectedly, and the air force were ordered back to base. Quadros' sudden resignation and the fear that his hardline left-wing deputy João Goulart would assume control put the Brazilian military on high alert. All military aircraft were grounded and the banks were closed. Hemming was stranded, with his supplies, but without money or a plane.

Hemming finally persuaded a farmer with a light aircraft to fly him to Rio after bribing him with a bottle of whisky given to him as a gift by the British ambassador: 'There were still a few commercial planes flying, and I discovered the cost of the air ticket to Rio was 1,740 cruzeiros. So I found a drunk air force sergeant in a bar, showed him a second bottle of the malt whisky, told him, "This is the finest thing you've ever tasted, and you're going to buy it off me for 1,740 cruzeiros," which he did, and that's how I paid for my ticket.'

In Rio, Hemming secured an urgent meeting with the air minister's deputy, who explained that all military planes were grounded but one plane used for air-sea rescue was still permitted to fly, and could take him to Cachimbo. Within twenty-four hours Hemming was travelling in darkness in the hold of what he calls a 'flying boat' through the middle of a storm: 'There was thunder and lightning and the plane was being buffeted from side to side, when suddenly the door opened and one of the pilots came back to me.' The pilot informed Hemming that news had just come over the radio: his camp had been attacked and all of his companions had been killed. 'There was,' he says, 'something Wagnerian about it all.'

When he finally arrived, Hemming discovered that only Richard Mason was dead. Mason had been carrying supplies from Cachimbo to a new riverside camp, when he'd been ambushed by a hunting party from the Pánara tribe, also known as the Kren Akarore. In the Pánara's language there was only one word for both 'stranger' and 'enemy'.

'We believed the area to be uninhabited,' says Hemming. 'But it clearly wasn't. This hunting party had stumbled over our trail, which to an Indian must have looked like a bloody motorway.' Hemming later discovered that the Pánara had also been made aware of Mason's presence by the sound of his trousers rubbing together as he walked. These naked tribesman had never seen a white man before, or a man wearing clothes. They shot Mason with arrows, before smashing his skull with clubs and beating him to death.

When Mason didn't return to camp, Kit Lambert went looking for him. A day's walk from camp, he discovered his school friend's battered and bloodied corpse, around which his attackers had arranged their arrows and clubs as a warning to other strangers. Lambert and the rest of the party made their way back to Cachimbo, terrified that they could be ambushed at any moment. 'Kit was in a bad state when I got there,' says Hemming. 'He'd lost an awful lot of weight and was covered in insect bites.'

Back in England, the BBC had broadcast the news of Mason's death. Robert Fearnley-Whittingstall met with Lambert's mother Florence: 'She told me, "We must rescue Kit. I'm going to talk to Harold Macmillan and get him to send a gunboat . . ."' Within days, a reporter from the *Daily Mail* arrived in Cachimbo. 'And Kit started pouring out his emotions and thoughts to this dreadful hack,' says Hemming. An hour later, another plane arrived carrying a *Daily Express* writer. He had barely spoken to Lambert and Hemming before discovering that the *Mail*'s reporter had beaten him to the story, whereupon he flagged down the plane he'd arrived on as it taxied down the runway, and returned to Rio. The *Daily Express*' report on 7 September 1961 stated that Mason had been killed with a poison dart from a blowpipe, and quoted a school friend who described him as 'a man's man'.

Eventually a team of medics and soldiers arrived in Cachimbo to help retrieve the body. Hemming and Lambert accompanied them to where the corpse had lain for nearly a week. 'In the rainforest everything decomposes very quickly,' says Hemming, 'and the animals move in.' The expedition party had been carrying machetes as gifts for any Indians they encountered. As a peace offering and a gesture of extraordinary goodwill to the Pánara, Hemming left the weapons at the site of the ambush. Mason's decomposing corpse was embalmed, wrapped in canvas, and carried for two days out of the jungle. He was buried in a plot in the British cemetery in Rio.

Lambert attended the funeral and recuperated in the city. 'He told me that the one thing he absolutely craved after being in the jungle was sugar,' recalls Fearnley-Whittingstall. As a guest of the British ambassador, Kit's dietary needs were well catered for. But he had other cravings and by the time he left for London, Lambert was also suffering from an anal infection contracted in a Rio brothel.

Back in England, John Hemming spoke about the expedition at the Royal Geographical Society and wrote articles for the *Sunday Times*. Unfortunately, the whereabouts of the footage Lambert shot on the trip remains unknown. Hemming believes that Kit may have still had it up until his death in 1981. Fearnley-Whittingstall suggests, only half-jokingly, that 'Kit may have left it in the back of a taxi.'

However, both Hemming and Fearnley-Whittingstall dispute the suggestion that Lambert was in love with Richard Mason; a theory mooted by several people who came to know Kit later on, including Terence Stamp. 'We didn't even know Kit was gay,' points out Hemming. 'It was a friendship forged when they were boys,' says Fearnley-Whittingstall. 'It certainly never occurred to me that they were gay, or that Kit had any feelings towards Richard.'

'I don't think Kit wanted to dwell on his time in Brazil,' he adds. 'I think coming back to London and civilisation was also about coming back to normality.' The two men moved into a flat in Curzon Place, near Piccadilly Circus. What Kit now wanted, he said, 'was to be rich'. After a short stint selling advertising, he decided that the surest route to achieving his aim could be found in the film industry. Those who knew him well suggest that Kit was more interested in the idea of making a movie than the work involved. Nevertheless, just three months after his life-threatening experience in Brazil, Lambert had landed a job in cinema.

Over the next two years, he worked as a director's assistant and production manager on several films, including Judy Garland's final movie *I Could Go on Singing* (1963); Sean Connery's second James Bond thriller, *From Russia with Love* (1963) and director Bryan Forbes' version of W. Somerset Maugham's drama *Of Human Bondage* (1964). Lambert's tasks ranged from preparing actors' call sheets to assisting with the sets to running menial errands for the talent, including, he once said, emptying Judy Garland's chamber pot. None of the work was going to make him rich, but it allowed him to travel overseas and brought him into contact with the kind of creative individuals that he believed might help him to realise his dream.

Kit Lambert encountered his future business partner and The Who's co-manager Chris Stamp in 1962, after they were hired as director's assistants on producer Richard Attenborough's romantic drama *The L-Shaped Room* (1962). The pair met at Shepperton Studios in Surrey. One of Lambert's jobs was to ensure that the star, French former ballerina Leslie Caron, was on set on time; which was easier said than done considering Lambert's wayward approach to timekeeping. Stamp, meanwhile, ensured that he was on set, mainly because he was utterly smitten with Caron.

As with Richard Mason, Chris Stamp was the apparent antithesis of Lambert. Yet he was intrigued by what he called 'Kit's worldly sophistication' and his background in a 'West End bohemian artistic family'. Lambert, meanwhile, at least initially, was attracted by Stamp's good looks and his working-class upbringing.

Christopher Thomas Stamp and his five siblings were the children of merchant seamen Tom Stamp and his wife Ethel Perrott. Their eldest son, Terence, would go on to become a film actor and writer. Their second son, Chris, was born in Stepney, east London, on 7 July 1942. Tom spent the war years as a stoker in the merchant navy. It was a harrowing experience that Chris would refer to in interviews many years later, and which helped him identify with Pete Townshend's notion of a generation damaged by war.

On several occasions, Tom Stamp's merchant vessel was caught up in a skirmish and its crew forced to abandon ship. More than once, Ethel went to the shipping company's office to collect her husband's wages, only to be told there weren't any as Tom's ship had gone down. During the Blitz, his crew received a wire informing them that London was under attack. When Tom received a second wire, he was so sure it would tell him that his wife and son had been killed in an air raid, that without opening the telegram, he tried to throw himself overboard. His shipmates restrained him while one of them read the message, telling Tom that Ethel and Terence were safe and had been evacuated to Yorkshire.

On a voyage from Ireland to Iceland, Stamp's father's vessel sailed into a force 10 gale. Tom and his fellow stoker spent twelve hours shovelling coal into the ship's boiler, while up to their waists in freezing water. The Iceland voyage would be the tipping point. By the end of the trip, Tom Stamp's jet-black hair had apparently turned white. He was psychologically scarred and, for a time, struggled to settle down to life in peacetime before taking a job as a tugboat man on the River Thames.

Ethel Stamp had raised Terence while his father was away at sea, and Tom focused much of his attention on his second son. 'Dad decided to bring Chris up himself, or at least to influence him as much as he could,' wrote Terence in *Stamp Album*, the first volume of his auto-biography. Tom soon taught Chris how to fight and, as a teenager, encouraged him to enter a school boxing championship. He made it through to the quarter-finals before being beaten. After the bout at Plaistow Town Hall, Stamp waited outside for his opponent and promptly knocked him unconscious. 'Chris was a natural fighter,' wrote his brother, 'but a street fighter.'

Chris Stamp left Plaistow Grammar School in 1958. Together with a group of friends, he bought a Daimler Hearse in which they rode around East End dance halls offering to quell any trouble in exchange for free entry. Among his friends was fellow ex-Plaistow Grammar schoolboy Bill Curbishley. In 1971, Curbishley was given a job with The Who and later succeeded Lambert and Stamp as the group's manager. According to Terence Stamp, talking to Andrew Loog Oldham in Oldham's book *Stone Free* (2013), the gang's activities had attracted the attention of east London's notorious criminal twins, Ronnie and Reggie Kray 'who were always on the lookout for young likely lads'.

In 1960, Ethel Stamp told Terence she was worried about Chris' involvement with the gang and urged him to intervene. Terence had moved out of the East End to a flat in Harley Street and was trying to break into acting. He summoned his brother to the flat where Chris begrudgingly told him that the only thing he was interested in was girls. Terence loaned Chris his theatre employee's union card enabling his brother to get a backstage job at Sadler's Wells Theatre: 'Two months later he rings up from Glasgow, and says, "I've just shagged all of the corps de ballet. The last one's here — she wants to say hello."' Despite the perks of the Sadler's Wells job, it was only when Chris was hired as a prop man on the West End production of Leonard Bernstein's musical *West Side Story* that he realised he'd found his ideal career. 'It changed his life,' said Terence. 'From that moment on he knew he wanted to be in show business.'

Like Kit Lambert, Stamp had a steely charm and fearlessness that enabled him to talk his way into jobs without having the necessary experience. A year later, Lionel Bart, the songwriter behind the West End hits *Fings Ain't Wot They Used T'Be* (1960) and *Oliver!* (1960), met Chris backstage and was instantly besotted. Terence assured Bart that his brother was heterosexual, but agreed to arrange a meeting. Chris told Terence, 'I know about queers,' and met with the songwriter who promptly hired him to run his publishing company.

Stamp had gained another foothold in show business, but the hand-to-mouth nature of the industry was evident in his living conditions. The writer Christine Day (née Bowler) met Chris in 1962 when he shared a flat with her brother, Clive Colin Bowler, an actor who'd appeared with Terence Stamp in the TV drama *Term of Trial*. Stamp, with his jeans, leather jacket and gruff East End accent made quite an impression at the Bowler family home in Wembley.

'Chris and my brother's fortunes seemed to fluctuate,' says Christine now. 'For a time they rented a room in Ladbroke Grove, when Ladbroke Grove was an absolute no-go area. My mother sent me down there with a bag of groceries because they had no money at all. I think there was this thing in the 1960s of wanting to dabble in an authentic lifestyle rather than thinking you were actually down and out.'

Not that this penury impacted on their social life. One evening, Christine, joined the pair on a trip to gatecrash a party in west London. The partygoers set off in Clive's newly acquired second-hand Jaguar, the bonnet of which was secured with a length of rope but floated off as they crossed Hammersmith Bridge. Once at the party, Stamp emptied the contents of the host's well-stocked fridge into the boot of the car.

Nevertheless, their fortunes changed soon enough, when the pair moved into a chic penthouse flat at 23 Cadogan Gardens, near Sloane Square. This new residence soon became a magnet for Chelsea's beautiful people, with models, actors, photographers, gamblers and debutantes regularly passing through. Mim Scala, a young film agent, shared the flat with Stamp and Bowler, and wrote about it in his 2012 memoir, *Diary of a Teddy Boy*: 'The most desirable girls in the world traipsed through these portals on a daily basis.'

Scala, whose parents ran an ice cream parlour in Fulham, also observed a crumbling of social barriers: 'For the first time since the days of the Regency Bucks, the riff-raff and the aristocracy mingled freely. Etonians acquired strange cockney accents, and cockneys started speaking posh. It had become completely credible for well-bred young girls to have naughty King's Road boyfriends.'

Among the regular visitors to Cadogan Gardens was John Fenton, who would go on to work with Lambert and Stamp, and would soon become involved in a lucrative deal to sell Beatles merchandise. 'We were hanging around the King's Road Chelsea set, doing three or four parties a night,' says Fenton now. 'Forget *La Dolce Vita*. Our lifestyle was twenty-four-seven. I liked Chris Stamp because, like me, he came from a serious working-class background.'

At Cadogan Gardens, Christine Day witnessed her brother and Stamp's mod-like attention to detail, when Clive came padding down the stairs in wet jeans he'd been wearing in the bath to shrink to fit: 'They were both absolutely obsessed with getting the perfect shape on their jeans.' This obsession led to Terence Stamp, now a star after his lead role in the naval drama *Billy Budd* (1962), treating his brother and Clive to a stay at Hampshire's Forest Mere Health Farm. 'Terry paid for it, so that the pair of them could eat fruit and get really fit and healthy, and look great in their clothes,' says Christine.

According to his older brother, by the time Chris Stamp worked on *The L-Shaped Room*, he was subsisting on a diet of apples in an attempt to shift some extra weight and impress Leslie Caron. In the end, though, it was Kit Lambert's eye that he caught. 'It never surprised me that those two got together,' says Robert Fearnley-Whittingstall. 'It may have seemed like an implausible partnership, but only superficially. It was a meeting of minds. They both wanted to make money, and nothing binds people together closer than that.'

What Lambert and Stamp also had in common was a willingness to take risks. Christine Day had noticed this attitude in Stamp early on: 'My brother and Chris were extreme, in that they thought everything was funny, everything was a laugh. Society at that time was very cold in a way. Most people were very conventional, so anyone in the arts was considered to be different. And anyone who was that way inclined would feel quite out of place. I think Chris reflected that.' Stamp, meanwhile, admired Lambert's blasé disregard for convention or doing his job properly on *The L-Shaped Room*.

In the summer of 1963, Lambert was hired as production manager on the Walt Disney thriller *The Moon-Spinners* (1964), a film that attracted a degree of prurient interest as it featured former child star Hayley Mills performing her first screen kiss. Lambert flew to Crete to organise the construction of a road for one of the film's sets. 'He was out there for about three months,' recalls Fearnley-Whittingstall. 'He brought me back a dreadful bottle of wine, but became fluent in Greek.' In a later interview, Lambert said that Walt Disney was so impressed by his organisational skills that he doubled his salary. However, others claim Lambert was unable to account for a significant shortfall in his production budget; a forewarning of future business practices.

When Lambert returned to England, he saw that The Beatles had just played the Royal Command Performance, and that 'rock 'n' roll had taken London by siege.' In summer 1964, with the help of director Richard Lester, the Fab Four would extend their success to cinema, indulging their skewed humour in the group's debut film, *A Hard Day's Night*. Until then, pop music movies were still defined by Cliff Richard and the Shadows' recent box office success *Summer Holiday*, by which point the hint of sexuality evident in Cliff's breakthrough hit 'Move It' had long since been excised. His films, like his music, were strictly wholesome, family entertainment.

Lambert and Stamp realised that they were working on movies that could cost as much as £1 million to make, but which were being overshadowed, in terms of ticket sales at least, by the likes of *Summer Holiday*. The pair decided to find a group of their own and then film themselves and their band struggling to make it in the music industry. Unlike Cliff's recent big-screen adventures, this would be an uncompromising, down-to-earth documentary; an anti-*Summer Holiday*. 'I wanted to make a film that was about the reality,' said Stamp, 'the pills and the mods and the sweat and the tears.'

With his perfect-fitting Levi's and chic haircut, the twenty-one-year-old Stamp looked like a man who belonged in the pop business. At first glance, the twenty-eight-year-old Lambert, with his crumpled aristocratic demeanour and what Richard Barnes calls 'a Savile Row suit covered in fag burns' did not. But then the same was true of Brian Epstein. By Christmas 1963, Lambert and Stamp were sharing a cramped ninth-floor flat at 113 Ivor Court in Gloucester Place, near Baker Street. Lambert commandeered the bed, Stamp took the sofa, and later, a bed, in the hall. Andrew Loog Oldham occupied the flat downstairs and observed his budding rivals with interest. 'Kit Lambert reminded me of a naughty sulking schoolboy,' wrote Oldham, 'who had either been deprived of his food or his first crush.'

Lambert's determination to find a band in London was driven by his belief that fans wanted the next challenge to The Beatles to come from the capital, blithely ignoring the existence of the London-based Rolling Stones and The Kinks. As a throwback to his days in the Royal Artillery, Kit acquired a Shell map of London on to which he pinned markers to divide up different areas of the capital. The pair began scouring the music papers and the local press, and made a habit of scribbling down any band names, pubs and dates they spotted on flyposters. By day they worked at Shepperton, but most evenings they would both head off to a different part of the city to investigate whatever group was playing.

Soon after, Stamp enlisted old school friend Mike Shaw to assist. Shaw was a twenty-one-year-old mod and lighting technician. He moved into Ivor Court, where his 'bed' was an armchair, and began riding his scooter around the capital's pubs looking for a new Fab Four. Unfortunately, he fared no better than Lambert or Stamp.

By June 1964, funds were running low and Chris Stamp took a job in Ireland on the movie *Young Cassidy* (1965), a drama starring his brother's future girlfriend Julie Christie. While he was away, Lambert drove his Volkswagen Beetle around north-west London, stopping at any pubs with scooters parked outside. When he spotted the Vespas and

Lambrettas crowding the car park of the Railway Hotel – 'a scruffy looking pub in Harrow' – he decided to investigate.

Once inside the Railway, Richard Barnes directed Lambert towards Pete Meaden. In Meaden's version of events, Lambert didn't mention making a film. 'He lied to me, he said he was a promoter looking for a band, to put in his club,' claimed Meaden. 'So I gave him the hard sell – "This is absolutely where it's at. You cannot fail on this, squire . . . If you'll just listen to me, you can make a lot of money out of this . . . because they are the people, they are the hippest numbers in town, there's no one quite like them."' As Meaden later realised: 'I hard sold myself right out of a band.'

In conversation with the *Observer*'s Tony Palmer three years later, Lambert talked up his first sighting of The Who. He spoke of how Keith Moon 'battered away for all his life was worth', and acclaimed the overall performance as 'revolutionary' and even 'Satanic'. But even allowing for hyperbole, his argument that the High Numbers 'had to be the face of the late 1960s' was perceptive considering how the band would develop.

Robert Fearnley-Whittingstall says that Kit appeared to own only two records at Oxford: a recording of *Façade*, with his father and Edith Sitwell reciting Sitwell's poems to William Walton's score, and Frank Sinatra's *Songs for Swingin' Lovers!*. Lambert also admitted that at first he could only tell a bass guitar from any other guitar by counting the four heads at the top. Yet in other ways, his ignorance was an advantage. Lambert approached pop without preconceptions. When Townshend and Daltrey were schoolboys worshipping Lonnie Donegan and The Shadows, he'd been pondering his father's critically doomed ballet *Tiresias* or fearing for his life in the Brazilian jungle. He had little prior pop knowledge and therefore very few prejudices.

Back at Ivor Court, Lambert called Chris Stamp in Ireland and told him he'd found the band they'd been searching for. Stamp caught a plane to London and joined Lambert for the last twenty minutes of the High Numbers' set at the Watford Trade Hall on 18 July. Stamp was as impressed as Lambert, but noticed something else: the audience. 'I was knocked out,' he recalled. 'But the excitement I felt wasn't coming from the group. I couldn't get near enough. It was coming from the people blocking my way.'

Lambert and Stamp moved quickly, and arranged a private audition at a school in Holland Park. As well as giving them the chance to watch the High Numbers without an audience, it was their first opportunity to meet the band. 'The great thing about The Who is that they had this incredible, distorted, dysfunctional energy,' said Stamp. 'Pete was cerebral, John was very isolated and shut down, and Roger was Roger – his anger came through in his voice. It moved because of Keith – his energy energised them.' For Stamp there was also something very appealing about the band's collective attitude. 'Totally up yer arse, up yer cunt, down with the motherfuckers,' as he later put it.

'On Kit's side, what was evident was that he was gay,' said Pete Townshend, recalling his first meeting with the pair. 'If not obviously gay, certainly gay enough that he was like Brian Epstein, who had masterminded The Beatles. Chris Stamp was a beautiful man, very sharp, also a mod. He'd grown up around people like the Krays, and knew how to handle himself. I completely and totally and utterly fell in love with both of them.'

It seems it took barely a week for Lambert and Stamp to adjust their plan. They still wanted to make a documentary about an unknown group, but now they wanted to manage that group as well. Robert Fearnley-Whittingstall recalls Kit taking him and his wife, Jane, to watch The Who at the Railway: 'He told us he was thinking of managing this band. It wasn't my kind of music but what I was impressed by was that the kids were listening to the music and not just dancing.'

In the meantime, Pete Meaden decided that the group's set-list needed sprucing up, and took them to visit the Scene club's DJ, Guy Stevens, who had one of the best record collections in the country. It teemed with obscure imports, offering rich pickings for up-and-coming bands in search of new songs. Lambert tagged along to the meeting. An excited Stevens played them Link Wray's 'Rumble', James Brown's 'Please, Please, Please', and every Motown and Stax single he could find. 'Townshend, Daltrey, Entwistle and Moon sat there for three hours drinking tea looking like little schoolboys,' said Stevens in a 1979 interview, 'and I'm playing the records going, "Jesus Christ! Wake up!"' What nobody seemed to realise was that what the High Numbers needed was *original* material, and that Pete Townshend, despite his faltering early attempts at songwriting, was capable of providing it.

Instead, Lambert offered Stevens £5 to make a two-and-a-half-hour tape of songs for the High Numbers to cover.

While Lambert and Stamp were circling the High Numbers, Helmut Gorden was out of the country on holiday. Pete Meaden wanted to retain his hold on the group but knew that Gorden was a poor manager. Despite his earlier jealousy of Andrew Loog Oldham, Meaden steered his former business partner towards the group, believing that Oldham's involvement would strengthen his own position. 'Madame Loogy' watched the High Numbers playing Tamla Motown covers at a club. He liked what he saw, but spotted his fellow Ivor Court tenants Lambert and Stamp in the audience, and declined to embroil himself in Meaden's confused power struggle.

By the beginning of August, Lambert had acquired copies of the High Numbers' agreement with Helmut Gorden and surreptitiously passed it on to The Beatles' lawyer David Jacobs, who pointed out that Cliff and Betty Townshend hadn't counter-signed the contract, and that it was therefore invalid. Lambert later told a journalist that he landed the management of the High Numbers after a game of brink-manship in a Chinese restaurant. When the band laughed at his promise to get them a top-twenty record, he offered them a wager: 'I said, "Listen you cunts, I'll bet your wages and more I can." I actually threw down the gauntlet on the Chinese tablecloth.'

In Lambert's account of the story, he bet £120 of his money against the cash they'd make from ten gigs, at £12 a night. Townshend refused to take the bet, Entwistle said he'd bet £10 only, but Daltrey and Moon took the full wager. Lambert then said he'd take over paying their wages, worth £1,000 a year each. That he didn't actually have the money seemed not to deter him. In the end, he sold Christopher Wood's 1926 portrait of his father to raise the funds.

Asked about it now, Richard Barnes still remembers the band hesi-tating over whether to dump Gorden and Meaden and sign with the film-makers. 'Townshend and I really liked Pete Meaden,' he says. 'But by then, we knew he had no money and we knew his weakness.' That weakness became even more apparent once on a stroll around Soho, when Meaden suddenly stopped outlining his plans for world domina-tion and started retching in the middle of Berners Street. They later found out, he'd popped a handful of pills on an empty stomach.

The High Numbers had wanted Meaden to help them emulate the Rolling Stones' management model. 'The Stones had Eric Easton, who put up the money but left the management to Andrew Loog Oldham, and got a return on his investment,' explains Barnes. 'That's what we wanted. Have Helmut Gorden put up the money and let Meaden manage the band. But Gorden wanted to be Brian Epstein, and when 'I'm the Face' flopped, it was obvious that he was going to interfere even more.' What finally convinced the High Numbers to sign with Kit Lambert was their mistaken belief that he was rich. Also Roger Daltrey's latest girlfriend, Cleo, was Constant Lambert's god-daughter. 'The story of The Who is full of all these incredible coincidences,' says Barnes.

Cleopatra Sylvestre was the teenage daughter of one of Constant's mistresses, Soho cabaret artist Laureen Sylvestre. When Laureen became pregnant, Constant and his friend, the Labour MP Tom Driberg, agreed to become her child's godfathers. By 1964, the teenage Cleo was an aspiring actress and singer, and had just recorded a version of Phil Spector's 'To Know Him is to Love Him' with the Rolling Stones as her backing group. 'My memory is that it was Cleo who convinced them to go with Kit,' says Barnes. 'She was the one that told them it was the right thing to do.'

Cleo Sylvestre first met Daltrey and the rest of the High Numbers at the Scene, but she had no idea at first that the 'Kit' in question was her godfather's son. 'Constant died when I was about six,' she says now, 'and although I'd met Kit, my mother always referred to him by his real name, Christopher.' It was only when Daltrey mentioned that Kit's father had been a conductor at Sadler's Wells that she made the connection. Daltrey gave her Lambert's phone number and she called him up, jokingly telling him, "I think we're related. I'm your fairy godmother."'

Helmut Gorden returned from his holiday to find a letter at his mother's house informing him that he was no longer managing the High Numbers. In desperation, he telephoned Doug Sandom: 'He asked if I could help get him back in,' says Sandom, 'the bastard!' When Gorden realised the band had wriggled out of the contract because of Townshend's parents' missing signatures he sued his lawyers. A year later, Gorden began managing Episode Six, a group whose lead singer was former Acton County pupil Ian Gillan. In 1969, Gillian and Episode

Six's bass guitarist, Roger Glover, were poached by Deep Purple, and Helmut Gorden's hopes of becoming the next Brian Epstein were dashed once and for all.

With Gorden gone, Pete Meaden's hold on the High Numbers was more tenuous than ever. In desperation, Meaden tried to get Phil the Greek to intimidate the new managers by flashing a knife at them during a band rehearsal. But Lambert and Stamp weren't easily intimidated. In July 1964, the *Daily Mirror* had written about the 'homosexual relationship between a prominent peer and a leading thug in the London underworld' under the headline, 'PEER AND A GANGSTER – YARD ENQUIRY'. Unknown to the public, the newspaper had acquired a photograph of the well-known Conservative MP Lord Boothby with Ronnie Kray and Leslie Holt, a cat burglar and male prostitute with whom Boothby had been having a sexual relationship.

It later transpired that Boothby and Tom Driberg were regular guests at Ronnie Kray's Walthamstow flat, where, as Driberg's biographer Francis Wheen wrote, 'rough and compliant East End lads were served like so many canapés.' Compared with some of the people Lambert and, especially, Stamp knew, the likes of Phil the Greek and Reg the Butcher, were small fry. 'I knew gangsters,' said Chris Stamp in 2002. 'These were half-baked tea leaves.'

In the end, it was Daltrey who broke the news to Pete Meaden that Lambert and Stamp were now managing the High Numbers. Meaden met Lambert at a restaurant in Soho's Frith Street, where he'd once had a job peeling vegetables, and was offered £500 in an envelope as a pay-off: 'I learnt later that I was supposed to accept £5,000, but I just said, "Yeah, that's alright, that'll do – thanks a lot."' Later on, Lambert boasted that he'd deliberately stuffed the envelope with crisp new banknotes to help lure his prey.

With the High Numbers now officially theirs, Lambert and Stamp formed a company, New Action Ltd, and had new contracts drawn up. For the third time in as many years, the band's parents were given a document to sign. Lambert turned up at Fielding Road one Sunday carrying a bunch of flowers on a charm offensive. The Daltreys agreed to sign, but the contract marked the beginning of the end of Roger's already precarious marriage. Lambert knew that pop fans wanted their idols to be single. The Rolling Stones' bassist Bill Wyman and drummer

Charlie Watts and Beatle John Lennon were encouraged to keep their marital status quiet. Lambert wanted Daltrey to do the same. Roger's son Simon was born that summer, but Daltrey was soon spending more and more time away from the Wandsworth council flat he shared with his wife and their new baby. As the photographer Colin Jones, who took some of the most famous photos of The Who, recalled, 'Roger fancied women something rotten, and he had them all over the place. He really tucked into it.'

Kit Lambert's charm offensive continued at Woodgrange Avenue, where he assured the Townshends that he was going to help make their son rich and famous. This time, Cliff and Betty signed the contract, but only after Cliff had struck out a clause guaranteeing the managers a percentage of Pete's future songwriting royalties. It was a decision that would, in time, help make his son a wealthy man.

With their parents' signatures in place, the High Numbers signed to New Action Ltd with a deal guaranteeing Lambert and Stamp forty per cent of the band's earnings, with the remaining sixty split four ways. It was a deal that reinforced the view that the managers were, as Daltrey put it 'the fifth and sixth members of the band'.

Their management takeover now complete, Lambert and Stamp returned to the idea of making a film, and arranged to shoot one of the Tuesday night gigs at the Railway Hotel. The 16mm footage shot by Lambert and Mike Shaw offers a crude but brilliant snapshot of the primitive Who performing Jessie Hill's 'Ooh Poo Pah Doo', Howlin' Wolf's 'Smokestack Lightning' and the Guy Stevens-approved Smokey Robinson and the Miracles' 'Got to Dance to Keep From Crying'.

Daltrey, wearing sunglasses and with his chest puffed out, growls into the microphone, while his straw-coloured hair starts to curl in the heat. Behind him, a sweat-soaked Moon's arms flail as he performs frantic laps of his kit. To his right stands Entwistle, hunched over his instrument, his gaze settled on a point somewhere in the middle distance. Lurching over the cymbals to the left of the drum kit is Townshend whose body twists and turns, a mess of right angles, bent elbows and twitching knees. His head sways from side to side and his eyelids close for a few seconds, as if in the grip of some fleeting reverie, before snapping open again. He looks, at times, like a man trying to escape his own body.

Just as striking as the High Numbers are the audience. On the dance floor, mod girls with elfin hairdos and desert-booted boys in voguish striped T-shirts dance in their own private spaces, their staring eyes and clamped jaws suggesting a mid-week amphetamine jag. One youth, Lee Gaish, a friend of 'Irish' Jack's from Shepherd's Bush, accompanies the band on a harmonica, while his brother, Martin, another Goldhawk Club regular, throws shapes beside him.

The Railway audience as a whole, though, is a microcosm of mid-1960s youth. Behind the mods, huddled around the bar, are lads clasping half-pint glasses of beer and wearing the traditional uniform of sports jacket and closely knotted tie. The next morning they will go back to work in either the local offices or the nearby Kodak factory. Alongside them are boys probably moonlighting from Harrow County School, a five-minute bus ride away in Gayton Road, who, in turn dance inches away from the black-clad, aspiring existentialists from nearby Harrow art college.

Several future pop stars and music entrepreneurs would pay their three shillings and sixpence to see the High Numbers that year. Among them were former Bo Street Runner and soon-to-be Fleetwood Mac drummer Mick Fleetwood; budding Face and Rolling Stone Ronnie Wood, who was then playing with Ealing mods The Birds; and the ex-Pinner County grammar school boy turned blues pianist Reg Dwight, who would go on to reinvent himself as Elton John. Another Railway attendee, Malcolm Edwards, who would shortly change his surname to McLaren, was studying at Harrow Art School in 1964. McLaren first met his future wife, Vivienne Westwood, at the Railway. At that time, her then husband, Derek Westwood, worked part-time for Bob Druce. McLaren would refer back to the aggression and anger of the High Numbers at the Railway when he launched the Sex Pistols in the mid-1970s.

Word of Lambert and Stamp's coup soon reached Bob Druce, whose services had also been dispensed with. There was just one problem: the High Numbers hadn't finished paying him for their van. On the night of filming, Pete Townshend took roadie Reg Bowen aside: 'Pete said, "Look we've got some people coming down here, but I've heard there might be trouble." He said, "One of them is Chris Stamp, he's Terence Stamp's brother." I thought, "God, he must be somebody." As soon as they arrived and the place started filling up, Bob Druce's bullyboys arrived.'

Former Detour Pete Vernon-Kell's new group, The Macabre, supported the High Numbers that night. 'Their big green Commer van got repossessed,' recalls The Macabre's ex-guitarist Chris Downing. 'Bob Druce's lot turned up and took it away. So all the High Numbers' equipment had to go in our old Dewhurst butcher's van.'

The Macabre supported the High Numbers on several dates that summer. Chris Downing worked at the tax office with Queenie Entwistle, but he swiftly discovered her son John's band were not like his. 'At the Railway, Keith Moon's playing was so intense he took off his T-shirt after the gig and wrung it out into a pint glass,' he recalls. An astonished Downing also watched as a bored Pete Townshend casually pushed his amp down a flight of stairs into a venue rather than carry it himself.

There were other more serious differences. The Macabre spoke to each other; the High Numbers didn't: 'The High Numbers were like four individuals who came together to play. It always felt as if Roger and Pete came from dysfunctional backgrounds. John and Keith didn't and were easier to talk to, and I didn't recognise the wild man Keith became. Roger was angry, though, and I got the impression there was some sort of criminal element there. He wouldn't talk to me. But Roger didn't even talk to his own band.'

One night, Daltrey's father-in-law strode into the Railway just as the High Numbers were due to go onstage. 'He was looking for Roger who hadn't been home for a long time,' says Downing, 'and when he found him, he took him outside the pub and punched him.' The Macabre had to go back onstage and fill in until the fight was over. When Daltrey reappeared, he joined the rest of the High Numbers and sang the set as normal. His band may have been deeply dysfunctional, but, as Daltrey explained, 'They came before everything.'

Writing in 1969, the pop critic Nik Cohn reflecting on The Who's early years, described them as 'the last great fling of super-pop'. The first sign of how they were already gearing up to become what Lambert had called 'the face of the late 1960s' came on 16 August when the High Numbers shared the bill with The Beatles at the Blackpool Opera House.

Lambert was determined to maximise the High Numbers' impact. Mike Shaw was now working as the band's production manager, and produced lighting cues for the theatre's reluctant in-house technicians to follow. At Blackpool, the High Numbers performed their two-song set to lights that flashed on and off and changed colour. Compared with the extravagant light shows of the late 1960s, it was a charmingly primitive display. But in 1964 it was ground-breaking. When The Beatles played later, they did so beneath a simple followspot and in front of a row of footlights.

Yet the din of screaming girls drowned out the first few bars of The Beatles' opening number, and didn't stop until they were offstage. It was a sobering reminder of what the High Numbers had to live up to. 'Beatlemania was extraordinary,' says Richard Barnes, who watched from the side of the Opera House stage. 'But it's hard to express just how loud and how powerful that screaming was when you experienced it up close.' From their vantage point, Barney and the band watched a grinning John Lennon blithely telling the crowd to shut up and fuck off, knowing that they were far too hysterical to hear him.

By the end of The Beatles' set, the whole venue smelled of urine. 'Every single girl in the audience must have pissed themselves,' said Townshend, who later watched the theatre ushers spraying the sodden seats with eau de cologne. Townshend recalled the incident later in the lyrics to The Who's 1973 hit '5:15' ('Ushers are sniffing/Eau-de-cologning'). When the High Numbers were loading up their van after the gig, a gang of teenage girls mistook them for The Beatles, or decided that in the absence of the real thing, they'd do. In the ensuing hysteria, the sleeve of Daltrey's mod-approved Madras cotton jacket was torn off. Kit Lambert, convinced he'd just been mistaken for Brian Epstein, was overjoyed.

Two weeks later, the band were headlining Glasgow's Kelvin Hall Arena above balladeer Dave Berry of 'The Crying Game' fame and fifteen-year-old singing schoolgirl Lulu. After the gig, the band accompanied Lulu to her parents' flat for a party. An accordionist played downstairs while Townshend disappeared upstairs with one of Lulu's girlfriends. 'She was a beautiful girl, but she had this strange coat on,' he recalled. 'I remember getting one button undone and then another, and looking down and there were like forty buttons on this military coat. I thought, "Give me a week and I may have got somewhere."' These strange incongruous gigs came as a culture shock after the Goldhawk and the Scene. 'We felt,' said Townshend, 'as if we were on another planet.'

When they came back to earth, the band discovered that New Action Ltd had printed hundreds of promotional flyers. In a shrewd ploy for attention, the flyers abandoned standard advertising hyperbole and proclaimed the High Numbers as 'the Worst in Family Entertainment'. With Commercial Entertainments dispensed with, the group needed to find new venues in which to play. New Action's plan was to break the band in areas outside their usual west London strongholds. But it would prove more difficult than they imagined.

On 23 September 'the Worst in Family Entertainment' played Greenwich Town Hall in south London. DJ Jeff Dexter and his business partner, the songwriter Ian 'Sammy' Samwell, had been holding a weekly record hop in the hall since the end of 1962. Dexter was unimpressed by most of what he calls 'the dodgy beat bands' that ended up on the bill in between the records. The High Numbers did little to change his mind. 'I thought they were fucking rubbish,' he says. 'They didn't seem to be tuneful or solid enough. Pete Meaden had told me about this great mod group from Shepherd's Bush. But this wasn't it.'

The summer of 1964 had seen several crucial developments in The Who/High Numbers' story. Yet the two most significant were yet to come. One would be partly driven by embarrassment, the other by simple envy. On 4 August, The Kinks released their new single, 'You Really Got Me'. Pete Townshend recognised the song's truculent riff from when both groups shared the bill with The Beatles in Blackpool. The Kinks' stage outfits of blood-red hunting jackets and white ruffled shirts had amused him. But their new song was no laughing matter. 'That sort of music usually came from over the water,' said Townshend. 'The Kinks had filled a hole we wanted to fill.'

In September, the High Numbers auditioned for EMI at Abbey Road studios. Kit Lambert had persuaded his friend, the pianist and light entertainment TV star Russ Conway, to ask EMI's A&R rep John Burgess to audition the group as a favour. One of New Action Ltd's more ridiculous ideas was to have the High Numbers play as Conway's backing group, a notion that may have owed something to Lambert having persuaded the pianist to invest in the company. It didn't happen, but the High Numbers did get an audition.

The group were thrilled to be performing at Abbey Road where The Beatles had recorded their hits. The difference was that the High Numbers were still playing other people's songs. The Beatles had just reached Number 1 with their own composition 'A Hard Day's Night', and Andrew Loog Oldham would soon lock Mick Jagger and Keith Richards in their kitchen until they wrote a song of their own. John Burgess wrote to Kit Lambert later, saying that he was unsure about the High Numbers, and wondered whether they had some of their own material to offer instead.

In the meantime, the band's Tuesday night residency at the Railway remained an important weekly date on any discerning Ealing art student's social calendar. Several of the college's 'lovely, fizzy girls' often made the trip to Harrow and Wealdstone. Their presence was partly responsible for what happened next.

Just like Keith Moon's entrance into The Who, the story of how and why Pete Townshend first smashed his guitar onstage has acquired a life of its own. In *Who I Am*, he added another twist by writing that he destroyed the instrument the first night Kit Lambert saw the High Numbers at the Railway. But most people believe it happened at least six weeks later. 'I saw it happen,' says Richard Barnes, before hesitating. 'Or did I? I'm not sure. I know we had to pay for the ceiling.'

What isn't in dispute is why it happened. The High Numbers usually extended the Railway's stage with upturned beer crates, but had just paid for a collapsible wooden stage which they planned to take with them to all their gigs. What the band didn't realise was that this new stage was higher than what they were used to at the Railway.

As the night wore on, Townshend ran through his repertoire of moves: jamming his guitar against the amp to create howling feed-back, playing it upright like a banjo and, finally, thrusting it above his head. This last move was accompanied by a scream of feedback fol-lowed by a splintering sound as the top of the guitar collided with the Railway's nicotine-stained ceiling. Townshend had held his guitar overhead many times before, but had forgotten that the distance between the ceiling and the new stage was significantly reduced.

Laughter rippled through the crowd. Townshend squinted into the darkness and saw girls from the art school pointing and sniggering. In one account, he claimed another of his college friends was doubled up with laughter in front of the stage. Flushed with embarrassment and with all thoughts of the outstanding hire-purchase payments forgotten, Townshend seized the guitar, wrenched it out of the ceiling and wondered what to do next. The audience, meanwhile, seemed indifferent. 'I was expecting everybody to go, "Wow, he's broken his guitar!" but nobody did anything,' Townshend later told *Rolling Stone* magazine, 'which made me angry, and determined to get this precious event noticed. So I proceeded to make a big thing of breaking the guitar.'

In the few seconds it took to reduce the instrument to a mess of tangled wire and splintered wood, Townshend felt a rush of excitement and validation. Over the years, he would compare this destructive act to Gustav Metzger flinging acid on to canvas, the Japanese youth attacking a painting with a samurai sword, and Malcolm Cecil sawing through his bass – but taken to a more extreme conclusion. And after he began to talk publicly about his childhood abuse, he would tell journalists that destroying a guitar was a way of exorcising his demons.

On the night, Townshend followed his violent act by calmly picking up his spare, twelve-string Rickenbacker and playing the rest of the set as if nothing had happened. He was brought back to reality as soon as the gig was over. An unimpressed Daltrey told him that he could have mended the broken guitar: 'And I was standing there thinking, "That's *not* the point!"' Not for the last time, Townshend's big artistic ideas had run up against Daltrey's hard pragmatism. What neither man yet knew was the dramatic effect this spur-of-the-moment act would have on the High Numbers' fortunes.

When the band returned to the Railway the following Tuesday, Townshend could see the anticipation on the audience's faces as soon as he walked onstage. But he refused to oblige. Instead, Keith Moon kicked over his drums at the end of the set. The drums didn't break, but the act itself was theatrical enough to shock. 'After Keith Moon smashed up a drum kit, we had it – we had that *thing*,' said Townshend. 'Even on days when we weren't going to smash anything we just had to look as if we were, and the crowd would be like, "Oh my God". There was this tension. It was all very, very punk and very, very dangerous.'

Two weeks on from the original incident, the crowd's patience was amply rewarded when both Townshend and Moon destroyed their instruments. There was no turning back. In the space of a fortnight, Townshend had smashed two guitars, with hire-purchase payments outstanding on both. As The Macabre's Chris Downing notes: 'It was an incredibly daring thing to do. My Rickenbacker cost me £169 and I was earning seven pounds a week at the tax office.' Kit Lambert's reaction to the wanton violence was one of admiration tempered with fear. Lambert was shameless in his pursuit of publicity but was also aware of how little money New Action Ltd had. Kit's grandmother Amy had died earlier that year and left him a substantial share of her estate. But Lambert and Stamp were spending far more on the High Numbers than they were making. Now, as well as a new van and new stage clothes, the group needed new instruments.

Word of Townshend's auto-destructive art also found its way to Marshall's. 'We went to Jim Marshall's not long after the Railway and Pete said, "I need a new guitar,"' says Richard Barnes. 'And they said, "No way, we know what you've done." So Pete grabbed one off the wall and ran out of the shop.' The guitarist soon became adept at ducking into the store, helping himself to a new instrument, and dashing out with a shouted promise to 'Pay ya later'. On other occasions, he sent Reg Bowen to do the deed for him. 'Marshall was owed a fortune,' says Bowen. 'So I'd grab the guitar, and jump on my scooter and drive off before anyone could say anything.'

Not wanting to lose the business or the publicity, Marshall's would soon start mailing hire-purchase agreements to Townshend. 'I think at one point he was paying for seven guitars on HP,' says Barnes. Before long, Townshend was trashing guitars just enough to impress an audience but not enough to be unsalvagable. On those occasions, the damaged guitars would be returned to Marshall's to be repaired.

'I fixed some for him,' recalls Terry Marshall. 'But I remember these three wonderful Gretsch Country Gentlemans that came into the shop. Pete said he wanted one to use onstage. I said, "OK, but for God's sake, don't bugger it up" – and he did. He broke the neck. I could repair that. Then he took it out again and broke the head, and there was no chance of fixing that. I couldn't believe it.'

Entwistle had found his niche as the unflappable bassist who played like a lead guitarist. But with Moon and Townshend smashing their instruments, there was now added pressure on Daltrey. In time, the singer took to accompanying Townshend's feedback and adding to the noise by striking Moon's ride cymbal with his microphone (something Keith apparently hated). Later on, Daltrey would discover what would become his trademark stage move: whirling the microphone lead over-head, like a cowboy lassoing cattle. 'The trouble is at first he kept smashing the heads off the mics,' says Terry Marshall. 'He'd come into the shop to get them repaired, and they'd look like a bunch of bananas.'

The group had stumbled on a visual gimmick that set them apart from every other band in the country. New Action's dogged attempt to bring 'the Worst in Family Entertainment' to the farthest reaches of London continued, with Stamp showing promoters an edit of the 16mm footage they'd shot of the group playing the Railway. More High Numbers dates followed in dance halls in Essex and Kent, and there was another visit to Greenwich, but it was still a struggle to find an audience.

Among the few regulars at Greenwich Town Hall was Plumstead teenager June Clark, who, along with her friend Deirdre Meehan, would later help run The Who's fanclub. 'The stage was about six inches off the floor and there was no one there,' she says now. 'But the music was different. Just the sound of it was so heavy compared to the poppy stuff that was around at the time.' June and her friends stood on chairs around the edge of the hall watching the band play as if the venue was full: 'Keith was breaking drumsticks and throwing them into the audience, even though there was hardly anybody there to catch them. At the end of the gig they all sat on the stage, and I went up and spoke to then. No one was too important.'

The violence of their stage act came as a surprise, though: 'I was shocked when Keith accidentally broke his drumsticks. When I later saw Pete break a guitar, I thought, "That is crazy. Nobody does that." I didn't find it exciting. It made me think, "My God, that man is angry."' June Clark also noticed how seriously Kit Lambert took the High Numbers' audience: 'Kit made a fuss of the fans and took them seri-ously. He thought they had something worthwhile to say.' Lambert would exploit this connection with the fans soon enough.

By the end of 1964, Chris Stamp had taken a job in Norway on an upcoming Kirk Douglas war movie *The Heroes of Telemark* (1965) in order to raise some much-needed funds. Over the coming months, New Action's extended family would expand beyond Mike Shaw to include Stamp's personal assistant Patricia Locke and long-serving roadies, Alan Oates and Dave 'Cy' Langston. Lambert also hired a secretary, a striking looking thirty-year-old brunette named Anya Butler, who would soon begin a clandestine affair with Pete Townshend. But Anya struggled to maintain order at the Ivor Court HQ, which now resembled a cross between a printworks and a military bunker with maps, flyers, music papers and posters strewn around the room.

Having turned down the offer to become the High Numbers' road manager ('I didn't know what that was, but it sounded like hard work'), Barney was now producing silk-screen posters advertising the band's gigs. His latest artworks were often hung up to dry in the flat. Lambert conducted his business on the phone while chain-smoking cigarettes and trying to ignore the chaos. 'He had this little Irish cleaning lady, who'd walk in, see what was going on and shake her head,' says Barnes. 'Kit would be ranting down the phone, spot her, and shout, "Boiled egg, dear."'

By late autumn, the chaos, and bailiff's letters, had become too much, and Lambert relocated to 84 Eaton Place, just around the corner from Lord Boothby in upmarket Belgravia. Lambert shared Pete Meaden's love of a fine postcode. But the chaos of Ivor Court soon followed him to his new SW1 address. Since Bob Druce's departure, New Action were acting as the High Numbers' managers and promoters. When it came to hustling new gigs, Lambert had to weigh up the pros and cons of telling the promoter that his band's drummer and guitarist had a penchant for destroying their equipment. There was also another problem: the band's name. The 'Worst in Family Entertainment' flyers had failed to have the desired effect, with some promoters mistaking the High Numbers for a bingo game. The name also evoked their non-hit single 'I'm the Face' and already sounded out of date; the worst crime in the mod world.

By November, The Who were again calling themselves The Who. 'It was,' insisted Townshend, 'the name we were supposed to have all along.' It was also a name that lent itself perfectly to the new logo

Townshend had designed. The Detours' name, as painted on the side of their old van, had included an arrow. Townshend co-opted this and added it to the letter 'O' in The Who's logo, turning it into the universal gender sign for the male sex. It was an arresting image that demonstrated Pete Meaden's ethos of 'neat, sharp and cool' more powerfully than the High Numbers ever had.

In November 1964, the group began what would become a residency at two London clubs. The first was at the Ealing Club. 'I knew Pete Townshend as the boy from the college,' says the club's former owner Fery Asgari. 'I'd seen The Who before, because they'd come to the club on their nights off to watch the Stones and Manfred Mann. Kit Lambert came to see me, drank lots of Scotch and told me he wanted to me to try out The Who.

'The Who's style was different from the other groups,' he adds. 'They really worked the audience hard. On the first Saturday, the crowd weren't sure. But by the fourth Saturday, there was a queue going around the corner, the club was full to capacity and we'd doubled our usual takings. Kit would be in there every Saturday, drinking all my whisky and practically dead on his feet, drunk, by ten o'clock.'

Three days after their Ealing Club debut, The Who played the Marquee. To advertise the gig, their new logo was put to use on the next round of promotional flyers and posters. The club had moved from its old Oxford Street premises to a new site at 90 Wardour Street, just down the road from the Flamingo. The High Numbers' Tuesday night run at the Railway had ended, not long after Townshend first stuck his guitar through the pub ceiling ('I think we broke some rule or other,' says Richard Barnes). Chris Stamp convinced the Marquee's owner, Harold Pendleton, to let The Who play on Tuesdays, traditionally the slowest night of the week, in exchange for sixty per cent of the door takings.

Although random gigs at Greenwich Town Hall and the Rochester Corn Exchange were forcing The Who out of west London, they weren't attracting a bigger following. A central London venue such as the Marquee was more prestigious and could potentially attract an audience from all over the capital.

Kit Lambert commissioned a friend in advertising to produce an eye-catching monochrome poster for the show. The Who's new macho logo was set above the words 'Maximum R&B' alongside an arresting image of Townshend with his arm up, poised to strike his guitar. 'That was daring,' says Barnes, 'putting the guitarist on instead of the singer' – even more so when the singer was Roger Daltrey. The image was printed on to over two thousand handbills and fly-posters, and still remains one of the most recognisable Who motifs.

In the space of a year, the band had replaced amateurish hand-drawn flyers with a poster that predicted the style and typography soon to be seen in the fashion title *Nova*, which launched the following year. The legend has grown over five decades, but the 'Maximum R&B' image also made its mark at the time. 'It looked amazing even then,' says Roger Spear, who wasn't completely sold on what he calls The Who's 'flashing noise'. 'The card with Maximum R&B and The Who logo on it was on the mantelpiece of my flat for about four years.'

The Goldhawk and the Scene were soon littered with handbills, and west London plastered with posters. To help spread the word further, Stamp devised the idea of an exclusive club made up of The Who's most dedicated fans, who would be given reduced admission to the gigs in exchange for distributing flyers. Among this so-called elite was 'Irish' Jack Lyons, who had first encountered Lambert at one of the Hammersmith Palais' mod nights.

The Savile Row-suited Lambert immediately stood out among the youths peacocking on the dance floor. 'He had a scarf furled over his shoulder,' he recalls, 'and wore a fancy double-breasted jacket. When he spoke he sounded like he was from the BBC.' Jack had watched his favourite band dispense of Helmut Gorden and now Pete Meaden, and was suspicious of this latest interloper. But he was impressed when Lambert solicited his opinion on which band name was best – the High Numbers or The Who – and seemed genuinely interested in what he had to say.

Before long, Jack and his friend and fellow Goldhawk regular Martin Gaish had been summoned to Eaton Place for a meeting with the new managers. The grandeur of the spacious, top-floor flat didn't go unnoticed by the two Shepherd's Bush youths. Inside, the pair were introduced to Chris Stamp, who, said Jack, 'looked aristocratic but spoke with a cockney accent'.

Stamp picked up where Lambert had left off at the Palais by asking if the boys would help spread the word and get their friends from the Goldhawk to go to the Marquee. When Gaish asked if they'd get paid, Lambert, through a fog of cigarette smoke, cunningly offered free admission to some of The Who's later gigs as a reward. Minutes later, Stamp had proposed the idea of an exclusive club for fans. Lyons and Gaish watched as the two men batted the idea around 'like two college professors discussing philosophy, and chain smoking at the same time'. 'How about calling them "The Hundred Faces"?' said Stamp in the end.

Sir Arthur Conan Doyle's fictitious Edwardian detective Sherlock Holmes conscripted a gang of street youths called the Baker Street Irregulars to run errands for him. By sending their own version of the Great Detective's scouts out on to the streets, Lambert and Stamp could publicise last-minute gigs, but also establish a very human connection between The Who's existing audience and potential new fans. It was a perfect example of the management's promotional nous and innate understanding of The Who's fanbase.

However, as 'Irish' Jack points out, the problem with the Hundred Faces is that they didn't exist: 'It was an idea that Chris mooted to Kit but in reality it was never formed. Yet loads of mods told you they were a member of the exclusive Hundred Faces.' The idea had tapped into the mods' love of elitism; their constant need to stay one step ahead of the pack. 'There were never a hundred faces,' confirms Richard Barnes, 'more like thirty. But it sounded good.'

The Who's first Marquee date was on 24 November. Prior to the show Lambert enlisted Jack and the Gaish brothers to hand out concession cards, granting half-price entry for two shillings and sixpence. Lambert resumed the role of junior field officer and ordered Jack on to Oxford Street with instructions to give a card to anyone young and fashionably dressed. It was pouring with rain and the usually teeming thoroughfare was almost deserted. In the end, he only managed to coax a couple of teenage girls into the club with the promise of free admission.

When he returned to the Marquee there were between thirty and fifty people in a club that could hold over 500. Few of the Goldhawk's regulars had been tempted to make the trip into the West End on a wet Tuesday night. The Marquee also lacked a drinks licence. To avoid an exodus to the Ship public house down the road, Lambert was soon scurrying around handing out tots of whisky. Knowing that the club was almost empty, the mood in the tiny dressing room was subdued. 'The Marquee meant nothing to me when we started,' said Townshend. 'I thought it was a jazz club. It was a dump.'

The Who's support bands included a Kentish Town mod group called The Boys (who'd soon change their name to The Action) and the latest incarnation of The Mustangs, now a three-piece playing soul covers and renamed The Footprints. 'Roger Daltrey phoned up and offered us six weeks at the Marquee,' says their ex-guitarist Alan Pittaway. 'The money was virtually nothing, but we weren't going to say no.' As their former drummer Peter Amott says, 'We had the unenviable task of following The Who.' Prior to the show, Amott spotted a jittery, chain-smoking Kit Lambert in the Marquee foyer and persuaded him to give up one of the Maximum R&B posters as a memento: 'We later discovered that Kit had pawned some of his late grandmother's jewellery to get The Who into the Marquee.'

Despite the poor attendance, Harold Pendleton agreed to have The Who back the following week. Lambert's 'Baker Street Irregulars' went into action and the crowds increased each Tuesday in the run-up to Christmas. 'Lambert and Stamp were unbelievable,' said Pendleton. 'They were the originators of promotions and stunts and spin and they built that night up.'

'We called what they were doing WOMP – word of mouth publicity,' says Richard Barnes. It was a revolutionary idea in the age before groups could directly text message and email their fans. 'It was incredibly forward thinking, but the message was mobile. The mods had scooters so they could spread this information around London, and get fans to the gigs. Eventually it worked.'

The Who's Marquee residency ran for twenty-two weeks. Playing though a backline of Marshall cabs beneath the club's chintzy striped stage decor, The Who produced a sound that, according to one eyewitness, 'hit you in the head as well as the guts'. They played 'Smokestack Lightning', 'I'm a Man' and a combative version of Martha and the Vandellas' 'Heat Wave'. Just as they'd previously done with the blues they were now taking unknown soul songs from Guy Stevens' record collection, and twisting them into bold new shapes, strafed with feedback, clanging power chords and Daltrey's Goldhawk Road-meets-Mississippi Delta howl.

'My eyes popped out of my head,' says Max Ker-Seymer, who had his second Who sighting at the Marquee. 'I had never seen or heard anything like it. It was light, it was dark, the colours were revolving. It was extraordinarily loud and I started feeling nauseous. It was that overwhelming.' Lambert's expedition companion John Hemming accepted Kit's invitation to the Marquee and was similarly taken aback. The intrepid explorer, who'd braved months in the Brazilian jungle, was shocked by the noise. 'I was amazed by the loudness,' he says. 'It hit you in the face.'

Keith Altham, who would oversee The Who's PR in the 1970s, but was then a writer for the pop magazine *Fabulous*, had his first sighting of the group at the Marquee. 'I wandered into the club and caught the end of The Who's set,' he says now. 'I thought I was seeing things. They were like a four-man demolition squad. Pete was trying to ram his guitar into the amp speaker cabinet. Roger was trashing his microphone and Keith was kicking his drums over. It was the loudest thing I'd ever heard. I can't honestly say I thought it was amazing, I didn't. I thought it was dangerous and they were doing *something* but I wasn't sure what it was.'

According to Altham, the destruction was being carried out for the benefit of a *Daily Express* journalist that Kit Lambert had lured to the gig: 'I think Pete had already smashed a guitar, but Kit had told him to do it again.' What had been a spontaneous act two months earlier had unavoidably become a gimmick The Who could deploy whenever they needed to shake up a complacent audience or shock a journalist into writing about them. After the gig, Altham tried to make a hasty exit but was spotted: 'Kit grabbed my arm and said, "Ah, Keith from *Fabulous*, you must come and have a brandy and talk to the boys." So I waited for them outside the dressing room.'

Fabulous, like all the pop papers, was used to presenting a flattering picture of its subjects. But The Who made little attempt to present a façade to Altham: 'The first one out was Keith Moon with his bag packed trying to head out the door at great speed. He said, "I can't stop, the singer's trying to kill me." I asked why? And he said, "Because I told him he can't sing for shit."'

Earlier, Altham had seen Daltrey throw his microphone at Moon, who'd retaliated by flinging his drumsticks back. It was Altham's first glimpse of Moon and Daltrey's fractious relationship; a simmering tension that would rip the band apart months later.

Onstage, The Who's set now included a short, brutish instrumental version of The Kinks' 'You Really Got Me'. It was as if Townshend was tormenting himself by playing the song's circular guitar riff over and over again. As well as sounding like the kind of song The Who should be writing, 'You Really Got Me' had also reached Number 1. The failure of 'I'm the Face', EMI's rejection letter and his envy of The Kinks gradually convinced Townshend that The Who needed songs of their own.

Just as The Who were preparing for their Marquee debut, the Essex pop group The Naturals released a version of the Townshend composition The Detours had recorded a year earlier, 'It Was You', as the B-side to their single 'Look at Me Now'. The single came and went. But it was a good omen. Townshend had started writing songs again, and had turned one of the spare bedrooms at Woodgrange Avenue into a makeshift recording studio. However, the conversion had been poorly thought out.

Townshend had initially approached Roger Spear's flatmate, a BBC cameraman and electronics wizard named Chris Glass, for advice about soundproofing the studio. 'I think Pete wanted somewhere Keith Moon could smash up his drums in peace,' says Glass now. 'The bedroom was about six by eight – just big enough to put a drum kit in. To soundproof it, I suggested they made a false floor with old tyres and then put a hardboard floor on top, and that they brick up the window.'

The advice went unheeded. Instead, Townshend bought sheets of heavy, straw-filled soundproofing material called Stramit boards. 'But we never got around to putting them up,' says Barnes, 'so these boards were left lying around, all over the flat.' After asking another friend for advice, they ended up with the studio floor covered with a thick layer of cement. To Cliff and Betty Townshend's alarm, the ceiling in their flat below started to buckle under the added weight. 'I always thought Pete's family liked having us in that flat,' says Barnes now. 'But years later Pete's brother Paul told me that his dad fucking hated having us there.' Nevertheless, Townshend now had his studio. Using a mono tape recorder and a microphone, he began experimenting.

As a frequent visitor to the flat, John Challis became a guinea pig for some of these experiments. 'Pete had this analytical approach to music, which I still think had something to do with Roy Ascott's ground-course,' he says. 'He would make you lie on the couch, put a speaker on your chest, play you something and ask you how it felt. Or he'd put a big pair of headphones over your ears and play something at deafening volume until you couldn't stand it any longer. It was all a bit sadistic. But there was a point to it – he was playing with your mind.'

Challis heard what would become The Who's first single 'I Can't Explain' being composed in the flat: 'I could hear Pete playing that tune down the passageway, while a gang of us lay around stoned in the front room. I thought, "What's that?" He was playing it on an acoustic guitar and it was close to how it sounded when the record came out.' The riff to Townshend's composition though was certainly familiar. 'Pete was trying to play the riff to The Kinks' "You Really Got Me",' said John Entwistle. 'But what he came up with was "I Can't Explain".'

By the time The Macabre's Chris Downing heard the song, Townshend had recorded a demo in the spare bedroom-cum-studio. 'John Entwistle played us the demo,' says Downing. 'It was the same tune but the lyrics were different and it was called 'It Must Be Spring'. We were sat there, me, John and Peter Vernon-Kell listening, but all thinking there was something wrong with the words. It sounded too happy.'

According to Richard Barnes, 'I Can't Explain' started out sounding like a Bob Dylan blues number: 'Pete had gotten into Dylan, especially the *Another Side of Bob Dylan* LP. There was a song on it called 'It Ain't Me Babe'. The subject matter was what you might call Townshend-ish.'

The lyrics of 'It Ain't Me Babe' had a similarly indignant air to the final lyrics for 'I Can't Explain'. 'I thought ['I Can't Explain'] was about a boy who can't explain to a girl that he's fallen in love with her,' Townshend said. 'But two weeks later I looked at the lyrics and they meant something completely different again.' The confusion made sense. Besides Dylan, the inspiration for lines such as 'I feel hot and cold down in my soul' came from The Who's frustrated, inarticulate and invariably male audience; 'The dislocated boys' as Townshend later called them.

One of Roy Ascott's preoccupations had been society's changing semiotics. Townshend was now convinced that pop music had a new function, which was to tap into the emerging language of its audience: 'Boys that were often in love with the girl on the other side of the room, but didn't want to go up and say, "Hey babe do you wanna dance?"'

The other challenge Townshend faced as a composer was writing words Roger Daltrey would be willing to sing. Surprisingly, for a song that The Who were still opening their shows with in the twenty-first century, Daltrey was unsure about 'I Can't Explain': 'I felt uncomfortable when I had to sing it, because it wasn't like anything we'd done before.' The 'dislocated boy' voicing his insecurities about girls, sex and life in general wasn't an easy character for Daltrey to assume. Knowing this, Townshend presented The Who with other songs. One of these, 'Call Me Lightning', had a lyric that exuded machismo and confidence. But it wasn't as good as 'I Can't Explain'.

It was Townshend's vulnerable song that first piqued the interest of The Kinks' producer. Sheldon 'Shel' Talmy was a Chicago-born studio engineer who'd moved to London in 1962. Showing a similar flair for a good hustle as Kit Lambert and Chris Stamp, Talmy arrived in Britain with several acetates, including the Beach Boys' 'Surfin' Safari', which he successfully passed off as his own productions. Decca Records hired him as an independent producer and A&R man. A year later, he'd produced the hit single 'Charmaine' for Irish harmony group The Bachelors.

Despite their success, Talmy wasn't interested in The Bachelors' cloying pop. Still only twenty-six, he wanted to find a British rock 'n' roll group. The Kinks fulfilled that ambition, but Decca in the UK, showing the same short-sightedness that had led them to turn down The Beatles, said no to The Kinks. Talmy took them to Pye Records instead. He scored a hit with 'You Really Got Me' and followed it with another top-five single, 'All Day and All of the Night', in October 1964. Both singles were the sort of records The Who should have been making.

Talmy's approach to record production differed from that of his British counterparts. He wanted more noise, more energy and more confrontation. In the studio, he insisted microphones were set up next to the drums and amplifiers, instead of relying on the in-house mics suspended from the ceiling. Like Townshend and Jeff Beck, The Kinks' lead guitarist Dave Davies was a fan of distortion and feedback and, encouraged by Talmy, he slashed the cone of his amp to create a dirtier sound. However, Talmy supplemented such rawness with session players, supposedly hiring twenty-year-old session ace and future Led Zeppelin guitarist Jimmy Page to play rhythm on The Kinks' debut album. Although as recently as 2014, Dave Davies was still insisting that Page never played on 'You Really Got Me'.

Talmy heard about The Who through Anya Butler, who was friends with his wife. He watched the group play a church hall in Shepherd's Bush, and was impressed. 'After hearing the first eight bars, I was convinced that at last I'd found a kick-ass English rock band,' he says. 'It was a no-brainer.' After a second audition in the former home of skiffle, The 2i's Coffee Bar, Talmy offered to pay for a recording session, which he would then shop around the record companies. The band, with Lambert and Stamp producing, had already cut a demo of 'I Can't Explain' at the Marquee's studios. But Talmy insisted the song needed reworking.

In November, Talmy joined The Who and engineer Glyn Johns at Pye Records' studio in London's Marble Arch. Talmy might have believed that The Who were a 'kick-ass English rock band', but he wasn't taking any chances and had hired the Ivy League, a male vocal trio, to sing harmonies on the track. 'The Who didn't do backing vocals,' Talmy explains. 'Or, to be more precise, they did them badly.'

The Ivy League weren't the only hired hands at the session. Interviewed in 2002, Chris Stamp said that 'Talmy didn't really want to use The Who, he wanted to use Jimmy Page and some drummer, but we said, "No fucking way."' In 2013, Page confirmed that he was present at the session, but that his contribution only amounted to 'playing the riff underneath' Townshend's lead guitar, and that he was barely audible. However, as with The Kinks, rumours circulated that it was Page, not Townshend, who had played on 'I Can't Explain'. The session musicians' code of silence meant that for years, nobody, including Jimmy Page, was inclined to put the record straight.

Talmy, however, strongly denies wanting to replace Keith Moon. 'Nothing could be further from the truth,' he says now. 'I *never* thought of bringing in a session drummer. Moonie was the best rock drummer of all time.' Nevertheless, Townshend, Daltrey and Entwistle all backed up Stamp's allegation. 'Keith told the session drummer, "Get out of the fucking studio, or I'll kill ya!"' said Townshend. Entwistle claimed the producer wanted to replace him as well.

Shel Talmy believed it was his job to make the best record he could, and had little interest in becoming friends with the band. 'Pete, for whatever reason, had two chips on his shoulders. To get on with him, you had to be twice as sarcastic,' he said. 'Moon I was very good friends with, John never spoke and Daltrey I never connected with at all.' But he found their management a bigger problem. 'Kit Lambert was out of his fucking mind,' Talmy told journalist Richie Unterberger in 2010. 'I think he was certifiably insane. If he hadn't been in the music business he would have been locked up.'

Asked about The Who's ex-managers now, Talmy offers a more measured response: 'I never found out what the hell Chris Stamp was doing,' he says, before describing Lambert as 'mad, bonkers, demented, deranged, potty, daft, incompetent, unhinged and pixelated.' The friction was probably inevitable: Lambert thought he should be producing The Who's records, because that was what Andrew Loog Oldham was doing with the Rolling Stones. But Talmy didn't want Lambert in the studio and, according to Townshend, he was reluctant to enter into dialogue with the band. An hereditary condition meant that Talmy had extremely weak eyesight. 'Recording with him, we were also blind,' said Townshend. 'We never knew what we were doing.'

However painful the process, with 'I Can't Explain' Talmy helped create a commercial pop record that still retained some of the bile and fury of The Who's live show. It was a compromise, but it worked in a way that 'I'm the Face' hadn't. Like The Kinks' 'You Really Got Me', The Who's debut single showed off both Talmy's noisy, revolutionary production but also a new style of songwriting. Townshend's stabbing guitar riff controlled the song and everything else, including Daltrey's vocals, followed that riff. This wasn't the sort of record The Beatles were making. Instead, like 'You Really Got Me', it was a template for the kind of heavy rock Jimmy Page's Led Zeppelin would build a career from in the 1970s.

Such confrontational originality meant the record companies would be hard to win over. Just as they'd done with The Kinks and The Beatles, Decca in the UK turned down The Who. But Talmy had a standing arrangement with the company's US wing, and called in the favour. 'They were a very nice bunch of guys, older men who had no idea what rock 'n' roll was,' he recalled. 'But they said, "If that's what's supposedly selling, then we'll go out and try and sell it."'

Talmy secured a one-off deal for The Who with Decca in America, which traded as Brunswick in the UK. However, neither The Who nor their managers were aware that Decca UK and Decca US were separate companies. New Action had also naively signed a deal with Talmy's production company, which tied The Who to him for five years, gave him control over all their recording and production, and would earn the group a paltry two-and-a-half per cent royalty rate (the industry standard was between four and six per cent).

Talmy had also written the B-side for 'I Can't Explain', 'Bald Headed Woman', a song The Kinks had already covered, thereby guaranteeing himself further royalties. Talmy's argument was that neither Lambert nor Stamp knew how the record business worked, he did, and was therefore entitled to a payback for financing the recording, and landing The Who a deal, albeit one with an American label that had little long-term interest in them. It would be a while yet before the band and their managers realised the full ramifications of the deal.

In the meantime, with Christmas 1964 approaching, Kit Lambert began courting the music press. Christine Day was now working as a writer for the teenage magazine *Boyfriend*, when Lambert contacted her. 'I met him in a Soho coffee bar,' she says. 'He was trying to get The Who written about in the "upcoming British bands" slot. When he realised I already knew Chris, I think he thought that gave us a kind of bond.'

Stamp and Lambert's chalk-and-cheese partnership came as no surprise to Christine, who'd witnessed Chris's hustling abilities when he'd shared a flat with her brother: 'Kit and Chris were both part of that very sixties thing – of not staying within your own class, and that idea that anything goes.'

Over coffee, Lambert outlined his plans for The Who. 'He told me they had this campaign to put arrows that just said "The Who" – nothing else, no explanation – all over London. I remember being terribly impressed. No other managers were doing anything like that.' It was the sort of viral marketing strategy record companies would embrace forty years later. Yet despite the fact that The Who had a record coming out, Lambert was still fixated on the idea of making a film about the band. 'That was still the master plan,' says Christine. 'They wanted to launch the group and make enough money that they could then make this movie. Their main interest didn't seem to be pop music, it was movies.'

Christine went back to the *Boyfriend* office and wrote a story talking up The Who and their new single. 'I Can't Explain' snuck out largely unnoticed in the US in November 1964 and was released in the UK on 15 January 1965. Lambert threw a launch party at Eaton Square, inviting everyone he knew. 'Kit had hired waiters in suits who walked around with champagne and canapés on silver trays,' says Christine. 'They just kept playing 'I Can't Explain' over and over again. It all seemed terribly funny because The Who were just hanging around, drinking the champagne, and basically looking like yobs.'

Halfway through the party, Kit grabbed Christine's hand and led her into his bedroom. Pinned to the wall above his bed was her *Boyfriend* article about The Who: 'He was so pleased, so proud.' Later, when the champagne was gone, Christine discovered that the lavish party had been something of a charade. Letters from bailiffs had been arriving at 84 Eaton Place. Once again, Lambert and Stamp were being threatened with eviction.

CHAPTER SIX
GOOD YOBS

'In an atmosphere of brooding sexual menace, the total effect is like crossing pop with science fiction.'

The *Observer* describes The Who, June 1965

'If we liked each other we probably wouldn't exist.'

Pete Townshend on the key to The Who's success, 1965

'All great art is crap.'

Kit Lambert

On 24 January 1965, Britain's wartime prime minister, Sir Winston Churchill, died at his home in London's Hyde Park Gate. He was ninety years old, and had recently suffered a stroke. Churchill had served a second term as prime minister in the mid-1950s. But it was his time leading the country during the Second World War for which he would always be remembered. Following the news of his death, radio and TV programmes were cancelled to make way for memorial broadcasts. Six days later, Churchill's coffin, draped in the Union flag, was carried on a gun carriage through streets lined with people, from Westminster Hall to St Paul's Cathedral, for a state funeral service. In 2012, Pete Townshend summed up his attitude towards the British establishment in the mid-1960s like so: 'They're all cunts and Winston Churchill is a bastard.' But the country's loss was The Who's gain.

Five days after Churchill's death, The Who made their first appearance on ITV's *Ready Steady Go!*, a pop TV show that had picked up where *Six-Five Special* and *Oh Boy!* had left off. *Ready Steady Go!* began broadcasting on Friday evenings in August 1963. A year on, the show's slogan 'The Weekend Starts Here!' had become a national catchphrase, and The Beatles, The Kinks, the Rolling Stones and The Animals had all passed through its central London studio.

In 2013, the programme's former editor and producer Vicki Wickham described *Ready Steady Go!* as being run by 'young people who knew nothing about TV'. The exception to the rule was its thirty-five-year-old host, radio DJ Keith Fordyce. But it was Fordyce's co-presenter, Cathy McGowan, who became the show's figurehead. McGowan was nineteen years old, and had been offered the job after answering a press advert for 'a typical teenager'. TV executives and older viewers winced as she fluffed her lines and missed her cues. But McGowan's charm and fashion sense appealed to a teenage audience, who soon nicknamed her 'Queen of the Mods'. Rather like The Who, Cathy McGowan was her audience.

With the release of 'I Can't Explain', Kit Lambert became aware of Decca Records' failings and decided to promote the record himself. Among those he called was *Ready Steady Go!*'s programme editor. Pete Meaden had previously pestered Vicki Wickham into considering the High Numbers for a slot on the show. But she'd been put off by their contrived image. Lambert invited Wickham and the show's director Michael Lindsay-Hogg to watch The Who at the Marquee. Impressed by the noise and the energy coming from both the band and its fans, they decided to book the group.

Lambert was aware that *Ready Steady Go!* employed a scout to visit clubs and ballrooms, and handpicked the programme's young audience. 'They wanted people who could dance and looked good,' says one of the show's regular dancers. 'They didn't want it be like *Top of the Pops*, with kids standing around chewing gum and looking vacant.' When Kit discovered that the scout was off sick, he promised Lindsay-Hogg that he could fill the studio with teenagers from the Marquee. Lambert then scavenged over a hundred tickets for the show, which were hastily distributed among the Goldhawk and Marquee 'faces'.

Shortly before The Who were due to make their TV debut, Lindsay-Hogg's team were informed that their usual studio at Television House, Kingsway, WC2, was needed for a Winston Churchill memorial broadcast. The team were moved to the larger Rediffusion studio in

Wembley, much closer to The Who's stamping ground. By the time the group arrived for rehearsals, their fans were already marshalling, like a sharply dressed army, outside. 'We basically took over their show,' said Roger Daltrey. 'We nicked their tickets and filled it with our audience.'

The acts that evening also included the Mancunian beat group The Hollies and the self-styled 'British Dylan', singer-songwriter Donovan. A forward-thinking Lambert had supplied The Who's followers with scarves, to ensure that they stood out from the rest of the crowd on TV. When Donovan and The Hollies performed, they did so to an audience dominated by The Who's scarf-waving fanatics. Like the oversized speaker cabinets with which they'd once intimidated rival bands, it was another example of the group's psychological warfare.

The High Numbers had made their low-key TV debut the previous autumn on BBC2's *The Beat Room*. That day, John Entwistle had threatened to walk out after discovering he was hardly in shot during the performance. It was *Ready Steady Go!*'s policy to include the whole group. On the night, The Who nervously lip-synced through 'I Can't Explain' – 'all hand clapping and gum chewing,' said Chris Stamp. But when Townshend mimed the song's final chord, the fans threw their scarves towards the stage where they ended up draped around the band like garlands. As Daltrey explained, '*After Ready Steady Go!* everything took off.'

Next, Lambert and Stamp gambled £350 they barely had to make a promotional film of The Who, which they then sold to the TV pop show *That's For Me*. The further exposure helped 'I Can't Explain' begin its slow climb into the top thirty. By now Stamp was following Kit Lambert's lead, and repeatedly phoning the new pirate station, Radio Caroline, to request the song. The Irish entrepreneur, Ronan O'Rahilly, who also managed Georgie Fame and the Scene Club, had set up Radio Caroline in spring 1964, motivated by the BBC's refusal to play Fame's first single (it was an independent release and the Beeb favoured major labels).

Stamp's persistence had the desired effect. Daltrey and Townshend had first heard Bill Haley and Elvis Presley on Radio Luxembourg. Ten years later, there was an illicit thrill to be had from hearing their own music illegally broadcast, albeit from a decommissioned passenger ferry moored off the Essex coast. The station's support worked: 'I Can't

Explain' finally cracked the top thirty, and The Who were asked to play on the BBC's *Top of the Pops*.

'It's incredible how fast everything happened,' says Richard Barnes. 'From playing some shitty boozer in Shepherd's Bush to *Top of the Pops* in what felt like six months.' The Who's appearance on the show came about only because another group had cancelled, and the producers needed some bright young things to fill the 'Tip for the Top' slot. But it worked. 'I Can't Explain' had made achingly slow progress but finally peaked at Number 8, sandwiched between The Supremes' 'Stop! In the Name of Love' and Bob Dylan's 'The Times They Are a-Changin''.

'I never doubted we were going to make it,' Daltrey told the author. 'I don't know whether it was over-confidence or me thinking, "I don't know why but this is what I've got to do." I felt like I was the man in *Close Encounters* [*of the Third Kind*] building a mountain. There were never any doubts.'

Not everyone was pleased. The Kinks returned from a US tour to hear 'I Can't Explain' on the radio. For a few confused seconds, they thought they were listening to themselves. The High Numbers had supported The Kinks on a number of occasions, and to singer Ray Davies the borrowing was apparent. 'I felt a bit appalled,' he said. 'The only reason I let it go was because I'd seen Keith Moon play, and he was such a funny, nice, original guy.'

The single's success had an immediate effect on The Who's finances. They could now charge as much as £300 a night, but with New Action running up sizable debts, the increase was laughable. The company had opened accounts with several different London banks, and squeezed at least £500 out of each thanks to their SW1 address, Lambert's public-school accent, and telling the managers what Chris Stamp called 'a load of old bollocks'.

Cheques were always in danger of bouncing, but the money enabled the managers to pay for The Who's promotional film, photo sessions, posters, flyers and new clothes. Lambert was determined to present a moneyed image to the outside world, whatever the cost. Just as he'd pawned his grandmother's jewellery to front the money for The Who's first Marquee gig, now he pawned a set of Constant's cufflinks to pay a dentist to fix Roger Daltrey's crooked front teeth. In the meantime, he cruised between business meetings in a hired Rolls-Royce, the bill for which was always overdue. 'Kit gave up taking buses early in life,' points out Robert Fearnley-Whittingstall.

In the meantime, Pete Townshend was photographed trying on clothes in Just Men, a hip boutique near the King's Road, and looking every inch the elegant would-be pop-star-about-town. New Action fed the music press with bogus facts and figures suggesting The Who were more affluent than they were. 'The group have a £50-a-month repair bill,' reported *Melody Maker*. 'The usual clothes-buying form is for two or three of the boys to go to London's Carnaby Street, and spend £200 in one visit.' 'That's how we built up the debt that we were in,' said John Entwistle. 'Buying clothes by day and smashing up equipment at night.'

The Who had managed a top-ten hit, but soon realised just how poor their deal with Shel Talmy and Decca Records was. After everyone else had taken their cut, the band made just £1,000, from which New Action then deducted their managerial forty per cent. Lambert and Stamp browbeat the record label into upping the group's royalties from two and half to four per cent for the next single. But the managers' already prickly relationship with Talmy would only get pricklier.

It hadn't made him rich, but Pete Townshend had written a hit single. If he needed proof that quitting art school had been the right thing to do, it was there in black and white in the *New Musical Express* charts. 'I Can't Explain' had been composed specifically for The Who's audience. Townshend realised he'd achieved his aim when a deputation of mods, led by 'Irish' Jack Lyons, appeared in the Goldhawk club's dressing room. 'I remember saying to Townshend, "You're writing about us",' said Jack. 'And he said, "That's what I'm trying to do."' Neither was Townshend's achievement lost on Kit Lambert. With the band about to start recording their debut album, Kit knew he had to nurture the songwriter.

But to do so, he would have to remove Townshend from his natural habitat. The scene that greeted every visitor to Pete and Barney's flat was one of casual squalor. There were LPs, guitars, amps, mattresses, bedding, over-filled ashtrays and Stramit boards scattered everywhere. The curtains were drawn and a haze of dope smoke hung over everything like a dull mist. The flat's occupants were so used to the mess, they barely noticed it. Lambert made a suggestion: 'That he take Pete out of our squalor,' says Richard Barnes, 'and into his.'

In reality, despite his plush SW1 address, Lambert was still living beyond his means. Bailiff's letters arrived, which he ignored, until the bailiffs themselves turned up. 'It's very depressing when you're managing a group and you're supposed to be making money and you arrive and there's a big furniture van on the steps of your office and a big bloke's carrying out your desk,' he later admitted. Invariably, Lambert would scrounge together enough cash to retrieve his possessions, and then the whole cycle would commence again.

In the 1987 biography *The Lamberts*, Kit's secretary Anya Butler told author Andrew Motion how Lambert always ordered her to hide a valuable bust of his father whenever the bailiffs arrived. Anya would stash the sculpture in the lavatory, then sit above it with her knickers around her ankles until they'd gone. This farcical ritual would be repeated several times.

Unaware of the extent of Lambert's financial chaos, Townshend accepted his offer 'to rescue me from my art school friends' and moved into Eaton Place. As soon as he arrived, Townshend noted the connecting door between his and Lambert's bedrooms. But he was unfazed. At Ealing, Townshend had been convinced that his effeminate appearance and inexperience with women had led many students to presume he was gay. 'And I didn't care,' he told the author.

Despite Shel Talmy's impression that 'Lambert was hot after Townshend', it seems Kit wanted to groom his nineteen-year-old protégé, not seduce him. 'I was disappointed Kit didn't fancy me,' Townshend admitted. 'But only because I wanted his absolute approval. Kit didn't like pretty boys, if I was a pretty boy in any sense of the word. He preferred street urchins and rent boys.'

At Eaton Place, Townshend would sleep late, and then disappear in the early evening to play the Marquee or a late-night mod dive on the south coast, only returning in the early hours. More than once he wandered out of his bedroom the next day to find some sullen youth he'd never seen before gulping tea and scoffing scrambled eggs at the table. There would be an awkward silence, before Lambert offered some implausible explanation: 'This unfortunate boy had a terrible accident and hurt his foot, so I had to put him up for the night . . .'

'We all wanted to be Acker Bilk.' Alf Maynard's New Orleans Jazzmen, circa 1961 (from left): Rodney 'Griff' Griffiths, Barry 'Bas' Smith, Chris Sherwin, Alan 'Alf' Maynard, John Entwistle and Phil Rhodes. © Chris Sherwin

'We all wanted to be The Shadows.' The Detours, circa 1963 (from left): Roger Daltrey, Doug Sandom and Pete Townshend. © Doug Sandom

above: 'We all wanted to be Lonnie Donegan.' The Sulgrave Rebels, Wormholt Park school, Shepherds Bush, 1958 (from left): Alan Pittaway, Reg Bowen, Roger Daltrey, Mike McAvoy and Derek 'Del' Shannon. © Alan Pittaway

left: 'Keith was the one you noticed.' The Beachcombers, 1963 (from left): Keith Moon, Norman Mitchener, John Schollar, Tony Brind, Ron Chenery. © The Beachcombers

top right: The High Numbers/Who show off their new mod makeover, near Piccadilly Circus, London, 1964. © tracksimages.com

right: The Detours, circa 1963 with ex-vocalist/bassist Gabby Connolly (centre): 'Our gigs were huge jamming sessions with everyone swapping instruments.'
© Gabby Connolly

'We wanted to make it like a nightclub-cum-bordello.' The High Numbers/Who, Railway Hotel, Harrow & Wealdstone, summer 1964. © tracksimages.com

'You've got to be different from the other "haddocks".' Mods and police at Clacton pier, Essex, summer 1964. © Popperfoto/Getty Images

'They really worked the audience hard.' The Who with Ealing Club owner Fery Asgari (second left), March 1965. © Fery Asgari

above: 'Nothing binds people together closer than making money.' The Who's managers Chris Stamp and Kit Lambert, January 1966.
© Colin Jones/TopFoto

right: 'I was looking for a kick-ass English rock band.' Keith Moon, producer Shel Talmy and Pete Townshend, the My Generation LP recording sessions, October 1965.
© Colin Jones/TopFoto

left: 'It was full of blokes that had just come out of the nick.' The Who on stage at The Goldhawk Club, Shepherds Bush, 1965.
Photograph by David Wedgbury, © Not Fade Away Archive

below: 'We live pop art!' The Who with Jasper Johns- and Peter Blake-inspired pop-art clothing winter 1965.
Photograph by David Wedgbury, © Not Fade Away Archive

right: Ready for a swift getaway: Roger Daltrey and his Volvo P1800, Chelsea Barracks, London, November 1966.
© Tony Gale/pictorialpress.com

below: Portrait of the artist at home: Pete Townshend in his home studio, Old Church Street, Chelsea, 1966.
© Colin Jones/TopFoto

above: Clown prince: Keith Moon, Saville Theatre, London, October 1967. © tracksimages.com

right: Tower of power: John Entwistle and Marshall stack, Chelsea Barracks, London, November 1966. © Redferns

above: The Who 'leave a wound': Pete Townshend, Pembroke College May Ball, Oxford, May 1967. © Redferns

below: TV stars: The Who performing 'Pinball Wizard', spring 1969. © TopFoto

'It was make or break time.' The Who with Kit Lambert, recording *Tommy*, IBC Studios, London, October 1968. © Baron Wolman Photography

'I felt like a workman in a lunatic asylum.' Pete Townshend and Roger Daltrey, on stage, Woodstock Festival, August 1969. © TopFoto

The Who knew about their co-manager's sexuality, even if he wasn't completely open about it. Townshend believed it gave Lambert a better insight into how The Who's audience worked. 'The audience were ninety per cent boys,' he told Andrew Motion. 'He picked up that the link between our audience and the band was a sexual one. He used that piece of secret knowledge to make the band – in dress and manner – more androgynous.' This manifested itself over time in Lambert encouraging The Who to adopt a more flamboyant look and to wear a little make-up onstage. In Townshend's mind, they were tapping into something that was already there in their mod fanbase waiting to be explored.

'A lot of my mod friends from the Goldhawk tried being gay,' he said. 'They tried it out because it was a fashionable thing to do, but also because in that little mod circle, we thought Rod Stewart was gay because he performed with Long John Baldry who was openly gay. We thought David Bowie was gay and we thought Marc Bolan was gay because Marc had said "I was a rent boy", which was a radical thing to say.'

At first, Townshend also believed Chris Stamp was homosexual: 'Because he was even better looking than his brother Terence.' Later, when Townshend joined Lambert and Stamp for dinner dates in Chelsea, he relished the attention they attracted: 'We would walk into a restaurant and all the men would look round and think that I was Kit's boy or, better still, Chris's. The frisson that created, especially with women, was quite extraordinary. What women would do was break into what they saw as a gay triangle.'

The first woman to break into that triangle was Anya Butler. 'It was the first really profound sexual affair I had,' Townshend told the BBC in 2011. 'Profound because it was so exciting and disturbing. Anya was ten years older than me, and just wanted to crash into this frisson.' The pair would have sex at the flat, until a disapproving Kit found out, and insisted that Anya set up Townshend in a place of his own. There was one condition: it had to be close to Eaton Place.

Lambert's reaction to the affair was hardly surprising. His insight into The Who and their male audience was partly born out of his own obsession. 'Gay managers like Kit regarded their groups as their family,' says Keith Altham. 'The "straights" that went home to their wives and children did not have the same time to offer their bands. Gay managers did.'

What Townshend called his 'toy boy relationship' with Kit's secretary fizzled out after Anya found him a flat at 8 Chesham Place, close to Sloane Square. Townshend moved his mattress, his records, his guitars, his clothes, a Marshall amp and his two tape recorders into the bare flat. There was nobody living next door for him to disturb, but also nobody to disturb him. He worked alone and often late into the night: 'The only thing in my life at the time was Who gigs and my tape machines.'

Townshend was now further away than ever from The Who, in every sense of the word. Entwistle was still with his mother and stepfather in Acton (Kit now referred to the forthright Queenie as The Who's 'shop steward'); Moon was renting a flat above a laundrette in Alperton but would soon move back to his parents' house in Chaplin Road, and Daltrey was technically homeless. Now separated from Jackie (whom he'd eventually divorce), the singer was living in the band's converted furniture van. 'It was no different to being a lorry driver kipping in your cab,' he said. 'I loved it. Park it up anywhere, get washed up at a mate's place . . .'

Daltrey claimed he spent six months living in the van, an impressive achievement considering Townshend and Barney only managed three weeks in their ambulance. But Reg Bowen insists that he no longer had the option of living at his parents' house: 'Rog lived in the van because his sister had pinched his old bedroom.'

With Chesham Place barely a minute in the chauffeur-driven Rolls from Eaton Place, Lambert could still keep tabs on Townshend: 'Kit would recommend books to read, music to listen to – great think-tank sessions.' Kit had the use of a private box at the Royal Opera House in Covent Garden, which Townshend was soon using to watch operas by Benjamin Britten, Verdi and Mussorgsky, whose challenging work *Boris Gudunov* proved a little too much: 'I drank champagne, lay on the floor and fell asleep.'

Townshend's collection of John Lee Hooker, Bob Dylan and Charlie Parker LPs now shared floor space with records handpicked by his manager. These included music by Kit's godfather, William Walton, the Italian violinist Arcangelo Corelli and Henry Purcell, the seventeenth-century English composer, whose work would soon have an impact on Townshend's writing.

These records also gave Townshend a glimpse into Lambert's childhood, and his relationship with his late father: 'This was the music Constant had introduced Kit to. This was the music of his childhood.' Constant had been a distant presence in his son's life, and most of the stories Kit told about his father had come via those who had known him better. Nevertheless, Kit had studied Constant's life and work and while he already shared his father's hedonistic tendencies, he also displayed his forward-thinking attitude.

Constant had infuriated the classical establishment by favourably comparing Duke Ellington with Ravel and Stravinsky. Similarly, Kit believed that pop was as valid an art form as classical music. But he also understood the importance of image in selling that art form. 'Constant deserted Kit as a child, and I always thought Kit was trying to appeal to the ghost of his father,' said Townshend. 'To try and acknowledge the musical genius, the entrepreneurial genius. Kit wanted to do all of that.'

Townshend was soon demoing as many as three or four songs a week on his Vortexion stereo tape recorders, and Kit was soon pacing around the flat, chain-smoking and critiquing the work: 'The wilder I got in my songwriting the more he supported me.' During these visits, Lambert would notice the pictures decorating the wall. They were pages torn from a pop-art book Townshend had stolen from the college library. The next stage in The Who's music and image would emerge from those pictures.

At the High Numbers' first Greenwich Town Hall gig in the summer of 1964, Jeff Dexter remembered Townshend playing with the Union flag draped over his amp. At Woodgrange Avenue, Townshend had filled notebooks with doodles of flags, targets, medals, chevrons and roundels, partly inspired by the British artist Peter Blake.

Blake was a thirty-three-year-old painter, who had grown up in the shadow of the Second World War. He liked Hollywood movies, comic books, Elvis and Chuck Berry, and expressed his love of pop culture in his work. In 1961, he produced *Got a Girl*, using images of Presley and other 1950s pop stars alongside military medals and chevrons. In the same year, Blake painted a self-portrait in which he wore a denim jacket adorned with badges. 'I had Peter's pictures cut out of books and magazines on my wall,' recalled Townshend. 'That was the image that I felt informed the way that I wanted to write.' Blake inspired more of The Who's imagery with *The First Real Target*, in which he reproduced a traditional archery target in vivid colours with additional typography, and his series of *Roxy Roxy* artworks, featuring portraits of female wrestlers framed with images that include the Union flag.

Blake wasn't the only pop artist working with this kind of iconography. The American Jasper Johns had created artworks from a target and the US Stars and Stripes nine years earlier. The English optical artist Bridget Riley was also using bold stripes and chevrons in her work. Blake and Riley both had their work displayed at Robert Fraser's Duke Street gallery throughout 1963 and 1964. Fraser was an Eton-educated former King's Rifles officer turned art dealer, and a confidante of the Rolling Stones. His exhibitions attracted pop stars, models and actors, and drew together worlds that had once seemed utterly disparate.

Fraser wasn't the only gallery owner to spot the new trend. Graphic designer Pearce Marchbank was a Marquee regular in the early 1960s. 'There were two fantastic art exhibitions in 1964,' he told author Jonathon Green in the social history, *Days in the Life*. 'There was this great big show called the Gulbenkian and there was 54–64 at the Tate [Painting and Sculpture of a Decade 1954–1964], which had a whole room full of American pop art: Rauschenberg, Jasper Johns, targets and flags.' Marchbank would leave the exhibition to go and watch The Who play: 'And you'd put two and two together. There seemed to be direct line between what was on at the Tate and what was on at the Marquee.'

'The art scene was almost closer to pop,' said Townshend. 'People like Jasper Johns and [Roy] Lichtenstein, people that were actually painting pictures, seemed to understand popular culture more than the people in the music industry.' American pop artist Roy Lichtenstein's comic strip-style works *Whaam!* and *As I Opened Fire* were loud and explosive and partly inspired by the Second World War. There were parallels to be drawn with the explosive song that became The Who's second single, 'Anyway, Anyhow, Anywhere'.

After 'I Can't Explain', The Who wanted to release something more representative of their uncompromising live show. Unlike that first single, 'Anyway, Anyhow, Anywhere' wasn't the result of one of Townshend's meticulous demo sessions. Instead, he arrived at the Marquee one afternoon with a scrap of an idea, which the band worked on during rehearsal. It was fast and spontaneous. Townshend later said that the song title had come to him while lying on his bed listening to the freewheeling jazz saxophonist Charlie Parker. 'He was a soul without a body,' he said of Parker, 'riding, flying, free on music . . . I wanted us to be like that.' But Townshend would have to run all this freedom past The Who's lead singer first.

Roger Daltrey had felt uneasy singing the vulnerable lyrics of 'I Can't Explain' so Lambert suggested that Townshend involve Daltrey in writing the words to the new single. 'Roger didn't want pop music, and Pete was also getting all the kudos,' says Richard Barnes. 'The politics of 'Anyway, Anyhow, Anywhere' was to placate Roger and get the live act on a record.'

The group were booked to record the track at IBC Studios in Central London's Portland Place on 13 April. Townshend and Daltrey stayed up most of the night before finishing the song. By the morning, its protagonist was no longer the blissful free spirit of Pete Townshend's imagination, and more reminiscent of the teenage Roger Daltrey, squaring up to 'Basher' Hurse in the classroom at Acton County. The final lyrics talked of breaking through locked doors and not caring what was right or wrong. Townshend's dreamy abstract vision had been dragged back to Shepherd's Bush. 'I toughened the song up,' insisted Daltrey.

'Anyway, Anyhow, Anywhere' became even tougher in the studio. To achieve a live sound, Shel Talmy miked up Townshend's amp from three different positions, and stuck twelve microphones around Keith Moon's drums. This time, there was no sign of the Ivy League or Jimmy Page, only session man Nicky Hopkins, whose bluesy piano fills would snake through the whole song. 'I suppose if I'd tried to sell another guitarist, I would have gotten a lot of hassle,' admitted Talmy. 'Nicky brought something unique to the recording without angering anybody else.'

After a conventional first minute or so, the track seemed to collapse in on itself, leaving Townshend to fill almost forty seconds with distortion and feedback, the sound of his plectrum scraping along his guitar strings, and the bleep of the emergency Morse code signal, which he created by flipping the selector switch on his guitar back and forth.

The Beatles' Number 1 hit 'I Feel Fine' in winter 1964 had begun with a five-second squall of feedback, but The Who were the first to make feedback a feature of a track. It was an extremely daring noise to use on a pop song that lasted two minutes and forty-four seconds; even more daring considering it was only The Who's second single.

As far as the group were concerned, the single had served its purpose. 'The intention was to encapsulate The Who's stage act,' said John Entwistle. 'To illustrate the arrogance of the mod movement and, through feedback, the smashing of the instruments.' Decca Records weren't convinced. When they first heard the track, they presumed they'd been sent a defective copy. 'I got a cable from them, saying, "We think we got a bad tape,"' recalled Shel Talmy. 'But I assured them that was the way it was.'

Brainstorming ways to promote the single, Kit Lambert stared at the pictures on the wall of Chesham Place, and informed the press that that The Who had just made 'the first pop art record'. 'I used to talk to Kit about pop art a lot,' said Townshend in 1966. 'And suddenly, he came out with this idea. He told us, "Keith is going to have a bull's-eye on his T-shirt, Pete is going to wear badges."'

According to a 1966 *Observer* article, radio DJs were sent early copies of the single in a garish yellow and orange sleeve with a message inspired by Roy Lichtenstein's comic-strip imagery: 'Pow! Don't walk, run to your nearest record player.' 'Townshend was intellectual,' wrote Nik Cohn in 1968, 'and Lambert wasn't exactly intellectual, but he had the jargon off. Between them, they looked at the things The Who did and analysed them and thought up sassy names for them.'

The press bought into it. Christine Day recalls The Who traipsing into the *Boyfriend* office in London's North Audley Street for an interview. Townshend assumed control, the others, she recalls, stood around combing their hair in the mirror. 'Pete was clearly the leader,' Christine says now, 'and he used to be moving all the time, so animated, up and down and walking in and out of the doorway while he spoke to you. He never stopped.' As Richard Barnes points out: 'I took an awful lot of pills around that time, and so did Pete.' 'The Who are everything that is 1965,' wrote Christine in *Boyfriend*, before comparing 'Anyway, Anyhow, Anywhere' to 'jets flying, cars roaring along the new motorway, the noises of the streets.'

Kit Lambert had schooled the band, particularly Townshend, to feed the press with good quotable lines and what Chris Stamp might have called 'old bollocks'. In Townshend's case, this was no great leap. 'We live pop art,' he proclaimed, before dropping Peter Blake's and Roy Lichtenstein's names in interviews. The message spread beyond the music press to Fleet Street. A column in the 27 June issue of the *Observer* described The Who as 'the first group to employ distortion and out-of-tuneness as an intrinsic part of their music'. Townshend played along, telling the *Observer*: 'From valueless objects – a guitar, a microphone, a hackneyed pop tune – we abstract a new value. We take objects from one function and give them another. And the auto-destructive element adds immediacy to it all.'

But The Who knew that namechecking a few modern artists wasn't enough. 'We're anti-middle age, anti-boss class and anti-young marrieds,' Townshend bragged to *Melody Maker*. Even Daltrey sounded uptight and desperate. 'I never want to grow old,' he said in *New Musical Express*. 'I want to stay young forever. If I wasn't in a group I don't know what I'd do with myself. I think I'd do myself in.'

Townshend had just turned twenty; Daltrey was twenty-one. Such angst might seem faintly ridiculous in 2014, but in 1965 it set The Who apart. Even the Rolling Stones didn't sound this disenfranchised. Kit Lambert's pop-art marketing strategy was rewarded. *Ready Steady Go!* started using 'Anyway, Anyhow, Anywhere' as their theme tune, and after twelve weeks in the charts the single reached Number 10. After 'I Can't Explain's success, this came as a disappointment, but The Who had made their point: this was a song that didn't sound anything like The Kinks.

Although he had succeeded in bottling what Entwistle called 'mod arrogance', Townshend was already distancing himself from the youth cult that had so fascinated him six months earlier. In a way, *Ready Steady Go!*'s championing of mod music and imagery had taken away the very thing on which the movement thrived: elitism. 'We think the mod thing is dying,' Townshend told *Melody Maker*. 'We don't plan to go down with it, which is why we've become individualists.' The paper's readers wondered what an individualist was, and how they might become one.

The Who's individual new look had been developing onstage for some time. 'Mod was fantastic and fashionable, but it was all very controlled, not flamboyant,' points out Richard Barnes. 'After a while, The Who wanted to become more colourful onstage.' The Who's new look was revealed on television in July during their third appearance on *Ready Steady Go!*. Townshend wore a jacket with medals from his mother's shop pinned to the front, and Keith Moon's shirt sported a vivid target image.

Over the next few months, *Ready Steady Go!* would reflect similar influences as the show's designer Nicholas Ferguson began copying his favourite pop artists and painting bold stripes on to the set. In the meantime, more stripes, targets, medals and chevrons found their way on to The Who's clothing. It was mod with a subversive twist, slyly echoing the icons of the British Empire and the Second World War.

Townshend and Richard Barnes's art-school friend Michael English (who died in 2009) had designed a pair of sunglasses with a Union flag underlay on the lenses for the Carnaby Street boutique Gear. 'Michael also did Stars and Stripes sunglasses and some with bull's-eye targets on them,' recalls his ex-wife and former Ealing student Angela Brown. 'They had fine see-through dots all over them so that you could see through them. He just bought cheap sunglasses and silkscreen-printed them.'

The Who followed suit. A Union flag draped over a Marshall amp become a Union flag cover on a Marshall amp, and a Union flag jacket. Sir Winston Churchill would have been appalled. 'Kit came up with the idea for the jacket,' said Roger Daltrey. 'Prior to that the Union Jack had only been flown on buildings as a flag. When we walked into a Savile Row tailor and said, "Will you make a jacket out of this?" they said, "No." They thought they'd go to jail.' Townshend said he had five jackets made, which he and, occasionally, Entwistle wore on and offstage.

A typical picture of The Who in 1965 might show Townshend baiting the establishment in his Union flag jacket, Entwistle modelling a shirt decorated with military insignia, and Moon in a target T-shirt and a jacket to which he'd pinned an oversized 'Elvis is Everyone' badge, in homage to Peter Blake. Which just left Daltrey, the man Pete Meaden might have called 'the red sheep in the flock'.

In fact, Daltrey became The Who's biggest individualist, and made a fashion statement worthy of Vivienne Westwood's early punk designs, by accessorising his clothes with electrician's tape of the kind commonly found in factories. Before the gig, Anya Butler would cut the tape into different shapes, which Daltrey would then stick to his clothes: 'I'd go onstage in a knitted jumper with tape stuck on it so it looked like something else,' he said. The strips would curl up and flake off in the heat, and it wasn't a flattering look. But that didn't matter: 'The idea was, "This is my statement, nobody else's."'

However, offstage The Who were now moving too fast for Daltrey's liking and not in the direction he wanted. Townshend had written enough songs to fill The Who's debut album, but Daltrey wanted to include the numbers they played live. At the IBC sessions for 'Anyway, Anyhow, Anywhere' The Who had recorded James Brown's 'Please Please Please', Bo Diddley's 'I'm a Man' and Martha and the Vandellas' 'Heat Wave', among others.

The album was due for release in the US in the summer. Shel Talmy played *Beat Instrumental* journalist John Emery an early acetate. 'One thing hit me slap in the face,' wrote Emery. 'The lack of originality in the choice of material.' He went on to describe The Who's version of 'I'm a Man' as 'monotonous'. Lambert panicked, and released a statement to the press explaining that the album was being delayed, that The Who were ditching R&B covers and focusing on what he called 'hard pop'.

With the gift of hindsight, it might be difficult to understand why Daltrey didn't want more original material on the album. But 'Anyway, Anyhow, Anywhere' hadn't been a major hit, and, although he'd change his opinion later, Daltrey regarded 'I Can't Explain' as soft pop. He was adamant that The Who on record should accurately reflect the band live. Furthermore, the Rolling Stones' recently released debut album had included the Chuck Berry and Jimmy Reed numbers they played live, and The Kinks' first LP was predominantly covers with just a handful of Ray Davies' originals.

But under the terms of the 'proclamation' Townshend had drawn up over a year before, The Who had to be different. 'We could have sung the blues and been a much bigger band much quicker,' said Chris Stamp. 'But everybody was doing that.' The management's decision to delay the album and replace the covers with more Townshend originals did little to endear it to The Who's lead singer.

Daltrey was now becoming isolated in what had once been his band. As well as Townshend's songwriting and his closeness to Lambert, he also had to contend with Kit's growing influence on Keith Moon. The drummer was intrigued by Lambert's worldliness and sophistication, and shared his love of booze and spending money. Lambert, meanwhile, was attracted to Moon's wild energy and, some suggest, his good looks. According to Chris Stamp, Keith turned Kit on to pills, and Kit turned Keith on to expensive champagne.

'Keith was a terrible social climber,' said Townshend. 'He once said to Kit, "Suppose I'm in a nightclub with The Beatles and want to impress them by ordering the best champagne, what should I get?" And Kit said, "Dom Pérignon 1926" or something . . . And the next thing we're in this nightclub and you hear Keith shouting "Dom Pérignon 1926!" And next there's an £8,000 bill!'

Simon Napier-Bell maintains that, 'Kit gave Keith licence to be himself. Keith's madness was an outward and visible expression of what was in Kit too.' To others, though, it seemed as if Moon was taking aspects of Lambert's character and making them his own. 'I remember Keith in the very early days and he was this young good looking sub-Beatle who had this very ordinary cockney accent,' says 'Irish' Jack. 'Then, little by little, Keith's accent began to take on Oxford tones. You'd ignore him and take no notice and tell yourself, "Well, he's probably drunk." But after a while you might speak to him and he'd be stone-cold sober and he's going, "Yes, quite, absolutely dear boy." And you'd be looking at him and thinking, "What the fuck?"'

Daltrey's isolation was compounded by the fact that Moon, like the rest of The Who and their managers, took drugs. Daltrey smoked and drank, and had tried amphetamines, but pills dried out his throat and affected his voice. He also hated the effect they had on his bandmates.

With the album on hold, The Who returned to what they did best: playing live and often. It wasn't unusual for them to follow a gig in the provinces with another performance the same evening at an all-night mod club in the capital. One favourite venue was Tottenham's

Club Noreik, where 'French blues' and 'bombers' were readily available, and the doors stayed locked, keeping the outside world and the crippling comedown at bay, until the morning. To cope with the frantic schedule, and for their own entertainment, Entwistle and Moon had formed an especially close drug-taking partnership. Pills would be counter-balanced with alcohol, followed by more pills to sober up. And so it went on.

'Moon would pass out before a gig,' said Entwistle, 'sober up just before we went on, play like a maniac, and go back on the bottle as soon as we finished.' After a performance in Reading that summer, the drummer sidled up to Richard Barnes and asked 'whether I had anything in the upward direction, dear boy?' Barney had a stash of twenty-four purple hearts that were meant to last him for the next three weeks. Moon swallowed the lot: 'I was pissed off, but incredibly impressed at the same time.'

The Who's first trip to France, to promote a French EP of 'Anyway, Anyhow, Anywhere' and 'I Can't Explain', included a gig at the Parisian equivalent of the Marquee, Le Golf-Drouot. At the same time French TV show, *Seize Millions de Jeunes*, screened a documentary about English mods that included footage of The Who, an interview with Townshend and a fluently French-speaking Lambert. Entwistle and Moon managed to stay awake for the duration of the three-day trip by consuming six phials of liquid methedrine. The Who wowed the French audience, but Lambert was forced to borrow cash from Chris Parmenter to pay for his train fare home.

Wherever they were played, be it a festival, mod club or a suburban town hall, one thing remained constant: the audience now wanted The Who to smash their equipment. Christine Day and Keith Altham had watched Townshend destroy a guitar at the Marquee, aware that he was doing it partly for their benefit. What had begun as a spontaneous act of destruction had now become a theatrical stunt that could be performed to order.

The Who's air of aggression, real or otherwise, didn't work everywhere, though. At the Public Hall in Barrow-in-Furness, Lancashire, the audience objected to Daltrey's swearing and cockney accent, and pelted the band with bottles and coins. Penguin-suited bouncers ended up positioned onstage to deter a further onslaught. 'The people there didn't know what we were trying to do,' complained Chris Stamp. 'Most nights ended up with a violent punch-up.'

Yet not every northern gig ended that way. Film-maker Richard Stanley would later work with The Who, but first encountered them when he was an art student and the High Numbers played Leicester's Granby Halls in summer 1964. 'Humphrey Lyttelton was headlining,' says Stanley now. 'Another group were meant to play but didn't, so The Who came instead. I was sat in the bar with Humphrey, being a typical jazz fan and thinking The Who were just some pop band, not really my thing, when my friend came running in, very excited and said, "The guitarist is bleeding all down his white trousers!"' Townshend had smashed his hand against his guitar and had drawn blood.

Stanley didn't take that much notice until The Who played his college, Leicester School of Art, the following spring. That night, he projected a film he'd made on to the stage as the band performed. *Sleeping and Digging*, a 'weird film with stop-motion', showed bicycles being ridden over slumbering bodies. 'Pete kept turning round while he was playing to look at what was going on,' says Stanley. 'Afterwards, he came up and asked who had been projecting the films. He wanted to know everything about it.' When Stanley told him he was about to move to London to study at the Royal College of Art, Townshend gave him his address and insisted he call.

But it was the release of 'Anyway, Anyhow, Anywhere' that made Richard Stanley a convert: 'It felt like the beginning of a new genre,' he says. 'There was pop art happening and exhibitions at the Tate Gallery. But that song was the start of it. It seemed more powerful than The Beatles or the Stones.'

What also struck Stanley was Pete Townshend's 'absolute curiosity' about the film he'd made, and the guitarist's interest in his ideas and his course at the Royal College of Art. When Stanley invited Townshend to a party he was throwing for his college friends, he realised that a pop star's life wasn't as glamorous as he might have imagined: 'Pete said, "That would be fantastic because no one invites me to anything anymore."'

In the press statement released with 'Anyway, Anyhow, Anywhere', The Who vowed, 'If this disc is a flop, we're going to make another just

like it, only harder hitting.' Although the song hadn't been a flop, it
hadn't been the hit The Who needed either. If 'Anyway, Anyhow,
Anywhere' aimed to capture The Who's live sound, then Kit Lambert
believed that The Who's next single needed to make a grand statement,
and the grander the better.

Townshend recalls jotting down the lyrics to what became 'My
Generation' in the back of a car. The socialist playwright David Mercer
had just published a trilogy of his work, *The Generations*, which gave
Townshend the title for the song. Its inspiration also came from an
incident that highlighted the social gulf that separated Townshend
from his Belgravia neighbours.

In summer 1965, Townshend had bought a 1935 Packard V12 Hearse.
One day he returned home to find the car missing from outside his flat.
The police informed him that it had been towed away on the orders of
the Queen Mother, who'd complained after seeing it on her regular
journey from Clarence House to Buckingham Palace. She'd taken
umbrage, as it reminded her of her late husband, George VI's funeral
car. The incident fuelled Townshend's ire at the Royal Family and the
British class system in general. 'I was outraged,' he said. 'This was the
world we were living in.'

'I'm not pretending we were the Arnold Weskers or John Osbornes
of our age,' he insisted. 'But certainly what we did followed on from
what was happening with the angry young men in the theatre.' 'My
Generation's' grand statement was, he said: 'All right you motherfuckers, I am going to have you. I am going to be bigger and richer, and I'm
going to move into your neighbourhood.'

The song came together over the summer. Unlike the spontaneous
'Anyway, Anyhow, Anywhere', it developed out of demos on which
Townshend sung and played every instrument. Copies were then given
to Lambert, Stamp and the rest of the band. Townshend later com-
pared the first demo with Mose Allison's 'Young Man Blues', Bob
Dylan's 'Talkin' New York' and 'Jimmy Reed at ten years old suffering
from nervous indigestion'. 'It was much slower,' recalled Roger
Daltrey. 'Very Bo Diddley – jink-a-jink-ajink, jink-a-jink-ajink.'

Nobody was overly impressed. But Stamp heard something he liked
and urged Townshend to persevere. Lambert, meanwhile, told him to
make the song bigger and more grandiose. The second demo included

handclaps, backing vocals, a lead vocal in which Townshend deliberately stuttered some of the words and a bass solo that John Entwistle would later turn into an integral part of the song. At Lambert's suggestion, the third demo threw in several key changes that Townshend told *Rolling Stone* magazine were 'pinched, again, from The Kinks'.

The one dissenting voice belonged to Roger Daltrey, who was still fixated on playing soul and R&B songs. Just as Townshend's grand statement started coming together, The Who started falling apart. The friction between Daltrey and the rest of the group reached a violent peak on a run of European and Scandinavian dates.

September 1965 started badly, and would only go downhill. In an effort to make The Who's van more secure, roadie 'Cy' Langston had visited south London's Battersea Dogs' Home to enquire about an Alsatian guard dog. When he came out, the van containing several thousand pounds' worth of gear had been stolen. The irony of the situation wasn't lost on The Who or their crew. When the vehicle was recovered, there were only two smashed speakers still left inside.

The Who had gigs lined up in Holland and Denmark. Chris Stamp assured them they could borrow equipment, forgetting that the fans would expect to see some damage inflicted on a guitar or amp as part of the act, and that none of The Who could speak Dutch or Danish. The borrowed gear broke down during the second Dutch gig. Two days later, in Elsinore, Denmark, when another set of borrowed equipment malfunctioned, tempers flared and, according to one eyewitness, Daltrey and Moon came to blows backstage.

A day later The Who were booked for two evening shows: one in the port town of Aarhus, the other in neighbouring Aalborg. Of course, Townshend, Entwistle and Moon had scored pills for the trip. Already frustrated at using equipment that didn't work properly, Daltrey now had to contend with everyone taking drugs, sharing in-jokes and chattering incessantly. Worst of all, the drugs were affecting the band's performance. 'The music was going down the tubes,' he said. 'It was fucking dire.'

The atmosphere at the Aarhus-Hallen that night was reminiscent of the Wild West or the Peckham Paradise in 1962. The hall was filled with around 4,000 young farmers, most of who had been drinking steadily and were itching to let off steam. Townshend had recently declared, 'The Who is a band chopping away at its own legs, and we will succeed.' This, then, was the moment when what he called his 'pseudo-intellectual ambitions' might be realised. The Who would 'destroy the bourgeois tools of production' (their instruments and equipment) before throwing themselves at their audience's mercy.

But when the drunken farmers greeted The Who with a volley of chairs and bottles, Townshend quickly forgot his pseudo-intellectual ambitions and made a run for it. The band played half a song before fleeing to the dressing room for safety. The audience invaded the stage and smashed the bourgeois tools of production themselves. The mob then ran riot through the town. 'We heard afterwards that they'd done £10,000-worth of damage,' said Townshend, 'and made the front page of all the Danish papers.'

Inside the dressing room, Daltrey's frustration at the abandoned gig, the faulty equipment and his drugged-up bandmates spilled over. 'You're all fucking junkies!' he shouted, before grabbing Keith Moon's bag of French blues and pouring the contents down the toilet. Distraught at losing his precious stash, the drummer picked up a tambourine and started hitting Daltrey with it. According to Townshend, 'Roger lashed out, bloodying Keith's nose, turning what would have been a minor spat into a melodrama.' Others claim the singer beat Moon unconscious. 'I almost killed Keith,' said Daltrey. 'It wasn't because I hated him. It was because I loved the band so much and thought it was being destroyed.'

Whatever the severity of the assault, the fallout was Daltrey's dismissal: 'They told me to fuck off and not come back.' Nevertheless, in a curious repeat of the circumstances surrounding Doug Sandom's dismissal, it was agreed that he would remain with the group long enough for them to finish the album and record another single. A fortnight after the bloodshed in Denmark, The Who went into IBC Studios and, in a whirlwind session, recorded what would become their debut LP and their next single, 'My Generation'. Perversely, considering he'd been so opposed to the song, Daltrey helped make 'My Generation' the grand musical statement Kit Lambert had hoped for.

Townshend had stuttered some of his vocals on the song's earlier demo version, a trick he'd copied from bluesmen John Lee Hooker and Sonny Boy Williamson. But when Daltrey stuttered his lines, dragging out the words 'fade away' and 'generation', he sounded less like a black American bluesman and more like one of the Goldhawk's 'dislocated boys', a pilled-up English mod struggling to articulate his feelings. Unlike 'Anyway, Anyhow, Anywhere', 'My Generation's' message hadn't been twisted to fit Daltrey's macho voice and personality. Daltrey's voice and the existing lyrics were already a perfect fit.

Behind the singer, Townshend's guitar howled and Moon and Entwistle played as if they were trying to drown their bandmates out. Even more audacious was the decision to include a bass solo. Entwistle tried three different instruments and sets of strings before finding the sound he wanted, which was then finessed by engineer Glyn Johns positioning the bass amp on a paving slab. The key changes that Townshend had ripped off from The Kinks made the song more grandiose, but also more frantic. 'My Generation' sounded every bit as fraught and combustible as The Who themselves.

By the early morning of 13 October, the group had recorded their next single and a further seven Townshend compositions. But it hadn't been easy. 'I was aware of the tension,' says Shel Talmy, who couldn't have cared less. 'I'd heard a rumour third or fourth hand that Roger had been asked to leave, but I wasn't interested enough to suss out the truth.' The tension increased when Talmy again banned Kit Lambert and The Who from the control room. Townshend persuaded Glyn Johns to let him in so he could hear a playback, presuming Talmy's eyesight was so poor he wouldn't even notice he was there.

The Who emerged from IBC blinking into the daylight. Twenty-four hours later their petty squabbles would be thrown into perspective by the news that production manager Mike Shaw was in hospital. Shaw, who had been ferrying equipment to Liverpool, had fallen asleep at the wheel and crashed into a lorry. He was left paralysed from the shoulders down and would be confined to a wheelchair until his death in 2012.

'The effect of his disablement on The Who and Kit and Chris was terrible,' wrote Townshend in *Who I Am*. Shaw was Stamp's childhood friend, and the first member of The Who's extended family after their managers. His work ethic, his patience and, crucially, the respect he earned from all four members of the band had been an invaluable asset. The severity of Shaw's accident, at a time when The Who's relationship with Daltrey had already deteriorated to breaking point, served to ratchet up the tension within the group still further.

'My Generation' was released at the beginning of November with an excitable blurb from Decca Records: 'This is a cry from the heart, penned by The Who's lead guitarist Pete Townshend and shouted by lead singer Roger Daltrey.' Lambert and Stamp, already afraid they might not have a band for much longer, were further frustrated when the BBC refused to play the A-side. When Daltrey stammered 'f-f-f-f-fade away' it sounded as if he might be about to shout an expletive instead, but it wasn't this hint of profanity that made the BBC nervous, rather it was the fear that the vocal might upset stutterers. However, the corporation soon backtracked when pirate stations started playing the record.

Naturally, it was 'My Generation's' confrontational lyrics that attracted the most scrutiny. The Rolling Stones had sounded disgruntled and frustrated on their recent hit '(I Can't Get No) Satisfaction'. But The Who sounded even more disaffected, as if they might explode at any second. Even if Townshend hadn't meant the line 'I hope I die before I get old' to be taken literally, he stood by the sentiment. Talking to the *Observer*'s George Melly he explained that the shocking lyric was necessary as The Who 'had to be drastic and violent to reach the audience'. At times, Townshend's message might have seemed contradictory, but it reflected the contradictory mindset of the people he was trying to reach.

Pete Townshend would spend the next fifty years being asked about lyrics he'd written as an angry young man. His response would vary: sometimes he'd defend them, sometimes he wouldn't, sometimes he'd make light of them and sometimes he'd evade the question altogether. But without that lyric pleading for an early demise, The Who's fortunes may have turned out very differently. By the end of November 1965, The Who's 'cry from the heart' was a Number 2 hit. Its success convinced them to carry on.

Townshend was now a successful songwriter, pop star and, in the eyes of his former tutor, an artist. Having left Ealing under a cloud, Roy Ascott was now promoting his controversial groundcourse at Ipswich School of Art. The future Roxy Music musician and producer Brian Eno was among his students. Eno vividly recalls Ascott arriving in class one day waving a copy of The Who's new single: 'He was saying, "You've all got to listen to this!"' Ascott applauded 'My Generation', insisting it was a direct product of what Townshend had learned at Ealing, and as valid an artistic statement as anything hanging in the Tate.

The issue Townshend and The Who now faced was whether to stay together and create more art. Just as 'My Generation' reached the charts, news of their internal strife reached the music press. *Melody Maker* ran a front-page story with the headline 'THE WHO SPLIT MYSTERY' and stated that Raymond 'Boz' Burrell, the twenty-year-old singer with the Boz People, was replacing Daltrey. Burrell denied the claim and witheringly described The Who as 'children playing with electronic toys'. 'Does anybody in their right mind think The Who would split up at a time like this?' blustered Chris Stamp at the time.

In fact, both the band and their managers had been considering other options. At first, Lambert and Stamp floated the idea that Daltrey should start a soul group, leaving The Who to carry on with Townshend singing lead vocals. 'When they kicked me out, I just thought, "Oh well, that was one band. Now I'll start another,"' Daltrey told the author. 'I was convinced that as the chemistry had found me once before, so it would find me again.'

Keith Moon, meanwhile, had another, stranger idea. Moon had first met drummer Ray Stock when The Beachcombers played with Stock's group The Shevelles at the American Air Force base at Lakenheath; a venue in which Keith's infamous pantomime horse had made an appearance. The Shevelles had since become the Flamingo's resident house band. 'Keith wanted The Who to have two drummers and two bass players,' says Ray Stock now. 'He wanted me to be the other drummer and Boz Burrell to be the other bass player. That was the plan. He said, "If this comes to be would you be interested?" And, of course, I said yes.'

The Shevelles and The Who had crossed paths before, but Stock had no idea how badly the group got on: 'Keith told me John Entwistle had got so angry with Roger at a gig a few days before, he'd smashed him in the ear with his bass. I was shocked. They all wanted Roger out of the band.' Ray Stock never made it as far as a rehearsal studio with The Who, and after Burrell's terse comments in *Melody Maker*, the idea was abandoned. 'I was disappointed,' he admits. 'But it was obvious that the management weren't going to let The Who split up. The pounds, shillings and pence soon took over.'

As managers of what was now a successful hit group, Lambert and Stamp persuaded Daltrey and the rest of The Who to try to resolve their differences. According to Townshend, the subsequent meeting was a humiliating experience for Daltrey, who was told he could remain in the band as long as he never resorted to violence again. Daltrey, who later described himself at this time as 'a bastard' and 'a real cunt', agreed to do as he was told. 'The problem *was* mostly me,' agreed Daltrey. 'I was the one who didn't know how to articulate my feelings. The only way I could solve anything was to have it out there and then. I had to learn to bite my lip and be a good boy from now on.'

Daltrey's acquiescence was an unusually conciliatory gesture from a man who rarely backed down from anyone or anything. It was borne out of simple pragmatism, though. Despite his initial thought that 'the chemistry would find me again' Daltrey had worked too hard to walk away from The Who. The thought of starting again or, returning to a 'proper job' in the steel factory, was at best daunting and at worst unthinkable.

Nevertheless, Daltrey's vow not to beat up his bandmates didn't resolve The Who's other problems, or quell his dissatisfaction with their live performances. 'Even in a stupor with all the speed he was taking, Pete knew that The Who's playing had gone downhill,' said Daltrey. 'The others needed reining in. It wasn't just me.' The rest of The Who acknowledged that their drug-taking was affecting the music, but carried on indulging as before. Meanwhile, Moon and Entwistle continued to upset Daltrey – and often Townshend – by playing too loudly. Keith knew he was now free to undermine the singer without risking getting punched in the face.

Daltrey wasn't the only band member feeling isolated. Townshend, who always wanted to be part of any gang, now felt excluded by Moon and Entwistle. 'Keith and John might have been like chalk and cheese but they got on,' says June Clark, who was soon helping to run The Who's fan club. 'The sense of humour bonded them. John was very humorous and dry, but he was tolerant and patient of Keith's idiosyncrasies, whereas Roger and Pete would get very annoyed with Keith and tell him off.'

Townshend's growing role as The Who's songwriter and mouth-piece would only heighten his sense of isolation. The Who were now a band without a leader, but with Townshend delivering the songs and shaping the band's image. The consequence was an uneasy democracy, every bit as dysfunctional as it had been under Daltrey's dictatorship. Meanwhile, their discontents were played out in public, with individual members bickering about each other via the music press. 'Roger is not a very good singer at all,' Townshend told *Music Echo*. 'We're not mates at all,' Daltrey informed *New Musical Express*. Before long, Townshend had come up with another perfect soundbite. 'Ours,' he said, 'is a group with built-in hate.'

The Who's reworked debut album, *My Generation*, finally appeared in the UK in December. The cover photograph was taken on a cold winter's morning at east London's unglamorous Surrey Docks. The group posed next to four large canisters of industrial propane, and looked as if they'd stopped rowing just long enough for photographer David Wedgbury to shoot a few frames. Wedgbury's photograph for the album's US edition, released the following spring, caught The Who looking even more sour-faced in front of Big Ben.

The music inside was similarly at odds with itself. James Brown's 'Please, Please, Please' and 'I Don't Mind' and Bo Diddley's 'I'm a Man' were still there, but they didn't quite fit with Townshend's compositions; part of the reason being that the guitarist's songs were so incredibly English. The white noise and splashes of feedback on 'Out in the Street' and the morbid sounding 'The Good's Gone' fulfilled Kit Lambert's promise of 'hard pop'. And although 'La-La-La-Lies', 'The Kids Are Alright' and 'A Legal Matter' were musically lighter, they were still a showcase for Keith Moon's frantic drumming and Townshend's deeply cynical lyrics.

'All the disturbing experiences of my childhood went into my composing,' he said later, when discussing *Tommy*. But there's already evidence of those traumas on *My Generation*. Every relationship Daltrey and Townshend sang about on the album seemed to be irreparably damaged, and everyone involved, particularly the women, was invariably a liar. *My Generation*'s overall message embodied the band and its audience's paranoia: trust nobody – girlfriends, boyfriends, mothers, fathers; the world, in fact.

The final track on the album's UK edition was 'The Ox', an instrumental credited to Townshend, Entwistle, Moon and Nicky Hopkins, and reminiscent of one of Keith Moon's favourites, The Surfaris' surf-pop hit 'Wipe Out'. But whereas 'Wipe Out' evoked blue Pacific waves and tanned beach bodies, 'The Ox' suggested Margate in the wake of mod-versus-rocker violence, with broken glass and deckchairs strewn across the sand. It was the perfect ending to a profoundly unromantic album. 'We weren't very good at doing love songs,' understated Daltrey. 'There was always more important things to sing about.'

In 2002, Townshend explained how The Who differed from The Beatles and the Stones in Andrew Loog Oldham's book *2Stoned*. 'The rules were laid down,' he said, as if alluding to 'the proclamation' drawn up in Michael English's flat. 'You do not sing about fucking love . . . These are songs about "I can't reach you" . . . "I'm gonna fuck you", but "we are in love" is a no . . .'

Nevertheless, unbeknown to the readers of *Boyfriend* or *Melody Maker*, Townshend did now have a reason to write a love song. He was in a relationship with Karen Astley, the daughter of Edwin 'Ted' Astley, a composer whose theme music for the popular TV drama *The Saint* could then be heard in living rooms throughout the country. Karen had first met Townshend when she was studying couture at Ealing Art College. 'She sat in the booth beside me at Sid's,' he recalled. 'She was very tall and beautiful.'

Karen Astley had now left Ealing and in January 1965 had modelled for the *Daily Mirror* under the headline 'A NEW KIND OF GIRL FOR THE NEW YEAR'. The photographer John French went into raptures about her 'small nose, good-quality hair and absolutely fabulous "sclerotics"', which the *Mirror* claimed were the 'blue whites-of-her-eyes'. A few months later, Karen met up again with Townshend at a Who gig in north-west London.

Despite Anya Butler's best efforts, New Action would soon be evicted from SW1, forcing Lambert to move his HQ back to Ivor Court. Before long, the inevitable eviction notice came for Townshend's Chesham Place flat ('We never paid the rent,' said Townshend. 'One didn't'). Townshend narrowly avoided having his tape recorders repossessed, squeezed some money out of Lambert and moved to a penthouse in Old Church Street, Chelsea. The tape recorders went with him, and the late-night demo sessions continued as before. But there was one important difference. 'Karen enriched my output as a writer,' he said. 'We made lots of friends and as a couple were more social than I had ever been on my own. My demos had a bigger audience.'

But not everyone in the Who camp was pleased for him. 'I found this beautiful girlfriend,' said Townshend. 'And Kit was particularly jealous. I think he found it an irritation that he didn't have the access to me that he once had.' The relationship was also difficult to sustain amid The Who's hectic touring schedule. Townshend would later admit to paranoia, worrying that 'my fabulous new girlfriend was deceiving me' whenever he was away with The Who.

It was an insecurity he shared with Keith Moon, if not on the same scale. Earlier that year Moon had met a sixteen-year-old part-time fashion model named Maryse 'Kim' Kerrigan, at a Who gig in Bournemouth, and was now in a relationship with her. Moon was smitten but also consumed with jealousy, terrified that the beautiful, blonde Kim would leave him for Rod Stewart, who was also pursuing her.

Moon once stormed on to the set of a boating magazine photoshoot at which Kim was the model, and threatened to punch her male colleague. Despite being a pop star, whose photograph was now splashed across the pages of numerous teen magazines, Moon remained as insecure as any of the dislocated boys described in Townshend's lyrics. Moon and Townshend were both young and in love, and struggling to make sense of their feelings. Neither did it help that Lambert was still determined to keep their respective relationships, especially pretty-boy Moon's, secret from the fans.

As soon as the *My Generation* LP was released Pete Townshend was telling journalists he didn't like it, calling the James Brown covers 'some old crap' but also distancing himself from some of his own songs. The press and the public took a different view. *Beat Instrumental* journalist John Emery praised the new version of *My Generation*, and applauded Townshend's unique songwriting. 'The Who haven't copied anyone,' he wrote. 'They are in a class of their own.'

The album made it to Number 5 in the UK. It was a modest victory. They still trailed behind the Stones, whose three LPs so far had all reached the Number 1 or 2 spots. And, shortly before Christmas 1965,

The Beatles' sixth album *Rubber Soul* would set yet another benchmark to humble the Fab Four's many rivals. Earlier that summer Paul McCartney had told the press that: 'The Who are the most exciting thing around.' But *Rubber Soul* was The Beatles' first step towards *Sgt. Pepper's Lonely Hearts Club Band*, and with it the idea of an LP as an artistic statement – something more than just a collection of random singles and filler – began to take hold.

Townshend's dissatisfaction stemmed from his conviction that both he and The Who could do better. *My Generation* would end up overshadowed by *Rubber Soul* but also by the big statement albums The Who released later in the decade, particularly *Tommy*. Its influence, however, would become more obvious over time: in the gnarly American garage bands that cropped up in its wake, and in the British punk groups of the late 1970s, some of whom cut their teeth playing early Who singles.

By the end of the year, the band members and their managers all seemed to be looking beyond The Who, as if conscious that the group might disintegrate at any moment. Townshend had followed his father's advice and in April he had formed his own publishing company, Fabulous Music. He knew that not everything he wrote would be accepted by The Who, and was also drawn to the idea of becoming a writer for hire, like some of the classical composers Lambert had turned him on to.

'Kit and I read that Mozart was doing commissions on motifs, numbered motifs, and selling his copyrights,' he said. '"Oh, the bloody prince of Denmark wants another piece of music, and I'm so busy. Give him fifteen of number twenty-two, six of number four, nine of number fifty-eight . . ."'

Townshend pitched one of his new compositions, 'Magic Bus', a song with which The Who would later have a hit, to an R&B group called The Fairies. Their drummer John 'Twink' Alder recalls drinking with Townshend in Blaises nightclub in Kensington before going back to his flat to hear the song. 'We were looking for a second single at the time,' he says. 'Pete said 'I think this will be good for you guys,' and it was 'Magic Bus', with exactly the same arrangement and the Bo Diddley beat as when The Who recorded it years later. It didn't click with us then because of that beat, because it sounded so very unlike The Who. Believe it or not, we said no.'

Among those who later recorded one of Townshend's songs were the Liverpudlian pop group The Merseybeats. Lambert and Stamp had started managing the band that summer. Having become The Who's managers almost by accident, they were reluctant to have them as their sole clients. But with Shel Talmy controlling The Who's studio output, Lambert also wanted a group of his own to produce. The Merseybeats had shared the Cavern Club stage with The Beatles and had enjoyed several hits, including 'I Think of You'. But by the time Kit and Chris approached them after gig in a London pub in early 1965 the hits had dried up.

'Lambert and Stamp said, "We would love to take you over and record you,"' recalls Merseybeats guitarist and vocalist Tony Crane. 'Chris said, "I work in films," and Kit said, "I've been an explorer." So I said, "That's all very well, but what's it got to do with music?"' Stamp then told Crane that his brother was Terence Stamp, and that they were about to break a new group called The Who. The Merseybeats agreed to consider their offer if the pair managed a Number 1 hit with The Who. 'A few months later, "Anyway, Anyhow, Anywhere" went to Number 1 in the *Disc* charts,' says Crane. '*Disc* wasn't as good as *Melody Maker* or *New Musical Express*. But I opened up the paper in the morning, saw that it was Number 1 and Kit rang me that afternoon. I was impressed.'

Lambert caught the train to Liverpool the next day and signed the band. As part of the deal, he insisted he had to produce their records from now on. The band and their label, Fontana, agreed. The Merseybeats' next single, the Lambert-produced 'I Love You Yes I Do', put the group back into the top thirty. 'I don't know how he did it,' says Crane. 'Because Kit didn't know anything about producing records. He let himself be guided by the engineers. But it worked.' Lambert was doing with The Merseybeats what he really wanted to do with The Who.

The Liverpudlians were swiftly introduced to New Action's glamorous but disorderly management style. The Merseybeats' bassist Billy Kinsley watched astonished as Lambert, after claiming he'd lost his wallet and chequebook, paid for an expensive meal in a restaurant by writing on a table napkin: 'He told the waiter it was legal tender and his bank would honour it – and they did.' 'Kit didn't have a clue financially. He'd wine and dine whoever to get a hit record, but beyond that he never thought about the money,' says Tony Crane, who first experienced London's nightlife in the company of the Stamp brothers and Terence's girlfriend, the actress and model Jean Shrimpton: 'Those nights on the town really opened my eyes to what went on.'

In October, just as The Who were finishing *My Generation*, The Merseybeats arrived at IBC Studios to record their new single, 'I Stand Accused'. Unfortunately, so did Keith Moon. 'Keith was there and tried to wreck the session,' says Crane. 'We'd booked the studio for three hours, the clock was ticking, and Keith was messing around in the control room, lying on the floor trying to make love to his girl-friend.' In a final attempt to keep the drummer occupied, Lambert and The Merseybeats agreed to let him play: 'Keith found a gong in the corner of the studio, and asked if he could hit it. I said "Yes, when I give you the nod," which I did, but he started hitting it and never stopped.'

The Merseybeats' 'I Stand Accused' with Moon's banging gong on the outro, was a minor hit. Lambert launched the single, just as he'd done for 'I Can't Explain', with a champagne-and-canapés reception at Eaton Place. 'It was *the* party to go to,' says Crane. 'It was filled with TV stars, DJs, actors and musicians. It must have cost a fortune.'

In the meantime, The Who's uneasy détente continued, observed by their new road crew and visiting journalists. After the incident at Battersea Dogs' Home, 'Cy' Langston had taken a job as a guitarist with Gary Farr and the T-Bones, although he'd work with The Who again later. His replacement was The Merseybeats' ex-roadie Neville Chesters. Despite being a slightly built man, Chesters was unusually strong. 'Neville's party piece was to come into the shop, put his hands on the counter and push himself up into a full handstand,' recalls Terry Marshall. 'He was the only person I knew who could pick up an eight-by-twelve cabinet on his own. We used to put casters on them, but the first thing Neville would do was take them off and then drag the cab down the road, so that by the time it was in the van, the bottom was down to bare wood.'

Chesters' ability to fix broken equipment under extreme pressure made him an invaluable asset to The Who. But he had other skills, which included entertaining Roger Daltrey. 'It didn't occur to me at the time, but Roger had nobody to talk to,' says Chesters now. 'There was this continual tension between Roger and Keith, which I walked into. But there were other things as well. The cost of the damages to equipment was being split four ways. So Roger was paying a quarter, and he hated it, absolutely hated it.'

'John Entwistle was always cool, and he was the one I was closest to,' he adds. 'Pete was difficult because he was a genius. But it depended on what mood he was in. He could be great. He could be awful. But I've tended to forget the awful times. Keith . . .' He hesitates, 'Keith was a fucking horror.' Quite how much of a horror would dawn on Neville a few months later.

Also joining the crew that summer was Richard Cole, who'd recently roadied for Unit 4 + 2, best known for the 1965 hit single 'Concrete and Clay'. 'With The Who it was £15 a week plus extra for food,' says Cole now. 'But I told them to make it a round £20 all in, because I knew I'd never get the extra cash out of them. Kit and Chris were great. But Kit was usually off somewhere being posh, while Chris was busy cultivating his cockney accent and shagging debutantes.'

Cole's first job was to drive Entwistle and Moon to Scotland, where The Who had three gigs booked: 'And that was my first introduction to those two lunatics. Unit 4 + 2 had been no trouble, but The Who were something else.' When they arrived in Edinburgh, Moon asked the new chauffeur to pull over outside a hardware shop: 'I didn't ask why. But I found out when we got to the hotel. I was downstairs ordering a plate of sandwiches, when suddenly all the fire alarms went off. Moon had made smoke bombs from mixing sugar with the weedkiller he'd bought at the hardware store, and now he'd let them off. We were thrown out of the hotel and Roger and Pete were not best pleased.'

The situation didn't improve. Cole soon realised that with Townshend and Daltrey travelling separately, he would always end up chauffeuring the rhythm section. 'I accidentally became their driver. But John and Keith had this resentment against Roger and also Pete, to a certain extent, and I ended up getting drawn into it. I didn't have a great relationship with Roger, and I could tell Pete didn't like me always being in the van with them two.'

Soon, Cole was joining Entwistle and Moon at the Scotch of St James, a late-night watering hole near Buckingham Palace, where Keith loved to hold court among the other pop dignitaries of the day:

'I was only a year or so younger than the band, so of course I loved it. It wouldn't be wrong to say The Who were yobs, but they were good yobs. It was great fun.'

Negotiating Pete Townshend's mood swings was less fun, however. During one Saturday night gig in the Home Counties, Cole dashed onstage to retrieve Moon's drumsticks, only to get kicked offstage by the guitarist: 'I don't know if Pete did it on purpose. Maybe he went into one of his trances. But I fell off and got caught between the stage and a radiator and ended up ripping all the hairs out of my leg. I was going to fucking kill him.' The gig climaxed with Townshend and Moon trashing their instruments, leaving Keith without a set of drums for the following night's show. Cole was also a drummer and agreed to loan Moon his own kit: 'And he smashed those fuckers up as well.'

The Who's financial problems were now becoming an issue for the crew. 'There was three quid spent to every one made,' says Neville Chesters. 'The money wasn't coming in quick enough, and it was either owed or hidden.' Or, in some cases, disappearing into roadies' or Keith Moon's pockets before it could be accounted for.

The Who acquired the services of a Liverpudlian roadie via The Merseybeats. 'He wormed his way in with The Who and got himself a job on the crew,' says Chesters. 'He turned up one day at my flat, where I kept the guitars overnight, before a gig. We loaded up the van, and then he asked me for the cashbox, which I also used to look after, and the van's keys. I asked him why and he told me the band had told him he was in charge from now on.' Chesters was furious at the newcomer being promoted after four weeks in the job, and punched him on the jaw — 'I broke my finger and he fell into the gutter' — before throwing the cashbox and keys on top of him: 'I went back to my flat and decided, that was it.'

Three days later Chris Stamp phoned Chesters: '"Where the fuck are you, Neville?" I told him what had happened.' Stamp replied that the roadie had been fired and said, '"Get yourself to Newcastle. Roger is looking after the cashbox and the keys now."' In *Who I Am*, Townshend wrote: 'The Who had several roadies from Liverpool who seemed to operate on the assumption that there was a moral gulf between London and their home city,' before claiming that several guitars and even items of hotel furniture went missing during this period.

The Who were now in the peculiar though not unique position of being pop stars, but still, to all intents and purposes, they were penniless — except for Pete. When Townshend received his first PRS (Performing Rights Society) cheque, he quickly realised how much better off he was than his bandmates: 'The other guys were still grubbing around trying to make money on the side from gigs and getting petty cash out of people that had no petty cash.'

Richard Cole witnessed this grubbing around first hand. After Mike Shaw's car accident, The Who hired a new production manager. 'We'd just done a gig in Hassocks, and this new guy collected the night's take. He was a bit green and said, "What do I do with the money?"' says Cole. 'And, of course, Keith said, "Oh you give it to me." So he did. John didn't mind, as Moonie probably split it with him. But those sort of strokes really didn't please the other two.'

Future *Melody Maker* journalist Brian Southall was a local newspaper reporter when he interviewed The Who at the Chelmsford Corn Exchange that winter. His first impression was formed after walking into their dressing room and spotting drink, drugs and groupies. 'There was booze and what I presumed were pills being passed around,' he says, 'and there were several young ladies in very short skirts, none of whom I'd never seen around town before.' In one corner of the room was Keith Moon, leaning over a chair, in the grip of a violent coughing fit, punctuated by equally violent bursts of swearing, while Kim tried to calm him down: 'Then, at some point, either Kit Lambert or Chris Stamp walked in, and opened a briefcase stuffed with money and doled out its contents. The four band members lined up as he handed them bundles of ones and fivers.'

Daltrey and Townshend told Southall that despite their earlier denials, the rumours of The Who splitting up were true: 'They said, "We were contemplating a break-up. We were bored, we hadn't had a hit record, and we weren't getting any money."' They'd changed their minds, because of *My Generation*, and the fact that they were now earning 'good hard cash again'.

On Friday 3 December The Who played the Goldhawk Club for the first time since April. It was a homecoming gig, a 'thank you' to those that had stuck with them through every incarnation of the band since the summer of 1963. The Who arrived straight from an appearance on *Ready Steady Go!* to find a queue trailing down the steps outside the building and along Goldhawk Road. The two warring elements in The Who's music would be captured right there in the audience that evening. In one corner of the club was the Italian film director Michelangelo Antonioni; in the other Roger Daltrey's criminal acquaintances.

Antonioni's recent film *Red Desert* (1964) had been a brooding commentary on post-war industrial culture, starring his girlfriend, Monica Vitti. The director was now seeking a fashionable pop group for his first English-language film, *Blow-Up*. He'd been introduced to The Who through Terence Stamp, who was due to take the film's lead role. The experimental director now found himself shoulder to shoulder with The Who's jittery, pilled-up fanbase, and various local villains, in a working men's club where a brawl was never more than a few minutes away from breaking out.

'The Goldhawk was very cliquey and very territorial,' says Max Ker-Seymer, who was in the audience that night, and later became an extra in *Blow-Up*. Towards the end of The Who's set a fight began on the dance floor: 'There was a bouncer there who had a wooden billy club about two feet long on a bit of string, and he would fling it to clear a circle and then drag out whoever it was that had been attacked.'

While The Who played, 'Irish' Jack remembers seeing as many as twenty mods moving in formation through the throng. 'It reminded me of a rugby pack powering its way over a goal line,' he said. 'Only this was an army of mods trying to kick some guy across the Goldhawk dance floor. The guy was using one of his arms to protect his head, leaving the rest of his body open to more flying boots. In the melee of bodies it was difficult to tell whether he was actually trying to roll his way out of trouble or being shunted along like a rag doll by the force of the kicking.'

Whenever a fight broke out at the Goldhawk, the bands usually stopped playing. Instead, The Who played on, as if, said Jack, 'they were part of the disturbance'. They supplied the soundtrack as the club's bouncers, which included local heavyweight boxer Basil Kew, tried to separate the victim from his attackers. 'The Who were almost nonchalant,' says Ker-Seymer. 'You could see that Roger Daltrey could handle himself. But the whole group's attitude was, "We are here, this is what we do, we are in charge." That's how they were different from every other band. They had the attitude and they had the authority.'

The Who's set ended with Townshend jamming the head of his Rickenbacker through the front of his Marshall cab. 'The guitar broke too quickly,' says Ker-Seymer. 'I remember Antonioni looked surprised.' It was still a suitably violent climax to the show. The broken amp was still feeding back as The Who trooped offstage towards the dressing room, and a battered body was carried off the dance floor. The club's manager opened the fire-exit doors to let some much-needed cold air into the room. When The Who re-emerged, 'Irish' Jack watched as a local villain and two of his sidekicks surrounded Daltrey as the singer made his way out of the club. As they passed, Jack glimpsed an object inside the villain's jacket: 'A fucking shooter. It was the first time I'd ever seen a real handgun, and the hairs were standing up on the back of my neck.'

In a 2011 interview Townshend claimed that Daltrey had jumped in to break up the fight at the Goldhawk, and returned to the stage with 'a sawn-off shotgun under his shirt'. Whatever the exact circumstances, this was a turning point for The Who, and also for the mod culture they'd once found so appealing. 'Something had shifted,' admitted Townshend. 'Things got darker and nastier. Some of the faces had got really old, and when they showed up at clubs they had become proper criminals.'

It would be the last time The Who played the Goldhawk. After the gig, Antonioni fled Shepherd's Bush for the sanctuary of his suite at London's Savoy Hotel. Shortly after, David Hemmings replaced Terence Stamp as the lead in *Blow-Up*, and The Who were passed over for The Yardbirds. 'Antonioni wanted us for the part,' said Pete Townshend. 'But we were too genuine.' Simon Napier-Bell insists, however, that Kit Lambert had offended the director with some unspecified act of rudeness, allowing him to take advantage of the situation to pitch his own act: 'I went to Antonioni's suite and persuaded him The Yardbirds would be the better group for his film.'

'A year later I was an extra on the set of *Blow-Up*,' says Max Ker-Seymer, 'and I got to watch Jeff Beck trying to break a guitar à la Townshend, and Antonioni had me standing in exactly the same position I had been in at the Goldhawk. It was very weird. Almost poetic.'

In The Who's usual contradictory fashion the violent curtain call at the Goldhawk was followed a fortnight later by a family-friendly appearance in *Ready Steady Go!*'s Christmas pantomime. Cathy McGowan played Cinderella, with Keith Moon her lovesick friend, Buttons. When filming was over, The Who dashed off to play Windsor's Ricky-Tick Club, only for Moon to pass out during 'My Generation'. This time, it wasn't just the booze and drugs that felled him; the drummer was diagnosed with whooping cough.

The Who already had a replacement on standby: Viv Prince, who'd just been fired from the hard-nosed R&B group the Pretty Things, for excessive behaviour. 'Viv was even crazier than Keith,' said Jimmy Page, who'd briefly played with him in the group Carter-Lewis and the Southerners. 'Viv was also the one who first coined the phrase "Moon the Loon".'

Moon, in fact, had been watching and studying Prince for several years. John 'Twink' Alder who'd later join the Pretty Things saw The Who with Prince deputising. 'Viv was Keith's hero,' he says now. 'Keith took a lot from Viv, who had entertainment value. He was over the top, always leaving his drums and playing the mic stand, the guitars, the floor, people's heads, while drooling from his mouth at the same time. That's probably why they got rid of him from the Pretty Things.'

Prince curbed his outlandish antics enough not to upstage the rest of The Who. Moon, perhaps fearful of losing his place to one of his drumming idols, soon recuperated and rejoined the band. It had been an eventful year. The Who had become pop stars and Pete Townshend a hit songwriter. They'd beaten each other up, ripped each other off, and fired and reinstated their lead singer. But 1965 would end as strangely as it had begun. Kim Kerrigan was pregnant and The Who's wayward man-child drummer was going to become a father.

CHAPTER SEVEN

THE FIRST CONCERT ON MARS

'Everything new, uninhibited and kinky is blooming at the top of London life.'

Time **magazine, 15 April 1966**

'The Who won't last that long. What I would like to do then is to go into writing musicals and operettas.'

Pete Townshend, October 1966

'Fuckin' hell! Who's he?'

Roger Daltrey meets Jimi Hendrix, November 1966

Pete Townshend, with his modish white shirt and gangly folded limbs, sits hunched on a stool in the middle of a television studio. It is January 1966, and he is facing his first TV inquisition on a new pro-gramme called *A Whole Scene Going*, the BBC's attempt to entice *Ready Steady Go!*'s viewers with a higher-brow take on pop culture. Over the next few minutes, Townshend will parry questions from the show's hosts, Barry Fantoni and Wendy Varnals, and a panel of teenagers, delivering his answers in what the *Observer* has recently described as 'classless cockney'.

The Who, says Pete Townshend, are sexless and unglamorous; yes, he meant it when he wrote the words 'I hope I die before I get old', and yes, he takes drugs, but admits they're not conducive to a good live performance. Townshend also reveals that he and John Entwistle had just listened to the latest Beatles LP in stereo, and thought the backing tracks were 'flippin' lousy'. Throughout the interview, he is articulate, outspoken and uppity.

The Who are also shown miming to 'Out in the Street' and 'It's Not True' from the *My Generation* LP. The unfortunate set design means that Moon, Townshend and Entwistle are playing on rostrums that are higher than Daltrey's, rendering the singer dwarf-like in comparison. In the light of the band's recent problems, it is hard not to wonder whether this is deliberate.

Like most television programmes from the mid-1960s, *A Whole Scene Going* is now showing its age and some. But in 1966 it marked the moment when the broadcasting establishment started to regard pop music as more than a silly fad. This was a sea change to which Townshend was well suited. With The Who still at war with each other, their songwriter daydreamed about writing a book, about the band, their fans and their relationship with pop. 'It was an audacious, and possibly even a pretentious position to take,' he said. 'But I really felt that after The Beatles, the Rolling Stones and Bob Dylan, the world was our oyster, artistically speaking, and that was what I wanted to shout from the rooftops.'

It wasn't such an implausible idea. *A Whole Scene Going*'s co-host Barry Fantoni quickly spotted that the twenty-year-old Pete Townshend was a perfect guest for the show. 'Because he was the sort of twenty-year-old we were aiming at,' says Fantoni now. 'The BBC wanted what *Ready Steady Go!* had, but wanted a magazine programme that didn't just present pop music but the pop spectrum as a whole. Pete Townshend *was* the audience.'

Townshend found plenty of common ground with Barry Fantoni. The then twenty-six-year-old host was a former jazz musician who'd been thrown out of art school for 'getting drunk and chasing birds'. He now painted pop art, wrote scripts for the establishment-baiting TV show *That Was the Week That Was* and composed songs with his friend The Kinks' Ray Davies. In 1963, Fantoni began drawing cartoons for the satirical magazine *Private Eye*, and was soon helping design what he calls 'those zappy, cool' pop art-inspired panels that formed part of the set of *Ready Steady Go!*. Fantoni embodied a new breed of creative people who moved easily between mediums. 'I was just an artist who moved into being on the telly,' he says.

It was Ned Sherrin, producer of *That Was the Week That Was*, who suggested Fantoni for *A Whole Scene Going*: 'Ned said, "That chap with the long nose and the long hair has the look of the people we are trying to reach,"' says Fantoni. He became friends with the equally long-haired, long-nosed Townshend and the programme changed his life. After Fantoni's fourth TV appearance, he was offered a record deal, and was soon flitting between *Private Eye*'s Soho offices and late-night soirees with Townshend, Ray Davies, or random members of The Beatles and the Rolling Stones. 'Pete Townshend was very bright, candid and a very driven young man,' says Fantoni. How driven became obvious when Fantoni joined Townshend for a recording session at Pete's Chelsea flat.

'I'd been offered this record deal,' he recalls. 'Pete had bought these tape machines and asked if I wanted to do one of my songs. It was called 'When I'm Sitting on the Fence'. We started recording, but the tape got stuck.' Townshend's response to this minor inconvenience was to pick up the machine and smash it on the floor: 'He smashed it in anger. Then he pulled what was left to pieces, picked up the tape and threw it out the window. There were these spools of tape everywhere.'

Townshend may have wowed the hosts and producers of *A Whole Scene Going*, but he was still brimming with anger; especially at The Who's deal with Shel Talmy, and their inability to break America. Townshend had watched The Beatles, the Stones and most recently The Animals crack the US market. The latter were a rugged sounding Geordie R&B band, with a gravel-voiced lead singer named Eric Burdon. 'Eric Burdon hates The Who, The Who hate Eric Burdon,' said Townshend, in a press interview, without telling his interrogator or his readers why. But The Animals' version of a traditional folk song 'House of the Rising Sun' had reached Number 1 in America, and the group were about to have another US smash with their take on the Nina Simone hit, 'Don't Let Me Be Misunderstood'.

Meanwhile, The Who's 'I Can't Explain' had limped to Number 93 in the US, and 'Anyway, Anyhow, Anywhere' had failed to chart at all. It hadn't taken long for Lambert and Stamp to realise that Decca had little or no understanding of the band. In the meantime, Lambert's resentment of Shel Talmy, the man who had brokered the Decca deal, had only increased. Kit told Simon Napier-Bell that when the producer had sent his chauffeur-driven Rolls-Royce to ferry Lambert to a business meeting he'd deliberately left thirty-seven cigarette burns on the vehicle's fine leather upholstery: 'Shel was so incensed,' said Napier-Bell, 'he refused to talk to Kit ever again.'

While Lambert concentrated on boosting The Who's profile at home, Chris Stamp tried to solve the American problem. When the 'My Generation' single stalled at Number 74 in the US, he flew to New York. Terence Stamp was due to start work on a new film there, and traded his first-class plane ticket for economy seats so that his brother could join him. The Stamp siblings set up base camp in a plush hotel suite provided by the film company. Over the next fortnight, Stamp arranged meetings with Sir Edward Lewis, the head of Decca UK, who was also in town, the vice president of the label's American division, as well as agents, publishers and DJs – anyone who would talk to him, in fact – in a determined effort to drum up interest in The Who.

Stamp, Lambert and The Who were determined to sever all ties with Shel Talmy. But Talmy had an arrangement with Decca, and the company had no intention of dumping him and relinquishing their grip on the group. When a sympathetic Sir Edward Lewis told Stamp there was nothing he could do to help, The Who's situation seemed even more desperate. While in New York, however, Stamp received positive interest from Atlantic Records. Atlantic were a forward-thinking label with a roster of fine soul and R&B acts. They offered The Who a £10,000 advance against a ten per cent royalty; the Decca/Talmy deal had only recently increased from two-and-a-half to four per cent. New Action's lawyer suggested a simple, but risky solution: break the contract with Decca/Talmy, but be prepared to face the consequences in court.

The Who had recently signed with an ambitious booking agent and aspiring music business mogul named Robert Stigwood. Like Lambert and Stamp, Stigwood sometimes appeared to live by his wits and was prone to extravagant spending sprees, despite being broke. Andrew Oldham had co-founded his own independent label, Immediate Records. Stigwood followed his lead and launched Reaction Records, arranging a UK distribution deal for the label with Polydor and US distribution via the Atlantic Records subsidiary Atco.

Stigwood offered to sign The Who to Reaction as a temporary measure. It was the lifeline they needed. Lambert and Stamp had soon relocated from Ivor Court and into the office next door to Stigwood's at Caroline House in Chesterfield Gardens, W1. The arrangement suited them all. Stigwood needed the rent money; Lambert and Stamp enjoyed his company, and benefited financially by borrowing the money back from him. In short order, Stamp was spending his Saturday afternoons with Stigwood betting on horses, while Lambert and The Who's new agent jointly indulged their mutual interests in fine champagne, fancy restaurants and attractive young men.

On 4 March, The Who fired the first shot in their legal battle with Shel Talmy by issuing their fourth single, 'Substitute', on Reaction. The Who had originally planned to issue the Talmy-produced 'Circles', but instead they re-recorded the song, retitled it 'Instant Party', and relegated it to the B-side. Talmy went to the high court to claim copyright infringement, on the grounds that his production was a significant part of The Who's sound on the single. 'I had always felt that the so-called Who sound, on record at any event, was a good deal my creation,' reiterated Talmy in 1989.

'We did two versions of 'Circles', which were identical, as they were both copies of my demos,' protested Pete Townshend. Despite Townshend's objections, the high court granted Talmy an interim injunction preventing Polydor from distributing 'Substitute' with 'Instant Party' on the B-side. After a fortnight's sales, The Who were forced to withdraw the single. To get around the ban, and Talmy's copyright claim, 'Substitute' was re-released with a new B-side, 'Waltz for a Pig', a song that didn't even feature The Who but another of Robert Stigwood's clients, the Graham Bond Organization, billed as The Who Orchestra.

Shortly after, The Who's original label, Brunswick Records, rush-released a Who single of their own, the aptly named 'A Legal Matter', in defiance of the band's broken contract. The Who were unable to stop the release, and found themselves in the absurd situation of having two singles in competition with each other on two different labels. Keith Altham, now writing for *New Musical Express*, visited the band during rehearsals at their old stamping ground, the White Hart. Daltrey confidently told him that 'the kids wouldn't want to know' about 'A Legal Matter', a song that had already appeared on the *My Generation* LP. Townshend, meanwhile, thought that the dispute was 'all good for publicity'.

Despite the circumstances surrounding their release, both singles caught The Who on a creative golden streak that would endure, almost unbroken until the end of the decade. Yet 'Substitute', arguably one of The Who's best singles, was, in Townshend's own words 'a rip-off'. The guitarist had recently taken part in *Melody Maker*'s Blind Date feature, where musicians were asked to review new singles without being told whom they were by. Townshend loved the riff on 'Where is My Girl', a forty-five by the long-forgotten Robb Storme and the Whispers, and decided to borrow it.

In fact, Storme's group had probably borrowed the riff from any number of Tamla Motown records, including The Four Tops' 'I Can't Help Myself (Sugar Pie, Honey Bunch)', a UK hit eleven months earlier. Townshend used it on The Who's new song and, as John Entwistle later pointed out, '"Can't Help My-self" became "Sub-sti-tute."' The Tamla Motown sound was everywhere in the spring of 1966. In February, Townshend and the Rolling Stones' Brian Jones saw the label's fifteen-year-old prodigy Stevie Wonder perform at the Scotch of St James club. 'It was a true Tamla mind-fuck,' said Townshend, who later declared he got so high on Wonder's music that he almost crashed his car driving home after the gig.

Ultimately, though, the song's biggest influence came from closer to home: the Rolling Stones. '"Substitute" was written as a spoof of "19th Nervous Breakdown",' said Townshend, who'd just heard an early mix of the Stones' song. The Who, with Townshend producing, recorded their new single at London's Olympic Studios, eight days after the Stones released theirs.

Interviewed on *A Whole Scene Going*, Townshend had talked about the importance of The Who moving forward. Rather than just trying to replicate the noisy outrage of 'My Generation', 'Substitute' was full of repressed anger, but all the more powerful for that. Its sunny melody was misleading. The lyrics required Daltrey to turn himself into an insecure young man who spends the song listing off his perceived weaknesses and defects. The character might have been an uneasy fit, but Daltrey didn't have a choice. He was still on probation.

Townshend's clever wordplay was the standout feature of 'Substitute'. In America, though, Atlantic Records worried that the line 'I look all white but my dad was black' would put off radio DJs. The

Who amended the lyric on the US version (to 'I try going forward but my feet walk back'), but with its talk of plastic spoons and plastic macs, 'Substitute' was seemingly too odd for America. It failed to chart, suggesting that The Who's lack of Stateside success wasn't solely down to their poor choice of record company.

It was a different story in Britain. Daltrey's prediction that The Who's fanbase knew best was confirmed when 'A Legal Matter' stalled outside the top thirty, and 'Substitute' reached Number 5. A 'Legal Matter' is, however, one of those great, but sometimes forgotten entries in the early Who songbook. A cheery country-blues, vitalised by Nicky Hopkins' piano playing, it was also a Trojan Horse, smuggling in a barbed lyric that supported Townshend's earlier comment about being 'anti-young marrieds'. The character in 'A Legal Matter' resents domesticity, fatherhood, wedding dresses, maternity clothes and his wife's wish for him to work in an office. It's hard not to see in him a commentary on Daltrey's marital situation, especially as Townshend sang the lead vocals, but, in truth, the song disguised more of its writer's insecurities. 'What the song was screaming from behind the lines was, "I'm lonely, I'm hungry and the bed needs making,"' explained Townshend.

Talking to *Melody Maker* after 'Substitute', Townshend took random pot shots at the world ('China is the only thing that threatens my life'), praised his new friends ('My favourite artists are Barry Fantoni and Peter Blake') and stated 'I always stand by Young Communist principles.' 'In 1966 that was a fucking nervy thing to say,' points out 'Irish' Jack, although unlike fellow Ealing art students Richard Barnes and John Challis, Townshend had never actually been a member of the Young Communist League. He also found time to lambast Keith Moon, whom he described as 'a little old man . . . who used to be lots of fun'.

Moon was in a terrible state. On 17 March, he'd married Kim Kerrigan. The secret registry office ceremony wasn't the wedding Kim had dreamt of, but Kit Lambert insisted on the couple keeping a low profile. Lambert had successfully thrown the press off the scent by stating that Keith had a new girlfriend, a dancer from *Ready Steady Go!*, but unfortunately he named the dancer in a magazine article, causing embarrassment, as she had no idea she'd been used as a decoy and was actually involved with Ian McLagan, keyboard player in the east London mod group the Small Faces.

Keith's seventeen-year-old bride joined her husband, his parents and two sisters at 134 Chaplin Road – and stayed there. Lambert didn't want Kim upsetting Keith's female fans by showing up in public with a baby bump. Moon, meanwhile, who hadn't yet turned twenty, was torn between wanting to look after his young wife and their unborn child, and his eagerness to savour everything that being in The Who had to offer. This tension displayed itself in drinking and increased drug use.

'He was on some weird downer pills,' John Entwistle told *Q* magazine. 'Someone had told him they were uppers but they made him paranoid.' This led to several disturbing, blackly comic episodes. After another marathon drink-and-drugs session, Moon came home late one night and decided he was going to commit suicide. He stuck his head in the oven and turned on the gas. Kim came downstairs, walked into the kitchen, and calmly told her gibbering husband that if he was going to gas himself he should close all the windows first.

It's a measure of how fragile Moon's state of mind had become that when he first heard 'Substitute' he didn't recognise his own playing. Instead, the drummer called Entwistle and began screaming down the phone: 'He shouted, "How dare you record without me?",' recalled Entwistle. 'He was convinced he hadn't been at the session.' In fact, Moon was so drunk he couldn't remember what he'd done. Entwistle told him to listen again. Apart from the fact that the drumming was unmistakably Keith's, he could also be heard shouting out after playing a particularly tricky fill. 'When he heard that,' said Entwistle, 'he realised just how far gone he was.'

Kit Lambert's attempts to drum up publicity for The Who were less problematic than his attempts to keep their drummer's private life private. On 20 March, The Who appeared on the cover of the *Observer*'s colour supplement magazine. Stories in the pop press and titbits in the tabloids were expected, but getting The Who written about in a broadsheet newspaper was a coup. The *Observer* story was the result of writer John Heilpern and photographer Colin Jones shadowing the band and their managers for over a month. It was full of Lambert-approved hyperbole, but it accorded The Who and New Action the gravitas they craved. Like *A Whole Scene Going*, it was another sign that the mainstream media were starting to take pop music seriously.

Colin Jones had met The Who in Manchester in January. At their hotel, Keith Moon liberated the Union Jack from the building's flagpole. Jones hung it on the wall of one of the rooms, posed the band in front of it, and took some pictures, before they got bored and wandered off. The photographs show four angry young men, with Pete Townshend in his Union flag jacket and Keith Moon wearing a T-shirt emblazoned with Bridget Riley's *Blaze Study*. The picture, which Townshend described as 'sinister and glamorous', was chosen for the cover of the *Observer* magazine and would become the defining image of The Who in the 1960s.

After the shoot, they dashed off to play a local club, the Jigsaw, where the band and their entourage consumed several bottles of Mateus Rosé. Towards the end of The Who's set, Townshend's Rickenbacker collided with the club's low ceiling in a repeat of what had first happened at the Railway Hotel. One eyewitness recalls the guitar spearing a photograph of Georgie Fame stuck on the club's wall, as if Townshend was symbolically bayoneting the pianist. A few hours later, the band were thrown out of their hotel for waking up the other residents. But for once, the culprit wasn't Moon. 'Roger fired a shotgun out the window,' said Jones. 'It frightened the daylights out of the other guests.'

Jones and The Who caught an overnight train back to London. Any hope of sleep was dashed when the photographer saw Moon chasing Townshend through the carriage, brandishing a knife and screaming, 'I'm going to kill you!' The murder threat had been prompted by minor spat at the Jigsaw earlier, which the paranoid drummer was now fixated on. 'I don't think I'd ever met a band who were so antagonistic towards each other,' said Jones.

In 1966 Townshend praised the article for proving 'pop is becoming accepted as an art form'. Writing about it in his autobiography, though, he complained that it was a puff piece for Lambert and Stamp, with The Who presented as 'braggarts, spendthrifts, dandies and scumbags'. Yet it was a persona they seemed more than happy to live up to at the time.

On 1 May, they played the *New Musical Express*' Poll Winners' Concert at Wembley Empire Pool, the same venue Keith Moon had once tried to set alight. The bill reflected the hierarchy of mid-1960s pop: The

Who played above their former heroes Cliff Richard and the Shadows, but below the Rolling Stones and headliners The Beatles. The Who had just two songs, 'Substitute' and 'My Generation', with which to make an impact. They detonated smoke bombs, Townshend attacked his amp and the set climaxed with Keith Moon booting over his drums. 'I think the drums even fell off the stage,' said Chris Stamp. 'He did it to top Pete and to make The Who's presence felt, make sure the Stones and The Beatles had to follow this.'

Though nobody in the audience knew it at the time, this would be The Beatles' final UK concert. But it could just as easily have been The Who's. Two days later, the band cancelled a gig at Malvern Winter Gardens, claiming their transport had broken down on the way to Worcestershire. This was a lie. Shortly after, Daltrey left The Who again, but this time of his own free will.

Daltrey missed several gigs over the coming fortnight, leaving the band to muddle on with Townshend and Entwistle sharing lead vocals. Daltrey apparently revisited the idea of putting a soul band together, but later cheerfully told the press, 'While they were out gigging I was probably shagging somewhere.' When the scaled-down Who played Kidderminster Town Hall, Led Zeppelin's future singer, seventeen-year-old Robert Plant, offered his services; Townshend subsequently joked that Plant had probably taken pity on them.

Meanwhile, Keith Moon was also considering a future outside the band, but wasn't sure who with. Although a pop star in his own right, the nineteen-year-old Moon was still very much a starstruck fan. 'At the height of The Who's fame, Keith would have dropped our band, just like that, to join The Beatles,' said Daltrey. But it didn't have to be The Beatles. Any group would do. In April, Moon approached The Animals in Soho's Le Kilt club. Their drummer had just quit, and Keith offered his services – which were politely declined. When The Animals hired the Nashville Teens' drummer instead, Moon asked the remaining Nashville Teens if they had a job for him, and went as far as to tell his old friends in The Beachcombers that he'd joined the group. On another occasion, at the Scotch of St James, Moon spotted his beloved Beatles and, after several whisky and Cokes, clambered into the booth where they were sitting. 'Can I join you?' he asked. When Paul McCartney pointed out that he already had, Moon replied: 'No, I mean, can I join the band?' McCartney drolly suggested that Moon have a word with Ringo Starr.

These drunken conversations in after-hours clubs rarely led to anything more, until the day Moon agreed to a jam session with Nicky Hopkins, The Yardbirds' guitarists Jeff Beck and Jimmy Page, and Led Zeppelin's future bass guitarist John Paul Jones. The Yardbirds' manager Simon Napier-Bell booked IBC Studios for 16 and 17 May amid great secrecy, only for Moon to show up wearing an attention-seeking disguise of dark glasses and a Cossack's hat. The result of this clandestine two-day session was 'Beck's Bolero', a reworking of the composer Maurice Ravel's orchestral piece Boléro. The instrumental pottered along gently enough until the one minute and thirty seconds mark when Keith Moon let out a bloodcurdling shriek, and attacked his drums with such force that he knocked a microphone off its stand. '[Moon] was the lead instrumentalist,' said Jimmy Page. 'If he wasn't the one that stood out at the beginning of the song, he made sure he was by the end.' But 'Beck's Bolero' was a powerful performance from all involved. Everyone in the room was convinced that there was a band in the making.

According to Page, there was even a discussion about who might be the lead singer in this new supergroup, with the popular choice being the Small Faces' frontman Steve Marriott. 'Jeff, myself and Keith were together after the session, and Keith started talking about forming a band,' Page told writer Nick Kent. 'Keith wanted to call it "Lead [sic] Zeppelin". I remember saying, "Great, can we use the name?"'

Moon made the suggestion after speculating that the band would 'go down like a lead Zeppelin' – instead of 'a lead balloon'. John Entwistle, however, said that it was he who came up with the name two years after 'Beck's Bolero', and that Moon had suggested the image of the burning airship used by Led Zeppelin on their first LP in 1969.

Despite their initial promise, management pressure and conflicting egos soon intervened, and the group never played together again. 'Beck's Bolero' surfaced as the B-side of Jeff Beck's 1967 hit single 'Hi Ho Silver Lining' and again on The Jeff Beck Group's Truth album, where Moon was credited as 'You-Know-Who'. Jimmy Page returned to The Yardbirds, but used 'Beck's Bolero' as a template for the sound of his next group, Led Zeppelin. As far as Townshend was concerned, the session had been 'a political move' by Keith Moon, designed to scare the rest of The Who into thinking they might lose him. But the song itself is built on the dynamic sound The Who had explored on 'Anyway, Anyhow, Anywhere' and 'My Generation'. 'I remember Townshend looking daggers at me when he first heard ["Beck's Bolero"],' Jeff Beck told Keith Moon biographer Tony Fletcher. 'He didn't want anyone meddling with that territory.'

In reality, Townshend was as disillusioned as his bandmates, and was wondering whether he shouldn't dump The Who, and stay at home writing songs and composing film scores. He would soon donate a song, 'Join My Gang', to one of Robert Stigwood's young charges, Oscar, a singer who, under the name Paul Nicholas would appear in the West End musical *Hair*, and become a successful TV actor. (Later, Townshend would offer several compositions, including 'I'm a Boy', to the American folk singer Sandy Darlington.)

In an attempt to save the band, Lambert and Townshend discussed merging the remaining Who with Brian Epstein's musical trio Paddy, Klaus and Gibson, whose bass guitarist Klaus Voormann had been a friend of The Beatles since their Hamburg days. But the idea never went beyond the talking stage. Similarly, Roger Daltrey's planned soul band never came together. In fact, even his demanding sex life wasn't enough to keep him away from The Who and the singer was back in time for a 20 May date at the Ricky-Tick club in Newbury's Corn Exchange.

This was Moon's first appearance with The Who since playing with Jeff Beck and Jimmy Page, but come the night he remained distracted. The Beach Boys' Bruce Johnston was in town, and for forty-eight hours before the gig Moon had been his hero's tour guide on a whirlwind trip around the London music scene. The pair had gate-crashed a performance by Moon's friend, the session singer Tony Rivers, much to the surprise of the promoter and the modest audience; Moon had introduced Johnston to The Beatles; and he had also arranged for the Beach Boy to be interviewed live on *Ready Steady Go!* on the day of the Ricky-Tick gig.

Bruce Johnston's TV appearance meant that Moon, who seemed reluctant to leave his side, was still in Wembley when he should have been on his way to Newbury. To compound the problem, John Entwistle was with him. As the clock ticked and the Ricky-Tick audience grew impatient, Daltrey and Townshend asked the bassist and drummer from the support group, the Jimmie Brown Sound, to fill in until their own rhythm section arrived.

The group's drummer, future *Melody Maker* and *Mojo* magazine writer Geoff Brown, recalled nervously sitting behind Moon's highly tuned Premier kit with its 'rifle-crack snare drum' and 'gong-like crash cymbals'. Brown played 'Ooh Poo Pah Doo' and had just started 'Heat Wave' when he saw that Moon and Entwistle had turned up, albeit drunk, with Bruce Johnston in tow. Geoff watched the rest of the set from the wings, but realised that something was amiss: 'Keith was out of his tree.' The Who's performance continued in a ramshackle fashion with an already furious Townshend glaring at the drummer every time he made a mistake.

During the 'My Generation' finale, Townshend stopped bouncing his guitar off his cab and flung it at Moon instead. The guitar connected with the drummer's forehead, and ended up blacking his eye. Moon retaliated by heaving a drum at Townshend, before falling backwards over his kit and cutting his leg, an injury that required three stitches. Bruce Johnston was impressed: 'I thought it was the best concert I'd ever seen.' The Who locked themselves in the dressing room, where they screamed at each other for the next hour. When the Jimmie Brown Sound were finally allowed inside, they found the window smashed, as if The Who had used it to make their getaway instead of the door. Lying among the broken glass was Keith Moon's leather waistcoat. 'Someone picked it up,' said Geoff Brown, 'and a cascade of pills of various hues scattered across the floor.'

Entwistle said that after the Newbury gig, he and Moon had gone looking for Kit Lambert to tell him they were leaving The Who, and had found him at Robert Stigwood's. The next day Townshend visited Chaplin Road to apologise, but the drummer refused to come to the door. Instead, Keith informed the press that he and Entwistle were starting their own band. 'We sat in different nightclubs and planned our new career,' said the bassist. 'I often wonder what would have happened if we'd gone away and formed Led Zeppelin.'

According to one old friend, Entwistle's dissatisfaction with The

Who stemmed, in part, from his own perfectionism. Dave Lambert, his fellow Boys' Brigade cadet and the future Strawbs guitarist, saw The Who play a tiny venue in Ealing that year. 'It was this little community centre, and they were great. But John was so self-critical. As soon as he saw me, he said, "Oh, we were rubbish." But this happened every time I saw The Who and spoke to him after a gig – "Oh, we were rubbish."' He often gave the impression of not caring very much, but I think that was a protection. I think he was fiercely proud of The Who.' When Clint Warwick quit the Moody Blues in June, the band asked Entwistle to join. He considered the offer, but, like Daltrey and Moon, drifted back, as if The Who's gravitational pull was impossible to resist. 'There was a sort of resignation we had with each other,' said Chris Stamp, 'that we were part of the same thing.'

Just as before, after the punch-up in Denmark, apologies were made, an uneasy truce called, and The Who were back on the road – earning money the best way they could, while Shel Talmy's injunction still hung over them. The Who's pop-star status meant that they could now charge £300 a night, sometimes as much as £500. In comparison, the Stones were going out for £450 and The Beatles could command as much as £1,000.

However, when roadie Richard Cole collected one speeding ticket too many and lost his driving licence, The Who found themselves a man down. Having been around at the 'birth' of Led Zeppelin, it was fitting that Cole would later become that group's tour manager, over-seeing some of the most debauched rock 'n' roll tours of the 1970s. But his time with The Who was a vital apprenticeship. 'The Who were exceptional,' he says. 'Four completely different individuals: different clothes, different drugs, different drinks. There was nobody else quite like them.'

Soon after, The Who hired the Walker Brothers' ex-roadie John Wolff (known as 'Wiggy' due to the Beatle-style wig he wore to disguise his premature baldness). Wolff had met The Who when Keith Moon had borrowed the Walker Brothers' drummer's snare, which he promptly destroyed. With The Who, Wiggy took over the tedious role of looking after 'the count'. This involved standing in the lobby of a venue with a hand-held clicker to record exactly how many people were coming in, and ensuring the promoter didn't rip the band off. As well as keeping his beady eye on 'the count', Wiggy knew how to work a spotlight and had a clean driving licence: 'If I was going a bit fast and the old bill saw me, I used to alter the position of the wig so they wouldn't recognise me later.'

Moon and Entwistle had just bought themselves a maroon and white Bentley. Wiggy became their chauffeur, and a willing accessory in their practical jokes by installing a microphone under the dashboard and a Tannoy under the car's radiator grille. 'They'd just opened another section of the M1,' he explains, 'and we were sick of people sitting in the inside lane, when we were late for a gig, so we decided to give them a little jolt.' Administering the jolt usually involved Keith Moon taking the microphone, putting on an authoritarian voice, and ordering the slow driver to change lanes. The shocked drivers presumed the Bentley was an unmarked police car and did as they were told, only to watch it cruise past with a couple of long-haired pop stars in the passenger seats and a young man in a lopsided wig behind the wheel.

As The Who's antics continued through what Pete Townshend later described as 'a summer of professional lunacy', Lambert and Stamp's fragile empire faced its greatest threat yet. Andrew Loog Oldham had been observing The Who's faltering progress with interest. The Rolling Stones were on a commercial high, having bagged another Number 1 single with 'Paint it Black' and having topped the album charts with their latest LP, *Aftermath*, a record Townshend was utterly smitten with.

Oldham had now sold his share of the Stones' management to their US business manager Allen Klein, a hard-nosed New Jerseyite who'd spotted how much money there was to be made from pop music, and how dangerously naive most groups and their managers were. Klein's cold business acumen and straight talking impressed Mick Jagger, which, in turn, would lead to Klein acquiring complete control of the Stones' early publishing, albeit without the group realising it. It would take the Stones seventeen years to extricate themselves from Klein's grasp. In the late 1960s, The Beatles would make a similar mistake when they appointed Klein to untangle their tortuous business affairs in a deal that resulted in him suing The Beatles and The Beatles suing each other.

Oldham could see that Lambert and Stamp were struggling with The Who, and made his move. In one of his rare interviews, Lambert recalled seeing Townshend and Moon climbing out of the Stones' manager's Phantom V Rolls-Royce: 'When the boys got to my flat I drew my old service revolver, an enormous Colt special, lined the boys against the wall, and asked "What's Up?" . . . The next time I saw the Rolls arrive, I jumped in and told [Oldham], "Hands off or else!"' As wonderful an anecdote as it is, none of the band have ever discussed Lambert threatening them with a gun, and Oldham insists Kit would have been more likely to 'wave a handbag' at him than a shooter.

Oldham intended to carry on producing the Rolling Stones, but was intrigued by The Who, particularly Moon and Townshend, whom he regarded as the stars of the band. In June he paid for Townshend to fly to New York and meet Allen Klein. The Stones' business manager informed Townshend that he could get The Who a lucrative deal with MGM Records, but that they had to dump Lambert and Stamp, and appoint Oldham as their manager. Townshend returned to England feeling confused and disillusioned.

Naturally Townshend's secret trip didn't remain secret for long. No sooner was he back in London, than the Scene DJ Guy Stevens and Island Records founder Chris Blackwell were at his Chelsea flat warning him off Klein and offering their services instead. In a scene worthy of a 1960s Whitehall farce, Kit Lambert unexpectedly turned up at the flat, and Townshend bundled Stevens and Blackwell into another room so he wouldn't see them. Unaware of their presence, Lambert then broke down and pleaded with Townshend not to desert him. 'He wept and wept and wept,' said Townshend.

Shel Talmy, meanwhile, had hired the pre-eminent barrister Quintin Hogg, the future Lord Hailsham, to represent him in court. When the fusty judge hired to hear the case mistook 'The Who' for an abbreviation of the World Health Organisation, the band's lawyers realised they were doomed. Outside the court Talmy informed The Who that he would renegotiate their deal, but only with Allen Klein handling that renegotiation.

In June, Townshend flew back to New York for another meeting with Klein, but joined by The Who's lawyer, Lambert, Stamp and Andrew Oldham. The rendezvous took place on a luxury yacht moored at New York's 77th Pier. Chris Stamp was well aware that in the film industry a yacht could be hired by the day, and was distinctly unimpressed. Recalling the meeting in 1974, Townshend was scathing: 'We ate [Klein's] caviar, had a look at the Statue of Liberty from his yacht, shat in his toilet and went back to England.' Back home, the encounter inspired him to write a song called 'Lazy Fat People'. He offered it to Helmut Gorden's new protégés, Episode Six, who turned it down.

Writing in 2002, Oldham explained that he wanted to keep Lambert and Stamp as The Who's producers, but act as their executive producer, with Allen Klein as their financial manager. What Klein wanted, however, was ultimately to manage The Who. He had the Stones and would soon have The Beatles; he was picking off the holy trinity of British pop groups, one by one. Lambert and Stamp demonstrated their love of brinkmanship by agreeing to hand over control as long as the contract was completed within twenty days. If not, then the deal was off.

News of the deal was even printed in the music press, where it was claimed that Oldham had 'scooped The Who's recording contract' and that Allen Klein had finalised a deal to sign The Who to MGM Records for the US and Canada. Lambert and Stamp then proceeded to stall the deal, creating petty complications and taking full advantage of the fact that they were in London and Klein was in New York. When the deadline passed Klein was out of the picture, for now, and The Who had reached an out-of-court settlement with Shel Talmy.

Under the terms of this new deal, Talmy would no longer produce The Who, but would still receive a five per cent royalty on their recordings for the next five years. At a time when few envisaged a pop group having more than a five-year lifespan, this might have seemed a small price for The Who to pay. In fact, it resulted in Talmy earning handsomely from later hit albums such as *Tommy* and *Who's Next*. For Talmy, though, this was payback for what he saw as his role in shaping The Who's sound and making them a commercially attractive proposition.

The Who were obliged to remain with Decca in the US, with Chris Stamp empowered to shake up the company's antiquated business methods, but they were now free to sign with any label elsewhere in the world. Decca also agreed to a $50,000 advance against future royalties. Meanwhile, The Who received £50,000 for signing to Polydor for the UK and the rest of Europe. While these sizable advances enabled New Action to pay off their sizable debts, there was another less attractive caveat to the deals. Once Lambert and Stamp had taken their share of the band's new ten per cent royalty, each member of The Who would receive just 1.25 per cent. This shortfall would be one of the reasons the band stayed on the road for the next fifteen years, where they would command enormous fees for playing arenas and stadiums.

Allen Klein's takeover of the Stones and his attempted hijacking of The Who was emblematic of how the music business was changing, of how big money was moving in, and of how Stamp, Lambert and Oldham were in danger of being swallowed up. In the outside world, though, these 'young meteors', as Nik Cohn had described them, were leading the charge in what the American news magazine *Time* called 'London: The Swinging City'. As the 15 April issue put it: 'In a decade dominated by youth, London has burst into bloom. It swings.'

Time's cover illustration was a departure from its usual gallery of granite-faced senators and world leaders. In their place was a rendering of Big Ben, a Rolls-Royce, a pair of Union flag sunglasses and a Who T-shirt. Inside, the writer Piri Halasz extolled a vibrant new London with its mod clothes shops and modish nightclubs. Halasz's statement that 'everyone parties with everyone else' acknowledged the sweeping social changes, where an Oxbridge-educated former public schoolboy and an East End tugboat captain's son could go into business together.

Just like 'mod', the phrases 'Swinging London' and 'the Swinging Sixties' have since fallen into disrepute. Pete Meaden's former associate, the photographer Philip Townsend whose archive captured many of the key players, maintains that the 'Swinging London' set actually comprised no more than 'about three hundred people', and that not everyone seen on the King's Road or Carnaby Street was young, hip and dressed in the latest fashions: 'I've got photos of Kensington High Street taken in the sixties, and it's full of old ladies wandering around.' The majority of London, never mind Britain, didn't swing. A look at the pop charts said as much. Even though The Beatles' 'Eleanor Rigby' and 'Yellow Submarine' were among the bestselling singles of the year, they still trailed behind Frank Sinatra's 'Strangers in the Night' and country crooner Jim Reeves' 'Distant Drums' – the two biggest hits of 1966.

But if you were among that select three hundred, London was the most exciting place to be. After Pete Townshend was evicted from Old Church Street for disturbing the neighbours, he moved into a converted film-editing suite, at the top of 87 Wardour Street, where he could make as much noise as he wanted. Townshend was now living five floors up in the heart of *Time*'s swinging city. It was easy to feel like a king. In the centre of the flat's living space was a large stone planter used as a makeshift dustbin. One day, Richard Barnes watched as Townshend casually picked up the pot and tipped its contents out of the window on to the street, impervious to who or what was below.

On another occasion, Townshend's art college friends gathered at the flat to drink, smoke and listen to music. When the beer ran out and one of the party offered to buy more, Townshend condescendingly asked whether they could afford it, before slowly tearing up a five-pound note in front of them. 'Pete had an extremely unpleasant side,' recalls one of his art college friends. It was something Townshend himself acknowledged, blaming it on his paranoia, his dope smoking and his massive ego. 'I wrote a song,' he said. 'It was a hit, and from that moment on I thought the world revolved around me.'

Being a pop star in 1966, though, put Townshend in a rarefied position. 'The world of the arts was like a chevron back then,' says Barry Fantoni. 'The spearhead was pop music, and everything else in the arts followed behind. It was a pyramid, but the richest and most revered at the top of that pyramid were the pop stars. I was as seduced by it as anyone else.'

Private Eye, encouraged by articles such as the *Observer*'s Who story, eagerly satirised the media's fascination with pop culture. *Evening Standard* columnist Maureen Cleave wrote a gushing weekly pop column and breathlessly told her readers that Chris Stamp was better looking than his film-star brother. *Private Eye*'s response to all this was a spoof column credited to one 'Maureen Cleavage', to go with 'Spiggy Topes and the Turds', a fictional pop group, created by Barry Fantoni and the comic writer and actor Peter Cook, and transparently based on John Lennon and The Beatles.

'We made fun of it at *Private Eye*, but the other people on the magazine were still fascinated by it,' insists Fantoni. 'Peter Cook was always interested in pop musicians. But the editor Richard Ingrams, although snooty about it now, was also pretty well captivated. I can remember seeing Ingrams, this patrician gentleman and grandson of Queen Victoria's physician, banging his hand arrhythmically on a filing cabinet and singing something by Adam Faith.'

For The Who and the rest of the pop establishment of 1966 and 1967, there was now a network of exclusive clubs where they could plot, gossip, drink, take drugs and swap band members and girlfriends. As well as the Scotch of St James, there was the Ad-Lib, in Leicester Square, the Bag O' Nails, a former brothel in Soho's Kingly Street, where bands could be guaranteed a drink and an unspectacular steak dinner after a late-night session or gig. ('It was in the Bag O' Nails that Keith Moon, smashed out of his head, stood up and just walked across the table and everyone's food,' recalls June Clark.) On the other side of Oxford Street was the Speakeasy, a basement in Margaret Street, originally decorated with gaudy pictures of the gangster Al Capone, where Moon supposedly stripped naked one evening.

Most of The Who soon became familiar faces on this late-night circuit. Occasionally, they'd venture out of Soho to Blaises, a basement in Kensington, or the Cromwellian in nearby Cromwell Road, a casino, discotheque and bar, where the clientele might include sundry Beatles, but also Sean Connery and Constant Lambert's former mistress Margot Fonteyn.

Barry Fantoni remembers Soho at this time as resembling a village populated by artists, actors, writers and fashion designers; a place where he could walk from one end of Greek Street to the other and be guaranteed to meet twenty like-minded individuals. 'You'd then go to one of three pubs or four restaurants, and you could stay there all day,' he says. 'Then you'd move on to Chelsea and it was the same. There was this restaurant on the King's Road, run by a funny Jewish woman who would only let you in if she liked you. The food was crap but there'd be all these people outside, pressed to the glass, trying to get in, just so they could eat in the same place as John Lennon or Michael Caine. Once you'd been on the telly and were a star you could have anything you wanted.'

Fantoni recalls sitting in Marianne Faithfull's flat, with her boyfriend Mick Jagger and Paul McCartney as they dissected the latest Kinks single. Fantoni considered Ray Davies a superior songwriter to both of them, as well as Pete Townshend: 'I always thought Ray was a genius, and I don't use that world lightly.' But, at the same time, he regarded Townshend as more clued-up and interesting than McCartney ('Paul affected an interest in art but I don't think it was close to his heart'), Jagger ('I always thought The Rolling Stones were rubbish') and the rest of The Who: 'The others in Pete's group were like footballers that sang. I saw a lot of Keith Moon but I don't remember a single word I said to him or him to me.'

That summer, Townshend received a £5,000 royalty cheque and decided to buy himself a flash American car, a left-hand drive Lincoln Continental. It was then that Barry Fantoni realised how privileged life was at the top of the pyramid. Fantoni accompanied Townshend to the car dealership in Balham, south London. The guitarist chose his vehicle, paid his money and then proudly drove the sleek, long-finned convertible out of the showroom. When Barry met him a few days later, Pete told him he'd already crashed his new toy: 'He didn't seem bothered by it. I remember him saying that he'd left it by the side of the road, and he'd probably get his chauffeur to take him down later so he could pick it up. I was astonished.'

Whether distracted by the professional lunacy surrounding The Who or simply because he was a careless driver, Townshend had crashed the Lincoln on the M1, an accident that resulted in a large fine. Later, he fell asleep while driving home from Sheffield and woke up in a ditch. To save his driving licence and potentially his life, Townshend hired an old friend and musician from Ealing named John 'Speedy' Keen to drive him around. Amid the blur of late-night motorway journeys and car accidents, Townshend was reminded of how far he'd come when The Who performed at the Isle of Man's Palace Ballroom, and he stood on the stage on which his father had once played every summer. The musical revolution that had started in 1958, with Pete pointing a home-made guitar at Cliff Townshend and thinking, 'Bang! You're dead!', had come full circle.

By now, though, both The Who and its audience had changed. For 'Irish' Jack, the turning point had been that violent Goldhawk gig in December 1965: 'The Who had come of age. They'd become untouchable.' For June Clark it was a gig in Eltham, south-east London, the following summer. 'I remember all the guys going crazy at the front of the stage, but all the women stood behind them,' she says. 'That's when I first saw the change. Nobody was dancing anymore. Now everybody just stood there and stared.'

In August, while The Who's lawyers thrashed out their deal with Decca, Brunswick milked another single from the *My Generation* LP, 'The Kids Are Alright' (a further Brunswick single, 'La-La-La-Lies', would follow in November). Reading between the lines, the lyrics of 'The Kids Are Alright' seemed to suggest its paranoid composer resigning himself to his ex-girlfriend having sex with his friends. The choirboy vocals evoked the schoolboy Townshend trying to recreate the celestial music whizzing around his younger self's head, while its baroque chord sequences were borrowed from Henry Purcell. This classical influence was no doubt lost on many Who fans, but Townshend would return to Purcell's work again and again. 'There was one particular piece of his called "The Gordian Knot Untied",' he said. 'The opening of which is deeply moving and tragic and profoundly sad.'

'The Kids Are Alright' was a subversive but charming pop song, yet it barely troubled the top forty. Still, there was something timely about its release. A few weeks earlier, Kim Moon had given birth to a baby girl, Amanda. When Keith eventually turned up to bring his wife and daughter home, he was in the final throes of a three-day drug binge. To Kim's despair, her disorientated husband wandered off into the field behind Central Middlesex Hospital, where 'Wiggy' Wolff had to talk him down. The Who's own overgrown kid was still coming to terms with fatherhood.

Aside from the spectacle of The Who beating each other up, Bruce Johnston's prevailing memory of his trip to England was meeting The Beatles. Initiated by Moon, the rendezvous had taken place in his suite at the Waldorf Hotel in Aldwych. After a few drinks, Johnston had played them the new Beach Boys album, *Pet Sounds*. Even with all the pills he'd consumed, Keith Moon could tell this was very different from their recent hits, 'Help Me Rhonda' and 'California Girls'. These new songs were mini-symphonies, created with harpsichords, flutes, violins, chiming bicycle bells and barking dogs. Keith Moon made appreciative noises, but the Beach Boys' new songs left him cold.

Its effect on The Beatles was very different. Paul McCartney would later declare one of these mini-symphonies, 'God Only Knows', as his favourite song of all time. The Beatles' *Rubber Soul* had inspired *Pet Sounds*, which, in turn, inspired the next Beatles LP, *Revolver*, released in August. *Revolver* was similarly complex and multi-layered and contained 'Tomorrow Never Knows', a song on which George Harrison played the Indian sitar. Although he'd revise his opinion later, at the time Townshend criticised *Pet Sounds* for being 'too remote and way-out'. And publicly, at least, he was still prone to making withering comments about the 'flippin' lousy' Beatles. But as Richard Barnes recalls, 'You waited for that new Beatles single and that new LP. You listened to it, and then you watched as everything changed and everyone else, including The Who, followed.'

Kit Lambert welcomed The Beatles' move away from simple pop, as he believed that The Who had more to say than could be contained in a two-and-a-half-minute song. It was this thinking that had prompted him to introduce Townshend to Purcell, Walton and Corelli, and to pack him off to the Royal Opera House. 'Opera as we know it is absolutely defunct,' said Lambert. 'One needs a completely fresh approach. I can see a Beatles opera on at Covent Garden; ten years from now, I bet you.'

In the meantime, Lambert urged Pete Townshend, who had already been fooling around with the idea, to get there first. When Townshend stayed at girlfriend Karen Astley's Pimlico flat, Keith Moon's old friend and occasional music journalist Ray Tolliday moved into Townshend's Wardour Street pad. 'Occasionally Ray and I got together and made spoof demos there,' said Townshend. 'For Kit's birthday, we made a kind of joke Gilbert and Sullivan opera called "Gratis Amatis".'

The ten-minute aria was an elaborate in-joke, aimed at Lambert and Stamp's friend, the songwriter Lionel Bart. 'The opening line was "Gratis Amatis, I love Lionel Bart-is", said Townshend, who had noticed Bart's presence at many Who gigs: 'Particularly when we played the Marquee, because he was after the boys.'

But when they played 'Gratis Amatis' to Lambert, he failed to see the funny side. Instead, Kit took Townshend to Wheelers restaurant in Old Compton Street and told him: 'There's something here. This is great. This model – with joined up pieces of music.' Lambert urged Townshend to create something similar but more serious for The Who.

His first step was to write a story set in 1999, a time when parents could choose the sex of their children. A couple request four daughters, but end up with three daughters and a son, whom they raise as a girl. Townshend called the story 'Quads': 'It was my first attempt at writing a mini-rock opera.' 'Quads' was never completed. Instead the story was condensed into two and a half minutes and became The Who's next single, 'I'm a Boy', in August.

Townshend introduced the story by singing about the three daughters, Jean Marie, Felicity and Sally Joy, in the first verse, before Daltrey assumed the role of their unfortunate brother, Bill, in the second verse. Sounding perplexed and angry, 'Bill' explained that it was a good day if his 'ma' let him wear trousers and didn't stick a wig on him. This tale of enforced cross-dressing featured more choirboy vocals, more Purcell-inspired baroque chord sequences and John Entwistle on tuba. 'I'm a Boy' was extraordinary and unique, and surprised their audience as much as their critics. 'No one else was singing about things like that,' says June Clark. '"My mum doesn't understand me and wants to dress me as a girl when I'm a boy?" But we could relate to it. The Who didn't do love songs, but there were still these hormones and confused feelings flying around in the music.' Despite their new deal, the single flopped in America. In Britain, where drag acts and comedies featuring men dressed as women were almost a national tradition, it reached Number 2.

But the song's darker side wasn't lost on the audience, or Townshend himself. His childhood abuse was finding an outlet in his work, even if he couldn't yet acknowledge it. 'Over the years, a couple of blokes came up and said, "That song saved my life,"' he said. 'They're not saying, "Oh you used to dress up as a girl as well, did you?" But that song came from somewhere in me, that had some empathy with them. We all have chunks of that stuff in different degrees. Some of us have one per cent that is vulnerable, with some of us it's twenty per cent. What has become clear to me is that the people that are really serious Who fans have a big chunk of fucked-up personality, equal to my own.'

The challenge for Roger Daltrey, though, was to find his place in Townshend's songs. 'I was unsure,' he told the author. 'I'd just been allowed back in the band. My ego had been crushed, and it showed in my voice. When I first heard those songs, I was like, "Oi, what's this about?" I didn't think I could find the right voice for them. You can hear it when you listen to them now.'

While Townshend pontificated in the press about rock operas, pop art and communism, Daltrey preferred to talk to *Melody Maker* about cars and women, although cars were better, he said, 'because they don't answer back'. Later that year, Daltrey acquired a yellow Volvo P1800, the same model that actor Roger Moore drove in the TV show *The Saint*. The vehicle, restored by a gang of Daltrey's Shepherd's Bush cronies that included 'George the Weld' and 'Nobby the Fibre Glass Kid', became his pride and joy. The Volvo, usually with a female companion in the passenger seat, was regularly seen speeding away from some provincial club's car park, as if the singer had just robbed a bank rather than played a concert. But Daltrey needed to get away fast. 'He was on his own in The Who,' says Neville Chesters. 'The others didn't talk to him.'

With Lambert busy clucking around Townshend like a mother hen, the street-savvy Chris Stamp helped bridge the gap between Daltrey and the management. 'Chris was the link between Kit and Roger,' believes Simon Napier-Bell. 'He was also a great editor of Kit's wilder ideas.' What Stamp brought to his partnership with Lambert, Daltrey would later bring to his with Townshend. 'Pete would come up with these amazing, complex ideas about ruling the universe and doing the first concert on Mars,' says Keith Altham. 'Then Roger, the practical one, would turn round and say, "That's great Pete, but let's start with Shepherd's Bush."'

For Altham, what he calls Daltrey's 'thug Teddy Boy persona' was a protective shield he'd adopted to cope with being in The Who: 'He *was* a proper Shepherd's Bush boy. But it was an image he sometimes played up to. There's so much more to Roger than that. But what he had then was presence, and that was a very good thing, especially when you were on tour, to keep everyone wary around you.'

For all of Townshend's complex ideas, that summer The Who were still a band that ran on a steady diet of sex and violence. At a gig in Örebro, Sweden, Keith Moon squared up to a policeman after the officer decided the audience were too rowdy and cut the power to the stage. Nine months after the Scandinavian dates, the Swedish model Elisabeth Aronsson gave birth to Daltrey's son, Matthias, confirming that The Who's singer was a lover as well as a fighter. (Although Aronsson would wait until 1980 to tell Daltrey that he had another child.)

At the Windsor National Jazz and Blues Festival on 30 July, The Who toughed it out on a bill that also included Robert Stigwood's new baby, Cream – a trio comprising former Yardbirds guitarist Eric Clapton, and the Graham Bond Organization's bassist Jack Bruce and drummer Ginger Baker. To paraphrase Jeff Beck, Cream were 'meddling with The Who's territory'. The Who rose to the challenge, but there was some truth in Townshend's growing fear that they were in danger of becoming a pantomime act. The managers threw smoke bombs from the wings, as Townshend and Moon set about their equipment, and Daltrey kicked out the lights at the front of the stage. John Entwistle, meanwhile, was so drunk he'd started playing a new song before his bandmates had finished the one before. The noise and violence egged on an audience already ecstatic at the news that England had beaten Germany in the World Cup final at Wembley.

When The Who returned to Europe later that summer, the chaos, violence and lack of money became too much for road manager Neville Chesters. At The Who's gig in France at Lyon's Palais d'Hiver, Moon threw his snare drum at Chesters in a fit of pique. Neville threw it back, resigned on the spot, but was talked into staying on by Chris Stamp.

Chesters then undertook a hellish journey from Lyon to Berlin, during which The Who's van broke down and Neville was repeatedly refused entry to Germany because New Action had failed to provide him with the correct paperwork. When he finally made it to Berlin, he was told there was no hotel room for him and he'd have to sleep on Roger Daltrey's floor.

Later, he joined Chris Stamp, Keith Moon and others on a tour of the local nightclubs. Before long, Keith had disappeared with a female admirer; unfortunately, her boyfriend and several of his friends objected. When they couldn't find the drummer they decided to take their revenge on his associates. 'Chris and I were about to get in the car and there were six guys waiting for us,' says Chesters. 'I took a bit of a pasting, but Chris knocked one of them senseless, and the rest of them ran. Keith had pulled the wrong woman and, once again, we'd been left to sort out his mess.' Ultimately, the gruelling journeys, the poor wages and Moon's behaviour had taken their toll. In October, Chesters accepted Robert Stigwood's offer of a job and left The Who behind.

Chesters' replacement was Bob Pridden, the John Barry Seven's roadie and a familiar face on the west London gig circuit. Pridden was initiated at Streatham Locarno, where, after watching The Who smash up most of their equipment, he was brusquely told to get the gear fixed for the following night's show. The Who may have burnt out his predecessor, but Pridden would outlast every other member of their road crew, going on to become The Who's sound engineer; a position he still holds today.

In August 1966, Kit Lambert finally realised his dream and was listed as an executive producer on a Who record, 'I'm a Boy'. Earlier, in the spring, Lambert had persuaded The Merseybeats' Tony Crane and Billy Kinsley to dump the rest of the band, hire a backing group and change their name to The Merseys. Having done so, they recorded the single, 'Sorrow'. It featured the cream of London session musicians, including Jimmy Page, and was produced by Lambert. Kit was now more convinced than ever that he should be producing The Who, but, in July, his ego got the better of him and he fouled up The Merseys' next single, 'So Sad About Us', a song written by Pete Townshend.

'John Lennon wanted to produce the follow-up single to 'Sorrow', says The Merseys' Tony Crane, 'and George Harrison and Ringo Starr wanted to play on it. It would have been the only time any of The Beatles played on anyone else's records and had a Beatle producing. We told Kit this, but he said no. We could not believe our ears. Instead Kit booked fifty session musicians and stuck all these timpani drums on the record that didn't suit it at all.'

'It was a Kit Lambert over-produced, overdone, egomaniacal catastrophe,' added the band's Billy Kinsley. 'So Sad About Us' flopped and Townshend told the press that he'd been opposed to The Merseys releasing it in the first place. 'It was a waste of a song,' says Tony Crane, who still sounds disheartened almost fifty years later. 'After that, Kit lost interest in The Merseys, The Who got bigger and bigger, and Fontana started producing our records again.'

Undeterred by The Merseys' failure, Lambert was now a dominant presence in the studio when The Who started recording new material for their second LP. Chris Stamp had arranged a deal with song publishers Essex Music, whereby Daltrey, Entwistle and Moon received an advance of £500 each for writing two songs apiece for the group's next album. The money was welcome: 'At the time we were on £20 a week,' said Entwistle. 'Which just about paid for the booze.' But the deal also empowered the three at a time when Townshend seemed to have become The Who's sole writer. It was good for band morale.

The Who's second album, eventually titled *A Quick One*, was recorded in fits and starts through September and November 1966 at several facilities, including their home-from-home, IBC Studios. Its centrepiece was Pete Townshend's first recorded attempt at a rock opera, *A Quick One, While He's Away*. But Townshend also contributed three short songs: 'Run Run Run', 'Don't Look Away' and 'So Sad About Us', minus the clunky orchestration that had blighted The Merseys' version. With their clipped harmonies and rumbling guitar sounds, all three demonstrated Townshend's latest description of The Who's music as 'power pop'.

Meanwhile, his bandmates' contributions varied in style and quality. Daltrey only managed one song, 'See My Way', a slight piece of Buddy Holly-inspired pop, on which Moon, according to John Entwistle, played a couple of cardboard boxes to achieve the sound the singer wanted. Entwistle, meanwhile, contributed 'Whiskey Man' and 'Boris The Spider'. Entwistle bought himself the same tape recorders as Townshend, and demoed 'Whiskey Man' at home, before playing it to his girlfriend Alison Wise. Townshend asked Alison what it was like. 'Oh it's lovely,' she apparently told him. 'Much better than your songs.'

There was something of Henry Mancini's theme music for the TV detective show *Peter Gunn* in 'Whiskey Man', but it paled next to his other composition. Entwistle had been drinking with the Rolling Stones' bass guitarist, Bill Wyman, and drummer, Charlie Watts, in the Scotch of St James one night. The drunker they became, the sillier the conversation turned, as the trio started thinking up names for different animals. Entwistle thought that Boris was a good name for a spider, a choice inspired by the horror-film actor Boris Karloff.

After hearing 'Whiskey Man' Townshend asked Entwistle if he'd written his second song yet. He hadn't, but lied and claimed that he had, saying it was called 'Boris the Spider', which he began improvising on the spot. The finished song's rubbery bass line evoked 'the black, hairy' arachnid of its lyrics, as well as childhood fairytales and the forbidden X-certificate horror films of Entwistle's Acton County schooldays. '"Boris the Spider" was the fastest song I ever wrote,' he said. Nonetheless, it marked the emergence of Entwistle as The Who's second songwriter. From here on, every Who album until 1982, barring *Quadrophenia*, would include at least one John Entwistle composition. 'The trouble was Pete had risen to the occasion first,' said Chris Stamp. 'So by the time John's songwriting was equal to Pete's, Pete was established as The Who's songwriter.'

Entwistle and Townshend both helped Keith Moon with his two compositions. 'Cobwebs and Strange' was, said Townshend, 'a rip-off' of a song called 'Eastern Journey' by the big-band drummer Tony Crombie. What The Who ended up with sounded like the Boys' Brigade on parade, albeit featuring a frantic solo from the company's drummer. Moon played a bass drum and cymbals, Townshend a banjo and penny whistle, Daltrey a trombone, and Entwistle the cornet and tuba. At one point, Junior Field Officer Lambert ordered them to march around the studio while they played. The whole song sounded as if it might collapse at any moment.

Moon's other contribution, 'I Need You', was more conventional. 'It's a musical illustration of a transport café,' he told *Beat Instrumental* at the time. 'If you listen to the whole thing you'll hear our transport café sound effects. We rustled bags of crisps and clinked teacups . . .' Breaking through its sing-song melody was the sound of Yorkshireman Neville Chesters mimicking a Liverpudlian accent (which led to press speculation that the song was poking fun at The Beatles).

What The Who created with 'Cobwebs and Strange' and the spoken-word segments of 'I Need You' was something unmistakably English. A quality only heightened by the fact that these songs featured on the finished album alongside Martha and the Vandellas' 'Heat Wave'. After spending three years immersed in American R&B and soul, The Who had started looking closer to home for inspiration. Much to Keith Moon's delight, the lugubrious comedian Max Wall had just compered the band's recent dates with The Merseys and Cream, and it was in Wall's customary home, the music hall, that The Who would find their new direction.

'Theatrical songwriting was always a part of my character,' said Townshend, 'because of my exposure to the Jewish music of the 1930s and 1940s in my upbringing with my father's music.' The Who weren't alone. The Kinks' recent hits, 'Sunny Afternoon' and 'Dead End Street', had incorporated elements of English music hall style, and The Beatles would do the same on the following year's *Sgt. Pepper's Lonely Hearts Club Band*. It was in the ether.

At IBC Studios the staff held fast to another very English tradition. IBC's disc-cutting engineer Brian Carroll oversaw several Who singles and albums from the mid-1960s until the early 1970s. 'It didn't matter what the bands were doing,' he says now. 'Every day, at 11 a.m. and 4 p.m. on the dot, the caretaker, Ernie Crimmins, would ring up each studio and say 'Tea's up', and wheel the trolley round. You'd then see The Who or the Bee Gees congregating outside waiting to be served. It didn't matter if you were in the middle of something important. Everything stopped for tea.'

On one occasion, when he wasn't dispensing hot beverages, Crimmins made an unfortunate discovery in IBC's Studio A: several hand-drawn penises on the sculptured cherubs surrounding the room's beautiful period fireplace. Much like the hoax fire at the Empire Pool, nobody could be certain that the guilty party was Keith Moon, but then again . . .

Despite The Merseys' misgivings about Lambert as a producer, The Who found themselves emboldened by his presence at IBC. 'Kit's greatest gift was to make us think that anything was possible,' said Townshend. It was Lambert's blind enthusiasm that enabled The Who to tackle Townshend's nine-minute-and-fourteen-second mini-opera. Instead of a meticulously crafted piece of music, *A Quick One, While He's Away* was cobbled together to fill a gap on the album. It contained six songs woven together to tell a story, in which a young girl is abandoned by her boyfriend and, while seeking comfort, encounters an old train driver, who promptly seduces her. The girl is later reconciled with her boyfriend, and confesses to what's she's done, asking for forgiveness.

A Quick One, While He's Away trialled some of the ideas The Who later used on *Tommy*, and three years later Townshend was describing it as '*Tommy*'s parents'. What's astonishing, though, is how much of it was inspired by its composer's childhood traumas, even though he never acknowledged it at the time. The opening section, 'Her Man's Gone', was, he said later, a flashback to when he was separated from his parents and sent to live with his grandmother. The second segment, 'The Crying Town', was the six-year-old Townshend weeping and wishing he was back with his family. Meanwhile, the story's predatory engine driver, Ivor, was an amalgam of the bus drivers Denny plied with cups of tea and chased for sex.

Townshend elaborated on the origins of this character in 2011, recalling a train journey from London to his grandmother's home in Westgate-on-Sea, during which the guard, in whose care he'd been placed, tried to molest him: 'I was about six, and he was trying to get into my pants. But I was an Acton boy and I knew what to do, which was to kick him in the balls. I ended up getting off at Westgate station and running into a policeman. And the man in the uniform said "this young child has abused *me*".'

He insisted, however, that he didn't make the connection when writing the piece. 'I was completely unaware of it at the time,' he told the author. 'At times I just thought *A Quick One . . .* was a silly story, but when I looked at it again I realised that it was a story many post-war kids share, of being sent away, of losing a precious loved one and being greatly changed when you returned.' The final movement, 'We Are Forgiven', acquired an added resonance when The Who played it live. Townshend sang the line over and over with increasing desperation, and, as he wrote in *Who I Am*, 'forgiving my mother, her lover, my grandmother, her lovers, and most of all myself'.

On one level, then, listening to *A Quick One, While He's Away* should have been a troubling experience. But until Townshend talked publicly about his unspecified childhood abuse, its meaning remained hidden by The Who's usual mordant humour and in-jokes. Impressed by The Beatles' use of a string octet on 'Eleanor Rigby', one of the standout songs on *Revolver*, Townshend wanted cellos on the track. 'But Kit Lambert said we couldn't afford cellos,' recalled Entwistle. 'So on the backing vocals, we sang "cello, cello, cello . . ." instead.' As when they later set some of *Tommy* in a holiday camp, this was The Who ensuring they didn't take themselves or their 'opera' too seriously.

In October, during a break from recording, The Who were given a sixteen-minute slot on *Ready Steady Go!*. Kit Lambert blustered away in the press about how The Who's performance would be comparable to the Theatre of the Absurd, the dark, satirical dramatic movement that included playwrights Jean Genet and Samuel Beckett. The Who's theatre of the absurd involved them miming to the theme tune from the TV show *Batman*, and John Entwistle smashing a bass filled with feathers and confetti for a finale of 'My Generation' and 'Rule Britannia'.

Three weeks later, they released an EP, *Ready Steady Who*. On one side was 'Circles' and a new Townshend song, 'Disguises'. On the other, their version of the *Batman* theme tune and covers of two of Keith Moon's favourite songs, Jan and Dean's 'Bucket T' and The Beach Boys' 'Barbara Ann', on which the drummer was allowed to sing lead vocals. 'Keith only seemed to like surf music,' said Townshend, 'so we did it to keep Keith happy. If you didn't keep Keith happy he would cause trouble.' If nothing else, then, *Ready Steady Who* captured the band's diversity. Onstage, The Who now played 'Batman', 'Heat Wave', the Everly Brothers' sweet-harmony pop song 'Man With Money', the transvestite anthem, 'I'm a Boy' *and* the death-wish rocker 'My Generation'. There wasn't another group around performing such an eclectic repertoire.

By December, it was as if The Who were making up for lost time, bombarding their audience with as much new music as they could record. The single, 'Happy Jack', emerged at the beginning of the month. The Who had hoped to play their first American dates that summer, but the trip had been postponed, meaning the single and the new album would be held over for a US release the following spring. The idea that 'Happy Jack' would be the single with which The Who would relaunch themselves in America now seems foolhardy. Its stuttering tempo and nursery-rhyme lyrics seemed completely divorced from the blues and couldn't have sounded more eccentric and English.

The song revisited a more innocent time in Townshend's youth, inspired, he said, by some of the characters he'd encountered during his father's annual season on the Isle of Man. Towards the end, Townshend could be heard shouting 'I saw ya!' – his outburst wasn't aimed at the mythical Jack, but at Keith Moon, who'd been banned from the studio while the others sang backing vocals, and who was now pulling faces at them in the control booth. The promo film to accompany the single had nothing to do with the Isle of Man and featured the band dressed up as burglars and trying to crack a safe before starting a food fight. Filmed in Robert Stigwood's office, The Who took great delight in redecorating the premises with cake.

Again, Daltrey struggled to find a suitable voice for a song which seemed closer to German oom-pah music than Howlin' Wolf, and which he'd later describe as 'bloody ridiculous'; but the audience warmed to it. The Who's strange, charming new single reached Number 3, and the new album, *A Quick One*, released the same day, hit Number 4. 'Gone is the breezy, slightly aggressively youthful sound of four young mods,' wrote Penny Valentine in *Disc and Music Echo*. 'This is a group with the most interesting LP ideas since The Beatles.' Soon after, Townshend ran into Paul McCartney in a nightclub: 'He was really raving over the album, and saying that track *A Quick One* . . . was exactly the sort of thing The Beatles were working towards.'

Viewed retrospectively then, *A Quick One* is a time capsule of 1966. The cover illustration, by the *Sunday Times Magazine*'s Alan Aldridge, wasn't so different from the image on the front of *Time*'s 'Swinging City' issue. Talking about the album in 1995, Chris Stamp enthused about Carnaby Street, the Ad-Lib, the fashion boutique Biba and his brother's girlfriend Jean Shrimpton, as if they were all inextricably linked to the music.

It's easy to see why the album's working title was 'Jigsaw Puzzle'. *A Quick One* is made up of often brilliant little pieces, but they don't always fit together: a raucous Motown cover to keep the Hundred Faces dancing, some slapstick nonsense for Moon's benefit, half a rock opera to satisfy Lambert . . . 'It was all a long way from the clumsy, ventrilo-quial mumbling of the early British rock 'n' roll idols,' wrote George Melly, recalling The Who in 1966. Most importantly, *A Quick One* empowered the band and, especially, Townshend, to think even bigger.

In a *Melody Maker*'s end-of-year poll, Barry Fantoni was voted Best Male TV Personality above Cliff Richard and Tom Jones ('Can you believe that?' says Fantoni now), and *A Whole Scene Going* the second-best TV show behind *Ready Steady Go!* Yet neither programme would be recommissioned; their time had passed. The mod culture with which *Ready Steady Go!* was so identified had peaked, and the pop-art-inspired set designs were looking passé. 'We've finished with pop art,' said Pete Townshend at the time. 'We've passed that stage where we used it as a great promotional idea. We don't need that now.'

The Who performed in the final episode of *Ready Steady Go!* and played a bullish version of Johnny Kidd and the Pirates' 'Please Don't Touch', a British rock 'n' roll song that had helped shape their sound. Next to *A Quick One, While He's Away*, it sounded like something from a bygone age; like being back in 1956 and hearing The Squadronaires' elegant big-band jazz drifting out of the Douglas Palace Ballroom after being blasted by 'Rock Around the Clock' in the cinema next door. The clothes, the music, the drugs and the audience were changing again. The question now, was whether The Who could keep up.

While they were finishing *A Quick One* at IBC Studios, the group had been introduced to Kit Lambert's new discovery, an unknown black American guitarist named Jimi Hendrix. With his unkempt hair and clothes, Hendrix looked, said Roger Daltrey, 'like a raving madman'. Hendrix spoke softly to Pete Townshend about guitars and amplifiers and then wandered out of the studio as quietly as he'd wandered in. What nobody in The Who realised at the time was that their territory had just been invaded.

CHAPTER EIGHT

A NECKLACE OF
HUMAN TEETH

'I was seeing what Adam had seen on the morning of his creation
– the miracle, moment by moment, of naked existence.'

Aldous Huxley describes his first LSD trip, 1954

'It was a paradoxical fact that the beautiful aspirations of the
hippies and the spiritual music that grew from them were in a
large part funded by criminal connections.'

Track Records' artist Arthur Brown, 2012

'The Who didn't really do peace and love.'

Roger Daltrey, 2008

As a ten-year-old, Pete Townshend often joined his parents and
The Squadronaires on Sunday nights at the Norwich Playhouse.
Performing on the same bill was the singer Frankie Vaughan, whose
big-band number 'Give Me the Moonlight, Give Me the Girl' was a hit
in 1955. Vaughan had been performing in variety shows since he was a
teenager and, at twenty-eight, was an experienced song-and-dance act.
He sang, he danced and he rarely stopped smiling.

'He was the original bump-and-grind man,' said Townshend, who
watched as Vaughan charmed his female audience with his smooth
patter and permanent grin. When Vaughan performed his biggest hit
he punctuated the lyric by kicking out his leg to a chorus of approving
screams. 'I remember saying to my friend Jimpy, "You've got to come

and see him,"' Townshend told the BBC. '"He does this thing where he kicks his leg and all the girls all go mad."'

Frankie Vaughan's 'Give Me the Moonlight, Give Me the Girl' and its high-kicking routine were guaranteed to get the girls swooning, until one night at the Norwich Playhouse in the early 1960s when it didn't. 'He did the kick, and there was absolute silence,' Townshend recalled. 'All the girls had their arms crossed.' Townshend approached the singer after the show and innocently asked him what had gone wrong. Vaughan dolefully explained that the girls sitting in silence were there to see Mark Wynter, a handsome pop singer fifteen years Vaughan's junior, and that the girls were his fanclub. 'That was when the era changed,' said Townshend. 'Suddenly the old music didn't work anymore.'

It was Pete Townshend's first taste of a fickle audience and the speed with which a singer could fall out of fashion. The Who in December 1966 were hardly Frankie Vaughan, and Jimi Hendrix wasn't Mark Wynter. But, despite their inauspicious first meeting at IBC Studios, Townshend had good reason to feel threatened.

Born Johnny Allen Hendrix in Seattle, Washington, twenty-four years earlier, Hendrix had left the US parachute regiments and become a musician for hire, working the chitlin' circuit, where black artists performed during the era of racial segregation. Hendrix had worked with the sibling soul group the Isley Brothers, Little Richard, he of the 'music to make your liver quiver and your bladder splatter', and husband-and-wife duo Ike and Tina Turner. He was leading his own ensemble, Jimmy James and the Blue Flames, when The Animals' bass guitarist Chas Chandler came across him in New York.

It was Keith Richards' girlfriend, former Ealing art college student and model Linda Keith, who'd tipped off Chandler about Hendrix. The Rolling Stones were on an American tour when Linda met Hendrix. Keith Richards was apparently so jealous that he contacted Linda's father to tell him his daughter was going off the rails. Hendrix hadn't even set foot in England but he was already unsettling the Ealing blues set.

The Animals' tour manager Terry McVay recalled his and Chandler's first sighting to Hendrix biographer John McDermott in 1992: 'This guy was playing the guitar backwards, upside down and making all these strange noises . . . Chas Chandler asked me, "What did you think?" I said,

"I haven't a clue what he's doing but I think it's great.'" After much nego-tiation, Chandler agreed to act as Hendrix's manager, brought him to London in September 1966, and began casting around for a backing group.

John Entwistle was approached for the bass player's job but turned it down out of loyalty to The Who. Instead, the role went to a twen-ty-two year-old guitarist named Noel Redding, who, after hearing Hendrix play, quickly agreed to switch to bass. The next recruit was drummer Mitch Mitchell, a one-time Marshall's music shop Saturday boy who'd auditioned for The Who after Doug Sandom's departure. The fact that Mitchell played around the beat, just like Keith Moon, but, unlike Moon, was a jazz-trained musician, were further thorns in The Who's side.

Calling themselves the Jimi Hendrix Experience, the trio played a series of warm-up gigs on the continent. But Hendrix couldn't stop himself turning up to show off and jam at various London clubs. Hendrix was part African-American, part Cherokee Native American and part Irish. As a black man with an untamed Afro hairstyle, buckskin suit and a guitar, which he played upside down on account of being left-handed, he was impossible to ignore. Crucially, he wasn't a white English ex-grammar schoolboy playing a white English ex-grammar schoolboy's interpretation of the blues.

Hendrix wasn't a purist; he was putting his own spin on the genre. He knew his Howlin' Wolf and his Robert Johnson, but his speed and fluidity, and his use of effects pedals and feedback was a challenge to Clapton, Jeff Beck and even Pete Townshend, who'd always distanced himself from his virtuoso peers. Hendrix was wilder and freer in his playing and more overtly sexual onstage. 'He made Jagger look like Shirley Temple,' wrote the *Observer*'s George Melly.

The Jimi Hendrix Experience were formally launched with a press reception and performance at the Bag O' Nails on 25 November. Like the Sex Pistols' notorious 100 Club gig ten years later, the list of people who claim to have seen Hendrix at the Bag O' Nails and elsewhere in London that winter grows with each passing year. It includes John Lennon, Paul McCartney, Mick Jagger, Jimmy Page, Brian Jones, Eric Clapton, Jeff Beck and one Farrokh Bulsara, another musically inclined Ealing art student who'd turn himself into Queen's lead singer Freddie Mercury five years later.

The gathered pop stars and pop-stars-in-waiting watched as Hendrix deconstructed Bob Dylan's 'Like a Rolling Stone', sending the music spinning off into different directions, and played the guitar behind his head, between his legs and with his teeth. Many of his fellow guitarists emerged from the Bag O' Nails wondering whether they'd just become obsolete. 'Hendrix is a one-man guitar explosion,' gushed *New Musical Express*.

As well as Hendrix's innate showmanship and musical ability, Townshend had another reason to feel intimidated. Kit Lambert and Chris Stamp were obsessed with Hendrix, and Stamp was soon calling him 'the black Bob Dylan'. Within weeks of Hendrix's arrival, the pair had persuaded Chas Chandler to sign him to their new label, Track Records. The inspirations for Track were Robert Stigwood's and Andrew Loog Oldham's independent labels, Reaction and Immediate. Just as Lambert and Stamp had talked their way into managing a band, they'd now talked their way into launching a record company.

Lambert later told journalists that he'd studied the way washing powder manufacturers marketed their products, based on the theory that a box of washing powder was roughly the same size as a box of records; comparing a musical group to a mundane household product was a very pop-art approach to business. Once he'd completed his research, Lambert announced his intentions to Polydor Records and the hustling began.

Polydor were an affiliate of the German classical label Deutsche Grammophon, whose roster included the easy-listening bandleaders James Last and Bert Kaempfert. These middle-aged men in pastel knit-wear sold millions of records, but not to teenagers. Polydor's new managing director, former EMI executive Roland Rennie, was given the task of dragging the company into the modern age.

Like the other major labels, Polydor were wary of independents that might weaken their hold on the industry. But Rennie had seen the powers-that-be at EMI struggle to keep pace with the market and was receptive to new ideas. Knowing this, Lambert and Stamp proposed that Polydor invest in and distribute Track Records, whose hip new artists would, in turn, bolster Polydor's credibility. Rennie was impressed by what he later called 'these two lunatics'. 'They wanted a label,' he said in 2011. 'Was it ego? I don't know, but it worked, and I didn't have anybody with their nous. They were there for the money but they knew all the angles.'

In fact, Polydor wanted Jimi Hendrix, but Lambert got there first. Kit said he sketched out the terms of a deal with Chas Chandler on the back of a drinks coaster at the Scotch of St James. What partly swung the deal in Track's favour was Lambert's promise of a £1,000 advance and an appearance on *Ready Steady Go!*. Hendrix made his UK TV debut on 16 December, two weeks before the show went off air.

The Experience's debut single was released on the same day as their *Ready Steady Go!* appearance, and was an electrified cover of 'Hey Joe', a folk song about a man who shoots his cheating girlfriend. Even Pete Townshend hadn't gone that far in a Who song. In the end, 'Hey Joe' was issued on Polydor, as the Track deal was still being finalised. But by landing Hendrix, Lambert had showed Polydor what he was capable of. In the late Chas Chandler's wonderful but possibly apocryphal account, Kit bribed Polydor's pressing plant operators into producing extra copies of the single rather than more of a rival act's new forty-five. 'Hey Joe' was selling well, but Lambert wanted to ensure there were enough copies in the shops to keep it selling. The single eventually peaked at Number 6, and its success convinced Roland Rennie to commit to the new label. From now on, the Jimi Hendrix Experience would be a Track Records act.

The Who's records would also now be released on Track, on the understanding that the group would share in the label's success and profits, and that its members would act as talent scouts. The problem was: The Who's managers had now become The Who's record company, which could and would lead to a conflict of interest. Moreover, Stamp and Lambert had just scored a hit single with a new artist every bit as outrageous as The Who. Any band in The Who's position would have felt threatened, even more so considering they'd spent most of the past six months trying not to split up.

On 21 December, The Who played the opening night of boxer Billy Walker's east London nightclub, the Upper Cut. As soon as the gig was over, Townshend, Entwistle and Daltrey raced into London to catch the Jimi Hendrix Experience at Blaises. Eric Clapton had been upset to see Hendrix using what he believed was his trademark, a wah-wah pedal. 'If I'd started using a wah-wah pedal Eric would never have spoken to me again,' said Townshend. But as an outsider Hendrix was oblivious to this code of honour. Outside Blaises, Jeff Beck warned Townshend that he'd just seen Hendrix performing Pete's stage trick and ramming his guitar against his amp. 'But when he started to play, something changed,' admitted Townshend. 'Colours changed, everything changed.'

At the time, though, the admiration was still tempered by jealousy. John Challis was using Townshend's Wardour Street home studio to record a soundtrack for a college graduation film – 'about bikers who go ice skating at Alexandra Palace' – and had enlisted Townshend to play bass and drums. One day, John arrived at the flat to be told that Pete hadn't returned from the night before. When Townshend did appear, Challis could tell something was amiss: 'Pete looked a bit distraught. He said, "I went out last night and heard this guitar player who was just too fucking good. He shouldn't be allowed."'

A month later, Brian Epstein and Robert Stigwood hired Covent Garden's Saville Theatre for a series of Sunday night gigs. The Who were booked to headline with Hendrix in support. 'Kit had just signed Jimi to Track and put him on backing us up,' said Townshend. 'I couldn't really believe it. I thought, "Jesus Christ, what's going to happen?"'

The Who watched as the Hendrix trio powered through a forty-five-minute set that included a loose and thunderous version of The Troggs' hit single 'Wild Thing'. Towards the end of the show, Hendrix thrust his Fender Stratocaster against his Marshall amp. The guitar howled, the audience roared. John Lennon, Paul McCartney and Cream witnessed it all from the VIP seats. 'Hendrix took all my ideas and flung them back at me with knobs on,' said Townshend.

Brian Epstein threw an after-show party, but the mood among some of his guests was subdued. When Chris Stamp spotted the three members of Cream gathered in a huddle, whispering about what they'd just seen, he couldn't resist a joke. 'Don't worry boys!' he supposedly shouted, 'there will always be work for good white guitarists!'

The demise of *Ready Steady Go!* and the rise of Hendrix were sobering reminders of how a slower-moving pop group could easily become tomorrow's Frankie Vaughan. The Who were changing, but into what? Nobody, including the band, was sure. 'A lot of our contemporaries had something we didn't have – a continuity, an identity,' said Townshend. 'They seemed to know who they were, whereas The Who were a band that were trying to find themselves, partly because what had united us was a lack of identity. We'd invested a sense of identity in the audience, but the audience was changing.'

'The Who were in a void,' confirms fan Max Ker-Seymer. 'I'd gone to the Windsor festival in the summer of 1966 and it was all Cream, Cream, Cream. Then suddenly Jimi Hendrix was around. When The Who were an R&B band they were great, but they hadn't gone anywhere, they seemed to be losing their edge. Now everyone was talking about psychedelia.'

'Psychedelia', the new buzzword, had first been used in the late 1950s by the psychiatrist Humphry Osmond, who'd researched the use of mind-altering drugs as a treatment for schizophrenia. Osmond had coined the term from two Greek words, broadly translated as 'psyche', meaning 'mind' and 'delos' meaning 'clear' or 'manifest'.

By late 1966, the term was being used to describe pop music that evoked a mind-altering state, specifically that triggered by the use of the hallucinogenic LSD. Lysergic acid diethylamide (nicknamed 'acid') had been created in 1938. Swiss chemist Albert Hofmann was working for Sandoz Pharmaceuticals in Berne, and trying to create a product to treat respiratory and circulation problems. During his research, he synthesised a new compound from ergotamine, a chemical derived from a fungus found on rye.

After Hofmann synthesised the drug for a second time he accidentally absorbed some through his skin. 'At home I lay down and sank into a not unpleasant intoxicated-like condition, characterised by an extremely stimulated imagination,' he wrote. 'In a dreamlike state, with eyes closed, I perceived an uninterrupted stream of fantastic pictures, extraordinary shapes with an intense, kaleidoscopic change of colours.' Hofmann had experienced the first LSD 'trip'.

In 1947, Sandoz began manufacturing LSD as a drug for treating psychiatric patients. Meanwhile, in America, the CIA initiated a research programme, and began administering LSD to military personnel and prisoners in the hope that it could be used as a truth serum or as a chemical weapon. Even an infinitesimal amount administered orally or absorbed through the skin had a profound effect. The morning after taking his second trip, Hofmann felt as if he was looking at 'a world that was newly created'. Inevitably, LSD's ability to 'open' the mind, to help attain a state of higher consciousness and alter the way in which the user viewed the world, inspired many to use the drug recreationally.

In 1960, the American psychology lecturer Timothy Leary set up a programme at Harvard University to analyse the effect of hallucinogens. Michael Hollingshead, an Englishman working for the Institute of British-American Cultural Exchange, introduced Leary to LSD a year later. Leary believed he'd had a spiritual reawakening and described LSD as 'the centre of life'. Hollingshead returned to Britain in the summer of 1965 on a mission to preach what he called 'the psychedelic gospel'.

With the help of some rich bohemian friends, Hollingshead established the World Psychedelic Centre in London at a flat in Pont Street, Mayfair. Its manifesto was 'spiritual and emotional development through the use of LSD'. Hollingshead, like Leary, was convinced that the drug would revolutionise the world. Over the next few months, numerous actors, poets and writers arrived at Pont Street to experiment with LSD in a controlled environment.

The Mayfair flat's living-room floor was scattered with pillows, there was incense burning, gentle music playing and a slide projector showing soothing images on the wall. Hollingshead, in his role as psychedelic high priest, dispensed the sacrament, read from *The Tibetan Book of the Dead* (the Buddhist text regarded as the LSD users' manual), and assisted his guests on their voyage of discovery. His usual clientele were soon joined by the likes of Eric Clapton, Donovan, Paul McCartney and art dealer Robert Fraser. Some came to take LSD; others simply to observe.

LSD infiltrated the music industry throughout 1965 and 1966. John Lennon and George Harrison were introduced to the drug by their dentist, who dosed their coffee at a dinner party without telling them first. The pair spent a disorientating night in London, where they imagined that the Ad-Lib club was on fire and that Harrison's house had turned into a submarine. Lennon reported feeling 'stunned for a month or two' afterwards, but was soon taking acid regularly.

If mod music and fashions had been about neat, clean lines, then psychedelia saw those lines becoming multicoloured, blurred and wavy. LSD's shimmering after-effects could be heard in much of the music The Beatles made from *Rubber Soul* onwards. It was the difference between 'Can't Buy Me Love' and 'She Said She Said', a piece they'd composed after a particularly intense acid trip in the summer of 1965.

The Animals' lead singer Eric Burdon was typical of the LSD evangelists now preaching to the pop community. This tough Geordie rhythm-and-blues fan took a trip and became an instant convert: 'I talked with Buddha. I saw the crucifixion of Christ. I talked with God. I saw myself at the age of a hundred and three.' Burdon felt as if he'd been handed the secret of life. He wasn't alone. 'After acid, you walked around bulging with new perceptions,' wrote The Who's friend and journalist Nik Cohn. 'You thought you'd been someplace nobody else had ever seen.'

In typical Who fashion, though, the group contained conflicting views about the drug. While some users treated LSD with great reverence, others, including Keith Moon, did not. When Moon arrived to collect Kim and their newborn daughter from hospital, he'd been coming down from an acid trip and had no idea who his wife was. The drummer's quest for oblivion outweighed any desire for a spiritual reawakening. He took LSD for the same reason he took pills or drank to excess: to obliterate himself.

Although Entwistle often joined Moon on his quest for annihilation, LSD wasn't to his liking. Daltrey, meanwhile, regarded it as another dangerous distraction for bandmates who were already dangerously distracted. Daltrey wanted to remain in control, and LSD involved letting go. 'Acid never interested me,' he told the author. 'I let the others do it, and I was the escort. I was the one that had to shepherd them about.'

Pete Townshend, meanwhile, was soon fascinated by the drug, and particularly its effect on music. Hendrix's flamboyant guitar playing and peacock image were colourful and psychedelic. But Hendrix's music was still grounded in the blues. New groups were emerging, however, that made music that had little to do with Howlin' Wolf, and everything to do with LSD. Townshend was intrigued by what he was hearing.

Among these groups was the Pink Floyd, whose vocalist and guitarist Syd Barrett and bass guitarist Roger Waters had grown up in Cambridge, but were now living in London. The Pink Floyd's entourage included a number of other Cambridge émigrés, some of whom had taken over a spacious flat at 101 Cromwell Road, South Kensington.

Before long, 101 was rivalling Hollingshead's Pont Street apartment as a rendezvous for the bohemian set. Mick Jagger and Marianne Faithful were among the pop stars who visited the dark womb-like flat where phials of LSD were kept in the refrigerator and droplets dispensed on the tongue from a pipette.

Syd Barrett was now taking LSD regularly, often at Cromwell Road, and the Pink Floyd gradually swapped their repertoire of blues covers for elongated jams, including their signature song, a rambling instrumental entitled 'Interstellar Overdrive'. Although these lengthy improvisations reflected the distortion of time experienced during an acid trip, there was another, more prosaic, reason: most of the Pink Floyd were rudimentary musicians and Barrett knew he would never play guitar like Eric Clapton. Instead, he took his inspiration from The Who. 'It was the noises that Pete Townshend was making – squeaks and feedback – that influenced Syd,' said Roger Waters. 'So we started making strange noises instead of the blues.'

The Who and the Pink Floyd's worlds intersected on New Year's Eve 1966 when both groups played Psychedelicamania, a 'Giant Freak-Out All-Night Rave' at the Roundhouse in Camden, north London. Artist and former Ealing lecturer Gustav Metzger also appeared on the bill, demonstrating light projections, where heat-sensitive liquid crystals were placed between glass slides inside a projector, to provide a visual accompaniment to the music. Although Townshend smashed his guitar at the end of the show, he did so despite feeling, in his words, 'quite loved-up'.

The reason was that he'd taken LSD earlier with artist Michael English and walked the five miles from English's house in Notting Hill to Camden. Unlike Eric Burdon, he didn't talk to God or Buddha or see Jesus Christ. Instead, as he wrote later, 'I rediscovered everything I took for granted – stars, moons trees, colours, London buses.'

Townshend believed he knew why the drug was so popular with musicians. 'It makes you part of the audience,' he told *International Times*, a newspaper dedicated to covering the emergent counter-culture. 'You take it, you sit back and there's no work, and off you go. It's twenty-four hours of touring.'

Before long, London's LSD set were gravitating towards a fashionable new club, UFO, which had been set up partly to fund *International*

Times. Its founders were John 'Hoppy' Hopkins, a Cambridge-educated physicist who'd discovered sex, drugs, jazz and politics, and was now an arbiter of London's underground scene, and Joe Boyd, a Harvard-educated American who'd moved to London to set up a wing of Elektra Records.

UFO had developed out of a series of 'happenings' held in London venues throughout 1966, where the Pink Floyd and their friendly rivals, the Soft Machine, played their non-blues on the same bill as poets, jugglers, performance artists and Gustav Metzger. By January 1967, UFO had become a Friday night fixture at an Irish dance hall beneath the Gala Berkeley cinema on Tottenham Court Road. 'There was nowhere more alternative, counter-culture or psychedelic in the UK than the London UFO club,' recalls Richard Barnes. 'On an average night about twenty per cent of the audience would be on LSD trips.'

UFO soon became a place where musicians, writers, artists and hip pop fans could take hallucinogenic drugs, dance wildly or lie on the edge of the dance floor observing the liquid light show, as the LSD took effect and the world became warm and fuzzy. 'The first thing that hit me on arrival was the smell of incense, with trippy lights shining on the stairs,' recalls DJ, promoter and former mod Jeff Dexter. 'Inside you could hardly make out any detail, the place was bathed in moving coloured light and all the faces seemed to melt into one.'

In between the bands, the DJs played a mix of sounds and music. 'Anything from Bach to The Beatles, or the Mothers of Invention to The Mar-Keys,' says Dexter. But the lighting gantry at the far end of the club also projected Chinese animations and art-house films such as Bunuel's *Un Chien Andalou* on to the walls.

Townshend paid UFO a visit and was very impressed. A year earlier The Who had played Leicester Art College, where student Richard Stanley had projected his home-made films on to the band while they performed. UFO's organisers and clientele were bubbling over with ideas and had created a multi-sensory experience. 'There seemed to be no separation between the music and the audience,' says Dexter. 'The bands, audience or dancers had all become part of a people show, melting into one swirling kinetic mass.' In some ways, it was an extension of the ideas espoused on Roy Ascott's groundcourse; a fuller realisation of what Townshend had hoped to achieve with The Who.

One night, Townshend ducked out of playing a gig in Morecambe, Lancashire, after taking acid, and went with Karen Astley to see the Pink Floyd at UFO. Karen and a couple of friends, including Michael English's girlfriend Angela Brown, had formed their own company, Hem and Fringe, and were designing clothes for the new 'hippie' fashion boutiques such as Hung on You and Granny Takes a Trip, which were now filling the spaces where the mod shops had once traded.

Karen arrived at UFO in one of her own creations, a dress that Townshend said 'looked as if it had been made from a cake wrapper . . . and no knickers and no bra'. The couple soon found themselves surrounded by incredulous mods who'd come to the club to stare at the audience: 'They were going up to her and literally touching her up while she was dancing and she didn't know they were doing it,' recalled Townshend. 'I was just totally lost.'

Onstage, the liquid lightshow created distorted images as the Pink Floyd produced their Who-influenced squeaks and feedback. Townshend's paranoia worsened, and he was now convinced that Roger Waters was going to run off with Karen, 'whom he openly fancied'. Joe Boyd later wrote in his 2007 memoir, *White Bicycle: Making Music in the 1960s* of seeing The Who's guitarist crouched beside the stage, telling everybody that he was terrified Waters was 'going to swallow him'. For Townshend, it was an early indication of the pitfalls of this new so-called wonder drug.

The mods that surrounded Townshend and his girlfriend that night were a flashback to what was now becoming The Who's past. Just months earlier, the group had been given an armed escort out of the Goldhawk, after watching as a member of the audience was beaten senseless. There were no fights, bloodshed or sawn-off shotguns at UFO. It was a contrast that The Who's devoted fan, 'Irish' Jack, became aware of when he turned up at the club one night.

By the spring of 1967, all the old mod venues were closing down, and Jack felt lost. Walking into UFO, he was shocked to see his old hero wearing a woolly Afghan coat and a necklace. Townshend was just as surprised at what his number-one fan was wearing: 'He said, "Jack, You're still a mod."' Jack suggested they go to the pub across the road but Townshend refused. Instead, he stayed by the club's macrobiotic food stall, watching Karen serving soft drinks to tripping customers.

'The mods seemed like these little grey figures lost in this world of colour and Pink Floyd and inventive music,' said Townshend.

After another heady Friday night, Townshend and a group of friends, including UFO's macrobiotic stallholder Craig Sams, were walking through Victoria when a car pulled up alongside them. A head emerged through the open window and a voice rang out: 'Hi! Pete Townshend, I think your last album was fucking great!' No sooner were the words out, when the fan vomited copiously down the side of the car. As Sams told *Days in the Life* author Jonathon Green: 'Suddenly, you realised the huge distance between where we were going, into spiritual realms, and fifteen pints of lager, which is where a lot of the mods had gone.'

Townshend was aware of the distance, but wasn't wholly convinced that drugs would lead him to any such spiritual realm. 'I remember thinking, this is not going to do it for me,' he said. 'The mods are not going to do it for me, drugs are not going do it for me, I need something else.' Townshend would discover that something else through one of his UFO connections, just not yet.

The man who would help guide Townshend towards what he was looking for was Mike McInnerney, then working as an art editor at *International Times*. McInnerney and Michael English also designed posters for UFO and other underground happenings. English would go on to form Hapshash and the Coloured Coat, a design partnership with Nigel Waymouth, co-owner of the hippie fashion emporium Granny Takes a Trip. Between the three of them, their work would become a visual shorthand for the UK psychedelic era.

Before long, Karen Astley's image was being used on a poster for UFO, and she and Townshend had become close friends with Mike McInnerney and his girlfriend, Kate Lambert. Over the next few months, Townshend would spend many evenings with the UFO and IT crowd, often at Karen's basement flat in Ebury Street or McInnerney's apartment above the Shaftesbury Theatre in London's West End. 'It's hard to overstate how important people's flats were back then,' says Mike McInnerney now, 'because they were secure zones where you could take drugs. We found ourselves going round to each other's places all the time. They were little havens.'

An elite social set was forming, one marked by a suspicion of those who didn't use narcotics. 'It was Michael English who coined the phrase "the greys" for those who weren't doing it,' says McInnerney. 'It was an awful term, so divisive, so tribal. But I suppose it was a natural outcome of the things that made up the scene – all these people going round to each other's flats and spending so much time taking drugs together.'

This need for a safe haven was understandable. In April 1966, the World Psychedelic Centre closed after the police found heroin on the premises. In the same month, the Pink Floyd's roadie Russell Page and a New Zealand film-maker and 101 Cromwell Road resident John Esam stood trial at the Old Bailey for possession of LSD. It was a landmark case, as the drug was still legal. Instead, the prosecution argued that ergotamine was outlawed under the British Poisons act, and that the pair should be tried for dealing a poisonous substance. After a lengthy trial, in which Albert Hofmann was called as a witness, the case was dismissed.

Scare stories about LSD were now regularly appearing in the tabloid press. The *Daily Mirror* warned that Britain could soon follow America, a nation where, it said, 'a third of all college students were experimenting with LSD', and cited the case of two students found eating tree bark while under its influence. In the spring of 1966, Home Secretary Roy Jenkins announced that possession of LSD without a medical prescription would shortly be made illegal.

Proof that LSD was no longer a secret between pop stars came with the Christmas 1966 issue of *Private Eye*. The magazine included a free comedy record, 'Psychedelic Baby', in which the singer, Whispering Jim Narg, urged the listener to 'dip your lump of sugar in the LSD' and 'suck the blotting paper'. It was common practice to take LSD on a lump of sugar or blotting paper, and 'Whispering Jim' was Peter Cook's comedy partner Dudley Moore, an acquaintance of the same dentist that had turned John Lennon and George Harrison on to acid.

Stories about pop stars taking drugs were pursued and peddled with gusto by the press. The *News of the World* weighed in with an exposé of a party thrown by the Moody Blues at their communal house near Richmond Park. Pete Townshend and Cream's Ginger Baker were named as LSD users. As Townshend had admitted to taking drugs on *A Whole Scene Going*, this was hardly a revelation.

In their quest for more salacious gossip, however, the newspaper sent an undercover journalist to Blaises, where he gleaned some admission of drug taking from the Rolling Stones' Brian Jones. Unfortunately, the quote was credited to Mick Jagger, who was in Italy at the time. Although the paper acknowledged their mistake, Jagger's announcement that he was going to sue the *News of the World* made them all the more determined than ever to bring him down.

On Sunday 19 February 1967, the *News of the World* had their revenge. Acting on a tip-off from the paper, the police raided Keith Richards' country house, Redlands, in West Wittering, Sussex. Richards and his guests, including Jagger, Marianne Faithfull and Robert Fraser, had all taken LSD. When Richards heard a knock on the door and peered through the window to investigate he was convinced there was 'a whole lot of dwarves outside wearing the same clothes'.

To the visiting constabulary, the scene at Redlands must have seemed impossibly exotic. There was Marianne draped over Jagger on a couch and naked except for a fur rug; Robert Fraser's gallery assistant Christopher Gibbs floating around, wearing a pair of Eastern silk pyjamas, and Fraser's manservant Mohammed, clad in a traditional Moroccan *djellaba*, serving tea. There was loud music playing, and the smell of dope and incense lingered in the air.

The police searched the house and catalogued anything they considered suspicious. While this included some illegal substances, it also extended to Chinese joss sticks, Earl Grey tea leaves and sachets of shampoo that Richards had collected from American hotels. The policemen had never seen products packaged like this in Britain, and tore the sachets in the hope that they might contain drugs.

The raid failed to produce the bountiful haul the *News of the World* had hoped for, but, according to the police they had enough to make arrests. Richards was charged for allowing cannabis to be smoked on his property, Jagger for possession of amphetamine tablets legally purchased in Italy, and Fraser for amphetamines and heroin. One of the other guests, a mysterious American nicknamed 'the Acid King', who'd been supplying several pop stars with LSD, was found with a few grains of cannabis resin. Oddly, his attaché case containing LSD, cocaine and dope was never searched by the police, and he left the country soon after.

Shortly before the 'dwarves' came knocking, Keith Richards' hi-fi had been blasting out Bob Dylan's *Blonde on Blonde* and The Who's *A Quick One* LPs. With the whole of what Townshend called 'the artistic elite' now in the firing line, what better time, then, for The Who to leave the country.

On 22 March, The Who arrived in New York to play their first American concerts. 'Happy Jack' was about to be released in the US, and Chris Stamp had convinced Decca that the trip was vital to its promotion. The Who had just signed a three-year deal with a new UK agent, Kennedy Enterprises, who, in turn, had negotiated a deal for The Who in the US with Premier Talent, whose young booker Frank Barsalona had worked on The Beatles and the Stones' first American dates.

The Who had another good reason for leaving the UK. Track Records had just released their debut single: 'Purple Haze', by the Jimi Hendrix Experience. It was a great swirling psychedelic pop song and would soon become a top-five hit. But Hendrix hadn't broken America. Not yet. The Who saw their chance. 'America was musically naive,' said Roger Daltrey. 'It was like this ripe field ready for ploughing'

Townshend had been to New York twice to see Allen Klein. But for his bandmates, this was a world that only existed in films. Once they arrived in the bustling city, with its yellow cabs and skyscrapers, an awestruck Moon and Entwistle behaved as if their childhood selves had stepped through the screens at the Wembley Regal or Acton Gaumont cinemas and on to the set of a movie.

Chris Stamp had booked The Who into the upmarket Drake Hotel on Park Avenue, but quickly regretted his decision. After hitting the local clubs, Moon and Entwistle returned to the Drake with an entourage of hangers-on only too happy to order lobster, oysters and champagne on The Who's tab. In the space of four days, the pair helped run up a $4,000 room-service bill. Stamp intervened and moved the party to the less expensive Gorham Hotel, where Moon, apparently, smashed up his suite.

The Who were booked to play nine shows at the RKO 58th Street Theater, as part of the 'Music in the Fifth Dimension' season. The event was hosted by Murray 'The K' Kaufman, a New York DJ, who billed himself as 'the Fifth Beatle' and had the wig to prove it. Robert Stigwood agreed to let Kaufman have The Who and Cream for a cut price of $7,500. Townshend turned up at a press launch for the event wearing a jacket decorated with flashing light bulbs, and drolly told reporters that it was psychedelic and 'meant to blow your mind'. Townshend agreed to scores of interviews, where he repeatedly explained that The Who had come to America to 'leave a wound'.

At some point during the trip, Townshend agreed to record a radio recruitment ad for the US Air Force, with 'Happy Jack' as its soundtrack ('You too can fly the skies, reach for the moon and touch the stars in the United States Air Force . . .'). It was an extraordinarily misguided idea. 'Young Americans were being blown to bits in Vietnam and I, a naive English twit, came prancing over,' he admitted. 'And I really didn't give a fuck about what was happening to the American young men. I really didn't.'

The Who made their violent intentions known at the first rehearsal in New York. At home, they'd been trying to phase out their destructive stage act, but they knew it would help them to stand out in America. 'The Who came out and looked incredible,' recalled Track Records' publicist Nancy Lewis. 'Townshend had on his Union Jack coat, and they just did a twenty-minute set, and at the end destroyed all their instruments and blew up smoke bombs. It absolutely freaked people out.' Backstage, The Who were told that their designated four-song set had just been cut to two. 'One and a half minutes of "My Generation", one and a half of "Substitute",' said Keith Moon. 'Then smash your fucking instruments – and off.'

Despite the hip-sounding name, Music in the Fifth Dimension was a traditional variety show. The rest of the line-up included 'In the Midnight Hour' singer Wilson Pickett, the vocal harmony quartet the Young Rascals, a fashion show presided over by Kaufman's wife, and a comedy trio, the Hardly Worth-It Players, whose shtick included Bob Dylan and Beatles impressions.

The show started at 10 a.m.. Each act performed their routine, returned to the dressing room and waited until it was time to come out again, repeating the act as many as five times until late evening. It was conveyor-belt entertainment. Schools were closed for the spring vacation, and gangs of thirteen and fourteen year olds were free to hang around the theatre until they grew bored of the music, the jokes or Murray Kaufman's deathless patter.

Each day, The Who would appear onstage for a few frantic minutes, create mayhem, disappear and then do it all over again. 'Bobby Pridden was backstage permanently gluing guitars together,' recalled Daltrey. But it worked. Mrs Kaufman's fashion parade and even Cream's virtuoso hard pop couldn't compete with Townshend throwing his Fender Stratocaster into the air and watching it smash on the ground, or Moon sending his bass drum barrelling across the stage, to a soundtrack of screaming amplifiers and exploding smoke bombs. After a while, the audience started arriving when the theatre doors opened, and staying for the rest of the day. 'They stayed because they liked the music they were hearing,' said Townshend. 'And they wanted to hear it again and again.'

Naturally, The Who didn't go unnoticed by the other acts on the bill. Heather Taylor was a six-foot redheaded fashion model, who had grown up in Hammersmith before moving with her family to America. Heather was appearing in Kaufman's wife's fashion show, when she was introduced to the visiting Brits. Heather already knew several pop musicians, including The Monkees' Davy Jones, Jeff Beck and Jimi Hendrix, and had soon caught Daltrey's eye. The pair would meet up again in London, and begin a relationship that would eventually lead to marriage.

As the days wore on and the boredom set in, The Who's appetite for mischief increased. Murray The K's self-importance and ridiculous Beatle wig did not go unnoticed. When Kaufman told the band never to touch his personal microphone, Daltrey's eyes lit up. By the end of the run, the singer had smashed eighteen microphones after bouncing them off the stage, the amps and Moon's cymbals. For the final show, Cream and The Who planned to have an egg-and-flour fight onstage, but Kaufman heard about the plot and threatened not to pay them. Instead, a food battle ensued in the dressing room, which promptly flooded after Townshend left the shower running.

However, all that violence in front of impressionable teenagers paid off. The Who's 'Happy Jack' single reached Number 24, their highest placing in America yet. The album *A Quick One*, retitled *Happy Jack* and with the single in place of 'Heat Wave', received a belated American release and made it to Number 67. The Who had dealt a wound, albeit a minor one.

Back in England, the band grabbed a couple of days' precious recording time in London's Ryemuse Studios. Townshend was already telling journalists about his planned 'rock opera'. Now that Hendrix had stolen his stage act and the Pink Floyd were creating a new kind of pop music, he needed to think big. '[The opera] takes place in the year 1999, when China is about to take over the world,' declared Townshend in January 1967. 'The hero loses his wife and decides to go and live in this tiny country, which is about to be overrun by Chinese. The hero goes through hundreds of situations and there is music for each.'

Townshend's operatic ambitions would soon be put on hold, though. Less than a week after returning from America, The Who set off on a twelve-date German tour. Their support act was Simon Napier-Bell's protégés, an arty mod-pop group called John's Children. The group's new lead singer Mark Feld was the outspoken young mod who had featured in 1962's *Town* magazine article. Since then, Feld had remodelled himself as a Dylan-style folk singer and changed his name to Marc Bolan. Napier-Bell sensed that 'the little elvin vampire' had something, but wasn't sure what it was. While trying to work it out, he suggested Bolan join John's Children, who'd just sacked their guitarist and been dropped by Columbia Records.

Inevitably, The Who's success had led to imitators. After losing The Who, Shel Talmy had found the similarly agitated sounding The Creation, whose recent B-side, 'Biff Bang Pow', had a pop-art title and a riff similar to 'My Generation'. John's Children were also inspired by The Who, as was Bolan, whom Townshend had previously mistaken for a rent boy at the Scene.

Columbia objected to John's Children's wanting to call their next single, 'Not the Sort of Girl (You'd Like to Take to Bed)', but Kit Lambert didn't, and thought they'd be perfect for Track Records. Although thrilled at being asked to join the tour, the band and Simon Napier-Bell knew that they needed to upstage the headliners. The two groups and their similarly attention-seeking managers would prove a volatile combination.

At Townshend's suggestion, Lambert had invited film student Richard Stanley and Stanley's art school friend, photographer Chris Morphet, to join the tour. Morphet's group, The Contacts, had once shared the bill with The Who in Leicester. Morphet and Stanley were now studying at the Royal College of Art, and were hired by Lambert to shoot a promotional film and take pictures of the tour. 'In theory, we were being paid,' says Morphet now. 'But things were so much more casual back then.' Richard Stanley still has a letter from Lambert, 'Half a page of scribble promising us £10 a day out of which we will pay our own hotel bill.' But it was the thrill of touring with The Who, not the money, that ensured they were on the first plane to Germany.

The first date was at Nuremberg's Meistersingerhalle, a concert venue razed to the ground by the RAF during the Second World War, but since rebuilt and now being used by the local symphony orchestra. None of this mattered to Simon Napier-Bell, who persuaded John's Children to smash a chair during their set. This simple act of destruction provoked a domino effect, and the audience were soon recreating the RAF's devastation and destroying the concert hall's seating.

After the show, the German promoter demanded that Lambert pay for the damages, but he flatly refused. Instead, Lambert put on his best upper-class accent and dismissed the man as an 'inefficient little hun'. When the promoter followed Kit into the street and carried on berating him, Lambert seized his briefcase, which promptly flew open sending two hundred thousand Deutschmarks, The Who's fee, fluttering into the air.

Napier-Bell could only admire Lambert's nerve as he ignored the cash floating away and marched off into the nearest bar, with the promoter close to tears behind him. Once inside, Kit insisted that he pay The Who their fee in full, regardless of the damages to the venue or the fact that Lambert had just lost most of their money in the street. Napier-Bell recounted the incident in his 1983 memoir, *You Don't Have to Say You Love Me*: 'Kit seemed completely unaware that he was himself in any way responsible for the promoter's behaviour.' Astonishingly, he returned the next morning with The Who's fee in full.

Two days later, John's Children went one better than a broken chair and slashed open several hotel pillows onstage, covering the Herford Jaguar Club with duck feathers. They followed this by smashing up their drum kit, attacking each other and jumping into the audience. It was staged violence guaranteed to get a reaction, but The Who were unimpressed and told Lambert to throw the group off the tour. Kit refused, knowing his own group would have behaved the same way if they'd been the support act.

'The only members of The Who with a true sense of humour were

John and Keith,' said former John's Children vocalist Andy Ellison. 'And Roger really didn't like us at all.' As such, the mood in The Who camp became extremely tense, even by their usual tense standards. When a mob of youths swarmed around The Who's car outside a venue in Düsseldorf, Roger Daltrey cracked. 'It all got very nasty,' he told the author in 2008. 'Keith Moon went to get out of the car and this bloke booted the door. I got out and did four of them.' Despite Daltrey's beating, the youths later invaded the stage as The Who played. Roger squared up to them, again, and Keith hit one of his assailants over the head with a cymbal.

Lambert's way of coping with the stress of the tour was to take drugs and have sex, ideally at the same time and as often as possible. Kit was now fond of reminding his charges that their excessive behaviour was nothing new. 'He was always saying to us, "You fucking rock 'n' roll people think you've done all this first,"' Townshend recalled. Thereafter Lambert would gleefully regale them with stories of how Constant's classical music peers used heroin and cocaine, and how he'd once caught his father having sex with Margot Fonteyn in a lift at the back of a theatre.

In Düsseldorf, Lambert struck gold and found a gay brothel in which he could acquire pills – and narrowly escaped a beating after making a quick getaway without paying for his boy or his drugs. But Kit couldn't blot out his problems forever. In Ludwigshafen, the crowd rioted after John's Children's stage act. Lambert now had no choice but to do as The Who asked, and John's Children were sent home. In a letter to his girlfriend, Marc Bolan described the headliners as 'a drag' and claimed his group were out-playing them every night.

For Richard Stanley and Chris Morphet, the German tour was an eye-opening experience. Once again, Stanley became aware of Townshend's 'absolute curiosity' about the world. 'Early on in the tour Pete told us this story that he'd been put under hypnosis by a society dentist,' he says. 'This meant that he'd been programmed to always give the very best performance ever, no matter what happened. And Pete said he always felt that he had never been taken out of this hypnosis, and that he'd been given a trigger, which would always work, presumably a guitar.'

Stanley laughs at the story now and suggests that Townshend's imagination was getting the better of him. But in an Indian restaurant in Ludwigshafen, he and Chris Morphet listened spellbound as the guitarist discussed his recent LSD experiences. 'Pete was saying how it had been for him "really really really big!" That was his exact description,' says Stanley. 'He was trying to describe the visual effect of being on the drug, and this Indian restaurant had flock wallpaper, that had that typical three-dimensional effect, and that was something he used to describe it. What the Germans sat near us must have thought I have no idea, but Chris and I were gobsmacked.'

Despite Townshend's profound LSD experience and talk of futuristic rock operas, The Who's next single, was a consummate but simple pop song. 'Pictures of Lily', The Who's first Track Records release, appeared in April, and was, said John Entwistle, 'a song about wanking'. 'It's all about a boy who can't sleep so his dad gives him some dirty pictures to look at,' explained Townshend. 'Then he falls in love with the girl in the pictures, which is too bad, because she's dead.' Later, he said that the inspiration came from pictures of Edward VII's mistress, the popular First World War pin-up Lillie Langtry, which he'd seen pinned to the wall in Karen Astley's bedroom.

The Who had recorded and mixed the song between Ryemuse, Pye and IBC Studios before going to Germany. At IBC, Brian Carroll witnessed Kit Lambert's approach to record production while overseeing the final cut. 'I did "Substitute", "Happy Jack" and "Pictures of Lily",' says Carroll, 'and Kit would come into the control room to supervise.' Lambert asked the cutting engineer how loud he could make the record. Carroll told him that if the meter on the volume-control indicator went into the red then the track would distort. 'So Kit said, "I want it in the red."' Carroll refused, but Lambert insisted: 'Go into the red! Go into the red!' In the end, he obliged: 'I had a little speaker in the room like you'd have in a radio. So we'd played The Who's songs through that, because Kit needed to know what they'd sound like on the radio. He loved what he heard.'

Like 'The Kids Are Alright' and 'I'm a Boy', The Who explored the themes of sex and death with a breezy melody, rudely interrupted by Moon's busy drumming and Townshend's jagged power chords. The song took a sharp left turn with the inclusion of a short French horn solo, which Daltrey said was meant to sound like a First World War siren; a warning, perhaps, to the troops to stop masturbating as the Kaiser's army was on the move. 'I was insecure about "Pictures of Lily",' said Daltrey, who was convinced at the time and even years later that his vocals revealed that insecurity. He liked the song but thought it was a rip-off of The Kinks and that Ray Davies would have sung it more affectingly. He was wrong.

'Pictures of Lily' was released on 22 April 1967, five weeks after the Pink Floyd's debut single, 'Arnold Layne', a song about a fetishist who stole women's underwear from washing lines. There were clear comparisons to be drawn between the two: both sets of lyrics had a sexual undercurrent; both groups featured guitarists who'd been to art school (in Barrett's case, Cambridge and Camberwell), and didn't play with their eyes closed and their heads thrown back like Eric Clapton or Jimi Hendrix. Both songs also landed their bands in trouble. American radio stations refused to play 'Pictures of Lily', and Radio London banned 'Arnold Layne'. The Floyd single only reached Number 20; The Who Number 4, still one position lower than Hendrix's infuriating 'Purple Haze'.

'Arnold Layne' was pop music, but looser and stranger. Townshend understood why: 'LSD had released groups, like Pink Floyd, from the chains of aping black rhythm and blues to break into a new world of "we do what we want". LSD made music European.' He admired what the Pink Floyd were doing, but wasn't sure The Who could do the same. 'I couldn't see how to write about LSD, purple skies and free love,' he revealed. 'But something dangerous and new was happening in music and I wanted to be part of it.'

If there was one event that embodied Pete Townshend's new, dangerous musical world it was the 14 Hour Technicolor Dream, held in north London's opulent Alexandra Palace. The 'free speech benefit' concert on 29 April was a fundraiser for *International Times*, which had just been raided on a trumped-up obscenity charge. The event featured psychedelic light shows, the Pink Floyd, art films, poetry readings, a fibreglass tent in which one could smoke banana skins, and performance artist Yoko Ono reprising her act at New York's Carnegie Hall in which she invited the audience to cut off her clothes.

Between seven and ten thousand people are said to have attended the event. Among them were John Lennon, Pete Townshend and Kit

Lambert. The latter quickly discovered that peace and love would only get him so far. After Lambert was turned away for not having a ticket, he was given a black eye by one of the doormen when he refused to leave.

Surviving photographs and grainy film footage of the event now have an eerie quality about them. In some clips, the dawn light can be seen streaming through the Palace's vast windows, illuminating a ghostly parade of shell-shocked young people, dancing, staring, sliding down a fairground-style helter-skelter in the middle of the room, wandering aimlessly, or scaling the scaffolding tower at the far end of the hall.

Among the groups playing that night were Track Records' latest signing, the Crazy World of Arthur Brown. Their frontman, Brown, was a theatrical singer whose act involved African voodoo costumes, Japanese kabuki face paint and a crown filled with petrol, which occasionally set his hair on fire. He was a tireless showman.

'Pete Townshend told Kit Lambert about us,' Brown says now. 'His angle was, "You should come and see this piece of performance art."' Brown admired The Who – 'They were like Andy Warhol coming into pop' – and was impressed when Townshend picked him up for a business meeting in his Lincoln Continental. Brown's old friend John Fenton had been managing the band, but Fenton agreed to Lambert and Stamp taking over their management in exchange for the pair paying off his telephone bill.

Yet, despite being impressed by their energy, charm and ideas, Brown slowly became aware that Lambert and Stamp weren't entirely masters of their own destiny. 'I don't want to say too much because I don't want to end up with a hatchet in my head,' he says, only half-joking. 'But the money behind Track Records came from New York from connections of a certain nature.'

Andrew Loog Oldham once described New York music publisher and manager Pete Kameron, who died in 2008, as 'the kind of guy that gets presidents elected'. In the 1950s, Kameron co-founded a jazz and folk label and moved into song publishing, before arriving in London in the early 1960s.

'He was a very shrewd businessman,' says John Fenton now. 'This guy set up a publishing company and he had the rights to a lot of famous jazz and blues numbers. He came over to England, saw all this talent in the sixties and picked a few people out. It's a shadowy story but he mentored several people and I was one of them, and we all fell for it big time.' By 1967, Kameron had taken over the European wing of Essex Music, with whom Stamp had cut a publishing deal for The Who. 'Pete Kameron was the power behind Track,' Fenton adds. 'He was Chris Stamp's puppet master. He pulled the strings.'

On one occasion when Arthur Brown refused to go along with one of his managers' ideas, he was taken for a walk by what he calls 'one of the American gentlemen behind Track': 'We were by the River Thames, and he said, "Arthur, I was brought up on the street, and we had this ethic – 'If you don't do what you're supposed to do' . . . Well, see that water, Arthur, and think of concrete boots." There was no blustering, no knives, he just looked me straight in the eye when he said it.'

In the summer of 1967, Lambert moved Track's headquarters from Chesterfield Gardens to 58 Old Compton Street. 'In the early days, there was an air of power and sustainable expansion about Track Records,' says Arthur Brown, before offering a vivid, fanciful description of their new HQ: 'You'd never seen an office with so many criminals in in your life – an eclectic mixture of intellectuals, artists, businessmen, models, actors, English crime lords and American Jewish mafia.

'The Who might be ambling in or out or, in the case of Keith Moon, running up and down the stairs chortling merrily at the top of his pirate voice,' he adds. 'Hendrix might be there. Kit might be haranguing Polydor Records on the phone, and Terence Stamp might be holding forth about being on the frontlines when the revolution came. Tea was made, joints were smoked, and cannabis tincture was administered medicinally.'

While Brown wrote songs for his debut album, Townshend shared his latest ideas for a rock opera: 'He was considering calling it "Rael", and it was about China,' recalls Brown. 'Unlike the French, a lot of the English youth were not thinking about politics. So I thought that was incredibly forward thinking.' Townshend's story had evolved over the past few months. In this latest version Israel was invaded by China, whose population was now expanding so fast they were taking over the world. Townshend wanted to produce the opera outside of The Who, and even considered Brown for the lead role.

However, as with 'Quads', the composer was brought back to earth by the demands of being in The Who. Track Records wanted another Who album. The band had been recording sporadically since March, but there was no direction to be found in the material they'd produced so far: a jingle for a Coca-Cola TV ad, John Entwistle's aptly titled instrumental 'Sodding About', a souped-up version of Norwegian composer Edvard Grieg's 'In the Hall of the Mountain King' . . .

Alongside these oddities were some superior Townshend compositions, however, one of which he'd originally demoed around the time of *A Quick One*. 'I Can See for Miles' was a song Townshend regarded as 'a secret weapon', a composition that could be called upon at a time when The Who needed something extra special. Kit Lambert decided that time was now.

In late May, The Who booked into CBS Studios on Bond Street and cut versions of three songs: 'I Can See for Miles', 'Mary Anne With the Shaky Hand' and 'Armenia City in the Sky', the last written by Townshend's chauffeur and fellow songwriter, John 'Speedy' Keen. 'Mary Anne With the Shaky Hand' was another of what John Entwistle called 'The Who's wanking songs', an homage to a girl whose shaky hands made her irresistible to men. But both 'Armenia City in the Sky' and 'I Can See for Miles' suggested 'the LSD and purple skies' Townshend insisted he could never write about.

The former had a dense, droning intro that mirrored the sensation of hearing music while coming up on LSD. 'I Can See for Miles' suggested an acid trip, but also a gathering thunderstorm or an air raid, with Townshend's siren-like guitar flashing back to a time of gasmasks and bomb shelters. Townshend later described the song as 'Wagnerian', but its lyrics didn't shout and scream and threaten suicide like 'My Generation'. Instead, it was a quietly menacing song about frustration and the power of aspiration, and arguably the best song Townshend had written so far.

'"I Can See for Miles" already sounded like the finished song when Pete played us his demo,' says Mike Ross-Trevor, the engineer at the CBS Studios session. 'I remember thinking how strange this was compared to other bands' demos. That song already sounded beautiful.'

Ross-Trevor spent three days at CBS, with Kit Lambert beside him in the control room. 'Pete knew exactly what he wanted, but Kit was technically producing, always asking for "more compression on the drums" and things like that.' When he wasn't giving orders in the control room, Lambert lectured the band about taxation laws and money. 'He was having all these discussions with the guys about which countries to put their money in and how much they could save. I wasn't surprised that they were having that conversation, but I was surprised that they were having it in front of other people.'

The Who were easy enough to work with, but their engineer was always conscious of where Keith Moon was at any given moment in time. 'Keith was completely crazy,' he sighs. 'I've always felt there might have been something wrong with him, like a mental disorder. I actually found it scary to be in a room with him. You felt insecure, always worrying what he was going to do next.'

On the last day of the session and with the recording complete, Moon was letting off steam on the drums, when he suddenly fell backwards off his stool: 'There was a concrete floor in the booth and he hit the ground with real force. He just lay there. He couldn't move.'

Moon was taken to hospital. There was no permanent damage, but he was diagnosed with a hernia, caused by throwing his drums around at an Oxford College ball gig the night before. The Who scouted around for an understudy. John's Children's Chris Townson was one of two drummers hired to fill in. Townson experienced a baptism of fire: before the gig he was jeered at by youths who mistook him for Keith Moon; at the end, the roadies let off a smoke bomb under his drum stool as payback for John's Children's antics in Germany.

By the second week in June, Moon was back behind the kit. With another trip to America pending, The Who needed their regular drummer, even one who'd just had his stomach stapled and had been ordered by his doctor to rest. Once again, The Who couldn't have chosen a better time to leave the country: Townshend's counter-culture friends were being arrested and The Beatles had just made the greatest record of their career.

On 13 May, Mike McInnerney married his girlfriend, Kate. The couple held their reception in Hyde Park. Karen Astley designed the wedding outfits, UFO's Craig Sams served macrobiotic food and a West Indian steel band provided the music. The police arrived to break up the party, as it was illegal to play music without a licence, but the new Mrs McInnerney talked them round. Photos of the colourful, peaceful hippie wedding made the newspapers.

'There was a shot on the front page of the *Sunday Times*, with Kate, this diminutive girl, in her wedding outfit, persuading these three really tall policemen,' says McInnerney. 'It's so nice, a perfect kind of picture.' The goodwill didn't last long. On 1 June, McInnerney's best man, John 'Hoppy' Hopkins, was sentenced to nine months in jail for possession of a miniscule amount of marijuana.

The party at UFO was soon to end as well. A *News of the World* reporter visited the club and claimed to have witnessed all manner of debauchery. The newspaper's subsequent story was as ill informed as its headline: 'I SAW COUPLES INJECTING REEFERS!' But a week later, the ballroom's owner told Joe Boyd that UFO was no longer welcome on the premises. Boyd moved the club to the Roundhouse, but by October it had closed for good.

John Lennon had paid the original UFO a visit shortly before it closed, and had brought with him a test pressing of The Beatles' new LP, *Sgt. Pepper's Lonely Hearts Club Band*. Everyone stopped and listened. Pete Townshend had first become aware of the huge leap The Beatles were making when Brian Epstein played him their yet-to-be-released single 'Strawberry Fields Forever', in February. 'It was utterly bizarre, creative, strange and different,' he said. 'It was the moment The Beatles became truly anarchic in the studio.'

With *Sgt. Pepper* The Beatles had put a marker in the ground, but it was hard to imagine how anyone else, including The Beatles themselves, could better it. Songs such as 'A Day in the Life' had an unparalleled breadth and vision. The rest of the album was filled with wondrous, imaginative sounds and what Pete Townshend called 'atmosphere, essence, shadow and romance'. This extended to the collage-style cover, designed by Peter Blake and his wife, the artist Jann Haworth. Here, The Beatles appeared alongside images of more than sixty famous and infamous people, including the occultist Aleister Crowley, the underground writer William Burroughs and the comic actors Laurel and Hardy. The days when it was simply enough to stick a photograph of the group on an LP cover were over. *Sgt. Pepper* was a musical and visual statement.

Timothy Leary apparently played the LP and was convinced his mission to turn on the world was complete. You could hear the drug in much of the music. Lennon had taken LSD while recording the record. Two weeks after the album's release Paul McCartney admitted in *Life* magazine that he'd also used the drug. It was a brave statement to make with Hoppy in jail, and Mick Jagger and Keith Richards facing a possible prison sentence.

Sgt. Pepper provided the soundtrack to The Who's return trip to America in June. They flew into Detroit for a couple of warm-up gigs before heading to California. The Who were due to play two nights at San Francisco's Fillmore Auditorium. When promoter Bill Graham told them they were expected to play two one-hour sets of different material, the band panicked, and Chris Stamp had to borrow a record player so the group could re-learn their own songs.

The Fillmore was an impressive auditorium with a state-of-the-art PA, and was located in the Haight-Ashbury district, the very heart of San Francisco's hippie quarter. A sprawling community of musicians, artists, poets, students and LSD disciples populated the area. It was home to the likes of Jefferson Airplane and the Grateful Dead, folk and blues bands who'd fallen for The Beatles and the Stones, discovered dope and acid and were now feeding those influences into their music.

The 14 Hour Technicolor Dream had been inspired by an event in January when more than ten thousand people had gathered at San Francisco's Golden Gate Park for a 'Human Be-in'. The Grateful Dead played, Timothy Leary preached his psychedelic gospel and the police watched in amazement as nobody got drunk, robbed or stabbed. Meanwhile, the University Of California, in neighbouring Berkeley, was a hotbed of political activity – and with good reason. In 1966, the US government had sent over 400,000 young men to fight in Vietnam. Anti-war sentiment was escalating. But by the time The Who arrived it was already apparent that what Townshend described as 'peace and love – those borrowed second-hand catchphrases' weren't going to change the US government's mind. Meanwhile, Haight-Ashbury had become a tourist trap, a place for the 'greys' to gawp and giggle at the brightly dressed hippies selling beads and tie-dyed T-shirts.

Rolling Stone magazine's John Mendelsohn watched The Who's show at the Fillmore, and was shocked by Moon's 'enormous, maniacal bug eyes', Daltrey's 'ultra-bouffant orange hair' and the 'comically gangly' Townshend. Yet by the end he was impressed with the 'thundering, pulverising music . . . and superhuman feats of stamina, strength and even grace.'

Days later, on 18 June, The Who brought their thundering, pulverising music to the Monterey International Pop Music Festival at the Monterey County Fairgrounds, California. Among the festival's organisers were promoter Lou Adler, John Phillips of the harmony group the Mamas and the Papas and The Beatles' press officer Derek Taylor. It was the first high-profile pop music festival and would pave the way for Woodstock two years later.

The organisers had pledged their profits to charity, and the band were all asked to perform for free. As the event was being filmed for a documentary movie, the organisers argued that the publicity would be as good as, if not better than any fee. Most accepted, albeit grudgingly, except the Indian composer and sitar player Ravi Shankar who pocketed $3,000 for his afternoon performance.

As The Who had only just dented the US market, Chris Stamp agreed to them playing for nothing. Stamp had just had his hair permed to look like Jimi Hendrix, had also discovered LSD and was now swept up in what he later called 'love and communication . . . and all that shit.' But he was still *compos mentis* enough to know that this was a good opportunity for The Who. The other acts on the bill included Country Joe and the Fish; Jefferson Airplane; and Big Brother and the Holding Company featuring singer Janis Joplin; and Scott McKenzie, whose hit 'San Francisco (Be Sure to Wear Flowers in Your Hair)' had become an anthem for what critics were now calling 'the summer of love'. The stage was wide open for a loud, aggressive group from England.

The Who were due to play on Sunday evening, and arrived the day before. Townshend watched Otis Redding work his magic on Saturday night, but America's take on psychedelia left him cold. 'The effect of LSD on American music just made it crap, with very, very few exceptions,' he complained. 'I think the only reason Jimi Hendrix was so fabulous is because he came here [Britain]. If he'd tried to develop himself in San Francisco he would have ended up sounding like Country Joe and the Fish.'

If ever The Who had the opportunity to leave a wound it was now. However, they weren't the only Track Records act on the bill. 'The Who paid my fare home,' says Keith Altham, who covered the festival for *New Musical Express*, 'but Jimi Hendrix paid for my flight out.' To add to the frisson, The Who and Hendrix were both due to play on Sunday evening.

By then, as many 80,000 had either passed through the gates into the Monterey Fairgrounds or congregated outside in the hope of seeing and hearing something, anything. The festival had attracted unprecedented media coverage, with more than a thousand journalists besieging Derek Taylor's press tent. Poised in the audience were record company executives ready to snap up the next big underground group, including CBS mogul Clive Davis, who'd recently signed Donovan. After Monterey, Davis would sign Janis Joplin, turning Big Brother and the Holding Company into a US chart act. Behind the scenes, visiting Rolling Stone Brian Jones was heard whispering, 'They might think this is the age of free love but it is not free and it is not love.'

Backstage, the Grateful Dead's sound engineer turned chemist, Owsley Stanley was distributing free LSD trips and Brian Jones was drifting around dressed like a Regency prince, but looking, as Keith Richards once said, 'like a ghost about to leave a séance'. Daltrey recalls Jones joining him, Janis Joplin, the Mamas and the Papas' Mama Cass and Jimi Hendrix for a loose jam session in the dressing room under the stage.

'Jimi was playing "Sgt. Pepper . . ." on his guitar,' said Daltrey. 'But, and this was the amazing thing, he was playing all the parts. He would go from a bit of orchestration, to a vocal part, to a solo – the whole thing on one guitar.' The others stood and watched, accompanying Hendrix by beating out a rhythm on anything close to hand.

Others remember it differently. John Entwistle said that roadie Neville Chesters, who was now working for Jimi, had warned him earlier that 'Hendrix was going to go on first and steal our act.' Townshend recalled arguing with Hendrix about who would play first, as neither wanted to follow the other. At one point Hendrix stood on a stool in front of him to show off on the guitar, as if to say, 'Don't fuck with me you little shit.' In the end, John Phillips suggested they toss a coin. Townshend won.

The Animals' Eric Burdon, his Newcastle accent softened by California, or drugs, or both, introduced The Who as 'a group that will destroy you completely in more ways than one'. Behind him, the band crashed into 'Substitute' followed by Eddie Cochran's 'Summertime Blues'. It was hard to imagine anything more removed from the Mamas and the Papas' passive 'California Dreamin'' or anything else the audience had witnessed that weekend.

The Who tore through 'Pictures of Lily', 'A Quick One, While He's Away', 'Happy Jack' and 'My Generation'. Instead of peace, love and flowers, they offered wanking, pervert train drivers, adolescent turmoil and Pete Townshend hacking away at the stage with his guitar, like a lumberjack trying to dismember a log with a blunt axe. Watching their performance in the film *Monterey Pop*, you can hear the gasps from the audience as stagehands rush on to try and salvage the broken equipment. Ravi Shankar watched the performance and was apparently appalled by what he saw as a 'lack of respect for their music and their instruments'.

There was also an air of English decadence about The Who at Monterey. In their paisley jackets, Edwardian ruffles and puffed sleeves, the group looked like a gang of marauding dandies. In 2005, Keith Altham recalled that Moon had accessorised his outfit with a necklace made from human teeth. Even Daltrey, who'd rarely worn targets and chevrons in the pop-art days, had joined the revolution. The cape draped around his shoulders was an explosion of red, brown and burnt-orange hues, described in *New Musical Express* as 'a heavily embroidered psychedelic shawl'. In fact, it was nothing of the sort. 'It was a tablecloth I bought in Shepherd's Bush market,' Daltrey admitted. 'But it did the job.'

Later, Brian Jones introduced Jimi Hendrix onstage as 'the most exciting guitarist I've ever heard'. Townshend watched the set with Mama Cass: 'He started doing this stuff with his guitar, she turned around to me, and said, "He's stealing your act." And I said, "No, he's doing my act."'

Although Townshend has since achieved a Zen-like calm on the subject of Hendrix, Daltrey still sounds defensive. 'I always have to defend The Who when people start raving about Hendrix at Monterey, and what he was doing,' he said. 'It was totally nicked from The Who. Pete was doing that down the Railway Hotel.'

Daltrey was right, at least until Hendrix sprayed his guitar with lighter fluid, set it on fire and tossed the charred remains into the audience. Hendrix had just invented a new act. Keith Altham remembers running into a subdued Townshend at San Francisco airport the following day, and being warned not to write just about Jimi. 'Hendrix triumphed at Monterey,' Altham points out, 'but it was The Who that had drawn first blood.'

On the plane home, Keith Moon thought it would be a good idea to take the acid Owsley Stanley had given him backstage. Townshend, believing that it was better for Moon not to trip alone, decided to do the same. He split a pill, swallowed one half, but soon wished he hadn't. Stanley's LSD was a new compound, known in Haight-Ashbury as STP. It was considerably stronger and its effects longer-lasting than the LSD Townshend was used to.

While Moon seemed untroubled by the drug, Townshend found the experience horrifying. When an air hostess appeared to turn into a pig and, in his mind's eye, began scurrying up the aisle, Townshend tried to force himself back to reality. But it was too much. In every account of the trip Townshend insists that he had an out-of-body experience, and ended up floating by the ceiling of the plane watching himself and his bandmates below. Over the next few hours, he would 'return' to his body, only for the fear and hallucinations to begin again. The trip lasted for sixteen hours instead of the usual ten and was a harrowing experience.

Back in England, it took more than two weeks for Townshend's world to come back into focus. His belief that 'the drugs are not going do it for me, I need something else' was truer than ever – he would never take LSD again. The Who's summer of love was over before it had even begun.

CHAPTER NINE

PIRANHAS IN THE BATH

'Well, I'm finally twenty-one years old. Boy, did I have a raving party.'

Keith Moon, *Beat Instrumental*, **September 1967**

'I felt as if a bomb had gone off in my head . . . I had to find something to fill the empty space.'

Pete Townshend remembers 1967

'Teachers, prophets, sibyls, oracles, mystagogues, avatars, haruspices and mullahs roamed the land, gathering flocks about them as easily as holy men in nineteenth-century Russia.'

Bernard Levin on the rise of the guru,
The Pendulum Years: Britain and the Sixties, **1970**

On the afternoon of 29 June 1967, Judge Leslie Block of the West Sussex Quarter Sessions sent Mick Jagger, Keith Richards and Robert Fraser to prison. Jagger was sentenced to three months for possession of four amphetamine tablets; Richards one year for allowing his property to be used for the taking of illegal drugs, and Fraser six months for possession of heroin. As soon as the sentences were passed down, a hysterical teenage girl ran from the courthouse, alerting the crowd of protesters outside to the verdict. Jagger was taken to Brixton prison; Richards and Fraser to Wormwood Scrubs.

A day before the verdicts were announced, The Who recorded two Rolling Stones songs, 'Under My Thumb' and 'The Last Time', at Holborn's De Lane Lea studios. Kit Lambert published an announcement in the late 30 June issue of the *London Evening Standard*: 'The Who consider Mick Jagger and Keith Richards have been treated as scapegoats for the drug problem and as a protest against the savage sentence imposed on them at Chichester yesterday, The Who are issuing today the first in a series of Jagger–Richards songs to keep their work before the public until they are again free to record themselves . . .' Lambert pledged to give all profits from the single to the Stones' legal defence team. 'We did it as a gesture,' said Roger Daltrey. 'We thought it was a disgraceful sentence.'

On the same evening as Lambert's announcement, a crowd of pro-testors made their way from UFO in Tottenham Court Road to the *News of the World*'s offices in Fleet Street. Police with dogs and batons were there to meet them, as were Keith and Kim Moon. 'I bought a hundred broom handles and a bunch of cardboard and made signs that said "Free Mick and Keith",' said Moon. 'I gave them out to the crowd in front of the building from my Bentley,' he added, which said much about his commitment to the cause. Kim and Keith were photographed holding placards that read 'Free Keith' and 'Stop Pop Persecution', and looking every inch the perfect pop-star couple.

The Who's Stones single was an unusually supportive act from a group not generally known for being supportive of anyone, including themselves. But it would have been even harder to imagine the Rolling Stones doing the same for The Who. Nevertheless, by aligning The Who with the 'Free Mick and Keith' campaign, Lambert had drummed up publicity for his group. No sooner had he done so than Jagger and Richards' sentences were quashed in the appeal court.

Harold Wilson's Labour government had been voted into power on a manifesto that championed Britain's youth. In 1965, Wilson had been instrumental in The Beatles receiving MBEs. But the Rolling Stones, with their drugs, long hair and influence, remained anathema to many sections of traditional British society.

Nevertheless, in a surprising turn of events, on 1 July, *The Times* published an editorial, under the headline 'WHO BREAKS A BUTTERFLY ON A WHEEL?', in which editor William Rees-Mogg questioned the severe sentences meted out to the Stones, and the motivation behind them. 'There are many people who take a primitive view of the matter . . .' he wrote. 'They resent the anarchic quality of the Rolling Stones' performances, dislike their songs, dislike their influence on teenagers and broadly suspect them of decadence.'

It was a remarkable statement from a newspaper long regarded as a bastion of the British establishment. When the *News of the World* admitted to deliberately tipping off the police about drugs at Redlands, letters began appearing in the press from readers who were neither teenagers nor Rolling Stones fans but nevertheless believed that Jagger and Richards had been treated unjustly.

MPs from both sides of the house voiced their support, including Labour MP Tom Driberg. Constant Lambert's old friend, Driberg, had first met Jagger at a dinner party in 1965, where, after a few too many drinks, he'd suddenly blurted out his admiration for what he called Jagger's 'big basket'. Although Driberg clearly lusted after the Stones' singer, he also recognised his power and influence and later tried, unsuccessfully, to woo him into joining the Labour Party.

Within hours of being granted his freedom, Jagger was being interviewed on ITV's current-affairs programme, *World in Action*. His interrogators were four pillars of the establishment, including William Rees-Mogg and the Bishop of Woolwich. They were curious and sympathetic and approached Jagger, with his long hair and satin trousers, like scientists would a specimen under a glass.

The singer answered their questions in a roundabout fashion, but repeated the comments he'd made at a press conference earlier. He believed that there were many things wrong with society, and that rebelling against them was a good idea, but refused to align himself with any specific cause. 'My responsibility is to myself,' said Jagger. 'I don't propagate religious views such as some pop stars do. I don't propagate drug use as some pop stars do.' Interviewed in 1995, Jagger compared his drug use in the 1960s to little more than a youthful folly. 'It was just a bit of a bore really,' he said. 'Everyone took drugs the whole time and everyone was out of it the whole time. It wasn't a special event.'

Jagger's blasé attitude, even at the time, was very different from Pete Townshend's with his ceaseless handwringing about the function of The Who and the band's responsibility to its audience. Later, when asked what he thought of The Who recording a Stones song, Jagger offered a rather condescending, 'Peter, you're a gentleman.'

One member of The Who had managed to excuse himself from the

'Free Mick and Keith' campaign. John Entwistle was on his honeymoon after marrying Alison Wise at Acton Congregational Church. While being in The Who would put extraordinary demands on the marriage, it now meant that Entwistle was less available for endless nights on the town with Keith Moon. When the bassist first announced his engagement, Moon tried to dissuade him: 'He was always finding beautiful women,' recalled Entwistle, 'and saying, "Look, you won't be able to have this when you're married."'

By now, Keith, Kim and their daughter Mandy were living in a former doctor's surgery on Highgate High Street in north London. Although Moon was desperate for Entwistle to avoid domesticity, he himself remained a confused and possessive husband. He watched Kim's every move, flew into a jealous rage whenever a man spoke to her, and bombarded her with postcards and telegrams whenever The Who were away, begging her to get in touch with him. In the months ahead, though, every band member's relationship would be put under pressure. Monterey Pop was just the beginning; The Who were going back to America.

The events of The Who's first major US tour have long since become folklore. Even those who were there couldn't agree on what happened at the time. Nearly half a century later, little has changed. What is clear is that the die was cast from the moment The Who arrived in New York in July.

Chris Huston had been the lead guitarist in a Liverpool beat group called The Undertakers. When they ventured south to play the Goldhawk Club and Forest Hill's Glenlyn Ballroom in 1964 their support act was The Who. It was a culture clash. 'We were Scousers and real rockers,' recalls Huston now, 'and The Who looked very London, very mod, unlike anything we'd seen around Liverpool.'

Three years later, The Undertakers had split up, and Huston was house engineer at New York's Talent Masters Studios. The Who were due to begin a ten-week US tour but had squeezed in a two-day session for that urgently needed new album. It was the first time Huston had seen any of them since 1964. 'The Who came in and we did the vocals on "I Can See for Miles" and "Mary Anne With the Shaky Hand" and two or three others,' says Huston.

Among the others was 'Rael'. However, Townshend's idea for a grand rock opera had been shelved. 'Rael's cautionary tale of the marauding Chinese had now been pared down to between five and six minutes. At Talent Masters, session keyboard player Al Kooper, whose sterling organ work could be heard on Bob Dylan's 1965 epic 'Like a Rolling Stone', was hired to play on the track.

At the end of a long session with The Who, Huston placed the four-track master tape of 'Rael' on a shelf in the control room, and went home: 'Normally I would have put the tape in the box but that day I didn't.' It was also a cheap plastic reel without the protective metal flanges found on more expensive tape. To the untrained eye, it might well have looked like a spool of discarded tape. Which is why, when Huston returned the following morning, the tape was gone.

'I asked my secretary, "Where did you put the tape?" She said, "What tape?" We looked everywhere,' he says. 'In the end, the only thing we could do was get in touch with the kid that cleaned the studio. He lived with his grandmother in an apartment in Harlem with no phone. We tracked down someone who knew where he lived, and the kid told us he'd thrown the tape in the trashcan. The studio was on 42nd Street and the back of the building opened onto 41st Street, and right below was a dumpster.'

Huston had no choice but to climb into the dumpster, wade through the discarded food and household rubbish until he found the spool of tape. It was broken but salvageable. He returned to the studio, spliced the tape together but discovered that the beginning of 'Rael' was missing. Fortunately, Huston had made a mono recording of the track, and was able to salvage the intro and edit it into the four-track recording. But he still had to break the news to Townshend when The Who arrived.

'I told Pete what had happened,' he explains. 'He was mad, he was angry, and he had every right to be. But he got over it.' Huston's memory is very different from Al Kooper's. According to Kooper in a 1995 interview, when Huston told Townshend what had happened to the tape, he finished with the words: 'Pete, I'm sorry but sometimes these things happen . . .' To which Townshend supposedly snarled, 'Don't worry Chris, sometimes *these* things just happen,' picked up the engineer's chair and threw it through the glass partition in the control room.

'I talked to Al about this ten years ago,' says Huston. 'We went and had a coffee together. I said, "That didn't happen," and he said, "Ya ya ya, it's show business..." It's a good story,' concedes Huston. 'Absolutely. But it's not true.' Another dramatic Who legend had been created. But there would be many more before the tour was over.

Although *Sgt. Pepper* had inspired plenty of groups to buy sitars and Kaftans, there was still a thriving market for pop music unburdened by a desire to revolutionise the world or to challenge its audience. Among these were Manchester's Herman's Hermits. Their run of hits had slowed down in the UK, but, they'd recently enjoyed two US Number 1s. 'Mrs Brown, You've Got a Lovely Daughter' and 'I'm Henry the Eighth, I Am' were gauche pop songs in which the Hermits' boyish lead singer Peter Noone sang in a broad northern English accent. America fell in love with them.

On paper, then, Herman's Hermits and The Who seemed diametrically opposed. To promoters in 1967, though, both were simply pop groups. The Hermits' manager Harvey Lisberg had been partly responsible, through his involvement with Manchester's Kennedy Street Enterprises agency, for negotiating The Who's deal with Premier Talent. 'The two acts may have been incompatible audience-wise, but it didn't matter,' says Lisberg now. 'The Who needed to do the groundwork in America.'

Peter Noone insists that Herman's Hermits chose The Who as their support act: 'We'd had Wayne Fontana and the Mindbenders, then The Animals, then The Hollies. Anybody we liked we tried to get.' What The Who and Herman's Hermits had in common was their upbringing in post-war England, where the idea of being paid to visit America, never mind tour the country on their own private jet, would have seemed as likely as flying to the moon.

On 13 July, the two British bands, joined by the home-grown psychedelic group the Blues Magoos, set off from Calgary, Canada, on a chartered DC-9, with their names emblazoned across the fuselage. It was a childhood fantasy come true; but the jet had seen better days. 'I remember looking out the back once and seeing flames coming out the exhaust,' recalls Lisberg. 'We all freaked out because we thought the plane was on fire, but it turned out that happened every time it took off.'

Prior to making the trip, Townshend had made some caustic remarks about the headliners in an interview. 'These Herman's Hermits guys are the biggest band in America,' he told *16* magazine. 'I have a mission to rid the world of this shit.' But Townshend's mission was quickly thwarted. Night after night, The Who played to people who didn't know their songs and didn't know how to respond to their anger. 'People got really upset after seeing The Who smash things up,' explains Harvey Lisberg. 'You had all these Americans walking around afterwards saying, "What are these guys doing? We *lurve* the guitar!". But I thought it was clever promotion.'

In fact, Townshend had long mastered the art of smashing up his instrument just enough for it to look shocking, but not so much that the guitar couldn't be repaired later. When he held it by the neck and smashed the body off the stage or his amp, the guitar would split in two but not shatter. Backstage, the two pieces would be stuck together with wood glue, wrapped in tape and left overnight, ready for the following night's show.

Once The Who had finished demolishing their equipment, Herman's Hermits would pick their way through the rubble to sing about Mrs Brown's lovely daughter to a chorus of approving screams. Townshend's frustration was obvious. 'Herman? Nobody in England has ever heard of him,' he lied to a reporter. 'In England, I can't walk down the street. But America, oh the myth of America, where they make Herman . . . a star.'

Meanwhile, Keith Moon had been hired to 'write' a weekly column about the tour for *Beat Instrumental*. 'It was a tour of discovery,' he said later. The extent of the discovery became apparent when Townshend's old Ealing friend Tom Wright joined the party. Wright was now living in Florida when he heard 'Happy Jack' and recognised Townshend's voice shouting at the end of the song. He wrote to The Who's office and was invited to join the tour as an official photographer.

Wright met up with the group at their gig in St Petersburg, Florida. The following morning he took his seat on the DC-9. Glancing out of his window he saw a station wagon racing alongside as the jet taxied down the runway. 'We must have been doing eighty when the driver produced a double-barrelled shotgun,' he recalled in his memoir, *Raising Hell on the Rock 'n' Roll Highway*. 'He pointed it at the plane and fired twice.' The jet left the ground just in time to avoid the bullets: 'And this was just my first ten minutes on tour with The Who.' Wright later discovered that Keith Moon had spent the night with an under-age fan: 'We decided that the odds were pretty good that it was her irate father driving the chase car.'

During The Who's earlier New York residency, a reporter for the *Village Voice* had observed the gangs of very young and persistent group-ies crowding backstage at the RKO Theater. 'They bribe the doormen with a wink, a kid-giggle,' he wrote. 'You can never lock them out totally. They squat outside the dressing rooms, scratching like exiled cats.'

As pop stars neither Herman's Hermits nor The Who were unused to female attention, but in America the groupies were more forthright – and younger. 'There were millions of them,' sighs Harvey Lisberg, who recalls stationing a roadie outside the Hermits' hotel rooms to keep the younger ones away. 'Everywhere we went, there were women. The radio DJs had a lot to do with this. The DJs provided these girls; they turned up with them. Nobody knew where they came from and nobody cared.'

Roger Daltrey's comment on The Who's 1967 tour was a succinct: 'The shagging was good.' But the singer adhered to a strict moral code. In *Who I Am*, Townshend recalls chatting to a beautiful blonde who was hovering around him by a hotel swimming pool: 'Until Roger took me aside and whispered "jailbait".'

The bands had all been booked into the Holiday Inn chain of motels. But with their long hair and flamboyant clothes, they were rarely made to feel welcome. America was also a culture shock in other ways. 'We all loved black music,' says Lisberg. 'The Who and the Hermits had grown up on soul and rhythm and blues and Tamla Motown. But we were all genuinely shocked by the colour prejudice and seeing blacks being made to ride at the back of the bus.'

A combination of anger at how they were being treated, raging hormones and boredom soon led to outlandish behaviour. Keith Moon and various Hermits began daring each other to jump from their motel balconies into the swimming pools below. After discovering the force of the impact when they hit the water, everyone started wearing shoes before jumping. Of course, the jumps were rarely attempted sober.

One afternoon, the Hermits' drummer Barry Whitwam and guitarist Derek Leckenby were taking bets over who would jump from a second-floor balcony when Keith Moon plummeted past them. The drummer had jumped off the motel roof, tastefully dressed in riding boots, a cape and a top hat. All bets were off.

Barry Whitwam recalled another incident that typified Moon's wayward behaviour. 'Keith bought a piranha from a pet shop,' said the Hermits' drummer. 'When he got back to the hotel he put the piranha in the bath and ordered a raw steak from room service.' When the waiter arrived, Moon asked him to throw the meat straight into the bath: 'And, apparently, the fish choked to death.' 'I heard about the piranha,' confirms Harvey Lisberg. 'In fact, I think there was more than one.'

Moon's favourite new discovery, though, was the cherry bomb, a spherical-shaped firework that resembled the bombs he'd seen in cartoons and comic books. Moon decided to test their explosive power in his motel hotel in Montgomery, Alabama. The firework blew a hole through his suitcase and the chair beneath it. In a further moment of madness, Moon and John Entwistle decided to throw another cherry bomb into Moon's lavatory, thinking they could flush it away and it would blow up in a neighbouring suite. Unfortunately, the flush on Moon's toilet wasn't working properly. Instead, the cherry bomb spun around the bowl, as its burning fuse became smaller and smaller. The pair raced out of the bathroom just as the lavatory exploded, showering the walls with porcelain splinters and leaving a gaping hole in the floor.

'I received a phone call at two in the morning,' recalls Lisberg. 'It was the hotel manager in this broad Southern accent saying, 'Do you have a Mr Moon in your party? The toilet is missing from his room'. I think we had to pay a thousand dollars for the damage, but the bill went to Premier Talent. I tried to have a talk with Keith, and tell him not to do it again, but he was totally wacko. They was no reasoning with him.'

If the cherry bombs didn't kill him, it seemed the locals might. Later, in Chattanooga, Tennessee, Moon became involved in a fracas in a bar after he and the Blues Magoos' exotically dressed lead singer Peppy Castro were mocked by a couple of good old boys. Moon's response was to smash a chair over one of the pair's backs. A Peckham Paradise-style bar brawl broke out, which apparently only ended when the Magoos' strapping tour manager, an expert in martial arts, intervened.

Moon's bravado was admirable if foolish. It appears he was repeatedly punched, often for nothing at all. As the most photogenic member of The Who, he attracted the most female attention and the greatest animosity from their boyfriends. The Hermits' bass player Karl Green remembers the drummer being hit several times, simply because 'You smiled at my girlfriend.'

At least Moon was out of harm's way on the plane. Or so it seemed. Flying out of Providence, Rhode Island, in August, the dilapidated jet's engines began malfunctioning and the plane was forced to make an emergency landing. Two of the touring party had just taken LSD and were bewildered by the turn of events. Townshend promptly wrote a new composition, 'Glow Girl', inspired by the event. It was his attempt at a doomed lovers' song – like The Shangri-Las' 'Leader of the Pack' – about a young couple that realise their plane is about to crash. After spending hours flying, day after day, Townshend was grimly aware that the chances of The Who dying had greatly increased.

When asked about The Who/Herman's Hermits American jaunt in 2005, Peter Noone replied: 'The fact that we got through that is still a miracle to everybody. We had no idea what we were doing.' Noone's comments could easily apply to the events of 23 August 1967. More than four decades later, contradictory accounts ensure that nobody can know for certain exactly what happened at Keith Moon's twenty-first birthday party, but this was the occasion that cemented the drummer's wild man reputation forever.

Flint, Michigan, lies some sixty-five miles northwest of Detroit. The Holiday Inn at 2207 West Bristol Road, where Keith Moon woke up on 23 August 1967, later became a Days Inn, just one of several anonymous pit-stop motels dotted along the highway a few minutes' drive from Bishop International Airport.

Confusion reigned from the moment Moon opened his eyes that day. First of all, he'd knocked a year off his show-business age after joining The Who. Many, including best friend John Entwistle, genuinely believed that it was Moon's twentieth birthday, and that he was only pretending to be twenty-one so that he would be allowed to drink (which he started to do at 10 a.m.).

Moon was already in high spirits when The Who arrived at WTAC Radio for a live-on-air interview. To everyone's surprise, he stayed conscious for the group's performance on the sports pitch of the local Atwood High School, which culminated in Daltrey kicking a timpani drum between two goalposts.

The groups had hired the motel's rather tatty Ambassador Suite for a post-gig birthday celebration, on the understanding that any damages would be paid for and that the party was to finish by midnight. Beforehand, all of the furniture, barring a table, was removed. The Who arrived after the gig accompanied by an entourage of DJs, record company staff and a gaggle of starstruck fans. The suite's table was now filled with birthday cakes from Track Records, Decca and Premier Drums; Moon was now playing a customised Premier kit with 'Keith Moon Patent British Exploding Drummer' written across its two bass drums.

Tom Wright remembered Chris Stamp bringing in a record player on which he played acetates of The Who's new songs. There were frequent complaints about the noise from the manager who eventually pulled the plug out of the record player at one minute past midnight. In Wright's memoir, he describes how Moon responded by squashing a piece of chocolate cake into the manager's face.

Herman's Hermits recall the food fight starting earlier though, when Moon flicked cake at Karl Green, and the Hermits' bassist responded in kind. Within seconds, Moon had grabbed a whole cake and flung it at the wall. 'Then people started picking up the pieces and hurling it about,' the drummer said. 'Everybody was covered with marzipan, icing sugar and fruitcake.'

Nobody involved disputes that the food fight happened. Some even recall that the local sheriff, who helped chaperone the event, good-naturedly took a slice of cake in the face without arresting anyone. But memories diverge on what happened afterwards. According to Keith Moon, he ran out of the hotel to escape the fight and 'jumped into the first car I came to, which was a brand new Lincoln Continental'. Interviewed in *Rolling Stone* in 1972, Moon gleefully recalled how he released the handbrake and allowed the car to roll through the fence surrounding the motel pool and into the pool itself.

'The water was pouring in,' Moon told the magazine, 'coming in through the bloody pedal holes in the floorboard, squirting through the windows . . .' In Moon's account, he sat in the driver's seat until the car was almost completely filled with water, before taking a gulp of air, forcing the driver's door open and swimming to the surface.

When asked about the incident since, Townshend, Entwistle, Tom Wright and Herman's Hermits have claimed it never happened. But Roger Daltrey flatly contradicts them. 'We got the $50,000 bill for it,' he insisted. 'It flaming well did happen.'

Former WTAC DJ Peter Cavanaugh, who'd interviewed The Who that day and attended the party, backed up Daltrey's version of events in an interview with author Johnny Black in 2002: 'I heard the ruckus and I went outside and the first thing I saw was the vehicle in the pool. By this time we'd all had several beers and some other stuff too, so things can get a little cloudy, but I clearly remember seeing the vehicle in the pool.'

In Moon's account, he returned to the party streaming with water. Others have no memory of this detail, but do recall Moon pulling Karl Green's trousers down with such force that he tore the seams. Green retaliated, but in doing so ripped Moon's underpants as well as his trousers, leaving the drummer naked from the waist down. It was at this point, apparently, that the sheriff intervened.

Herman's Hermits remember the sheriff attempting to handcuff Moon, and the half-naked drummer wriggling free. Apparently Moon ran out of the suite but in his drunken haste, slipped on a piece of cake, fell flat on his face and smashed his front tooth. Others say he knocked out the tooth by jumping into the hotel swimming pool, which was empty. What isn't in dispute is that Moon ended up being driven to an emergency dentist to have the tooth fixed, and that the amount of alcohol and other substances coursing through his bloodstream meant he couldn't be given any anaesthetic.

Although the birthday boy had departed, others were determined to carry on the party. Some of the revellers liberated fire extinguishers from the hotel corridors, and began spraying the rooms and each other. The fight continued into the motel car park, where the protagonists quickly discovered that the foam was stripping the paint off the cars.

In Moon's fanciful account to *Rolling Stone*, Herman's Hermits and The Who later had a whip-round for the damages: 'It was like a religious ceremony as we all came up and dropped a thousand dollars into a big hat, and sent it off to the Holiday Inn with a small compliments card with 'BALLS' written across it.' In fact, after his visit to the dentist, Moon had spent the remainder of the night in a police cell, only to find out that the rest of the touring party had flown ahead to the next gig without him. According to Herman's Hermits, though, it was they who ended up footing the bill – which covered ruined wallpaper, paintwork and carpets – and, like The Who, they were banned from the Holiday Inn chain for life. Whatever the exact circumstances, Keith Moon's twenty-first birthday party has since become the biggest Who legend of them all.

The Who/Hermits tour ended with a concert in Honolulu. For Moon, who'd spent his adolescence listening to the Beach Boys, it was a boyhood dream come true. As it was, he nearly drowned, and almost scalped himself on a coral reef, during his first attempt at surfing.

Their gigs with the Hermits were over but The Who had been booked for one last performance. Ultimately, it would bring them more exposure than any of the shows they'd just played. On 15 September, they arrived at CBS Television Studios in Hollywood for an appearance on *The Smothers Brothers Comedy Hour*. Dick and Tommy Smothers were folk musicians-turned-comedians and their *Comedy Hour* defied the network's censors by sneaking political satire and references to sex and even drugs into an otherwise mainstream variety show. They also booked the hippest pop groups.

Tommy Smothers had compered at the Monterey Pop festival and wanted The Who to recreate their stage act on US television. On the night, Smothers introduced the band, who then mimed their way through 'I Can See for Miles'. So far so good. With his side-parted hair and double-breasted blazer, Smothers played up to his conventional image with expert comic timing. The Who, looking like four west London oiks who'd just robbed a King's Road fashion boutique, played along, sniggered and gave one-word answers to his questions.

When Daltrey mumbled the title of their next song, 'My Generation',

Smothers stared into the camera and deadpanned: 'I can really identify with these guys.' The Who mimed to a specially cut version of the song, which finished with Townshend ramming his guitar into his amp and bouncing it off the stage, and Moon kicking his drums over. It was business as usual, until a thunderous explosion shook the TV cameras and covered the set with smoke. The audience's loud collective gasp was followed by a ripple of nervous laughter, as Moon leapt off the back of the drum riser as if in fear of his life, and Townshend staggered through the smoke waggling his finger inside his right ear.

A silent Tommy Smothers reappeared holding an acoustic guitar. Townshend grabbed it off him and smashed it on the floor, as they'd rehearsed earlier. They kept the routine going, but Townshend looked genuinely dazed, and repeatedly ruffled his dishevelled hair as if checking that his skull was still in one piece. Smothers looked unfazed, but later admitted that his first thought after the explosion was that Townshend was injured. 'His head must have been about three feet from the cannon,' he said. 'It must have sounded like a siren inside his skull.'

According to some, Keith Moon had loaded one of his bass drums with an excessive amount of 'flash powder', a pyrotechnic concoction, often used in cherry bombs, which produces a loud theatrical bang. According to Tommy Smothers, though, the explosion came from a flash powder cannon near the drums. Moon had been told that under strict union rules he wasn't allowed to touch the cannon. Instead, a technician was given the job of loading it with a safe amount of powder. When it failed to function during the dress rehearsal a second amount was added. At some point after that, Moon secretly snuck in a third.

Whatever the circumstances, the effect was devastating. Townshend's art school fantasy – that The Who would one day blow themselves up onstage – had almost come true. In the end, the band escaped unscathed. Despite pretending to collapse after the explosion, Moon had only sustained a gash to his arm. Townshend's hair was singed, but he would later claim that the explosion marked the beginning of his hearing problems. The real victim, according to Townshend, was the actress Bette Davis, who was in the audience that night. So shocked was she by the blast that she fainted into the arms of fellow old-stager Mickey Rooney seated beside her. 'I don't know if that's true or false,' said Tommy Smothers. 'But let the legend grow.'

The Who's tour with Herman's Hermits had been chaotically good fun, but had left them some $5,000 in debt. 'It got us around America,' said Daltrey. 'But it did us no good at all.' Despite their ruthless touring schedule, Kit Lambert had also booked The Who into recording studios on their days off. As they travelled the US, Lambert would rifle through the local phone book and find any studio that had multi-track recording facilities. These had included Hollywood's Gold Star, where Brian Wilson had pieced together the Beach Boys' *Pet Sounds*, and Bradley's Barn in Nashville, once used by The Detours' hero Buddy Holly. Lambert and Stamp were desperate for a new Who album, even if that meant recording in fits and starts.

The first taster of The Who's new music, 'I Can See for Miles', was released as a single on 13 October 1967. The 'beautiful song' Mike Ross-Trevor had engineered at CBS Studios in the spring had since been finessed in several American studios. Thanks in part to the spectacle of The Who on national television, it broke into the US top ten. But Townshend considered that a hollow victory. Although the single made it to Number 10 in Britain, he'd been expecting at least a top-three hit.

'To me, this was the ultimate Who record,' Townshend told *Melody Maker*, 'and yet it didn't sell. The day I saw it was about to go down [the charts] I spat on the British record buyer.' Instead of 'I Can See for Miles', The Foundations' 'Baby Now That I've Found You', The Kinks' 'Autumn Almanac' and '(The Lights Went Out In) Massachusetts', the latest forty-five from Robert Stigwood's protégés the Bee Gees, hogged the top three.

Even a letter of appreciation from Kit Lambert's godfather Sir William Walton couldn't quell Townshend's disappointment. 'William Walton wrote Kit a letter congratulating *him* on how brilliant his song-writing [on 'I Can See for Miles'] was,' Townshend told the BBC. 'Then Kit passed it to me, and it started, "Dear Kit, your song is fabulous . . ."'

New Musical Express applauded The Who's return to their 'old knock-about style', but didn't recognise the song as a great artistic statement. Townshend, meanwhile, had hoped that 'I Can See for Miles' would rescue British pop from what he called 'post-psychedelic wetness'. Since *Sgt. Pepper*, it seemed as if every workaday pop group was wearing Kaftans and singing about their multicoloured dreams and visions. Even the Rolling Stones had turned. In August, they'd released the single 'We Love You', an insipid pastiche of *Sgt. Pepper*, and a complete volte-face from a band more usually given to expressing lust or violence.

The Stones jumping on the psychedelic bandwagon disgusted Townshend. 'I'll tell you who is going to be big next year – groups not afraid to make concessions and mock the whole process,' he told *New Musical Express*. 'I've heard all I want to of the last Beatles LP. 'Pictures of Lily' and 'Happy Jack' had simple tunes people could remember.' But Townshend's bravado couldn't hide the fact that he was now considering whether The Who were still a singles band, even though their attempts at a rock opera had been repeatedly thwarted by the need for conventional songs. When Chris Stamp presented him with a proposed tracklisting for the next Who album, Townshend panicked.

'I needed an idea that would transform what I regarded as a weak collection of occasionally 'cheesy' songs into something with teeth,' he said. After a brainstorming session with Stamp, Townshend devised the idea of turning the next Who album into a spoof pirate radio programme, complete with adverts recorded by The Who. It was a concept that would transform the new album into something more than a collection of unrelated songs.

At first Chris Stamp wanted to sell the space between the tracks to advertisers, who would then have a bespoke ad recorded by The Who: 'We initially thought the group would write commercials for amusing and weird products.' The group had already recorded a jingle for Coca-Cola, but the company were reluctant to advertise on a pop album. Other companies proved similarly reticent. Stamp's moneymaking scheme pre-empted the rise of corporate sponsorship, but ultimately failed. Undeterred, The Who decided to record the ads anyway.

The catalyst for the idea had been the recently passed Maritime Broadcasting Offences Act, which had declared pirate radio stations illegal. Stations such as Radio Caroline and Radio London had been championing pop music since 1964, whereas BBC radio's pop coverage was limited to just a few hours a week. The offshore stations also attracted a huge teenage following with their looser broadcasting style.

What they gave British teens was a skewed take on the US top-forty radio format, with its infuriatingly catchy jingles and breathless DJs chattering in the gaps between records.

Despite his later reputation as a tribune of the people, the Maritime Broadcasting Offences Act, which came into effect on 15 August 1967, had been proposed by the then Postmaster General Anthony Wedgwood Benn. The government argued that pirate radio stations were using wavelengths allotted to others and that their ships might be a danger to other legitimate vessels. In reality, the pirates' power troubled the BBC; the Beeb's response to their outlawing was to launch a dedicated pop station, Radio 1, six weeks later.

The Who, like every other British pop group of the early 1960s, had prospered from the support of the pirates. A shared love of Radio Caroline and a mutual disgust at its demise had the unusual effect of uniting The Who.

The others fully supported Townshend and Stamp's idea to make an album that sounded like a pirate radio broadcast. The Who spent the remainder of October playing mismatched gigs around the north of England with Traffic and the squeaky-clean groups Marmalade and The Tremeloes, and recording spoof ads for RotoSound Strings and Premier Drums, dreamt up by Moon and Entwistle in the pub next to De Lane Lea Studios.

Michael Weighell had worked with The Who on 'Happy Jack'. He was booked to engineer their new sessions at De Lane Lea, but found that the band, barring John Entwistle, had changed – and not for the better. 'They were riding high,' says Weighell, 'and their lifestyle consisted of setting their equipment up onstage and *being* The Who and having that attitude. That's fine onstage, but not in the studio.'

'John was no trouble,' he adds. 'But the others – Daltrey moaned all the time and Moon and Townshend wrecked my mics. They were just acting up. But I never found out why. I created a stink but the only response I got from Kit Lambert was, "Oh, put it on the bill."' Lambert's reply would come back to haunt him. But, despite alienating those around them, The Who's new album was finally taking shape.

In 1966, Alan Aldridge's illustration on the cover of *A Quick One* captured the essence of Swinging London. But the artwork for The Who's third

LP would be more cynical and wryly humorous than anything they, The Beatles or the Rolling Stones had previously conjured up.

Roger Law and David King were employed as a designer and art editor, respectively, on the *Sunday Times* colour supplement, when they were hired by Track Records. It's an indication of Roger Law's state of mind in 1967 that he only discovered years later that he'd played a policeman in the promo film for The Who's 'Happy Jack'. 'I don't remember a fucking thing about it,' says Law, who helped create the satirical TV puppet show *Spitting Image* in the 1980s. 'But I've seen the film. It looks like me and I've asked other people, and they say it's me. To be honest, it freaked me out when I first saw it.'

Despite, or perhaps because 'we were permanently stoned', Law and King were asked by Lambert and Stamp to design the artwork for the Jimi Hendrix Experience's second album, *Axis: Bold As Love*: 'We had seen Jimi around town, and you noticed him because of the hair and clothes. When he turned up for the shoot he had a badge on that said "Don't stare".'

Shortly after, they were asked by Stamp to suggest a concept for The Who's new LP cover. Law is certain that it was he and King who came up with *The Who Sell Out* as a suggested title: 'I've got a feeling we then had to sell the idea to the band, because "selling out" was a very controversial phrase at the time.' But it was just the sort of contrary statement that appealed to Pete Townshend: 'Oh, Pete got it straight away.'

The pair hired photographer David Montgomery and a studio in Chelsea's Edith Grove. According to Law, Jimi Hendrix had been 'charming and professional and always on time'. The Who weren't. But once Law and King realised never to book a photoshoot with the group before midday, the session went well.

On the day, The Who posed for four individual spoof magazine ads. Townshend was photographed with an oversized can of the deodorant Odorono pressed into his armpit; Moon applying the acne cream Medac to a fake blemish; and Entwistle as a Charles Atlas-style strong-man with a bikini-clad blonde model on his arm. Daltrey, who was the last to arrive, was asked to wear a Victorian bathing costume and sit in a Victorian hip bath filled with Heinz Baked Beans. 'I got the girl,' Entwistle said drolly. 'Roger got the beans.' But there was a problem.

'We didn't have enough beans,' says Law. 'So I had to send someone out to the supermarket to get some more. The trouble is, they'd been kept in the cold store.' The Who had recently returned from Hawaii, where Daltrey had been sunning himself on the beach: 'I said, "I don't like to complain but I'm fucking freezing . . ."' David Montgomery found a three-bar electric fire, which was then positioned behind the bath. 'I was in there for nearly two-and-half hours,' Daltrey told the author. 'I was cooking at the back, and freezing cold at the front. I think they enjoyed seeing me suffer.' Roger Law remembers Daltrey 'fucking moaning the whole time'. But the singer still maintains that he contracted pneumonia after the shoot.

With the photographs complete, the album's release was delayed for two months as Lambert and Stamp tried to get clearance from Medac, Odorono and Heinz, a legal nicety that until now had been overlooked. Heinz, for one, were initially unsure about having The Who's lead singer bathing in their product, but most of the companies finally acquiesced. The Who had, however, used a jingle for the now defunct Radio London pirate station, without permission from the company that had written it. The company announced its intention to sue, and Lambert and Stamp paid up before being taken to court.

Track Records geared up for Christmas 1967 with two major releases. On 1 December came *Axis: Bold As Love*; two weeks later the long-delayed *The Who Sell Out*. British pressings came with a free psyche-delic poster, but it seemed like an afterthought. It was the album's front cover, with Daltrey spewing beans and tomato sauce down his chin and a sneering, bare-chested Townshend offering his armpit to the record-buying public, which grabbed the attention. In contrast, the sleeve of the Rolling Stones' latest, *Their Satanic Majesties Request*, released the same month, showed the group looking self-conscious in gaudy satin capes and wizard hats. The Stones were trying too hard. The Who were, as Townshend had promised, 'mocking the whole process', including themselves.

'*The Who Sell Out* really is a sell-out,' wrote *Melody Maker*. 'In fact, it's almost "The Who drop out of everything that is supposedly fashion-able and therefore valid in 1967's flowery year."' Instead, there was something intriguing about the album's unfashionable preoccupation with consumer culture, and the way The Who juxtaposed 'I Can See for Miles' and 'Armenia City in the Sky' with cheery jingles for baked beans, acne cream and guitar strings. The songs were serious, but the jingles suggested Townshend the iconoclast was determined to pull the rug out from under Townshend the cerebral songwriter.

Reluctant to compete with Hendrix or Pink Floyd, Townshend had filled the record with what he called 'story-songs, cameos, essays of human experience . . .' The sweethearts in 'Our Love Was' admit their romance has been a fabrication, while on 'Sunrise', Townshend sings about a man unable to commit to the woman he wakes up to every morning.

John Entwistle had also contributed one of these story-songs, 'Silas Stingy'. But Daltrey hadn't been so lucky. Daltrey was now writing with guitarist and Who roadie 'Cy' Langston. The Who recorded the Daltrey/Langston composition 'Early Morning Cold Taxi', but Townshend dropped it from the tracklisting when he found out that it was all Langston's work. In doing so, he denied the album a fine song.

Daltrey was growing in his confidence and ability as singer, though. Just months earlier, he had fretted that he couldn't do justice to 'Happy Jack' and 'I'm a Boy', but on *The Who Sell Out*'s 'Tattoo' he gave one of his strongest ever performances. Townshend had written the song in an American motel room while trying to escape the madness of the Herman's Hermits tour. It was another flashback to his youth. 'When I was eleven or twelve, street guys always had a mass of tattoos down one arm,' he explained. 'You really felt, "Jesus, that's gonna happen to me sometime." It was such a relief when I finally got to be sixteen or seventeen, and you didn't have to do that anymore.'

Townshend was convinced that Daltrey would struggle with a song that questioned the nature of masculinity and expected the singer to suggest he sang it himself. When Daltrey didn't, Townshend was shocked: 'And he sang it really well. And I realised then, "Hey, he's got the same insecurities as me."' It was another example of how Daltrey was now inhabiting Townshend's songs, even if neither of them fully appreciated it.

What stands out now about The Who's homage to pirate radio is how much Townshend was hankering for his youth. It was as if, to escape Hendrix and LSD, he had returned to the early 1960s, and the innocent joy of hearing Eddie Cochran on a radio hidden under the bedclothes. Unfortunately, Townshend's nostalgic tribute failed to sustain its big idea. Instead, the radio jingles petered out halfway through, and the last part of the record felt divorced from the first. In this latter half was Townshend's semi-rock opera, 'Rael'. Its original tale of over-population and economic super-powers had been pared down and the result no longer made much sense. But if the rest of *The Who Sell Out* was inspired by the past, than 'Rael' certainly hinted at the band's future. It was a trailer for what would become their next album, *Tommy*.

For all its promise, *The Who Sell Out* sold slowly, peaking at Number 13 in Britain. Townshend was convinced America would love the album, as British pirate radio sounded just like American radio. Instead, the head of WTAC, the US' biggest radio network, described the artwork as disgusting, and said he wouldn't let his children have the LP in the house. *The Who Sell Out* barely reached the US top fifty.

Writing in *Queen* magazine in 1967, Nik Cohn compared the album to pop artist Andy Warhol's *Campbell's Soup Cans* and the American sculptor Claes Oldenburg's *Giant Hamburger*. At last, Townshend had made his pop-art statement. But Cohn also said that he'd been hoping for 'a wholesale ad fantasia, stuffed full of jingles and flashes and product-hymns, all done as fast and loud and vulgar as it could possibly be'.

In reality, The Who had run out of time. The album had been written by Townshend on the hoof in American motel rooms, while drummers plummeted past the windows, and it had been recorded on the run by a band whose ears were usually still ringing from the gig the night before. Nearly fifty years later, Roger Daltrey remains *The Who Sell Out*'s greatest supporter: 'I loved . . .*Sell Out* because we were trying to break moulds. We weren't getting put in a package that said "This is what The Who do." We did something different.'

Townshend thought it 'felt like half an album . . . like a great idea that needed more time' and later compared it with The Beatles' surreal short film, *Magical Mystery Tour*, screened on Boxing Day 1967, and roundly vilified in the press shortly after. Like *Magical Mystery Tour*, *The Who Sell Out* was 'going somewhere', said Townshend. It's just that nobody was sure where it was going.

Meanwhile, as Townshend failed to write his rock opera, others seemed to be getting there first. That summer, Keith West, lead vocalist with UFO club regulars Tomorrow, had a top-five hit with 'Excerpt From a Teenage Opera'. It was a quaint pop song that featured a children's choir, and sounded nothing like 'Rael'. But it was the first taste of its young composer Mark Wirtz's attempt to create what he called 'a movie on record'.

In the press, though, Townshend was still banging the drum for the merits of simple pop. 'I like people to enjoy and be entertained by what we put over,' he told *Melody Maker*, ' . . . not send them back to school.' Yet, the summer's soundtrack had been dominated, along with *Sgt. Pepper*, by Procol Harum's 'A Whiter Shade of Pale', a pop single based on Bach's 'Air on a G String' and filled with abstract lyrics that invited the listener to reach for their own interpretation. Pop music was sending its listeners back to school, whether Pete Townshend liked it or not. Was it any wonder he turned to religion?

On 27 August 1967, Brian Epstein died from an accidental overdose of barbiturates. At the time, John Lennon, Paul McCartney and George Harrison were attending a conference on transcendental meditation hosted by the Indian master Maharishi Mahesh Yogi at Bangor University in Wales. The Beatles' spiritual journey was cut short by their manager's death. But the group had acquired their own guru, and where The Beatles went others soon followed.

Maharishi Mahesh Yogi had begun espousing the benefits of meditation to westerners since the 1950s; long before the world's most famous pop group discovered him. George Harrison had been the first Beatle to explore Indian music and would do the same with Eastern philosophy after being given a copy of *The Complete Book of Yoga* by Swami Vishnu-devananda on the set of the film *Help!*. In March 1966, John Lennon declared his disaffection with conventional religion by telling the *Evening Standard*: 'Christianity will go . . . and [The Beatles] are more popular than Jesus.' Even the cautious Paul McCartney had informed the press early in The Beatles' career: 'None of us believe in God.'

The Beatles becoming disciples of an Indian guru was far more than a snub to traditional Western religion. It was also a reaction to LSD's failure to bring them the enlightenment so many believed it could. Shortly after Paul McCartney admitted to taking LSD, he denounced the drug and told the press: 'The answer isn't pot and it isn't acid. It's yoga and working and meditation and discipline.'

The Beatles weren't alone. Other pop musicians were now looking for answers they'd failed to find in either Western religion or hallucinogenic drugs. The singer-songwriter Donovan had joined The Beatles on their trip to see the Maharishi in Bangor, and in December 1967, Beach Boy Mike Love was introduced to the guru in Paris. Love and fellow Beach Boy Al Jardine would both study transcendental meditation under the Maharishi's tutelage. Pete Townshend's belief that 'Mod is not going to do it for me, the drugs are not going do it for me . . . I need something else,' now seemed truer than ever.

Townshend thought he'd found what he was looking for on the Herman's Hermits tour. The Blues Magoos had introduced him to the works of George Adamski, an American writer who claimed to have seen flying saucers over the Colorado Desert and to have been contacted by aliens. Adamski also believed that there was a race of spiritually perfect people living on another planet; just what Townshend wanted to hear at a time when The Who couldn't have been more spiritually imperfect.

Adamski wasn't alone. The British author and counter-culture pioneer John Michell had just published *The Flying Saucer Vision*, which became required reading for the underground set. Now the drugs weren't working, many went looking for the answer in UFOs, Arthurian legends and spiritual ley lines. Townshend was among them. Writing later in *Rolling Stone*, he said that he'd seen 'several flying saucers in the Florida area . . . and that they hold a key somehow to the future of humanity'.

When he returned from America, Townshend visited Mike McInnerney at his eyrie above Shaftesbury Avenue and shared his ideas. 'I was ranting and raving,' he said. 'But every time I came up with a world-wise theory that had taken me years of thought to get clear [Mike] would say, "That's such a coincidence, man, this guy Meher Baba said something similar to that in this book, *The God-Man*."'

The God-Man was British author C.B. Purdom's biography of the Indian master Meher Baba. Purdom had met Baba when he first visited England in 1931 and believed that he was 'the Ancient One, the highest of the High'. Meher Baba was born Merwan Sheriar Irani in Poona,

India, in 1894. Aged nineteen, he experienced an epiphany after being kissed on the forehead by Hazrat Babajan, one of the so-called 'perfect masters' — 'one who has himself reached the goal to which he directs others,' wrote Purdom, 'one who, pointing to God, has himself realised God.' Baba became impervious to the world around him, and spent five years studying under India's perfect masters, during which time he took a vow of silence. From 1925 until his death in 1969, he only communicated via sign language and an alphabet board.

Mike McInnerney was introduced to Baba's teachings by his design partner Dudley Edwards, the artist who'd famously painted the psychedelic swirls on John Lennon's Rolls-Royce. Edwards had seen a photograph of Baba torn out of a magazine. He had no idea of the identity of this beatifically smiling man, but he found himself inexplicably drawn to the image. Edwards took the photo, stuck it on his wall, and only discovered it was Meher Baba months later.

In the summer of 1967, Edwards invited Mike McInnerney to a Baba meeting at the Poetry Society in Earls Court, organised by the theatre actress and Baba follower Delia De Leon. Edwards also asked Paul McCartney, who turned him down because he'd already committed to an audience with the Maharishi. 'It seems men work on a first-guru-come, first served basis,' joked Townshend later.

'I was looking for answers before I took LSD,' says Mike McInnerney now. 'I was interested in religion before, but I didn't like Western religion. Taking drugs was all about heightened consciousness, about taking a spiritual journey. Drugs were a way in, but this was something else. The really impressive thing about that first Baba meeting was seeing this group of old people, and the way their faith was still being carried after all those years.'

Townshend's started reading *The God-Man* and was captivated. Meher Baba preached what he later described as 'practical spirituality — do your best, don't worry, be happy'. Baba didn't offer any magical solutions, but Townshend believed that his teachings left him better equipped to deal with his problems and find the solutions himself.

By early 1968, Townshend was living with Karen Astley in her flat in Pimlico. He offered Baba's followers the use of his Wardour Street studio for meetings, and was charmed by the sight of these genteel middle-aged men and women congregating in the same room where he'd taken numerous drugs and once nonchalantly emptied his rubbish out of the window into the street below: 'It was a group of old ladies, as far as I could see, who had been actors, artists and musicians and had met Meher Baba in the thirties. I felt completely at home.'

Some of these older followers had felt inspired by Baba after living through two world wars and witnessing the horror of Nazism. They had been looking for 'something' in an uncertain world, just as Townshend was now. Furthermore, they willingly accepted the long-haired pop star and his friends into their fold, despite the fact that most of Townshend and his associates had been, as he put it, 'doped up to the eyebrows for years'.

In 1967, Meher Baba turned seventy-three. He rarely left India, didn't court publicity and never requested money from his followers. In contrast, the Maharishi had an upscale headquarters in Beverly Hills, paid for out of the substantial fees he charged for his transcendental meditation courses. 'I've got a mental block to that cat,' Townshend told *International Times*. He was similarly suspicious of pop stars that adopted an Indian master as readily as they might acquire a chic new jacket from Granny Takes a Trip.

Townshend would sum up his feelings about Meher Baba in the sleevenotes of his 1972 solo album, *Who Came First*: 'Baba and what he teaches are universal. Baba gives no rituals or ceremonies . . . There are no churches, no designated teachers . . . There is no fee. True religion, in Baba's eyes, is not a card-carrying affair but rather a matter of the "heart".'

Yet as Townshend was beginning his love affair with Meher Baba, The Beatles' infatuation with the Maharishi was coming to an end. In February 1968, The Beatles, their wives and girlfriends, Mike Love and Donovan joined the Maharishi in his ashram at Rishikesh, near the foothills of the Himalayas. They meditated, slept in Spartan huts, abstained from cigarettes and alcohol, and ate only vegetarian meals; although Ringo Starr brought a suitcase filled with tins of baked beans, as his weak stomach couldn't manage spicy food.

For several weeks, The Beatles enjoyed not being The Beatles. But the Maharishi wouldn't let them forget so easily, and suggested a scale of fees for his spiritual services, reputedly based on ten per cent of their weekly earnings. Ringo was the first to go home, followed by Paul;

John and George wanted to stay longer. 'This is the biggest thing in my life right now,' said Lennon, 'and it's come when I needed it most.' But when word spread that the Maharishi had made sexual advances towards a woman at the ashram, Lennon and Harrison decided to leave. Harrison later insisted that the accusation was false, but The Beatles' flirtation with the Maharishi was officially over. Lennon felt disillusioned and vented his ire with a thinly disguised rant against the guru in The Beatles' song 'Sexy Sadie'. In the eyes of some, The Beatles had been taken for fools. As far as Townshend was concerned, they'd simply been following the wrong guru.

Pete Townshend's spiritual journey was frequently interrupted throughout 1968 by the chaos that surrounded The Who, and their pressing need to earn money. Nearly four years after discovering the band, Lambert and Stamp looked as if they might finally put The Who in a movie. Stamp told the press that the group would probably star in an American black comedy; *Disc* magazine announced that The Who and their managers would be appearing in a new US comic strip, and that John Entwistle was making a children's album ('*Horror Songs for Kids*,' said the bassist). Yet all three projects failed to materialise.

Nevertheless, Track Records was a successful operation. In its first twelve months, the independent label had scored several top-twenty singles and albums with The Who and Jimi Hendrix alone. The air of power and sustainable expansion that had so impressed Arthur Brown had led to a reputation for musical quality, modern production methods and imaginative promotion.

In 1966, the original Track team included Lambert, Stamp and music journalist-turned-publicist Richard Green. When Green left the following year, Vernon Brewer, an aspiring actor who'd recently been an extra in the Terence Stamp film *Far From the Madding Crowd*, took his job. As well as dreaming up imaginative ways in which to promote Track's new releases, Brewer's job description also extended to organising Lambert's shambolic private life.

'I got a phone call from Kit one Saturday morning at 9 o'clock, saying, "I want you to arrange a wedding party, and I want caviar and champagne and game pies,"' Brewer recalls. The party was for an old college friend of Kit's. 'I said, "When's the wedding?" He replied, "12 o'clock today." Kit had promised to organise the reception months ago, and then forgotten about it. His housekeeper had woken him up that day and reminded him. Brewer and the housekeeper took a mad dash around Fortnum & Mason, and had just finished laying out the food and pouring the champagne when the first guests arrived: 'I thought we'd never be done in time. But that was typical Kit.'

When confronted with a problem, however great, Lambert used to say, 'It's nothing. Once you've rearranged the entire seating of Lancing College Chapel to sit next to the boy you fancy, anything is possible.' It was the same ethos that had inspired him to arrange a last-minute aerial leaflet drop over Oxford to promote the drama society's production of *The Changeling*. He'd forgotten to publicise the play, the same way he'd forgotten to arrange a friend's wedding reception and forgotten to clear the fake ads on *The Who Sell Out*. But it didn't matter, because, once again, he'd got away with it.

Lambert brought the same flair and panache to Track Records, something that wasn't always evident at the major record labels. 'Track was nothing like EMI,' says Jeff Dexter. 'It was a bunch of mates sitting around, pushing buttons and trying to bash square pegs into round holes. It was creative. I loved it.' 'With all the shit that was going on in the rock 'n' roll business, there was a certain sophistication about Track,' adds John Fenton. 'No other company had that, except perhaps Chrysalis later on. I think it was partly because it was such a strange mixture of people.'

The problem with Track, though, was money. At the end of 1967, with two top-ten Jimi Hendrix albums to their name, Track were served with a lawsuit from Hendrix's early manager Ed Chalpin, who'd signed the guitarist to an exclusive contract in 1965. When Chas Chandler found out, he offered Chalpin $70,000 for the contract. Chalpin refused, preferring to wait as Hendrix's stock rose and his potential settlement grew. When the courts found in his favour, Chalpin walked away with a percentage of royalties from *Are You Experienced*, *Axis: Bold As Love* and all future Hendrix releases on Track. It was a harsh blow, but there were others that were self-inflicted.

Unfortunately, the money Track made was often spent just as quickly. John Field was the European financial accountant for Dictaphone when he accepted Lambert's offer to double his salary and become Track's accountant in 1968. 'Was the company run properly?' he muses. 'No, it wasn't.' Field was impressed by Kit's ability to tot up figures and percentages in his head without recourse to a calculator, but less so by where the money was going: 'When I first looked at the accounts, I'd never seen such a waste in all my fucking life. But when I looked harder and put myself about in the industry, I could see that it was necessary for the creativity. But at first I just saw expenses for booze, guitars and drugs, and I freaked out.'

Too much of The Who's income from tour fees and royalties was being swallowed up by the cost of replacing equipment and redecorating hotel suites. Moreover, in addition to their managerial cut, Lambert and Stamp were still taking a slice of profits from The Who's recordings. The band cared, but only so much. 'Roger asked questions, because he was the original material girl and he was seriously into money,' says John Fenton. 'Keith and the Ox were out of it all the time and didn't say anything. Pete would occasionally ask questions about where the money was going, but with Pete it was all about the art.'

'The Who earned and Keith spent,' adds John Field, who was working late one night when Moon arrived in his office unannounced. 'Keith came in for some money and the safe was empty,' he says. 'I had half a crown on me, and that was it. Keith went bananas, and wrecked the office. I just sat back in the chair and watched it. The next afternoon there was a tap on the door and a head came round. It was Keith with a bottle of champagne in one hand and two glasses in the other, saying "I think I owe you an apology . . ." But that's a fair example of the sort of thing that was going on.'

John Field wasn't the only new addition to the Track family. In the same year, Track acquired the services of Cambridge graduate Peter Rudge. In 1966, Rudge had booked The Who to play a university ball. When Lambert cancelled the booking the day before, Rudge turned up at Track Records' office threatening to sue. Lambert was so impressed he later offered him a job. Before long, Rudge would be setting up tours for The Who.

Moon and Entwistle had also acquired a new chauffeur. Peter 'Dougal' Butler, a seventeen-year-old west London mod, had been hired as a roadie in late 1967. Dougal quickly became au fait with The Who's way of doing business, and with Keith Moon's inability to manage money. The first time they'd met, Butler noticed that Keith's Petticoat Lane market fur coat was actually falling apart and moulting all over the office. 'He was still living in a rented flat above a doctor's surgery in Highgate,' says Butler, 'and it was shit. He and Kim had no money. He was always skint because he spent it all from those tours before he'd even earned it. Keith was a complete nightmare with money. It was chaos.'

Come January 1968, Moon was back on the road earning yet more money that would never make it back to his family. The Who, the Small Faces and former Manfred Mann singer Paul Jones had been booked for a whirlwind tour of Australia and New Zealand. The problems started before the plane had even left the ground. 'The first thing Pete did was walk off the plane at Heathrow because he hadn't got a first-class ticket,' recalls Wiggy Wolff, who was now The Who's production manager.

Wiggy paid to have Townshend's ticket upgraded. But no sooner was the plane airborne than the guitarist was ferrying free drinks from first class to his bandmates in economy. 'Roger went to sleep, he wanted no part of it,' says Wolff. 'But Keith, John and I settled down for some lunacy.' The drinks were chased with pills, then more drinks . . .

'Everyone else was asleep or wanted to be asleep. But Keith was getting louder and louder. I said to this stewardess, "Could we get another drink?" And she agreed, but a bit too quickly. The next thing I remember is waking up. Moon was on the floor and John and I were slumped over each other. This air hostess had slipped us each a "Mickey Finn" [a drink laced with a sedative pill]. We'd landed somewhere, but we weren't in Oz.'

The plane had stopped off in Cairo. In fact, the gruelling thirty-six-hour flight would be broken up by further stops in Bombay, Karachi and Singapore. 'We didn't care,' says Wolff. 'We thought we were world travellers, so we got our passports stamped in every country.' By the time they landed at Sydney's Mascot airport, everyone was exhausted and dishevelled: 'The moment we got off the plane, there were cameras flashing. Roger had the hump. Pete had the hump . . . The Who! Small Faces! Paul Jones! It was the biggest thing to hit Australia, but all we wanted was some sleep.'

The Australian media had been gunning for the bands as soon as the tour had been announced; asking why these pommy upstarts were taking work away from home-grown entertainers. 'Couldn't you even have brushed your long hair for your fans?' asked one reporter. The Who and the Small Faces responded with monosyllabic grunts.

The band flew on to Brisbane, where they were due to play the Festival Hall and where, for reasons unknown, Keith Moon had insisted on being given a rental car. He had no intention of driving it anywhere, except into the hotel itself. The venue's electric doors opened wide enough to let the vehicle in. Moon pulled up next to the reception desk and tossed the keys to the concierge with a simple instruction, 'Park it!'

Due to some ridiculous scheduling, the bands then had to return to Sydney for two performances at an old boxing stadium where the PA dated back to the Second World War. The combined weight of the bands' equipment proved too much for the venue's revolving stage, which turned halfway before jamming and leaving a section of the audience with an obstructed view. When the disgruntled fans began booing, The Who started shouting expletives.

It wasn't just the PA that was outdated. Wolff, Moon and Townshend decided to take an afternoon stroll around town and were accosted by a policeman. 'He kept saying, "Are you boys or girls?"' says Wolff, who'd discarded his wig because of the heat and was now covering his sunburnt bald head with a fedora. 'Then he started asking me what I was hiding under the hat. When we walked off he threatened to arrest us.'

Relations between The Who and the media deteriorated further at a press conference in Melbourne. When a reporter kept asking him 'What drugs are you on?' Townshend responded by throwing a punch. The absurdity of the situation was not lost on the guitarist who, when he wasn't hitting reporters and swearing at fans, was reading *The God-Man* and trying to become a more spiritual person.

The Small Faces' frontman Steve Marriott later admitted that The Who 'slaughtered us every night' on the tour. But Marriott was cocky and outspoken, and annoyed Townshend who was later seen pinning him to the floor in an armlock. However, Townshend found a kindred spirit in bass guitarist Ronnie Lane. Lane's girlfriend at the time was a Buddhist and he was currently reading a book about the mystical

Islamic tradition, Sufism. The two swapped ideas, and Lane would join
Townshend at several Baba meetings in England.

When a beautiful female fan in Melbourne told Townshend that
she too followed the Master, and handed him a badge showing Meher
Baba's face, the pair ended up in bed together. Townshend wasn't
entirely sure whether this was what the Master would have wanted,
but the encounter inspired him to write the song, 'Sensation', later
included on *Tommy*.

After a final gig in Adelaide, the groups boarded a flight to Sydney
with another stopover scheduled in Melbourne. The band would
encounter even more disapproval on the plane. 'Most of us went to
sleep, but a couple of Paul Jones' Australian backing band were awake,
playing cards and drinking beer,' recalls Wiggy Wolff. When a stewardess saw that they were drinking, she objected. 'They had a law in Oz
that you couldn't drink alcohol on an aeroplane if it was flying over a
dry state. The stewardess was getting more and more angry, until Paul
Jones, who was very posh and polite about it, said "Now, hold on,
young lady . . ."'

At this point, The Who's roadie Bob Pridden decided to speak up.
Pridden's girlfriend and future wife, Mia, was the daughter of the fifth
Earl of Gainsborough. 'Bob gets up and says, "Let me tell you that I am
in line to the throne of England,"' says Wolff. 'Now you'd have to kill a
lot of people first before Bob became king. But it was at this point that
the stewardess burst into tears and went to fetch the captain.'

The captain ordered the groups to remain in their seats. 'He said,
"You are now confined,"' says Wolff. 'As if we could go anywhere
anyway . . .' The police were waiting when the plane landed in
Melbourne. The bands were due to play two gigs the following day in
Auckland, New Zealand. Eventually, after a three-hour delay and a
promise to behave, the touring party, accompanied by two Department
of Civil Aviation officers, were allowed to board a plane to Sydney and,
finally, a flight to Auckland.

The Who received a warmer welcome in New Zealand. 'I don't
think they were too keen on Australians and didn't want us to think
they were as bad,' says Wolff. A haughty Townshend informed the
waiting journalists that The Who would never set foot in Australia
again; a promise he kept until 2004.

In rock mythology, it's usually Keith Moon who's credited as one of the first pop stars to have thrown a TV set out of a hotel window. Not so, according to Townshend. 'The first person I ever saw throw a TV set out a window was Steve Marriott,' he said. Marriott celebrated his twenty-first birthday on the tour, with a party at his hotel in Wellington. EMI New Zealand presented the Small Faces singer with a portable record player as a birthday gift. When it didn't work properly, he upended the player over the balcony outside his room. Before long, Marriott, Moon and Wiggy Wolff were picking up anything they could find and heaving it into the car park below. Eventually that included the television set.

Once most of the suite's furniture was gone, Wolff telephoned reception to complain that someone – 'a bald man' – had broken into the room and vandalised it. Marriott claimed that the deception worked, despite several guests witnessing the drunken pop stars and their bald accomplice tossing anything they could lay their hands on over the balcony.

Incredibly, by the following night, the hotel had replaced the furniture and repaired the balcony's smashed French windows. Keith Moon arrived to inspect the refurbishment. 'They've done a great job,' he declared, before flinging a glass ashtray through the brand new window. The chairs and TV set soon followed. This time the hotel manager called the police. Yet still the guilty parties evaded arrest. Instead, the cops pulled up a chair each – once they'd been retrieved from the car park – and spent the remainder of the night chatting with the musicians and playing records.

The Who's Australasian misadventure received scathing notices in the New Zealand press. 'The Who and the Small Faces did more harm to the British image in a few days than Harold Wilson and Edward Heath could do in ten years . . .' blustered one tabloid. News of their behaviour had also reached the Australian prime minister, John Gorton, who sent the group a telegram: 'Dear Who's [sic]. We never wanted you to come to Australia. You have behaved atrociously while you've been here, and we hope you never come back.'

'We were children,' said Pete Townshend, when asked about the trip many years later. 'As a rock star in a band like The Who, I often found myself in what felt like a spiritual testing ground.'

The flat Illinois landscape flashed past the window of The Who's tour bus as Pete Townshend spoke to a BBC interviewer. 'I am today's powerful young man,' he declared. 'I am today's successful young man . . .'

By 10 March, barely a month after leaving New Zealand, The Who were back in America. It was their first headlining tour, but their fourth visit in twelve months. Tony Palmer, the *Observer*'s pop music critic, joined them for a couple of dates in the Midwest. In October 1967, after John Lennon tipped him off about The Who, Palmer booked them for a new BBC comedy show he was producing. Among the cast of *Twice a Fortnight* were the future Monty Python stars Terry Jones and Michael Palin. 'I thought it would be interesting to blend what The Who were doing with their sophisticated humour,' says Palmer now.

Palmer ruffled feathers at the *Observer* shortly after by comparing 'I Can See for Miles' to Bartók and describing The Who as 'the Sir William Walton of pop music'. Palmer had produced a film about Benjamin Britten, and knew Kit Lambert from the Royal Opera House. It was Townshend's musical ambition that appealed to him: 'I could see that Pete was making a real attempt to come to terms with the world in which he found himself rather than just writing 'doobee doobee doo'. I didn't always agree with what he was saying but I sympathised with what he was doing.'

When Palmer was commissioned by the BBC to make a serious documentary about pop music, he approached The Beatles, Cream, Pink Floyd, Hendrix and The Who. After flying out to Los Angeles, he interviewed Kit Lambert sitting by his hotel pool and being chauffeured around Hollywood, before joining The Who in the less glamorous locale of Peoria, Illinois.

Pete Townshend was filmed, being outspoken and forthright, from his window seat on the bus. 'It's crucial that pop should progress as an art form and not return to the kind of factory-made, big agency-controlled rubbish that it was before The Beatles came along . . .' he said. Later, he told Palmer that he'd just made a tape in his home studio containing music that was 'more overwhelming than Mahler's "Ninth Symphony".'

These were bold words, and far from reflective of Townshend's daily existence at the time. As Palmer discovered, today's powerful young man was still travelling by bus to venues where he sometimes had to get changed in the bathroom because there was no proper dressing room: 'And in Pete's case trying to say something about the world in which they lived to an audience that just wanted to scream and yell and didn't really give a fuck.'

The BBC broadcast Palmer's documentary, *All My Loving*, later that year. Footage of Hendrix and Cream and their wailing guitar solos proved that 'rock', pop's serious older brother, had arrived. But the music was also accompanied by topical newsreel coverage, including a Tibetan monk setting himself alight and a Viet Cong guerrilla being executed in the street. Palmer intended these harsh images to reflect the combative mood of the times.

For the new music was beginning to wield a harder edge. The Who's American support band on this latest tour were Blue Cheer, a punishingly heavy rock trio managed by a former Hells Angel. Before Christmas 1967, The Who had played London's Saville Theatre with Vanilla Fudge, another new American rock group who, Townshend said, played at such volume they dislodged the plaster from the venue's ceiling. By the end of the year, even some of The Beatles' new music had acquired some muscle. Their self-titled follow-up to *Sgt. Pepper*, nicknamed *The White Album*, included 'Helter Skelter', a song whose churning riff blueprinted the heavy rock sound championed by the likes of Led Zeppelin in the 1970s. Decca Records, however, ignored the zeitgeist and in March released 'Call Me Lightning', a mod-meets-surf-pop song written in 1964, as The Who's next US single. It sank without trace.

On 4 April, The Who arrived in New York for a three-night stand at San Franciscan promoter Bill Graham's new east coast venue, the Fillmore East. Shortly after six o'clock that evening, the black civil rights leader Martin Luther King was shot in Memphis. He died later in hospital. Within hours, there would be race riots in several major cities including Washington DC and Chicago.

The Who wondered whether they should go ahead with the gig, before concluding that they should. Townshend told the venue's director that there was too much violence in the world and he wouldn't smash his equipment that night. But he didn't keep to his word. Instead, lost in the moment, he forgot all about King's assassination and smashed his guitar, as usual, before Moon did the same to his drums. The audience bayed with delight.

The Who's drummer had left another trail of destruction across America on this latest jaunt. As well as cherry bombs, Moon discovered the powerful adhesive Super Glue. Hotel maids were routinely confronted with toilet seats that wouldn't lift up, furniture stuck to walls and, on one occasion, a glass of urine attached, as if by magic, to a ceiling. At New York's Gorham Hotel, Moon tossed cherry bombs on to the street, resulting in the band being thrown out. When they moved en masse to the Waldorf Astoria, Moon responded by letting off more explosives.

Kit Lambert had recently confided in Tony Palmer about his own reckless drug taking and behaviour. It was a further extension of what he calls 'the physical, emotional, psychological brinkmanship' that Lambert thrived on. But Palmer thinks that Moon was also absorbing elements of Kit's personality.

Moon, himself, was not given to self-analysis. In Saskatoon, Canada, he took an axe to every piece of furniture in the room because 'when I get bored I rebel'. Entwistle and Townshend had become almost inured to Moon's activities; accepting the fact that they would be asked to leave hotels in the middle of the night, and that their drummer might blow himself or an innocent bystander up at any time. Townshend had walked out when Steve Marriott and Keith Moon started smashing up Marriott's hotel room in Wellington, but he now found himself prone to the same behaviour: 'Keith set the precedent, and once it was set, I fell into it, too.' Now, instead of getting out of his motel bed to turn off the TV, Townshend would sometimes throw an ashtray at it. There was nothing in *The God-Man* that said he couldn't.

Asked about Moon's antics today, Roger Daltrey can't always hide his disapproval. 'It wasn't so funny if you were on the receiving end of one of Keith's pranks,' he told the author. 'But the trouble is because of his mischievous personality and the way he was, we all fell for it and let him get away with it. But there was another side to him. Keith was a desperate little man.'

On the road in Illinois, Tony Palmer noticed that The Who's singer seemed to be permanently frustrated: 'You sensed that there was this burning thing inside Roger but he didn't know how to articulate it.

But what rock 'n' roll did in those days was free people of these inhibitions. I never thought he was a frontman to start with, but he certainly grew into it.'

Tom Wright described Daltrey in 1968 as resembling an 'Edwardian rich kid with big hair and a cockney accent'. In photographs from the time, Daltrey often countered his dandyish ruffled shirts and lacquered hairdo with a forbidding scowl, as if the flower-power garb was all a ploy and he was still ready for a fight down the Goldhawk. Night after night, though, on The Who's latest US trek, Daltrey helped win over audiences that were often indifferent and occasionally hostile. After all this time, he was getting good at it. While Townshend fretted about smoking dope and finding God, Daltrey was turning into a rock star.

Furthermore, 'the millions of women' Harvey Lisberg had witnessed on the Herman's Hermits tour were still around, and usually gravitating towards The Who's lead singer. 'Around 1968 there were a clique of groupies that were the best ever,' a misty-eyed Daltrey later told the press. Not for nothing did Townshend refer to America as 'Groupieland'. But the hardness of the new American rock music was matched by the hardness of these female fans. In his memoir, Townshend wrote about one girl 'who romped around naked for seven hours' on The Who's tour bus as it drove through Canada, and how Moon and Entwistle later paid her $100 to sleep with Townshend and give him 'the clap' as payback for what they considered his snobbery about groupies.

'The idea in all our heads was to ball every chick in sight,' The Animals' Eric Burdon told Tony Palmer. 'That was the prime, continual object: to have a permanent party.' Reflecting on the era in *All You Need is Love*, his 1976 study of popular music, Palmer suggested that what unified the groups and their fans in 1968 was impatience. 'An unwillingness to postpone any satisfaction,' he said. 'I want to make love – gonna do it now. Eat now; drink now; everything now . . .'

That autumn The Who returned from 'Groupieland' to find themselves booked into many of the same clubs and university halls they'd been playing for the past five years. After America, with its free drink, drugs, sex and sunshine, The Who were confronted by miserable old Blighty, mounting debts, suspicious wives and girlfriends, and the ignominy of playing Dunstable's misleadingly named California

Ballroom, a venue they'd first performed in as The Detours. Their career had stalled. Again. They needed a hit, and Townshend needed some new inspiration.

A few months earlier, Townshend had accompanied Richard Stanley to watch Pink Floyd play at the Royal College of Art. Among Stanley's fellow film students was Storm Thorgerson, who would later co-found the design agency Hipgnosis and create album artwork for Pink Floyd, Led Zeppelin and many others. At the time, Stanley was staying with Townshend and Karen Astley, while working on a film idea for his graduation course: 'In the evening Pete and I used to do a lot of playing around in the studio he had there, and somehow this script formulated.'

From these sessions came the idea for *Lone Ranger*, the story of a pop star and his wild, daydreaming brother. Townshend agreed to play the pop star and write the music for the film; something it's hard to imagine a Beatle or Rolling Stone agreeing to do for an art student's graduation project. Chris Morphet was hired as a cameraman, Storm Thorgerson as an assistant and one of Thorgerson's flatmates, Matthew Scurfield, to play Townshend's 'brother', Beaky. 'There was never a script,' Stanley admits. 'The film was a whole bunch of different situations, things I talked about with Pete and Storm, mostly connected with French nouvelle film-making. It all emerged very chaotically.'

The twenty-two-minute movie was essentially a day in the life of Beaky, a young man who wanders, childlike, through the world around him. Richard Stanley's 'bunch of situations' included the pair fooling around at the breakfast table as their impassive, pipe-smoking father reads his newspaper, and Scurfield jumping out of Townshend's Lincoln Continental in central London and appearing to feign a heart attack on the pavement. It was a piece of performance art redolent of Townshend's Ealing art school groundcourse. The story struck a chord with Townshend, who said that playing a pop star in a movie was no different from playing the part onstage, and that the childlike role allowed him to reach back and 'redeem the lost boy in myself'.

Stanley submitted *Lone Ranger* as part of his graduation course. 'It was a coup to have Pete Townshend in my film,' he says, 'but what we ended up with was closer to a music video. The film school initially refused to show it, as it wasn't what they expected.' A protest by the student body convinced the RCA to change their minds though, and *Lone Ranger* would go on to be shown at the Edinburgh Film Festival in September 1968.

Matthew Scurfield would become a theatre, film and TV actor and appear alongside Roger Daltrey in 1980's *McVicar*. In 1968, though, he was a star-struck young Who fan. Townshend took Scurfield to Birmingham where The Who were playing and introduced him to the rest of the band. It was a baptism of fire. 'The first thing Keith Moon did was sneak up behind me backstage and rip my trousers off,' says Scurfield now. 'I was wearing a pair of sailor's loons and the whole back of them was gone. I was standing there in my underwear, terrified.' Townshend found him a spare pair of trousers, but Scurfield drank so much free booze Townshend had to pull over on the way home so he could vomit: 'I felt terrible. Coming back, Pete tried to sober me up by playing Pink Floyd's first album [*The Piper at the Gates of Dawn*], which somehow made it worse. Pete had a fascination, which bordered on a kind of obsession, with Pink Floyd, especially Syd Barrett.'

By now Barrett had drifted out of Pink Floyd, and was living a rather cloistered existence in the same South Kensington flat as Scurfield and Thorgerson. Townshend invited the *Lone Ranger* actors and crew for dinner at Ebury Street, where the conversation soon turned to their mysterious flatmate. Townshend invited them all to a Who gig at the University of Essex, but asked them to bring Syd. 'I had the feeling that this was what Pete had been building up to,' says Scurfield.

On the night, Barrett obliged and even drove them to the gig. 'I don't think we stopped at one red traffic light on the way,' recalls Scurfield. Once they'd arrived at the venue, Barrett immediately disappeared. Scurfield remembers The Who playing Pink Floyd's *Arnold Layne* in his honour, but Syd was gone. Barrett was a Who fan whose guitar playing had been inspired by Pete Townshend. Now, just as his former hero was looking to him for inspiration, Barrett was retreating from the world. Neither was he the only rock 'n' roll casualty in 1968. Townshend's closest friend in the Rolling Stones, Brian Jones, had been busted for drugs, and was now turning up for Rolling Stones sessions too disorientated to play properly. Townshend's disaffection with LSD, and drugs in general, looked ever more prescient.

In contrast to the madness around him, Townshend joined the 'young marrieds' he'd once disparaged, and wed Karen Astley at Didcot registry office. The bride wore white; the groom a Meher Baba badge on the lapel of his dinner jacket. 'There's not even time for honeymooning when you're a busy pop star,' noted the *Daily Express*. Instead, Townshend joined the rest of the band at London's Advision Studios to record The Who's new single, 'Dogs'.

After moving from Leicester to study at the Royal College of Art, photographer Chris Morphet had learned to navigate his way around London via its dog tracks. 'I was fascinated by greyhound racing, and I went to all the tracks – Romford, Catford, Park Royal,' he says. 'So I took Pete to White City, and he loved it.' Townshend's father had taken him there as a child, and there was something comforting about returning to this arcane world of betting slips and Woodbine smoke as an adult. It was as if the so-called Swinging Sixties had never happened.

'There was a greyhound at White City called Yellow Printer, who was one of the fastest in the world,' recalls Morphet. Yellow Printer was expected to win the English Derby that year, but lost out to the Duke of Edinburgh's Camira Flash, 'and the punters were convinced it was a fix.'

Yellow Printer and Camira Flash turned up in the lyrics for 'Dogs', a sweetly tuneful homily to the joys of beer, family life and greyhound racing. Daltrey sang in a pronounced London accent, and Townshend assumed the persona of a Cockney old-timer scared that his wife would discover he'd lost his money at the track. 'Dogs' failed to reach the top twenty, unlike the song that inspired it: the Small Faces' 'Lazy Sunday', which featured Steve Marriott roaring in his broad cockney accent. 'You can see the influence,' admitted Daltrey. 'That was what Pete was listening to.' 'Dogs' left both The Who's audience and supporters in the press confused. Heard again now, though, it sounds startlingly similar to something the Britpop group Blur might have attempted in the mid-1990s.

'Dogs' as a hymn to working-class life, *The Who Sell Out*'s homage to pirate radio and *Lone Ranger*'s return to childhood were all examples of Townshend backing away from what he called 'the acid trips and funny clothes' in favour of something simpler and more innocent. He was reaching back to his past; a process he would take further on The Who's next album, *Tommy*.

Kit Lambert was still banging the drum for Townshend's idea of a rock opera, but in practice the band's managers left him little time to turn it into reality. Instead, The Who were booked to play more live dates and encouraged to record more singles. The brute financial reality was they needed to keep earning. 'It was a battle,' admitted Chris Stamp. 'Our expenses with The Who were twice our earnings.'

At Lambert's suggestion The Who had just recorded a few Townshend originals and some covers, including Johnny Kidd and the Pirates' 'Shakin' All Over', for a planned release, *Who's for Tennis?*, that Kit wanted to put out in time for that summer's Wimbledon tournament. 'It was a bit of a hotchpotch,' understated Townshend. When Lambert accidentally left the finished master tapes in the back of a taxi, the idea was abandoned.

'The Who were getting left behind in 1968,' says Richard Barnes. 'They were always on the road and Kit was pushing them too hard. Also Keith had got married, John had got married and now Pete had got married. Whether consciously or not they didn't spend all their time thinking about the band anymore.'

At times it seemed as if The Who had stalled by the side of the road, while the competition zoomed past them. In March, the experimental Californian rock troupe the Mothers of Invention, led by Frank Zappa, released *We're Only in It for the Money*, a satirical concept album with a cover that spoofed *Sgt. Pepper* and songs that mercilessly poked fun at hippies, left-wingers and Republicans in equal measure. Closer to home, the second side of the Small Faces' latest album, *Ogden's Nut Gone Flake*, was given over to a psychedelic fairy story about a boy's quest to find the missing half of the moon. Six months later, The Kinks released their homage to English country life, *The Kinks Are the Village Green Preservation Society*. 'That was Ray Davies' masterwork. It was his *Sgt. Pepper*,' said Townshend in 2004. 'Nobody was daft enough to call these "rock operas", but they were in a way: they were aural concepts.'

It didn't help The Who that just weeks after they released 'Dogs', on 14 June, the Crazy World of Arthur Brown's second single, 'Fire', reached Number 1. Townshend and Lambert had been working with Brown for months. 'Fire', with its Hammond organ riff and spoken-word introduction ('I am the god of hellfire and I bring you fire!') was the perfect pop single for 1968. 'Barbaric, bombastic and brilliant,' wrote Tony Palmer in the *Observer*.

'Fire' was based on Brown's childhood experience of hiding in the basement of his family's home in Whitby during a wartime bombing raid. Brown wanted to make a concept album about fire, hell and psychological conflict, but Kit Lambert vetoed the idea. They reached a compromise, with one half devoted to Brown's concept; the other to shorter songs and the Marvin Gaye and Screamin' Jay Hawkins songs he played live.

In the end, the Crazy World of Arthur Brown's debut album was a shrewd mix of voguish heavy rock and tried-and-tested cover versions. But the 'Fire' single was its standout track. 'We sent out these matchboxes to promote the single,' remembers Vernon Brewer. 'There were matches inside but also a bottle of firewater, anything at all to do with fire.' 'Fire' was a British hit but also gave Track what they hadn't had with The Who: a top-five hit in America.

Despite Chris and Terence Stamp having been arrested and charged in Malibu on 18 May for possession of marijuana, Chris was able to oversee what Arthur Brown calls 'an historical act of promotion'. 'They went to the AM stations and told them it was a novelty record,' he explains. 'Then FM radio started playing it because they thought it was an underground record. Then you had Jimi Hendrix throwing the record on the counter at black radio stations saying, 'Play this, motherfucker!' And they did, because my face was covered in make-up on the sleeve and they presumed I was a black man.'

While Arthur Brown was at Number 1, The Who were languishing outside the top twenty. But Lambert now had a plan. His objection to Brown's idea to make a concept album about fire, hell and psychological turmoil wasn't just down to his need for hit singles. He was, as he willingly admitted to Arthur, stealing his idea.

The Who *were* going to make their rock opera now, and Lambert didn't want anyone, including one of Track's own acts, standing in the way. 'Kit said to me, "Pete says he's doing this opera thing, which isn't really an opera at all. But I'm going to say it is,"' recalls Arthur Brown. '"So I'm using your concept, old boy!"'

CHAPTER TEN

A SOPHISTICATED
CIRCUS ACT

'A full-length rock opera that for sheer power, invention and brilliance of performance, outstrips anything that has ever come out of a recording studio.'

Leonard Bernstein on The Who's *Tommy*, 1969

'I must admit to finding it pretentious in content, and not worth a single chorus of "My Generation".'

George Melly on The Who's *Tommy*, 1970

'I don't want to spend the rest of my life in fucking mud, smoking fucking marijuana. If that's the American dream, let us have our fucking money and piss off back to Shepherd's Bush, where people are people.'

Pete Townshend on the Woodstock Festival, 1969

There was no escaping Jim Morrison's picture. The lead singer of the American psychedelic group The Doors had been photographed with his shirt off, his face framed by a halo of ruffled curls and his arms outstretched as if he was preparing for crucifixion. Pete Townshend had struck the same Jesus Christ pose onstage many times in The Who's early days. The difference was that the bare-chested Morrison looked like a hippie messiah, and Townshend had been a gawky art student trying to distract the audience from the size of his nose.

It was 2 August 1968, The Doors had just reached Number 1 in America with 'Hello, I Love You', and The Who had arrived in New York to support them at the Singer Bowl. 'The Doors had become meteoric,' said a glum Townshend, 'and Jim Morrison's Christ picture was all over fucking New York.'

The show started late and the 16,000-strong audience was already hyped up when The Who appeared. By the time The Doors arrived, they were even more stoned, drunk and excitable. The black-clad Morrison teased the audience between songs and relished his obvious power. By the end of the set, many fans had smashed up their seats and rushed the stage.

Pete Townshend told the press that he'd watched a young female fan rush up to touch Morrison during the gig, only to be thrown off the stage by his bodyguards with such force that she cut her face on one of the barriers. The unquestioning hero worship, the hero's indifference and the ugly violence inspired Townshend to go back to his hotel and write a song for The Who's next album.

Townshend had started to plot out what would become *Tommy* while the band toured America in the spring. Stuck on a bus for hours at a time (one trip from California to the next gig in Vancouver had taken three days), he had time to fill.

To begin with, Townshend wrote an essay about a young boy, who dies in a car crash and is spiritually reborn. The story was influenced by Meher Baba, but also by the works of the Sufi writer Idries Shah and the German author Hermann Hesse, whose 1922 novel *Siddhartha*, about a young man's quest for spiritual illumination, had become a set text in hippie circles. Townshend's young hero was a Hesse-like 'seeker' looking for answers, but his story flitted between real life and a dream state.

'I got a letter from Pete in Miami saying he had developed this idea called "the Amazing Journey",' recalls Richard Stanley. 'It was obvious that it was quite different from anything he had thought about before.' To help explain the story, Townshend drew a diagram 'to show the aspect of illusion and the aspect of reality' in which his hero existed. Back at Ebury Street, he showed the diagram to Stanley. 'He seemed pretty confused,' admitted Townshend. 'When I look at it today, I feel the same way.'

The next stage was to strip out what Townshend called 'the double-barrelled plot', and make the story more linear. At least that was the plan. Townshend wrote a lengthy poem, in which his young hero is taken ill, falls asleep and meets his spiritual master in a dream. After being abandoned by the master, the hero is reincarnated several times before waking from the dream and being reunited with him in what is presumably real life.

But the poem, like the essay and the diagram, was gradually discarded. Instead Townshend extracted a few lines to use in what became one of the finished album's songs, 'Amazing Journey'. The central character in the story had now become a deaf, dumb and blind boy who existed in what the composer called 'a world of vibrations', where he experienced touch and feelings as music. Townshend posited the idea that his disability was a metaphor for 'what the wise men of the East say – that we are essentially deaf, dumb and blind to our spiritual potential.'

This character gave Townshend's bandmates something they could latch on to. 'Pete's ideas and thoughts were so out there, he was always pushing boundaries,' Roger Daltrey told the author in 2014. 'But there would always be one sentence that came out of that rambling brain of his that made sense. With *Tommy*, it was – "Imagine living life and all you can feel are vibrations".'

Away from the band, Townshend used Richard Stanley and Mike McInnerney as sounding boards for his ideas. 'I think Pete saw people as bits of Lego,' offers McInnerney. 'He had this way of looking at people, and saying, "You're a bit of that person and a bit of that." I remember being in the kitchen at Ebury Street – I have these big memories of sitting in kitchens talking in the sixties – and Pete was talking about pulling together these ideas for *Tommy*. It was like Lego again – separate things happening.' There was something else emerging as well: 'You could see the influence of Meher Baba on this idea of the disabled kid. That intrigued me the most.'

Townshend went public with his ideas in a *Melody Maker* interview in May 1968. He was writing a rock opera; it might be called *The Amazing Journey*; it might be called *Journey Into Space*. He hadn't decided: 'The theme is about a deaf, dumb and blind boy who has dreams and sees himself as the ruler of the cosmos.' Shortly after, he settled on the name Tommy because it was a traditional post-war English name, but also, said Townshend, because the second and third letters 'o' and 'm' reminded him of the Hindu mantra, 'om'.

It wasn't until The Who went back to America that Townshend discussed the idea with a journalist again. A fortnight after The Doors concert, The Who arrived in San Francisco to play three nights at the Fillmore West. After the second show, Townshend found himself at the house of Jefferson Airplane bassist Jack Casady, with a group of Casady's friends, including *Rolling Stone* magazine editor Jann Wenner. In the absence of Richard Stanley or Mike McInnerney, Townshend turned to Wenner. The pair's late-night interview would be reproduced across two issues of *Rolling Stone*. At one point during the conversation, Townshend was convinced that his drink had been spiked with acid. 'He said he felt as though he were beginning an LSD trip,' said Wenner. 'But I hadn't slipped him anything.'

Townshend outlined his story, which Wenner was convinced 'he was making up as he went along'. It was still a jumble of ideas; some elements were hangovers from the essay and poem, but others were new. He told Wenner about the boy's father's frustration with his son's disability and how 'the father starts to hit him . . . and he doesn't feel the pain . . . he just accepts it', and how when the boy is left in his uncle's care, 'his uncle starts to play with the kid's body . . . and the boy experiences sexual vibrations'.

Wenner was quick to pick up on the trend in Townshend's songwriting; what he described, in the parlance of the late 1960s as 'a young cat, our age, becoming an outcast from a very ordinary sort of circumstances'. As the night wore on, Townshend told Wenner that when he was a child he'd spent long periods of time with his parents when other children's parents were at work; but that he'd also spent long periods away from them; and that they'd never stopped him playing music, smoking pot or having sex. He remained profoundly confused about his childhood: 'The whole incredible thing about my parents is that I just can't place their effect on me, and yet I know it's there.' He still wasn't making the connection between the sex and violence in Tommy's story and his relationship with his maternal grandmother.

The following day, he met up with Rick Chapman, a Californian who ran the Meher Baba information service from a PO Box in Berkeley.

While talking, Townshend rolled a joint. Chapman gently pointed out that Baba opposed all drug taking. Although Townshend had been telling the music press he thought dope should be legalised, he often sounded as if he was saying what he thought The Who's fans wanted to hear, not what he believed himself. Unlike The Beatles, The Who hadn't signed a recent petition in *The Times* calling for the legalisation of marijuana. Nevertheless, dope was an intrinsic part of Townshend's relationship with music, and had been since lying stoned on the couch listening to Jimmy Reed in Sunnyside Road. At Chapman's suggestion, he vowed to give up smoking dope and gradually weaned himself off the drug over the next few months. 'It was the biggest surprise of my life,' he wrote later, 'to discover that I could still get into music straight.' Townshend was changing, but it would be a while before his band-mates and his managers fully understood why.

The Who flew home from America at the end of August, 'flat broke and busted', as Roger Daltrey put it. Richard Barnes' observation that by 1968 they no longer spent all their time thinking about being The Who was borne out by their personal circumstances. The band members had all settled down with their respective wives and girlfriends, though some had settled more successfully than others.

Roger Daltrey had now moved out of London with Heather Taylor and into a fifteenth-century cottage in the Berkshire village of Hurst. The couple would eventually marry in 1971, as soon as his divorce from his first wife was finalised. In contrast to Daltrey's escape to the English countryside, John and Alison Entwistle had acquired a semi-detached house in Pope's Lane, in Ealing, all of six minutes from Entwistle's childhood home. The bass player installed a suit of armour in the hallway, and turned a box room into a studio.

In the meantime, the Moons were still ensconced in their Highgate flat which now bore a permanent reminder of one of Keith's reckless nights out: a champagne bottle embedded in the plaster over which he'd hung a fancy picture frame. Moon never told visitors that it was there because he'd thrown it at Kim during a drunken row. 'I would give any woman who lived with Keith Moon the Victoria Cross,' says his former driver Dougal Butler.

Pete and Karen's late-night conversations with the McInnerneys carried on as before, but in the kitchen of their newly acquired eight-eenth-century Georgian house in Twickenham, opposite Eel Pie Island. The couple's newfound domesticity prompted Kit Lambert to start referring to them as 'Lord and Lady Townshend'. 'Kit was particularly jealous of my relationship with my wife,' said Townshend. 'He found it an irritation that he didn't have the access to me that he used to have.' Lambert's hold on his protégé would weaken further still the follow-ing year when Karen gave birth to the couple's first child, a daughter Emma.

Lambert may not have approved, but others liked the change in Townshend. In 1967, Richard Barnes had left England and taken a road trip around Europe. He had fuzzy memories of spending a day in Istanbul on LSD and another on opium. When he met Townshend again, Barney thought that the idea of following a guru was passé but admitted that his friend seemed happier than he had done in years. 'Pete always seemed to be a bit torn anyway' he says now, 'between being this mad hellcat rock 'n' roller and wanting to go home and listen to classical music.'

Townshend had converted two rooms in his new family home into a studio, and covered the walls with pictures of Meher Baba. Even though they knew that it was the inspiration for The Who's next album, Townshend's bandmates didn't share his interest. 'It was difficult for the people around me to accept that I was leading a very different life,' Townshend told *Q* magazine. 'Roger and Keith didn't take the piss. John Entwistle would – I think he was embar-rassed by it.'

Daltrey confided that he found Townshend's obsession 'a bit of a puzzle'. Mike McInnerney remembers broaching the subject with Keith Moon, however, and being pleasantly surprised: 'I think he had a kind of spiritual side himself, Keith. He might have been mad, a spiritual fool, if you like. But I think he respected the kind of feelings that Pete was getting.'

The Who started recording *Tommy* at IBC Studios in mid-September, with producer Kit Lambert assisted by in-house engineer Damon Lyon-Shaw. It was make-or-break time. 'This was the one where we were going to sink or swim,' admitted Chris Stamp. 'We had to do some-thing big – had to risk everything.'

Stamp and Lambert's hopes of having a Who album out in time for Christmas were soon dashed. As always, Townshend had produced meticulous demos, which he brought to the studio and played to his bandmates. Of the songs that would make it onto the finished album, Townshend had already written 'Welcome', 'Amazing Journey', 'I'm Free', 'Sensation', inspired by the Australian groupie, and 'Sally Simpson', about the girl he'd seen mistreated at The Doors concert. But there were also gaping holes in the story and several scraps of half-finished ideas. At the end of a long day at IBC, Townshend would often return to Twickenham to make sense of these embryonic songs, turning them into demos in time for the next day's session.

It was an arduous process, but The Who worked uncharacteristically well together. When Townshend revisited the original tapes decades later, he was surprised by how much laughter he could hear between the takes. Kit Lambert, meanwhile, was in his element, overseeing the sessions with his shirttail hanging out, a Player's cigarette smouldering between his fingers and a bottle of something alcoholic open on the mixing desk. As well as firing off countless ideas and suggestions, Lambert turned up one day with a portable roulette table to keep the roadies occupied. He was also there to calm the situation when one of The Who's crew went on to the studio roof to smoke a joint, took the wrong staircase down and ended up in the Chinese Embassy next door.

The band's economic circumstances meant that they still had to play weekend gigs to pay for recording time. Come Friday night, The Who, with their heads still reeling from *Tommy*, would drive off to play their past hits and smash their equipment in a university hall, before pocketing the cash and driving home. More than once, they had to wait outside the studio until a Track Records cheque cleared IBC's bank account.

In the middle of the sessions, The Who released a new single, 'Magic Bus'. Except it wasn't new at all. The Bo Diddley-inspired song had been briefly considered as a follow-up to 'My Generation', and then abandoned. While drunk one afternoon at IBC, though, The Who recorded a new version. 'It was a gas, and had a mystical quality,' said Townshend, who nevertheless dismissed the song's freestyle lyrics as 'garbage'. 'Magic Bus' would become one of The Who's most popular live songs, but in 1968, it sounded like a throwback to the past.

To launch the single, Track's publicist Vernon Brewer hired an open-top bus, a baby elephant, a cockatoo and a lion. The bus carrying the animals, The Who and a pair of what *New Musical Express* called 'dolly birds with micro skirts' set off from outside the BBC's Lime Grove Studios, heading for the King's Road. Who songs blasted out of a pair of speakers as the band threw streamers and sweets at passing pedestrians, and posed for photograph with their menagerie. 'I'm not saying what Keith did to that elephant,' admitted Daltrey. 'But it staggered off the bus.'

'Magic Bus' was a modest hit in the UK, but became the first Who single to break into the US top thirty. After four years of doggedly trying to crack America, they had finally managed it with a song they'd once rejected. Having tired of waiting for a new Who album, Decca's American wing also put out a cobbled-together collection of studio tracks confusingly titled *Magic Bus: The Who on Tour*. To the band's chagrin, the LP went on to become the first Who album to reach the American top thirty.

Chris Stamp protested loudly about Decca's money-spinner, but Track put out their own Who compilation in the UK soon after. *Direct Hits* was another hotchpotch of singles and random studio tracks, although the legal bust-up with Shel Talmy meant there was no 'I Can't Explain', 'Anyway, Anyhow, Anywhere' or 'My Generation'. Track Records had a Who album out in time for Christmas, it just wasn't *Tommy*.

Instead, Track's biggest victory in 1968 would come courtesy of Jimi Hendrix. *The Who Sell Out*'s photographer David Montgomery shot a cover image featuring naked women of various shapes and sizes for Hendrix's third LP, *Electric Ladyland*. The nudity had been another Lambert/Stamp brainwave, and Track Records took over the window of the fashion boutique I Was Lord Kitchener's Valet on London's Piccadilly Circus to launch the album.

'We covered the window with covers except for one small area,' says Vernon Brewer, 'and then hired some scantily clad models to dance in the window. It stopped the traffic.' The police were soon called to disperse the crowds gathered outside, but the publicity stunt worked. *Electric Ladyland* became a UK top-ten hit in October and soon went to Number 1 in America.

Back at IBC, The Who worked hard on what Townshend was cautiously describing as 'a song-cycle with a spiritual theme' and Lambert was loudly declaring 'a rock opera'. Having used an orchestra on Arthur Brown's debut album, Kit wanted to do the same with *Tommy*. Townshend had been studying classical composition, but rejected the idea. 'I didn't want to make a studio masterpiece,' he explained. 'I wanted to make an album The Who could play live.' Instead of an orchestra, Townshend played keyboards and Entwistle the brass instruments.

Tommy was further delayed because every time Townshend came up with a new idea for it, the album became longer. As the narrative evolved, The Who had to tweak their existing songs or re-record them altogether. 'It just started to drive us mad. We were getting brainwashed by the whole thing,' said Entwistle, who also admitted that he had no idea what the album was about.

'Keith and I used to play cards with John and Alison when The Who were doing *Tommy*,' says Dougal Butler, 'and I can remember them talking. There wasn't conflict as such. It was more a case of, "Where *is* this album going?" Because it was all in Pete's head.'

Kit Lambert's task then was to tease the story out of Townshend and help turn it into something everyone else could understand. 'Kit suggested I bring the story into the real world, and make it about Britain and real life,' Townshend told the BBC, 'and drag it out of Persia and India and Sufism, and that I start the story at the end of the Second World War and bring it up to the modern day.'

Townshend agreed. In doing so, he gave Meher Baba a less prominent role, something that made the management feel more comfortable. 'We didn't want to be promoting a guru,' admitted Chris Stamp. 'We wanted to bring the theme of spirituality down to a more day-to-day rock 'n' roll level.'

Lambert also proposed making Tommy's sensory deprivation the result of a real-life trauma. This appealed to Townshend who had been considering making Tommy autistic. The medical profession had only acknowledged the existence of autism in the 1940s, and information about the condition was still scarce. In Richard Barnes' essay for the 2013 *Tommy* box set, Townshend explained he'd read that autism could be the result of a childhood trauma and heard about a therapist who used music as a way of connecting with autistic children.

The story of Tommy now began with Tommy's mother giving birth to a son, while her husband, Captain Walker, is missing, presumed dead, in the war. Walker reappears several years later and discovers that his 'widow' has a new lover, whom he murders in front of his son. Tommy's parents tell the boy that he didn't see or hear anything. He responds to the trauma by falling into a near-catatonic state, losing his sight and his hearing, but able to experience the outside world through a series of visions and sensations.

Neglected by his parents, Tommy is left in the care of others, and is tortured by his cousin and sexually abused by his uncle. A drug dealer takes the boy to a prostitute who gives him a hallucinogenic drug that she wrongly believes will awaken his senses. A doctor later convinces his parents that their son's symptoms are psychosomatic and tells them to put the boy in front of a mirror as part of his treatment. 'Somewhere I read about an autistic child who had stared constantly into a mirror, as though he was the only person in the world,' Townshend told Barnes.

Tommy repeatedly stares at himself in the mirror, until his mother smashes the glass in frustration. This violent act reawakens his senses and is interpreted as a miracle cure. Tommy goes on to become a spiritual leader, and attracts a devoted following, but his disciples turn on him when he fails to impart the meaning of life.

Interviewed in 2004, Townshend said that he didn't realise he'd been writing his own story until 1991 when he was involved in a Broadway musical production of *Tommy* and started asking his mother about gaps in his childhood memories. In his autobiography, though, he said that he found it tough to write about Tommy's sexually abusive uncle even in 1968, because it stirred up memories of Denny, and her 'half-deaf boyfriend', the man he was made to call 'uncle'.

Townshend first hinted at what had happened in an interview with *Q* in 1996: 'I think it's quite possible when I was with my grandmother, she had a boyfriend who came into my bedroom. I don't quite get what happened.' After that, he didn't speak publicly about it again for several years.

When it came to the songs about the abusive uncle and cousin,

Townshend asked John Entwistle to write them for him. Entwistle went home to his box-room studio and composed 'Cousin Kevin', a song about a school bully who burns Tommy with cigarettes and holds his head under the water in the bath, something Townshend later said that Denny had done to him. Entwistle was unfazed by the commissions, as he'd witnessed plenty of casual cruelty during his time at Acton County.

Entwistle's second composition was 'Fiddle About', a macabre nursery-rhyme-style song about Tommy's 'wicked Uncle Ernie', with lyrics in which he orders his nephew to pull down the bedclothes and lift up his nightshirt. Years later, Townshend explained how Entwistle understood the subject because they'd both known children who had been abused in the church choir and in the Boys' Brigade. 'It was discussed then,' said Townshend. 'But what hadn't happened was victims coming forward. We knew what it was, and there were shades of things that had happened to us. Someone would say, "In the scout camp, the scout master came in and his trousers were down . . ."' Then someone else would say, "Oh, that's nothing . . ."'

What Townshend ended up writing was a story about the experiences of many post-war youths, including himself, his bandmates and The Who's audience. 'I wrote the story,' he said, 'before I knew what I was writing about.'

Captain Walker's return from the war, in the song 1921, to a wife who had found someone else and to children who didn't recognise him, also struck a familiar note. 'These were the stories I grew up with in my neighbourhood,' said Townshend. His parents had split up for a time, and it was Betty Townshend's boyfriend, not his father, who'd brought him home from his grandmother's.

Tommy's parents ordering him not to speak about the murder was another familiar scenario. 'I remember growing up with boys that were four or five years old during the war,' Townshend told the author, 'and you'd know that something dreadful or bizarre had happened to them.' His suspicions would be confirmed years later at therapy groups for survivors of childhood abuse: 'Sometimes guys in the groups would take me aside and say, "I was shipped out in the middle of the war to Wales, and the guy that ran the farm believed the Germans were going to take over and he just had his way with all of us. And after the war we were shipped home and I said, 'Dad, Dad, that farmer . . .' But my Dad said, 'Shut it! He saved your fucking life. You didn't see it. It didn't happen.'"

Townshend's experiences with LSD fed into 'The Acid Queen' in which a prostitute gives Tommy a hallucinogenic drug in a failed attempt to restore his senses. He told *Rolling Stone* that the song was all also about 'how you get it laid on you that you haven't lived if you haven't fucked forty birds, taken sixty trips, drunk fourteen pints of beer – or whatever'. Again, it was partly a flashback to his childhood; to the social pressures Townshend felt as an adolescent, watching his schoolfriend trying to have sex with a girl in Hyde Park, and, failing to pick up on obvious sexual signals from women at art college.

Townshend also told the magazine that there was something 'sinister, feline, sexual . . . inherently female' about LSD. Interviewed in 2013, Townshend explained that the female in the song could have been a prostitute, but according to the lyrics she was also a gypsy, which was another allusion to his grandmother. 'My mother's mother was born of a gypsy girl,' he revealed. 'Her dad had left his wife to pursue this gypsy girl. My grandmother would do magic stuff. She would put curses on people . . .'

As *Tommy* progressed, the album became more and more of a melting pot for Townshend's pet theories and obsessions: identity, spirituality, family, sex, drugs and gurus. There was a line to be drawn between Tommy's sensory deprivation and the occasion Townshend wheeled himself around art college in a trolley and communicated by using an invented alphabet. Meanwhile, Tommy experiencing the world only through touch linked to another of Townshend's art school infatuations: the philosopher Marshall McLuhan and his study of the power of the senses.

When Tommy becomes a guru and attracts a cult following, however, Townshend was clearly drawing on his current experience as a pop star. The incident with Jim Morrison and the injured girl had made an impression. So too had the 1967 cinema verité film, *Privilege*. 'It was a film about a charismatic young man who was a pop star and started a cult,' said Townshend. 'It was part of the vernacular of the time to look at the responsibility you had if you put yourself on a pedestal and start preaching.'

Privilege starred The Who's touring partner Paul Jones and Terence Stamp's ex-girlfriend Jean Shrimpton. Jones played Steven Shorter, a pop star with such power that he's pimped out by his managers to help promote religion and patriotism for the government. *Privilege*, like Jim Morrison, encouraged Townshend's fascination with the way a charismatic pop star could manipulate his followers, but end up morally bankrupt.

While *Tommy* was Townshend's brainchild, the rest of The Who were pivotal to its creation. Initially, Townshend wanted to perform the role of Tommy's inner voice and act as the album's narrator, with Daltrey playing Tommy later on in the story. As the tale evolved, the roles became harder to define.

The most poignant moment on the finished album was the closing section of 'We're Not Gonna Take It!', later known as 'See Me, Feel Me'. Daltrey had already tried and struggled to master the song. Townshend was convinced that The Who's alpha-male frontman couldn't possibly do it justice. One afternoon, Townshend arrived late to the studio and heard Daltrey delivering the vocal in a perfect fragile falsetto. It was a revelation: 'I realised then that Roger had occupied Tommy.'

'Everybody has a longing in them to be understood to be loved, and that was what I tried to do,' said Daltrey. The insecurity that had plagued him for most of 1966 and 1967 had been officially dispelled: '"I Can See for Miles" was when it came back for me vocally. And Tommy was the beginning of the next climb.'

Pete Townshend was provided with another reminder of the pitfalls of being a pop star when The Who broke off from recording *Tommy* to appear in the Rolling Stones' Rock and Roll Circus. On 10 December, The Who joined the Stones, Eric Clapton, John Lennon, Yoko Ono, Marianne Faithfull, Jethro Tull and others, in a cavernous TV studio in Stonebridge Park, near Wembley.

Like The Beatles' *Magical Mystery Tour*, the Rock and Roll Circus was the Rolling Stones' brave attempt to break out of the conventional format of theatre gigs. With the help of former *Ready Steady Go!* director Michael Lindsay-Hogg, they'd turned the studio into a Victorian circus, complete with half a big-top tent, a circus ring, fire-eaters, clowns, dwarves and trapeze artists. The show would be filmed for a possible

TV programme, but if the circus format worked the Stones wanted to take it on the road.

The Who were the first group Mick Jagger approached. When Townshend turned up for a preliminary meeting with the Stones, he was shocked by Keith Richards' appearance. The guitarist's drug habits had recently progressed beyond pills, dope and cocaine, and now included heroin: 'He was, literally, yellow, like he had hepatitis. I remember thinking, this isn't going to happen.'

Richards managed to stay alive, but when The Who arrived at the TV studio the following day they found Brian Jones and Richards' girlfriend, the Italian model and actress Anita Pallenberg, similarly the worse for wear. Jones was swigging vodka and kept breaking down in tears, and 'Anita looked as if she was withdrawing from something'. Jones, the Stones' founder member and once its driving force, would be fired from the Stones a few months later.

Over the next two days, the Stones' drug habits and labyrinthine sex lives added to an already tense shoot. Jones had been Pallenberg's boyfriend before Richards. But Anita had just appeared in the film *Performance,* an art-imitating-life drama about an East End gangster and a psychologically damaged pop star played by Mick Jagger. Rumours of a sexual dalliance between Mick and Anita on set were rife, which did little to help the fragile state of mind of Jagger's girlfriend Marianne Faithfull. When a couple of policemen showed up in the Stones' dressing room, Marianne was convinced they were all going to be busted for drugs, again, and became hysterical. She only calmed down when the cops explained they were just looking for the canteen as they fancied a cup of tea.

Come showtime, the seats around the circus ring were filled with friends, roadies, critics — including regular Who watcher Keith Altham — and lucky *New Musical Express* readers, all of whom had been given garishly coloured ponchos and floppy hats to wear. The circus began with a loud fanfare and the Stones, The Who and the rest of the cast were ushered into the ring by clowns, acrobats and a cowboy on horseback. But the entrance scene had to be re-shot several times due to technical problems. The words 'Can we shoot one more?' would be heard again and again over the next eighteen hours.

With the show underway, Jethro Tull arrived and played their fidgety art-school blues, before Marianne Faithfull sang the ballad 'Something Better' while looking winsome in a floor-length gown. Later, a supergroup made up of John Lennon, Eric Clapton, Keith Richards and Mitch Mitchell, appeared and launched into 'Yer Blues' from The Beatles' recently released *White Album*. Towards the end of their set, Yoko Ono emerged, unannounced, from a sack in which she'd been hiding and began shrieking into a microphone. 'I remember feeling,' said Townshend, 'that you couldn't put a band of more impenetrable beings on the stage.'

Townshend was arguably all the more sensitive to their impenetrability because of the themes he was exploring in *Tommy*. 'Every talented person spends most of his time hiding his talent – or freakiness,' he later said. 'The reason is the remoteness it creates – the more remote they become, the more powerful they are as star figures.' Despite being pop stars themselves, The Who were still plagued by insecurity. 'I speak to Mick Jagger on the telephone all the time,' Townshend admitted, 'and I still can't be normal with him.'

Perhaps it was The Who's insecurity that made their performance that day so astonishing. Keith Richards, looking sinister in a top hat and eye-patch but no longer quite so yellow, introduced the group with a mumbled, 'And now ladies and gentlemen, dig The Who.' The band performed 'A Quick One, While He's Away'. Moon drummed with such intensity he almost toppled off his stool; Townshend thrashed his guitar so hard you feared he might impale his hand on its tremolo arm, and Entwistle played spidery fingered bass while looking, with his dyed black hair and leather T-shirt, as if he'd just stepped off the set of a Joe Orton play. Meanwhile, with his suede tasselled shirt and newly long curly hair, Daltrey's metamorphosis from 1960s mod to 1970s rock star was visibly under way. The Who had to play the piece three times but their energy never flagged. During the final take, as Townshend repeatedly yelled 'You are forgiven!' they looked as if they might combust.

That The Who were a hard act to follow became increasingly obvious as the hours passed with no sign of the Rolling Stones. In fact, the Stones didn't appear until the small hours of the morning, by which time many of the audience had handed back their hats and ponchos, and drifted off to catch the last bus out of Wembley.

When they finally appeared, Mick Jagger was primed and ready to go, but the rest of the band took a while to catch up. As they did, the sound or the camera angles needed adjusting, so they had to do everything all over again.

At 5 a.m., the Stones began playing 'Sympathy for the Devil', an eerie samba taken from their latest album, *Beggars Banquet*. The unconvincing cod-psychedelia of 'We Love You' was long gone. This new song cast Jagger as Lucifer recalling his exploits through history. As it built to a climax, the singer stripped off to reveal a painted devil's head covering his skinny torso. 'This resulted in the total collapse of a young lady near the stage,' recalled Keith Altham. It was pure showbiz. But even so, there was in Jagger's performance something of the ultimate 'powerful, remote star figure' that so fascinated Townshend.

Yet the Rock and Roll Circus was far from the triumph Mick had hoped for. According to one of the Stones' confidantes, the singer watched the footage a few days later, to be told by Allen Klein, 'The Who blew you off your own stage.' Klein secured the rights to the recording, and the Rock and Roll Circus remained unseen until the mid-1990s. 'The Who stole the show,' says Keith Altham now, 'which is half the reason Jagger never put it out. The Stones are good in it, but The Who are better.'

Nevertheless, come the middle of December, The Who had taken so long to complete their rock opera that another of London's crotchety R&B bands had beaten them to it. No sooner had the Rock and Roll Circus left town than the Pretty Things released their album, *S.F. Sorrow*. It told the unhappy tale of Sebastian F. Sorrow, an ordinary boy who drifts through a regular childhood, a mundane factory job and his first sexual experience before becoming engaged to a local girl. Sorrow is drafted into the army and survives the First World War, only to see his fiancée die in an airship crash. As part of his quest for self-discovery, he takes a hallucinatory trip into the underworld, is shown events from his childhood in a room full of mirrors, and ends his life broken and alone.

EMI fumbled the launch of *S.F. Sorrow* with a low-key advertising campaign. A problem with the Pretty Things' US label meant the album wasn't released in America until three months after *Tommy* in the summer of 1969. As a result, the band members would spend the next five decades insisting they got there first.

Rumours about *S.F. Sorrow*'s influence on *Tommy* have circulated forever. 'We were at Abbey Road making the album, and Pete phoned up to speak to [Pretty Things frontman] Phil May,' recalls former Pretty Things drummer John 'Twink' Alder. 'He'd heard about what we were doing through the grapevine, and told him that The Who were working on something similar.' However, Townshend has always gone to great lengths to insist that *S.F. Sorrow* had no bearing on *Tommy*. 'I actually heard *S.F. Sorrow* after hearing *Tommy*,' he insisted.

In reality, the Pretty Things and The Who were both trying to break out of the conventional pop format at the same time. With songs about fumbled adolescent sex, the war and the search for answers, there were parallels between the two albums. Though according to Phil May, the biggest clue can be heard in the *S.F. Sorrow* song, 'Old Man Going'. 'You've got the opening of "Pinball Wizard" completely there,' May told the *New York Times*.

The opening bars of both songs do sound similar, but there the comparison ends. 'Pinball Wizard', a crucial piece in the *Tommy* puzzle, was written late in the day after Townshend invited Nik Cohn to listen to the album so far. Cohn was now writing about pop music for the *New York Times*. He listened and then confirmed Townshend's worst fears: 'He said, "It's a bit po-faced, all this spiritualism. You need something to make it more fun."'

At the time, Cohn was an obsessive pinball player. So much so that Townshend would often join him at the Lots O' Fun Arcade on Charing Cross Road, near the Track Records office. On one of these trips, Nik introduced him to a fifteen-year-old girl whose pinball skills put theirs to shame. Cohn was now working on a novel inspired by this young prodigy entitled *Arfur: Teenage Pinball Queen*. When Townshend mockingly asked Cohn if he'd give the album a good review in the *New York Times* if there was something about pinball in the story, Nik told him he probably would.

That night Townshend went home and wrote 'Pinball Wizard'. Rather than the Pretty Things, Townshend later said that the song's main theme was inspired by Johann Strauss' 'The Blue Danube', which had just been used in the recent sci-fi movie, *2001: A Space Odyssey*. He then dashed off a set of lyrics in which his deaf, dumb and blind hero became a gifted pinball player: 'I thought, "My God, this is awful . . . Oh my God, I'm embarrassed . . ."'

Townshend returned to IBC the following day, expecting his bandmates to reject the song. Instead, everyone, including Kit Lambert, told him it was a potential hit. Only Townshend couldn't see it. In fact, Townshend had written a song that would define The Who for the rest of their career. Its effect on *Tommy* was immediate. 'It made the whole story lighter,' Townshend admitted, 'but it also made it more accessible.'

Turning the hero into a pinball player put a different slant on the rest of the story, though. Townshend started to worry that when Tommy regained his senses and is feted as a spiritual leader, the theme would become 'too establishment, too churchy'. He shared his concerns with his bandmates one night, and 'Keith said, "Well, I've been thinking that it would be a good idea to set the whole thing in a holiday camp."'

As a child, Townshend had joined The Squadronaires at Butlin's holiday camp in Filey, near Scarborough. He knew that world. With The Beatles not long back from the Maharishi's ashram, there was something wonderfully cynical about The Who's guru addressing his disciples in a place used for amateur beauty contests and knobbly knees competitions. It also gave the story a much-needed shot of self-deprecating humour. '*Tommy* got sillier because of The Who,' said Townshend. 'If it was just me, it would have been more serious, but probably wouldn't have been as successful.'

What the band needed now was to see the story written down, to help focus their minds. Chris Stamp recalled Kit Lambert producing a film-style script, entitled 'Tommy Walker 1914–1984', in one nocturnal, drug-fuelled writing session. 'The original story was a few words on the back of a Player's cigarette packet,' claimed Stamp. 'The script was a way to ground everybody, to remind us all that we were on the same side.'

Stamp suggested that Lambert should write the script early in the making of *Tommy*. Townshend remembers it being written after the album was completed, and that it was partly motivated by Kit's ambition to make a film of *Tommy*, something Townshend was unaware of at the time.

Lambert's other great contribution was to reassure Pete Townshend that his story wasn't a load of pretentious old tosh: 'He would just say, "Fuck them! Fuck them all!"' recalled Townshend. '"What does anybody know about opera?"' The story of Tommy was convoluted and, in parts, incomprehensible. But Lambert pointed out that many traditional operas were also convoluted and incomprehensible. Staying true to form, Kit urged Townshend to go further still; to start Tommy with an instrumental overture, which would quote the piece's main musical themes and make it seem even more like a traditional opera. Townshend did as he suggested. It was the final piece of the Tommy puzzle.

Director Cameron Crowe's 2000 film Almost Famous is a semi-autobiographical tale of a young music journalist, William Miller, and his rite of passage on tour with a 1970s rock band. Early on in the film, Miller's older sister passes her record collection on to him. After Pet Sounds and Axis: Bold as Love, Miller comes across Tommy. Inside is a note left by his sister that reads, 'Listen to Tommy with a candle burning and you will see your entire future.' It's difficult to imagine the scene working as well if The Who's album didn't have an LP sleeve as intriguing as the story itself.

Tommy was now a double LP, and while Lambert and The Who had been labouring over the music, Mike McInnerney had spent three months creating the artwork. 'Pete told me I was free to come up with whatever I wanted,' he says now. 'Kit met me and immediately said, "Great! The artist in the garret." That idea appealed to him, so he left me alone as well. It was a wonderful commission.'

McInnerney had copies of Townshend's poem, essay and tapes of his demos to refer to. He designed a globe floating in space, covered with geometric holes, like windows into another dimension. Surrealist art, spirituality and Meher Baba were all among the influences. But the geometric patterns also referenced optical art designs of the kind found on the set of Ready Steady Go! and on Keith Moon's Bridget Riley T-shirt in 1966.

As Tommy grew, so did the artwork until it became a triptych. The front cover, with its planet, clouds, flying birds and outstretched fist, suggested 'breaking out into freedom', says McInnerney. The grid surrounding the planet was the gateway through which the listener passed to reach the music. The inside triptych showed a hand reaching towards birds, trees and a light in the darkness, and represented Tommy's enclosed world. Mcinnerney also produced illustrations for a printed libretto that would be included with the LP. Printing the lyrics inside an LP cover would become standard practice for progressive rock groups in the 1970s, but was still unusual in 1969.

On 1 February 1969, Delia De Leon telephoned Pete Townshend to tell him that Meher Baba had 'dropped his physical body' the day before. Townshend and McInnerney agreed that the words 'Avatar: Meher Baba' (from a Hindu phrase meaning 'a manifestation of a deity') would be included in the final *Tommy* LP credits.

As the album neared completion, though, Townshend couldn't shake the feeling that its spiritual message had been diluted: 'Instead of having the guts to take what Baba said, "Don't worry, be happy. Leave the results to God . . ." I decided that people weren't capable of hearing that directly. They've got to have it served up in this soppy entertainment package.'

Other aspects of *Tommy* would niggle Townshend and his bandmates for the next five decades. The album had been Kit Lambert's baby, which made his decision to go to Cairo instead of overseeing the final mix especially odd. No one can remember why Lambert decamped to Egypt, only that he turned up at IBC, told The Who he had a plane to catch, and left the studio wearing what appeared to be a dressing gown. ('It wasn't unusual for people to turn up to work at Track still wearing their dressing gowns,' points out Arthur Brown.) Instead, Lambert left the final mix to Damon Lyon-Shaw. 'I interpreted many of Kit's excitable instructions during the sessions, many on the back of a cigarette packet,' Lyon-Shaw told Richard Barnes. One of these instructions was to make Pete Townshend's acoustic guitar 'sound like the colours of a rainbow'.

Although Roger Daltrey appreciated what he called 'Kit's quirky, cranky production' on The Who's early records, the band wanted something different for *Tommy*. Brian Carroll had cut several Who records at IBC with the volume control indicator's needle in the red: 'It distorted the sound, but that was what Kit wanted.' But Tommy had to be different.

The finished album was warmer, subtler and less distorted, but, as Keith Moon said, 'It was very un-Who-like.' Townshend defended Lambert's production; Entwistle grumbled that it wasn't powerful enough, and that Kit should have given them more time for over-dubs. After working on the album for eight months, Daltrey said he felt like 'a tiger trapped in a cage' and nobody was sure what sounded good anymore.

The public had its first taste of The Who's rock opera with the single 'Pinball Wizard' in March 1969. Former pirate DJ turned BBC Radio 1 employee Tony Blackburn decried the song as 'sick'. But that was the point. 'It was meant to be teenage-like and slightly sleazy,' said Townshend. 'Something a schoolteacher would disapprove of.'

Furthermore, the song Townshend had initially denounced as 'embarrassing' caught the public's imagination. Townshend might have been writing about sensory deprivation and childhood abuse, but The Who gamely promoted 'Pinball Wizard' with appearances on BBC's *Top of the Pops* and ATV's family-friendly *This is Tom Jones*. The exposure worked. Kit Lambert had predicted a hit, and 'Pinball Wizard' reached Number 4, the highest entry for a Who single since 'Pictures of Lily'. 'It was the song that saved us,' admitted Daltrey.

The Who planned to follow their renewed success with the launch of *Tommy* at Ronnie Scott's Soho jazz club. On 1 May, The Who took over the venue's cramped stage in front of an audience of what *Record Mirror* described as 'journalists, publicists and assorted ravers', many of whom quickly polished off the free drink Track Records had supplied. Townshend offered them an unflinching explanation of The Who's rock opera: 'It's a story about a boy who is born normal, just like you and me . . . Then he witnesses a murder and becomes deaf, dumb and blind. He is later raped by his uncle and gets turned onto LSD . . . It's not sick contrary to what one hears on Aunty [the BBC] . . .'

Record Mirror recalled The Who being greeted by good-natured taunts of 'Fuck off'. Later, talking to Who pundit Dave Marsh for *Mojo* magazine, Townshend remembered 'an audience of baying critics going "You fucking perverted asshole!" because it was about a deaf, dumb and blind boy.' The band ignored the heckling, turned their amps up even louder, and thundered through the whole of *Tommy*: 'By the end of the show they'd all had a lot of alcohol and we'd deafened them. Then it was kind of, "Well, this could be a hit." But the damage for me was done.'

Journalists who had previously worried that the story was distasteful were now cautiously supportive. However, the album's release was put back until the end of May, due to a problem with printing the elaborate sleeve. When it did arrive, *New Musical Express* damned *Tommy* with faint praise: 'Pretentious is too strong a word . . . Maybe, over-ambitious.' *Melody Maker* suggested that the story was 'disturbing, faintly vicious but generally compassionate', and the *Observer*'s Tony Palmer feared that The Who's greatest hurdle would turn out to be musical snobbery: 'For all we know [Townshend] could have written the greatest music of the twentieth century, but because he has to do it with pop music what he *does* write doesn't stand a chance of a fair hearing.'

Over the coming months, Townshend would talk himself hoarse discussing his new creation. Today, some of his comments about Tommy's sexual abuse would attract widespread condemnation. 'Tommy's awareness of the world is completely un-jaded,' he said in July 1969. 'He gets everything in a very pure, filtered, unadulterated, un-fucked-up manner. Like when his uncle rapes him – he is incredibly elated, not disgusted, at being homosexually raped. He takes it as a move of total affection . . . In Tommy's mind everything is incredible, meaningless beauty.'

In January 2003, Townshend was arrested on suspicion of possessing indecent images of children. From the outset, Townshend admitted trying to access a website containing indecent images but denied ever actually entering the website. He also made clear that this was over his concerns as to the shocking material readily available on the Internet and as part of his research towards a campaign he had been putting together to counter damage done by Internet pornography. When the police later established that he was not in possession of any downloaded child abuse images, he was cleared of the charge. In a statement at the time, Townshend insisted that the police had 'unconditionally accepted' that he was trying to look at the site as research for his campaign. Even so, Townshend's comments around the time of *Tommy*'s release and others like them, would become grist to the mill for journalists after his arrest.

However, as Roger Daltrey bluntly explained, in the 1960s,

'Nothing was off limits for The Who. There was no subject we wouldn't write about.' Since being arrested and subsequently cleared, Townshend has refused to back away from the uncomfortable aspects of the story, largely because it's his story: '"See me, feel me, touch me . . ." Where did that come from? It came from that little four-and-a-half-year-old boy in a fucking unlocked bedroom in a house with a madwoman. That's where it came from.'

What *Tommy* shares with *S.F. Sorrow* is an unhappy ending, if it has an ending at all. Just as The Who had challenged the prevailing ethos of peace and love in 1967, so they rejected the idea of a beatific Tommy guiding his disciples to spiritual salvation. Instead, Tommy gathers his followers together at the holiday camp, brusquely disregards his loyal fan Sally Simpson, and tells his apostles to reject a life of hedonism, plug up their eyes, ears and mouths and play pinball instead. After which he returns to his inner, fantasy world. Listeners were left scratching their heads and wondering what had happened.

Townshend usually directed those who wanted to know what it all meant to Meher Baba's instruction: find the answer yourself. The rest of The Who toed this party line. 'The ambiguity of *Tommy* allowed it to answer many things for many different people,' said Daltrey. 'But in fact it didn't really answer anything. That was the beauty of it.'

However, as the years passed and *Tommy* became a movie in 1975, and a stage musical in the mid-1990s and 2013, Townshend would try to explain the message. Naturally, it kept changing. In 1994 he told *Playboy* that 'Tommy has become a metaphor for post-war children . . . and the ordinary person, whose life, in its simplicity, is crying out for more.' In 2013, Tommy's sensory deprivation was 'a metaphor for how you feel as a teenager', while Tommy recovering his senses represents 'us breaking away from things we clung on to in childhood and assuming our powers as men'.

Not that this ambiguity was detrimental to sales, even at the time. By June, *Tommy* had reached Number 2 in the UK album charts. Like its titular character's real and illusory worlds, the record worked on two levels. Sometimes the lyrics didn't fit the music, and some of the music – and the story – came up wanting. But *Tommy* was big and ambitious and sounded like it meant *something*. That said, strip away the mysticism, and the listener was still left with some extraordinary three-minute pop songs, 'The Acid Queen', 'Pinball Wizard', 'I'm Free' and 'See Me, Feel Me'.

Every member of the group, especially Moon and Daltrey, had given an outstanding performance. But, at times, during the classically inclined instrumentals, The Who sounded as if they were reaching for something beyond their grasp. At their core, The Who were still the same ramshackle R&B band that used to play the Railway. What's astonishing, even now, is the way Townshend had taken the music they used to play and completely distorted it. Only The Who could have served up this strange brew of Sonny Boy Williamson's 'Eyesight to the Blind', Henry Purcell, old-English music hall, black humour and sexual perversion, and called it an opera.

Townshend believed that 'the pretention, the audacity and cheek' of *Tommy* was necessary to get The Who the attention they needed. Chris Stamp said that he'd satisfied his anti-establishment tendencies: 'It was the world we were trying to pull down, all those associations of conservatism.' Meanwhile, it gave Kit Lambert a stick with which to beat the critics that had mocked his father for daring to mix European classical music with American jazz.

'I once had a long conversation with Kit about a conversation I'd had with Igor Stravinsky,' says Tony Palmer. 'I'd asked Stravinsky, "Do you worry about the impact popular music might have on classical music?" And Stravinsky said, "No, absolutely not. There are only three kinds of music — good music, bad music and non-music." In other words, I don't give a toss if it's a concerto or a song by Lennon and McCartney.'

'Kit thought in a similar way,' he continues. 'Coming from his background, it didn't matter what you called it — rock 'n' roll, blues, jazz or show music — it didn't matter. Kit grasped that as a principle. He didn't think of rock 'n' roll as up here and classical music as down there — and he was thinking like that long before *Tommy*.'

Tommy was a hit, but was it a hit with the same dislocated boys and girls whose response made 'I Can't Explain' a hit? 'Only the mods would've lost the thread of The Who once we got passed at least 1967 and 1968,' offers 'Irish' Jack. 'I don't think too many mods, of those few that were left, had an idea of what the hell 'Dogs' or 'Magic Bus' were about. Yet this was all part of the evolution. Townshend could have written a grand opera about the women's union at the Ford Dagenham car-assembly plant, as long as the music was fresh and exciting I'd have been up for it.'

Others weren't so sure. For June Clark, who had once helped run The Who's fan club, *Tommy* was the end: 'I know it told a story and it was unique and new. But I remember writing about this in my diary at the time. I didn't like The Who's music anymore and *Tommy* bored me to tears. To this day I can't stand it.'

What neither The Who nor their audience realised was that *Tommy* was both the end of one chapter and the beginning of the next. By the time the album was released in Britain on 23 May, The Who were already in the United States. They flew to Michigan a week after playing Ronnie Scott's, with Townshend convinced that London had disowned them. Perversely, for an album so steeped in post-war British culture, it was in America that The Who's deaf, dumb and blind hero would truly come to life.

Keith Moon, in a rare moment of lucidity, once said, 'it wasn't until *Tommy*, when people started regarding us as a musical group in addition to a stage act'. The Who were reminded of how much they were defined by their stage act on 16 May, when they arrived in New York to play the first of three nights at the Fillmore East. They were nearing the end of their set when the more coherent members of the audience noticed smoke drifting through the venue. Understandably, they presumed it was all part of the act.

In fact, the smoke was coming from a supermarket next door. The shop's owners had refused to pay protection money to a local gang, and a Molotov cocktail had just been thrown through their front window. Wiggy Wolff was counting the night's takings in Bill Graham's office when he heard about it: 'My first thought was "Fire? Pay Me!"'

Mingling with the audience were several undercover policemen. After hearing about the fire, one of them jumped onstage and, without explanation, seized Daltrey's microphone. Daltrey threw a punch, and Townshend kicked the policeman in the groin.

It was only when promoter Bill Graham took the microphone and calmly told the audience they had to evacuate the building, that many realised it wasn't all part of the act. After all, The Who beating a man up onstage was the next logical step after destroying their guitars and amps.

Ironically, The Who had wanted to tone down the onstage violence for this latest trip and now there was a warrant out for their arrest. The band's agent Frank Barsalona pleaded their case, and told the police they hadn't realised the stage invader was a cop. Daltrey and Townshend handed themselves in the following morning. Barsalona posted bail and the tour was allowed to continue. The threat of cancelled visas and a year in jail, hung over The Who for the next two months.

By the end of May, though, 'Pinball Wizard' was in the American top twenty and *Tommy* had received Nik Cohn's promised glowing review in the *New York Times*: '*Tommy* is just possibly the most important work that anyone has yet done in rock,' he wrote. 'We really went from the ridiculous to the sublime,' admitted Townshend, 'being told we were musical geniuses when really we were a bunch of scumbags.'

While rehearsing *Tommy* for its launch at Ronnie Scott's, the band had been struck by the music's extraordinary, building energy. This only increased as the US tour progressed. The tipping point came halfway through a show at Chicago's Kinetic Playground when the audience stood up as one and remained standing for the rest of the performance. 'It took *Tommy* to do what several hit singles and countless tours hadn't been able to do,' suggested *Rolling Stone*'s John Mendelsohn, 'give the ordinary American rock fan a handle with which he could get a good grip on The Who.'

Yet *Tommy* also spoke to the 'extraordinary' fan, as Townshend discovered when he received a letter after one of the Chicago gigs: '[He] said, "Hey, Mr Townshend, I've got to tell you what happened when I first heard *Tommy* . . . I became Tommy and ever since I've been in this spiritual trance."' Townshend could relate to this, and later said that while performing the album, he experienced a natural high that transcended anything he'd had with illegal drugs: 'The finale of *Tommy* never failed to mesmerise me along with the rest of the audience.'

Performing *Tommy* would have a quite different effect on Roger Daltrey. In 1964, Kit Lambert had proudly described The Who as 'the ugliest [group] in London'. His description of Daltrey on Brighton beach was especially wounding: 'Roger, with his barrel chest and skinny legs and ribs showing, a real short arse . . .' Yet just as Daltrey had inhabited the role of Tommy in the studio, he now inhabited the role onstage. '*Tommy* gave Roger a part to play,' said Townshend. 'It made him an icon. It made him a rock god.' Certainly Daltrey sang *Tommy* with complete conviction. But there was more to it than that; Daltrey had turned the character into a sex symbol.

At some point in 1968, Daltrey had stopped lacquering his hair and let it grow out naturally. 'It was my wife's idea,' he said. 'I woke up one morning and she said, "Your hair, your hair . . ."' Daltrey's first panicked thought was that it had fallen out overnight. In fact, he'd simply gone to bed with his hair un-straightened. 'What she said was, "Your hair, your hair, it's beautiful." After that I stopped straightening it and let it grow.'

Daltrey dumped the gel and lacquer he'd been using since 1964 and was soon accessorising his new lion's mane with a selection of chi-chi neck scarves and fringed buckskin jackets cut away to reveal a lithe torso. The transformation reflected his growing confidence within The Who, and only served to bring Daltrey even more attention. 'Roger grew his hair, took his shirt off, and started to sit in the sun,' said Townshend, 'and instead of getting laid every couple of days he got laid every fifteen seconds.'

When The Who played Columbia, Maryland, their support act was Led Zeppelin, whose name had been gifted to them by Moon and Entwistle during a drinking session. At first glance Zeppelin's blonde, long-haired vocalist Robert Plant resembled a five-foot, eleven-inch version of The Who's lead singer. 'Robert was a bit Daltrey Mark II,' conceded Roger. 'But I was always more jealous of the fact that he was so fucking tall.'

The Who had their first taste of Zeppelin's imperious attitude at the Columbia gig when they played for so long that Wiggy Wolff pulled the plug on them. Zeppelin and The Who would trail each other around the US stadium circuit for most of the 1970s. Zeppelin's tumultuous heavy rock would make them millionaires and give birth to dozens of inferior imitators, but Pete Townshend would never become a fan. 'I like them all as people,' he said later. 'But I haven't liked a single thing Led Zeppelin have done.'

Unlike Daltrey and Robert Plant, though, Townshend was now dressing like an anti-rock star. In 1967, he'd been the dandy in ruffled shirts and a beautiful pearly king jacket. A year on, and he was arriving onstage wearing a boiler suit and work boots, like a plumber who'd come to fix a leaky backstage toilet. 'I used to go on wearing a boiler suit and Dr Martens in defiance of fashion,' he explained.

By the end of the tour, *Tommy* had become The Who's first US top-five album, but Daltrey and Townshend were still facing criminal charges. The pair flew back to New York for an appearance at Manhattan's Supreme Court. To their surprise, the charges against Daltrey were dismissed and Townshend was let off with a $75 fine, a small price to pay for kicking a policeman in the balls. Townshend told anyone who would listen that he never wanted to go back to America again. Yet by the following morning he'd agreed to play Woodstock.

The Woodstock Music and Arts Fair was being sold to groups and their managers as 'three days of peace and music'. The idea for the festival came about after two entrepreneurs, John Roberts and Joel Rosenman, placed ads in the *Wall Street Journal* and the *New York Times* declaring themselves, 'Young men with unlimited capital, looking for interesting, legitimate, investment opportunities and business propositions.' They ended up investing in what would become the biggest music event of all time. Vast sums of money would be made, but also lost. As Brian Jones said of Monterey, 'It is not free and it is not love.' For The Who, Woodstock would be the proof of that.

The festival was to be held over three days between 15 and 17 August 1969 on 600 acres of farmland near the small town of Bethel in upstate New York. But the organisers needed a big act to headline the show. The Beatles had stopped playing live in 1966 and the Stones were out of action as Mick Jagger was shooting another film. Woodstock's production co-coordinator was John Morris, Bill Graham's right-hand man at the Fillmore East. Morris told Frank Barsalona he wanted The Who.

Townshend agreed to have dinner with Morris in Barsalona's New York apartment. 'Frank was dying for us to do it,' says Wiggy Wolff, who was also present. 'There was a buzz and the feeling that this could be a big thing. But it was seen as a bit dodgy – out there in this big field – which is why a lot of acts wouldn't commit.'

Townshend, exhausted after weeks of touring and the stress of his court appearance, just wanted to go home to see his wife and baby. Morris and Barsalona tried to wear him down by keeping him awake all night. According to Townshend's autobiography, the persistent agent went so far as to lock them in his apartment and toss the keys into the street below, telling Townshend he couldn't leave until he agreed to play.

Wolff was also reluctant to commit to Woodstock, as The Who were already contracted to play Bill Graham's Tanglewood festival in Massachusetts a couple of days before. At the time Woodstock wasn't going to be a free festival, and Graham was paying The Who $12,500. Never one to take his eye off 'the count' Wiggy told John Morris that the band couldn't possibly play Woodstock without their freighting costs being covered.

Morris agreed to provide a helicopter to transport The Who between the two festival sites. But when Townshend asked for a fee of $15,000, Morris told him they only had $11,000 left in the budget. After further haggling, an exhausted Townshend finally gave in. 'Pete had agreed to do it but didn't really want to do it,' says Wolff now. If Townshend harboured any thoughts of reneging on the deal, they were quashed when Chris Stamp signed the contract a few days later. The Who were playing Woodstock, whether they liked it or not.

Asked about his plans for Track Records in 1967, Kit Lambert told journalists that Pete Townshend would be 'heading up a mysterious department called "Jazz and New Sounds"'. Despite his punishing workload with The Who, Townshend fulfilled his duties as an A&R man. After bringing the label the Crazy World of Arthur Brown, he signed Andy Newman, the jazz pianist who'd so intrigued him with his performance at Ealing art school, six years earlier.

Townshend was also trying to find a musical project for his friend, 'Armenia City in the Sky' composer John 'Speedy' Keen, and his latest discovery, a fifteen-year-old Scottish guitarist named Jimmy McCullough. Lambert had pointed out that he didn't have time to look after all of them, so Townshend decided to form a group for all three. It was another example of what Mike McInnerney describes as 'arranging people like pieces of Lego' to see what worked. But not all the pieces fitted. 'Pete Townshend jammed the three of us together,' says Andy Newman, who still sounds baffled by the arrangement, even now. 'We were a manufactured band. Like The Monkees.'

The disparity between the three men soon became obvious. Keen and McCullough had the long hair and general demeanour of late-1960s rock stars. But with his professorial spectacles and beard, the twenty-six-year-old Andy Newman resembled a schoolmaster. Andy was a talented Dixieland jazz pianist, not a rock 'n' roller. 'The Who were diametric to my ideas of music at the time,' he admits. In an attempt to stimulate Newman's creativity, Townshend invited him to his home studio, placed photographs of different objects, including a picture of a crocodile, on the piano, and asked him to play whatever came into his head. It was an idea that could have come straight out of Ealing art school: 'Pete suggested I play along to these pictures, though I can't say whether it made a lot of difference.'

The incongruous trio recorded their debut album, *Hollywood Dream*, in fits and starts throughout 1969. Speedy Keen wrote the songs, sang and played drums. Townshend produced and played bass under the pseudonym Bijou Drains. After casting around for a band name, Townshend borrowed Andy's nickname, Thunderclap Newman, a moniker he'd been given by his schoolfriends after his heavy-handed style of piano playing.

Newman had spent the past ten years working as a GPO engineer, and was wary of giving up a steady income. Nevertheless, he agreed to do so, in exchange for what he called, 'Track Records' meagre retainer'. But when The Who returned from America in July, Thunderclap Newman's first single, 'Something in the Air', was on its way to Number 1.

In June 1969, astronaut Neil Armstrong became the first man to walk on the moon; 'Something in the Air' captured the spirit of change and revolution in what was the final summer of the 1960s. 'It was the right moment for that particular song,' says Newman.

Unfortunately, the group's next single, 'Accidents', failed to reach even the top thirty, and their live shows proved to be a disappointment. Speedy Keen and Jimmy McCullouch fell out badly — the fact that the three band members had been, as Newman says 'jammed together' didn't help, but nor did the fact that Lambert, Stamp and Townshend were busy with The Who.

'I later realised that the problem with Kit Lambert was that he was just like his opposite number in Liverpool, Brian Epstein,' says Newman.

'He was a one-group manager. I have always suspected Kit Lambert wanted us to have a big crash and sell no records so he could turn round and say "You're finished." We had the hit, but they still didn't follow it up. They were dedicated to The Who, and our career was put on the back burner.'

Further evidence of Lambert's managerial shortcomings came when Townshend's other signing, the Crazy World of Arthur Brown, were on tour in America in July. Their follow-up singles had failed to match the million-selling 'Fire', and the band suddenly found themselves stranded in a New York hotel without any money.

'It was a sign of things starting to go wrong at Track,' says Brown. 'We were left in this hotel without a penny and with one hamburger to eat between the five of us.' Brown complained that Lambert and Stamp were 'off taking drugs somewhere'. This may have been true, but, by his own admission, Brown was also 'stoned off my crust'. It was the blind leading the blind.

Promoter Bill Graham took pity on the band and gave them money for food. Soon after, Brown was approached by a New York business-man who was looking to break into pop management. He'd concocted a deal with CBS and offered Brown a huge advance to make a soul album. After hearing about the offer, Lambert and Stamp suddenly arrived at the hotel and pleaded with Brown not to leave Track. 'They said, "Please, we were the guys who put you at the top, don't you think you have a moral duty to us to stay on the label?"'

Brown gave in, turned down the CBS offer and flew home to England: 'After that, Kit missed five successive business meetings with me in a row, at which point I thought, this has gone too far.' The Crazy World of Arthur Brown split up, but the legal and financial fallout from their contract with Track would drag on well into the twenty-first century.

While hardly drug-free himself at the time, Brown maintains that the decline of Track Records can be pinpointed to an increase in Chris Stamp and, especially, Kit Lambert's drug use. Simon Napier-Bell offered an unflinching description of Kit's average day in *You Don't Have to Say You Love Me*: 'He'd arrive at his office at eleven in the morning, having woken up with a good sniff of coke to brighten the day . . . As soon as he got to his desk, he'd light a joint. Then he'd take two dishes of pills out of a drawer and leave them sitting on the desk like cocktail snacks on a bar . . .'

'Unfortunately, by the late sixties, the white stuff [cocaine] had come in, and Kit, Chris and all of us were seriously supporting the Colombian economy,' admits John Fenton. 'But Kit was a gentleman and one of the few guys in rock 'n' roll with an intellect. Even when he was off his box, you'd put up with it because he was so entertaining and such a great raconteur.'

The culture of excess was escalating and now impacting on the business. Track's office was close to an Algerian coffee shop. 'I used to go into the entrance and you were always overwhelmed by the beautiful smell of roasting coffee,' recalls Andy Newman. 'As you went up the stairs, the smell of coffee faded and was replaced by the smell of cannabis. I eventually gauged that if the smell of cannabis was overpowering the smell of coffee at the bottom of the stairs, then you had no chance of doing any serious business.'

Lambert and Stamp would add to their roster in 1969 by signing Keith Moon's favourite comedian, wisecracking American Murray Roman, and singer Marsha Hunt, the star of the hippie musical *Hair*. But these acts struggled to sell records in the way The Who, Hendrix, Arthur Brown or Thunderclap Newman had. In the meantime, any money made continued to leave the office faster than it was coming in.

'There were a lot of people at Track haemorrhaging money, not just Kit and Chris,' states John Fenton. 'I can remember going back to the office at Old Compton Street at four in the morning with a group of Track employees, where we played poker until nine o'clock. When they ran out of money, they just opened the safe and helped themselves to more. I went home and woke up at my flat in Knightsbridge, and I was covered in £20 notes. The last thing I remembered was that safe being opened.'

This culture of excess would soon claim its first victim. On 3 July, Brian Jones drowned in the swimming pool of his Sussex farmhouse. Pete Townshend was backstage at *Top of the Pops* with Thunderclap Newman when he heard the news. The pair had spent many nights swanning around the Speakeasy and the Ad-Lib together, before their respective workloads and Jones' drug habits pulled them apart. 'Brian died a drunken muddle with no one trying too hard to look after him,' said Marianne Faithfull. 'A little bit of love might have sorted him out,' ventured Townshend. But it was too little, too late.

There was no time to grieve, for the Rolling Stones or The Who. Their lives were moving too fast. Three days after Jones' death, the Stones went ahead with a planned free concert in London's Hyde Park. A large photograph of their ex-guitarist was positioned at the side of the stage. They delivered a so-so performance that included Jagger reading Shelley's poem 'Adonaïs' and releasing white butterflies over the crowd as a tribute to their former bandmate.

When the gig was finished, many of those who had been backstage at Hyde Park drifted over to the Royal Albert Hall where The Who were playing the inaugural Pop Proms. Also on the bill was Chuck Berry. 'The Who loved Chuck Berry, we all loved Chuck Berry,' says compére Jeff Dexter. 'Unfortunately Chuck was a cunt to everybody else.'

The problems had begun during rehearsals in the early afternoon, when Berry berated his group for not playing his songs 'the way Chuck plays 'em'. Berry's next target was The Who. Berry had opened for the band in New York a few weeks earlier, and was reluctant to do so again. A compromise was reached: Chuck would close the first set in the afternoon and The Who would close the second in the evening. But The Who hadn't reckoned on their past life as a mod group coming back to haunt them.

In 1964, Townshend and Barney had gone to see Chuck Berry at the Hammersmith Odeon. That night, mods and rockers alike had paid homage to one of rock 'n' roll's founding fathers. But when The Who arrived to play their matinee set at the Albert Hall, they faced a group of die-hard rockers and Teddy Boys with long memories. 'Chuck was still attracting the leftovers who considered The Who a mod band,' says Dexter.

Within seconds of The Who's arrival, the Teds were trying to block the stage. The irony was that Daltrey, with his enormous hair and tasselled suede outfit, couldn't have looked less like a mod if he'd tried. When the rockers started throwing sharpened pennies at the band, one of The Who's roadies took the drastic step of firing a mace gun into the front row. It was a formidable display of power. But when a flying penny cut Daltrey above his eye, the singer waded in. 'The guy who did it was wedged up against the stage,' he recalled. 'By then I could swing the mic so accurately I could take a cigarette out of someone's mouth.' Daltrey swung his mic like a lariat and struck his assailant full in the face.

When Jeff Dexter's female assistant was knocked unconscious, the DJ dashed to the front of the stage to try to calm the situation: 'I started trying to preach peace and love. "Hey, we all love Chuck Berry . . . and we all love The Who . . .".'

The police managed to round up most of the culprits, frogmarching them out of the venue, and the show carried on. To pacify the remaining rockers, The Who played Eddie Cochran's 'Summertime Blues' and Johnny Kidd and the Pirates' 'Shakin' All Over', like parents trying to soothe an infant with its favourite lullabies. Standing by the side of the stage watching it all was Townshend's favourite painter, Peter Blake. The Who's past world of mods, rockers, Teddy Boys and pop art had converged in one afternoon.

The Who played their second set that evening to a peaceful audience, including Mick Jagger, resplendent in the same white frock, borrowed from Marianne Faithfull, that he'd worn onstage at Hyde Park. 'The Who were on brilliant form,' says Jeff Dexter, 'because they were playing to their peers. They were the best rock 'n' roll group we had. The Stones had become satellites of each other, whereas The Who were constantly on the road. They played and lived and shagged together. They were unified.'

The four disparate individuals who had failed to impress Dexter at Greenwich Town Hall four years earlier had changed. Nevertheless, The Who's lingering reputation for violence made the Pop Proms' organisers uncomfortable. Promoter Roy Guest didn't want to see smashed guitars and amps on the Royal Albert Hall stage, and came up with a diversion.

'Roy suggested we give them bunches of flowers, just like they do at the classical proms,' says Dexter. 'My assistant gave Daltrey a bunch and I gave another to Moonie. He was so taken aback he forgot about smashing his kit. I don't think anyone had ever given The Who flowers before.'

Pete Townshend climbed into the limousine taking The Who from their hotel in Liberty, New York, to the Woodstock festival site and had his first inkling that something was wrong. According to his chauffeur, all helicopters in and out of the site had been grounded, as the charter company hadn't been paid.

The organisers, Woodstock Ventures, had sold 186,000 tickets for the three-day festival, and had expected an additional 30,000 people to turn up over the course of the weekend; but by the second day there was somewhere between 400,000 and 500,000 people on-site. The company didn't have the manpower to disperse that many or charge them entry. Woodstock had become a free festival, and Woodstock Ventures were in no hurry to pay the bands, which now included Jimi Hendrix, the Grateful Dead, Crosby Stills Nash & Young, Santana and Jefferson Airplane. The event was also being filmed and recorded for a documentary and live album, for which Woodstock Ventures would be paid an advance in excess of $1 million.

Unfortunately, nobody involved with the festival had considered the problems that would arise from having half a million people squatting for three days on a farm. By Saturday, when The Who arrived, food and water were in scant supply, the Port-O-San toilets had proved woefully inadequate and persistent rain had turned much of the farmland into a quagmire. The road leading to the site was inches deep with mud, leading to twenty-five-mile tailbacks and scores of abandoned vehicles. 'We got as far as the car could go,' said Townshend. 'Then it became the hundred and ninety-fifth limo to get stuck.'

'It was a morass, mud up to the knees,' recalls Wiggy Wolff. 'Pete was pissed off as he'd brought over his missus and his young kid, and that was why he had agreed to do the gig in the first place.' After reaching the backstage area, and surveying the chaos, Karen wisely opted to take their baby daughter Emma back to the hotel, where they remained for the rest of the weekend. Townshend, meanwhile, wondered what he'd let himself in for. At which point he glanced up to see a poster of Meher Baba's face pinned to the top of a telegraph pole.

'It was a wonderful symbol,' he said. 'Then this young man, blonde-haired, Germanic looking, in his underpants, obviously on a trip, ran across and shinned up this pole like an athlete and touched the picture. At this point I was like, "Wow cool, man!" I was still in hippieland. And he touched this picture and went "Aaargh!" as though his hands had been burnt.' The Baba disciple had touched a live power line and been electrocuted. He fell backwards and landed on an ambulance stuck in the mud below. 'His head was moving, but his body was completely static,' recalled Townshend. 'He had broken his neck. I don't know if he survived.'

In just a few seconds, any good vibes Townshend felt had been extinguished. To add to his unease, he realised that the coffee he was drinking had been made with water spiked with LSD, albeit heavily diluted LSD. John Entwistle had taken the precaution of bringing his own bottle of bourbon, but mistakenly let someone fill his glass with ice cubes from the backstage area. His response was to guzzle as much bourbon as he could to stave off the effects of the acid. Moon, meanwhile, was on LSD under his own volition. Once again, the no-nonsense Daltrey was at odds with the world around him. 'Everything was spiked,' he grumbled. 'You were scared to take a drink.'

Now trapped on-site, The Who discovered that they weren't due to play for another fourteen hours. The view from the stage was breathtaking: a sea of bodies that stretched as far as the horizon. To keep such a vast crowd happy, the organisers had decided that music should start in the early evening and carry on through the night. Food and drink might have been in short supply but drugs weren't. The medical tent was soon full of disorientated young people in the throes of bad acid trips, with one area reserved for those LSD users who'd scorched their retinas from staring at the sun for too long while under the influence.

Most of the musicians were in a similarly heightened state. The Grateful Dead's guitarist Jerry Garcia later discovered that the ball of light rolling in front of him on the stage was electricity and not a hallucination brought on by acid. Garcia was electrocuted and blown several feet back into his amp. When Jefferson Airplane finished their set, guitarist Paul Kantner found that he was unable to move. Kantner was tripping on LSD, and convinced that his legs had turned into tree trunks and had taken root in the stage.

The backstage enclosure seemed to be populated solely by people who were high, whether by accident or design. Everywhere Townshend looked, they lurched into view, grinning inanely or spouting gibberish, before ducking back into the shadows. 'As a cynical English arsehole, I wandered through it all and felt like spitting on the lot of them,' he said.

The day got worse as it wore on. At some point in the afternoon John Morris sheepishly told Wiggy Wolff that he didn't have The Who's money. 'Because of the flower-power people, all you ever heard at this time was, "Free, *man*",' says Wolff, dismissively. 'Free love, free music, free concerts, and it was getting out of hand.'

Wolff reminded Morris of their agreement: that The Who wouldn't set foot onstage until he'd received their fee in cash: 'He said, "You can't do that, there are almost a million people here and there will be riots." I said, "Yeah, there will be riots. But you will remember I said, we need to get paid or we wouldn't have come."'

Morris argued that it was a Saturday, the banks were closed, and it was impossible to raise the cash. When Wolff refused to back down, other bands' managers tried to appease him. 'They were all like, "Come on, *man*." But I didn't care. They kept saying, "We can't get the money out of the bank because it's Saturday and the safe has a time lock on." I said, "Well, get the bank manager up. He can override it." I didn't know what I was talking about. I was completely bullshitting. But in the end, they did.'

Joel Rosenman telephoned the manager at the White Lake branch of Sullivan County National Bank. When the manager informed him that the roads were too blocked with cars for him to get to the bank and to the site, he was told to wait in his back garden and a helicopter would pick him up. 'They got him to the bank,' says Wolff, 'got him to override the time lock on the safe and got me my money.'

News that The Who had been paid spread through the backstage area. Suddenly the same managers who had been telling Wolff to stop being a capitalist pig were queuing up behind him trying to get cash for their own groups. 'Creedence Clearwater Revival's manager tried to ask for the same,' says Wolff, 'and they pummelled him, because he was an American. The organisers pointed at me and said, "He's a Limey, they're all horrible, but you . . ." My name was shit but I didn't care.'

Wolff now had the unenviable task of keeping more than $10,000 safe and stopping his weary, drug-addled band from falling asleep on him. The Who had been due on at 10 p.m., but as Saturday night turned into Sunday morning 'they kept sticking more bands on ahead of us'. The Grateful Dead were followed by Creedence Clearwater

Revival, Janis Joplin and the Kozmic Blues Band, and, finally, Sly and the Family Stone.

By 3 a.m. Sly Stone's exuberant soul music had blasted the crowd out of their torpor, but, having done so, the band refused to stop. A one-hour set had become a two-hour set. 'I realised that if they carried on any longer, The Who wouldn't be able to perform,' says Wolff. 'I actually said to the organisers, "We're too tired. We're not playing. Here's your money back."' Again, Wolff's bullishness paid off. 'They cut Sly Stone's set short,' he says. 'Not by that much – I can't take all the credit – but they did cut it short.'

It was close to 4 a.m. when The Who finally climbed the steps on to the darkened stage. 'Once again, providence went our way,' says Wiggy 'because Sly and the Family Stone were a horrible band to follow, but at least they'd woken the audience up.' Despite the shivery after-effects of the LSD and the crushing boredom of the past fourteen hours, The Who exuded an almost super-human energy. Sly Stone's limbous funk suddenly gave way to some twisted English blues. Townshend, in a boiler suit and boots, grinned, gurned, scowled and windmilled his guitar, while Daltrey, an explosion of blonde curls, suede fringes and bare flesh, lassoed his mic lead around his head.

When film-maker Michael Wadleigh appeared holding a camera, Townshend pushed him into the press pit without a second thought. However disgusted he claimed to be by the aloof behaviour of his rock-star contemporaries, Townshend was guilty of the same. Later, his extreme reaction to another stage invader anticipated *Time* magazine's description of The Who at Woodstock as 'slicing through the flower power like a chainsaw in a daisy garden'.

Among those backstage and high on acid was Abbie Hoffman, a strident anti-Vietnam War protestor and one of the founders of the vociferous Youth International Party. His fellow activist and leader of the White Panthers, John Sinclair, had just been sentenced to ten years in prison for possession of two marijuana joints. Hoffman watched The Who from the wings and in his already heightened state began brooding over Sinclair's plight. Without warning, he dashed on to the stage to protest in the middle of *Tommy* and barked into the microphone: 'I think this is a pile of shit while John Sinclair rots in prison.'

'Fuck off! Fuck off my fucking stage!' Townshend replied in a braying cockney accent. According to Who mythology and several eyewitnesses, he then struck Hoffman with his guitar, knocking him into the press pit. 'If I'd hit him with a guitar he'd be dead. I used the guitar neck to sweep him off the stage,' Townshend later insisted. The cameraman was changing film at the time and missed the altercation. After dealing with Hoffman, Townshend delivered a personal promise to the crowd: 'The next fucking person that walks across the stage is gonna get fucking killed, all right?'

Townshend later felt guilty. He knew who Abbie Hoffman was and wasn't unsympathetic to John Sinclair's plight. But he was also obsessively territorial about The Who's stage. The incident was still on Townshend's mind when he wrote about Meher Baba in *Rolling Stone*, two years later: 'I see me writing columns like this, then going and kicking Abbie Hoffman's little ass in a proud rage . . . I am my own worst enemy.'

Despite Townshend's violent outburst, The Who's Woodstock performance was a victory. As they reached the grand finale of *Tommy*, Mother Nature chose to smile on the band, giving them a crucial advantage over all the acts that had come before. 'During "See Me, Feel Me", the sun started to come up fast,' says Wiggy Wolff. 'You could not have asked for anything better. Some guy actually came up to me and said, "How the fuck did you do that?" And I said, "I had God's help."'

Almost twenty-four hours after they'd left, the exhausted band returned to their hotel in Liberty. By then, the state governor had arranged for military helicopters to bring emergency food and medical supplies to the festival site. Jimi Hendrix was supposed to play on Sunday night. By the time The Who's nemesis arrived onstage, it was Monday morning, and the farmland was strewn with abandoned tents, clothes, blankets and the bodies of those too exhausted or stoned to move.

Despite the drugs and the disorganisation, the music press declared Woodstock a triumph. 'The largest groupings of Americans in history has to be taken as a political event,' wrote Danny Goldberg in *Billboard*. 'Political, without the fear, clichés, and martyrdom of other political events. Its candidate was music and peace.'

By Monday morning, even the mainstream media were forced to report that half a million people had managed to co-exist peacefully for three days. There had been fewer than a hundred arrests for drug-related offences and a single accidental death, caused by a tractor crushing a youth asleep in a field. As a reporter for *CBS News* noted: 'These long-haired mostly white kids in their blue jeans and sandals were no wild-eyed anarchists.'

After the backstage squabbles over money, John Roberts and Joel Rosenman had run up an overdraft that threatened to consume almost all of their 'unlimited capital'. The advances they received for the film and album rights would save them from bankruptcy, but Woodstock Ventures would spend the next eleven years paying off their debts.

The whole experience, however, had left The Who cold. 'Woodstock was the end of that era,' said Pete Townshend. 'The whole of the rock community divided into three camps. There was the John Sinclair/Abbie Hoffman camp – the revolutionary politicos. There were the hippies, which is, "Oh man, oh man, you gotta try this and then throw yourself out of a tree." Then there were the Brits – people like us. We came here to work, and then go home and rest and write. Somehow we felt eminently boring at the time. Maybe that was why I had the conflict with Abbie Hoffman. He had something to say, he had something to do, something to be passionate about, and I just felt like a workman in a lunatic asylum, come to fix the plumbing.'

Townshend thought The Who didn't deserve their victory at Woodstock, and Daltrey declared it 'the worst gig we ever played'. But the subsequent documentary movie would preserve their performance forever, and elevate their standing around the world. The Who were on the verge of rock stardom.

After the communal madness of Woodstock, the Isle of Wight festival at the end of August was a quaintly sedate affair. Bob Dylan was booked to close the festival, with The Who headlining above Joe Cocker, the Bonzo Dog Doo-Dah Band and Track labelmate Marsha Hunt.

The Who's choice of transport to the festival site was a reminder of their now elevated status. There would be no hiking through the mud this time. The Who came by helicopter instead. Unfortunately, their grand entrance didn't quite go to plan. As their craft descended backstage, one of the wooden boards comprising a makeshift landing pad flipped up and smashed into its rotor blades. The helicopter landed with a loud bump before disgorging four laughing band members. Nobody cared about the damage. Track's financial profligacy was such that a new, bigger helicopter arrived to replace the broken one, and Peter Rudge was soon offering backstage guests a ride back to London for £25 a head.

Meanwhile, The Who's 2,500-watt PA was so large it came with a warning notice to the audience not to venture within fifteen feet of it. Unlike at Woodstock, The Who were able to avoid any peripheral distractions backstage. 'We didn't spend time getting into the vibrations,' said Townshend dismissively. Instead, they performed *Tommy*, with brutal efficiency, before flying home in time for Moon to catch last orders at The Speakeasy.

The following day, festival compére Jeff Dexter was shocked to see Bob Dylan and his manager, Albert Grossman, on their knees in a backstage cabin, counting piles of crumpled ten-bob notes and towers of coins. Like The Who at Woodstock, Dylan wasn't setting foot on the stage until he'd had his fee — in cash. 'There I was, feeling spiritual, and there was Dylan counting money,' says Dexter. 'But it was at that moment that hard commerce slipped into the trip.'

The dissenting voices that had greeted *Tommy*'s release had now been silenced. Before long, *Melody Maker* was loftily declaring The Who to be 'the band against which the rest of rock must be judged'. The Who received similarly glowing notices when they returned to America in October, and played a six-night stand at the Fillmore East in New York.

Waiting for them backstage after one of the shows was Leonard Bernstein. The *West Side Story* composer had heaped praise on *Tommy* after first hearing it. 'He shook me and said, "Do you know what you've done?" said Townshend. 'Of course, what he was talking about was that I was going the next step in what he had done with *West Side Story*, which was creating a popular song cycle, a musical that was really rooted in street culture.'

Townshend could afford to bask in the praise. For Kit Lambert, though, the final blow to the musical establishment was yet to come.

The Who began 1970 with a punishing workload and a terrible accident. Pete Townshend woke up in Twickenham on New Year's Day to find a *Melody Maker* reporter waiting downstairs to do an interview.

Four days later, after a heavy drinking session, Keith Moon accidentally killed his chauffeur.

Moon had recently bought a mock-Tudor pile in Winchmore Hill, a place of moneyed stockbrokers and manicured golf courses deep in suburban north London. Moon couldn't afford it, but believed he was due a sizeable royalty cheque for composing the song 'Tommy's Holiday Camp'. His marriage was in turmoil, but, if nothing else, he was determined to keep up appearances. Dougal Butler was currently driving John Entwistle, so Moon hired a new chauffeur, Neil Boland, to shepherd him around town in the trusty Bentley.

On 4 January, Moon was invited to open a discotheque in Hatfield, Hertfordshire. Neil Boland drove the drummer and his entourage to the club, where Keith gave a speech and proceeded to get roaringly drunk. Despite being hassled by a gang of skinheads, Moon insisted on staying at the venue and carrying on drinking. At closing time, the same gang followed the party into the car park and were soon screaming abuse and banging on the roof of the Bentley.

Boland climbed out to remonstrate with them, but was knocked to the ground. In a panic, Moon clambered into the driver's seat and started the vehicle. The car was several hundred yards away before Keith realised that his chauffeur was trapped underneath. Boland died in hospital shortly after. Eight youths would later be charged with causing an affray, and Moon for driving without a licence and insurance while under the influence of alcohol. Thanks to his persuasive and, presumably, very expensive lawyer, Keith was let off with an absolute discharge due to 'mitigating circumstances'. Boland's family never forgave him, and, according to many, Moon was tortured with guilt for the rest of his life.

Moon's response to the accident was to blot out the pain with yet more drink and drugs. But the mischievousness and charm that had allowed Keith to get away with so much in the 1960s wouldn't be enough to sustain him in the new decade. Soon it would become hard for even close friends to identify who the real Keith Moon was. 'The only time he was himself was when he shut himself off at home and relaxed with Kim,' says Dougal Butler. 'You could actually talk to him then, because he wasn't in the music scene. But as soon as he opened that front door and went into town he turned into "Keith Moon".'

John Schollar had stayed in touch with Moon since their time together in The Beachcombers. The Who's touring schedule made meeting up difficult. But when they did, Moon was the same as ever, as long as they were on their own. 'He came round especially to see my parents when he found out they were moving house,' says Schollar. 'This would have been in the late sixties, and they were so pleased to see him.' Schollar's mother couldn't help noticing that Keith's dilapidated fur coat was being held together with a safety pin. 'Yes,' said Moon, proudly. 'But it's a *silver* safety pin.' During these visits, Schollar would sometimes take Moon to the same pubs and bowling alleys they used to frequent in the early 1960s: 'And it would be fine to start with. But then after about ten minutes, he'd be buying all the lads drink and showing off. Keith couldn't have a quiet life.'

In some ways, it's easy to see why Moon struggled with fame. Gushing praise from the likes of Leonard Bernstein meant that in America, especially, The Who were now being feted as serious musicians; a group that had bridged the gap between rock 'n' roll and opera. Moon recalled the change in perception in an interview with *Rolling Stone*: 'Before, if we were sitting backstage, people would just barge in and help themselves to a drink. Now, they knock at the door, and when they come in, we're sitting with champagne on ice that's been provided by the management . . . People would treat us slightly differently,' he added. 'They talked in whispers.'

Rock music was now being regarded in some quarters as 'art' and *Tommy* was partly to blame. Just as *Sgt. Pepper* had encouraged lesser bands to start writing about imaginary LSD trips, The Who's rock opera ushered in the era of the concept album: a story set to music, regardless of the quality of the story or the music.

In November 1969, a new British group King Crimson released their debut album, *In the Court of the Crimson King*. Their often-brutal jazz-rock prompted one *Melody Maker* critic to accuse them of creating 'an almost overpowering atmosphere of power and evil'. King Crimson played at the Stones' Hyde Park concert. During their set, the six-foot-high picture of Brian Jones at the side of the stage fell over hitting lead vocalist Greg Lake on the head. It was as if the dead Rolling Stone was wreaking posthumous revenge on these art-rockers with their howling saxophones and crooked time signatures.

King Crimson supported The Who a few weeks later at the Plumpton National Jazz and Blues festival. Pete Townshend thought they were wonderful, and wrote a critique of *In the Court of the Crimson King* to be used in press ads for the LP. 'An uncanny masterpiece,' he wrote. 'A friend listening to the album from a room below says, "Is that a new Who album?" Deeply, I'm ashamed that it isn't, but I'm also glad somehow . . .' Townshend compared the album with Mahler's 'Eighth Symphony', but also wondered whether it should even be described as rock music.

But the idea of what rock music was or wasn't was changing, yet again. By 1970, it could be The Who thrashing away at 'My Generation' or King Crimson scaring the critics with what Townshend described as 'a million bloody Mellotrons that whine and soar like sirens down a canyon'. In 1968 Tony Palmer was pilloried by large swathes of the *Observer*'s readership and some of his fellow critics for comparing The Beatles' *White Album* to the great works of Schubert. Had he made the same comparison after *Tommy*, the reaction might have been different. The term 'progressive rock' was now being used by the press to describe King Crimson, Pink Floyd and new groups, including Family and Yes, that pulled influences from jazz and classical as well as pop music, and all of whom would make concept albums in one form or another.

By the new year, though, The Who were growing sick of *Tommy*. In America, the album had become bigger than the band. Roger Daltrey was now so closely identified with the character that many of the fans, waitresses and airhostesses he met in his everyday life called him 'Tommy'. The album had made Daltrey a star and seen Townshend acclaimed as a serious composer. But their bandmates were less enamoured of its effect on the group. 'John Entwistle got so sick of playing *Tommy* and talking about *Tommy* that he started to resent it,' admitted Townshend.

There was also a polarity between the grandness of *Tommy* and the modest venues The Who were still playing in the UK. After performing to half a million people at Woodstock, The Who's next gig was in front of a few hundred at a theatre in Shrewsbury. But they'd turn this to their advantage. In fact, it was all part of Lambert and Townshend's plan to subvert the grandeur of *Tommy* and bring The Who back to earth.

The group had arranged for many of their recent US dates to be recorded for a possible live album. When sound engineer Bob Pridden told Townshend that he had no idea which of the shows was the best, a petulant Townshend ordered him to burn the tapes and announced that The Who would record their live LP in England instead. Two shows were earmarked, at Leeds University on 14 February and the day after at Hull City Hall. It was a decision that would affect the The Who's future in more ways than they could possibly have imagined.

Kit Lambert once told Tony Palmer that he believed pop would usurp classical music and that The Beatles would stage an opera one day. Instead it was The Who. Lambert had dreamed of launching *Tommy* with performances at the world's most famous opera houses, starting with Moscow's Bolshoi Theatre. Unsurprisingly, the Soviet government was reluctant to sanction a visit from a decadent western rock group, even one that had written an opera. But Lambert was stung when Sir Rudolph Bing, director of the New York Metropolitan Opera House, turned him down as well. However, Kit wasn't so easily put off.

The English National Opera had recently moved from Sadler's Wells Theatre, where the teenage Chris Stamp had once talked his way into a job, to the London Coliseum in Covent Garden's St Martin's Lane. Lambert persuaded the management to let The Who play at the ENO's new home. On 14 December, The Who walked out onstage in the same venue that had recently hosted productions of Wagner's *Die Meistersinger von Nürnberg* and Mozart's *Don Giovanni*. Townshend bashfully told the 2,500-strong audience that it felt a bit odd being there, before finding his usual confidence, and announcing, 'Now we're going to take over!'

The London Coliseum was just the start. Lambert, with the help of Cambridge graduate Peter Rudge, had soon sweet-talked the managers of some of Europe and Scandinavia's greatest opera houses into letting The Who perform. Before long The Who were booked to play *Tommy* in the Théâtre des Champs Elysées in Paris, the Royal Danish Theatre in Copenhagen, the Stadt Opernhaus in Cologne, Hamburg and Berlin, and at Amsterdam's Concertgebouw throughout January 1970.

The Théâtre des Champs Elysées was the home of the Paris Opera and the venue in which Igor Stravinsky had first staged his controversial ballet *The Rite of Spring* on 29 May 1913. The audience were so shocked by its experimental rhythms and choreography that a riot broke out during which the orchestra was pelted with vegetables. There was something fitting then about The Who being the first pop group ever allowed to play there.

For Kit Lambert, it had all been leading up to this. 'Kit wanted to create change and revolution in the establishment,' said Chris Stamp. 'That's what we all wanted. So we came up with the idea of raiding the opera houses, the thrones of the bourgeoisie, with our people – the scruffy, long-haired fucks.'

For The Who, though, it was a bittersweet victory. Instead of their die-hard audience of 'scruffy, long-haired fucks', Townshend found himself peering at rows of record-company bigwigs, minor royals, bored classical music critics with their fingers in their ears and, in Cologne, the West German president Gustav Heinemann. Instead of beads, denim and a stoned grin, The Who's audience were now wearing bow ties, dinner jackets and a look of confusion, even hostility, at what they were hearing.

The Who took Lambert and Stamp's cultural revolution in their stride, but regarded it with both cautious pride and outright disdain. 'I see The Who as a sophisticated circus act,' offered Townshend. 'We take our failings very seriously and our successes ecstatically.' When challenged about the authenticity of their rock opera, Townshend made no attempt to justify it. 'I can remember playing it in Hamburg or somewhere like that that, and opera critics came backstage after and said, "Mr Townshend. This is a very impressive evening, but this isn't actually an opera is it?"' he recalled. 'And I'd say, "Yes it fucking is, mate" – or whatever rock stars were supposed to say in those days. And they'd say, "No, no, no, it's a *cantata*. More like a song-cycle . . . Do you mind if I say it is a rock cantata?" They missed the irony. That whatever we call it, it is. I'd say, "Rock cantata? It's a rock banana, mate, OK!"'

Having conquered Europe, Kit Lambert sent Peter Rudge to New York to talk to Sir Rudolph Bing again. His opinion of *Tommy* had softened since the previous summer. 'I didn't understand a thing about *Tommy* myself,' Bing said. 'But I didn't understand everything about *Don Giovanni* either.' He finally agreed to let The Who play.

On 7 June 1970, The Who became the first rock group to play the New York Metropolitan Opera House. They had always thrived on incongruity, and there was certainly something incongruous about the sight of Keith Moon's battered drum kit and the paraphernalia of a touring rock 'n' roll band alongside the regal gold and velvet furnishings of this prestigious theatre.

The clash of cultures was everywhere. Co-promoter Bill Graham had drafted in staff from the Fillmore East to help the venue's regular ushers with problems they wouldn't have experienced during the Met's recent staging of *Tosca*. By showtime, thick clouds of marijuana smoke had shrouded the ornate chandeliers, and Graham had already marched a ticketless fan out of the theatre and been denounced as a 'fucking capitalist' for his troubles.

In 1965, Kit Lambert instructed Pete Townshend never to walk on to the stage, only to run. Townshend was arguably the first musician to ever run on to the stage of the Metropolitan Opera House, and certainly the first to do so wearing a boiler suit. Townshend informed the audience that this would be the last time The Who performed *Tommy* in its entirety. It wouldn't be. But he wished it was.

The Who then blasted through their rock 'cantata' before reaching the emotionally charged finale of 'See Me, Feel Me'. The Met's shell-shocked ushers cowered from the noise, and 4,000 fans cheered through a fug of dope smoke. After the two-and-a-half-hour matinee show, The Who did it all over again in the evening. When the gold stage curtain came down after the second performance, the audience stood up and applauded for fifteen minutes. The Who didn't play encores but Bill Graham persuaded an exhausted Townshend to go back and talk to the crowd.

'I went to speak,' he said, 'and someone threw a can of Coke at me.' When Townshend explained that the show was over, some of the audience began booing. Townshend threw his microphone into the orchestra pit and stalked off. The Who could have been back at The Goldhawk or The Oldfield, squaring up to the truculent drunks slopping beer and itching for a fight. Everything – and nothing – had changed.

Keith Moon later described the performance as like 'playing to an oil painting'. For Roger Daltrey, it was just another gig: 'A hole with a stage. It had chandeliers, so what?' Meanwhile, Townshend railed against the Met and said that it was 'full of dead ideas, dead people and too much fucking reverence.' But even he was forced to admit that 'a snotty pop group playing opera houses' was something of a *coup d'état*.

Soon after, *Life* magazine declared that The Who's performance at the Met had 'installed rock as a maturely rounded art in the shrine of the great European classics . . . Best of all, it afforded The Who the opportunity to do brilliantly what no other rock group ever dreamed of doing.' The Who's rock opera, rock 'cantata', rock *banana*, even, had paid off. Pete Townshend and his 'bunch of scumbags' were being hailed as musical geniuses.

Kit Lambert had achieved what he'd set out to do ever since stumbling across the High Numbers at the Railway Hotel in summer 1964. In a little over five years, he and Chris Stamp had helped transform a jobbing pub band into a top-ten singles and albums act, and turned their art school student leader into a songwriter to rival Lennon and McCartney. Now, to top it all, they'd taken that group and its composer's angry commentary on sex, drugs and violence into the last remaining bastion of the classical music establishment.

'Can you imagine that?' says Tony Palmer. 'Kit Lambert, the son of Constant Lambert, the founder of the Royal Ballet, had presented an opera at the New York Metropolitan Opera House.' For the working-class would-be revolutionary Chris Stamp it was a kick in the balls to the bourgeoisie; for Kit Lambert, it was a vengeful act against the naysayers who'd hounded his father in the last months of his life.

Three weeks before their performance in New York, however, The Who had released the concert album, *Live at Leeds*. Whereas *Tommy* had arrived in a grandiose sleeve, this one came in a brown paper bag. The music on *Live at Leeds* included pumped-up versions of 'Summertime Blues' and 'Shakin' All Over', the same songs The Who used to pacify the Teds and rockers at the Royal Albert Hall. The energy they imbued in these songs and versions of their own hits was a stark reminder of their power as a live act. *Live at Leeds* cued up the next stage in The Who's career, one that would see them become one of the biggest rock 'n' roll bands in the world, capable of casting a spell over a stadium full of people.

For the three men who'd met as boys at school over ten years earlier, it would always be an uncomfortable alliance. What had started as Roger Daltrey's group had long since slipped out of his control. But by

1970, Daltrey recognised the importance of his role as a mouthpiece for Townshend's songs; as Townshend's voice even. After years of struggle, Daltrey ended the 1960s knowing who he was and where he fitted in.

Tommy, meanwhile, would mark the beginning of Pete Townshend's rapid ascendance as a pop songwriter. The insecure art student recruited to join an older, feared schoolboy's band had taken over. Townshend's ideas would become more ambitious and far-reaching as the 1970s progressed. But he would have to fight ever harder to get his bandmates and the managers who'd nurtured his talent to understand those ideas.

John Entwistle's role in The Who had been set in stone long before 1970. It never changed. Entwistle was the Who's engine room, its unsung hero and certainly its unsung songwriter. Beneath the stoic exterior, there was a frustrated rock star trying to get out. By the time The Who made *Tommy*, Entwistle had reconciled himself to his position, but that didn't stop him wanting more.

Despite the best efforts of his bandmates, his wife and his friends, Keith Moon's demise already seemed inevitable. The hopeless schoolboy with the uncanny powers of mimicry had become an idiot savant: a gifted drummer, an extraordinary comic and arguably the most famous member of The Who. But Moon had been acting for so long, he was now more confused than ever about who the real Keith Moon was.

And if 1970 was the beginning of a new chapter for The Who, then it marked the beginning of the end for Kit Lambert and Chris Stamp. Their time as The Who's mentors was drawing to a close, even if nobody involved yet knew it. Lambert once said, 'Just to succeed in life is banal to the point of failure. The purpose of success is to have something substantial to wreck, and the ultimate triumph is to create a magnificent disaster.'

The Who's raid on the world's opera houses would turn out to be their management's last great victory. 'I should have resigned then,' said Kit Lambert, after *Tommy*. 'I knew I couldn't do anything better than that.' The Who would go from strength to strength in the 1970s, but the two men who'd put them on course would end almost wrecking what they'd worked so hard to create. For Lambert and Stamp, the war was over. The challenge now was how to survive in peacetime.

AFTERWORD

The Questors Theatre in Ealing is a modest brick and glass affair tucked away behind the main shopping thoroughfare. It's a gentle stroll from what was once Ealing art school and the house in Sunnyside Road where Pete Townshend conducted his earliest drug experiments. The art school is now the University of West London, and the former student drug den an elegant town house with an immaculate front garden.

It is a crisp Sunday afternoon on 16 February 2014, and four hundred people have arrived to hear Pete Townshend discuss his life and career as part of the Ealing Music and Film Festival. The man tasked with interviewing Townshend is a familiar face, Tony Palmer, now an esteemed film director, but in the mid-1960s the *Observer*'s pop critic and a staunch advocate of The Who's music.

Townshend lopes onstage, wearing a smart suit and a hangdog expression. 'Ah, back on duty,' he says, with a Tony Hancock-style comedy sigh. Yet with very little direction from Palmer, Townshend spends the next sixty minutes talking about The Who and the men he describes as 'real stars in their own right', the now deceased Kit Lambert and Chris Stamp.

As the conversation wears on, Townshend makes self-deprecating asides and describes himself as 'a big-nosed bastard'. But he also silences the room with his admission that 'there are times when I wake up feeling incredibly depressed and want to commit suicide'. At one point he bellows the words 'fuck all of you!' so loudly that a theatre usher beside me gasps. Yet as Townshend explains afterwards: 'That explosion of swearing was to show you that I'm still as interesting as I was when I was younger.'

The past casts its spell over Townshend and The Who in 2014, just as it always did. In the 1960s they came of age, absorbing and expressing the restlessness of the time in a way that ultimately propelled them to the triumph of *Tommy*. The 1970s would present the band and their contemporaries with a new challenge: how to survive. On 10 April 1970, Paul McCartney announced that he was leaving The Beatles. By the end of the year the group had officially broken up. They had stopped touring four years earlier but had continued to set the agenda in the studio. For Townshend, their split was about more than just the music.

'The Beatles never said that they would promise anything,' Townshend explained. 'But we had expected them to come up with some answer that would have a political and social consequence for us all – and it didn't happen.' There was now a void to be filled: 'Suddenly, they broke up, and you were left with The Who, The Kinks, the Rolling Stones . . .'

In 1964, The Kinks had been the inspiration for The Who's emotionally charged debut single, 'I Can't Explain'. Later on, Townshend had praised 1968's *The Kinks Are the Village Green Preservation Society,* their songwriter Ray Davies' portrait of a lost England, telling journalists that Davies should be appointed the nation's poet laureate. The Kinks initially wowed America, but by the mid-1970s their fractious relationship with each other and Davies' growing discontents had slowed their progress.

In contrast, no amount of in-fighting, drug abuse and even death could derail the Rolling Stones. With Brian Jones' replacement, gifted guitarist Mick Taylor, in the fold, the Stones, like The Who, were soon reconfiguring themselves for the decade ahead. Unlike The Who, the Stones would never fully abandon the rhythm and blues that had served them so well in the 1960s. The music remained the same. It was just that the amps, the lights, the stage and Mick Jagger's persona became bigger.

Indeed, size was to be one of the dominant themes of the new decade: bigger concepts, bigger shows, bigger venues and, inevitably, bigger money. In the studio, the dramatic approach The Who first used on *Tommy* would become the model for 1970s anthems such as 'Won't Get Fooled Again' and 'Baba O'Riley'. These were big songs for the big audiences The Who routinely played to from 1971 onwards. Yet their inspiration came from the 1960s and even earlier.

'Won't Get Fooled Again' was the sound of Townshend, the 1970s rock star, railing at his peer group's failure to right the social and political wrongs committed by the previous generation. 'Baba O'Riley' addressed the unease he'd felt about the drugs and self-destruction of the 1960s; the 'teenage wasteland' he'd witnessed at Woodstock.

There were echoes of Roy Ascott's revolutionary groundcourse, Bertrand Russell's impassioned speech at the Aldermaston march, and Meher Baba's philosophy in these songs. Townshend worked strenuously to convey his message. But onstage, simply raising his right arm and bringing it down on to his guitar, like a windmill's sail, was invariably enough to win over a stadium. Inevitably, in all that excitement, the message was forgotten. 'One windmill and I've got a thousand people in my pocket,' he admitted.

Three years after *Tommy*, the Who released *Quadrophenia*, an even more ambitious work that told the semi-autobiographical tale of a mod's coming of age in the early 1960s. It addressed Townshend's obsession with post-war English youth culture more explicitly than anything The Who had done before. But in 1972 *Quadrophenia* was already a work of history. For The Who what was once an audience of a hundred mods at the Railway Hotel in 1964 had become thousands at Charlton Athletic football stadium by 1974, all waiting for Townshend to smash his guitar. However hard The Who worked to bridge the gap between them and their followers, the intimate connection Townshend had with his audience in the 1960s, became much harder to sustain.

At the Questors Theatre in 2014, Townshend discussed The Who's plans for a tour to mark their fiftieth anniversary. It would be their last he insisted. The Who had said that before, in 1982, when the remaining band members were in their thirties; Townshend will turn seventy in 2015 and Daltrey seventy-one.

Their bandmates and mentors hadn't survived the journey with them. Keith Moon died on 7 September 1978, his body having buckled under the drugs and alcohol he'd been pouring into it since the early sixties. In the end, it was an overdose of clomethiazole, a sedative prescribed to alleviate the symptoms of alcohol withdrawal, that killed him. Even in death, Moon maintained a complex relationship with the truth. A clerical error on his death certificate gave his birth year as 1945. Moon was born in 1946, but had spent his adult life telling his bandmates and interviewers he was a year younger. By the end, nobody was quite sure what to believe.

Moon's early demise meant that he would remain forever frozen in time: the permanently grinning, gurning man-child flailing away at the drums on *Ready Steady Go!*. His name remains a byword for rock 'n' roll excess, but for Roger Daltrey the public image of 'Moon the Loon' is misleading: 'Keith was a Shakespearean character, a troubled man,' he said. 'He was a genius on the drums, but the other side of his character was incredibly destructive.'

Moon's closest friend in the band, John Entwistle, would remain with The Who until his own death. He was there when they hastily reconvened with Moon's replacement, former Small Faces drummer Kenney Jones, just seven months after Moon's death, and he was there again each time they reunited in the 1980s and 1990s. Despite his indomitable public persona, at the time of his death Entwistle was battling alcohol and cocaine addictions, and living beyond his means.

Home for The Who's bass player was a seventeen-bedroom mansion in the Cotswolds, which he shared with an extensive collection of medieval suits of armour and stuffed fish. 'I have to keep working with The Who if I want to maintain my ridiculous lifestyle,' he admitted. In his final years, he was forced to sell off his guitars to make money whenever The Who weren't working.

After an evening spent drinking and taking cocaine, Entwistle passed away on 27 June 2002, in a Las Vegas hotel suite. The groupie he had gone to bed with woke up to find him dead. Entwistle was about to start another Who tour, which had been organised to help him pay off his considerable debts. 'John had a wonderful wit and a very dark sense of humour, and I miss him,' said Daltrey in 2014. 'But he had his insecurities, partly because he was always overshadowed by Pete and I. He died a very rock 'n' roll death.'

Shortly before The Who's victorious raid on the world's opera houses in 1970, Kit Lambert began adding heroin to his daily drug cocktail. With the onset of addiction, his control of The Who and Track Records started slipping away. By the early 1970s, Chris Stamp had also lost himself in what he later called 'the neurotic drug culture' of the era.

Before long, even Townshend could no longer ignore the financial chaos that surrounded The Who, and was forced to turn his back on the men who'd helped make him one of the world's most famous songwriters. In 1971, Stamp's childhood friend Bill Curbishley took a job at Track Records. Curbishley entered the organisation with the clearest of heads while everyone else appeared to be losing theirs. 'Kit and Chris were totally out to lunch, and Bill was very much at lunch,' points out John Fenton. 'I could see that Bill was a man with a mission.' Five years after Curbishley's arrival at Track, he was officially appointed The Who's manager; a position he continues to hold today.

In the end, Kit Lambert lived up to his assertion that the ultimate triumph in life was to create what he called 'a magnificent disaster'. Track Records had become that disaster, and the once-magnificent label closed down, leaving behind a murky trail of debts and missing royalties that some of their former artists would still be chasing in the twenty-first century.

Chris Stamp's story would have a happier ending. Stamp entered a drug rehabilitation programme in the 1980s, and he later became an addiction counsellor and therapist, specialising in psychodrama therapy, where clients work through their problems through role-play and by recreating real-life situations. Stamp described his experience of working with The Who as 'an apprenticeship' for his later career. By the mid-1990s, he'd made his peace with the band and was, said, Townshend, 'handsome and white-haired, looking like a god and behaving like one.' Stamp died of cancer on 24 November 2012.

Lambert was less fortunate. Like Stamp, he never discovered another group to match The Who, and his wilful spending and drug addiction took its toll on his career and personal life. In 1976, he was made a ward of court to head off bankruptcy proceedings. That said, his closest friends maintain that however desperate Lambert became, he never completely lost the wit and spark that had once made him such an irresistible force. 'He was the most extraordinary, clever, amusing and knowledgeable person I'd ever met,' says Simon Napier-Bell.

Shortly before he died, Lambert hatched a plan to stage a new production of his father's most famous ballet, *The Rio Grande*. Meetings were held with the ballet's original choreographer Sir Frederick Ashton, but the project never came to fruition. It was another reminder of how much Kit's career had been driven by his desire to prove something to the man he'd never really known. 'He had this terrible wound he was carrying,' said Townshend, 'which I think was to do with the fact that he never managed to have a proper relationship with his father.'

Lambert died on 7 April 1981. He'd been beaten up two days earlier, supposedly over a drug debt, in the toilets of a gay nightclub in Earls Court. He made his way to his mother's house in nearby Fulham, where he drank too much brandy and later fell down the stairs. Kit was taken to hospital, diagnosed with a cerebral haemorrhage and never regained consciousness. He was forty-five years old, the same age at which his father had died.

A memorial service was held at St Paul's in Covent Garden, the church in which Constant's memorial had taken place. An orchestral group played music by Kit's father and Henry Purcell alongside extracts from The Who's *Tommy*. After the service, a few of the guests repaired to a studio in the West End to snort cocaine and toast Kit's memory. The sharp contrast between the ceremony and the wake seemed to encapsulate Lambert's conflicted life and character.

Lambert and Stamp had been brilliant managers in the 1960s, but their imagination and bravado wasn't enough to sustain them in the 1970s. Their great success story was The Who. But The Who outgrew them, just as the Stones outgrew Andrew Loog Oldham and The Beatles would almost have certainly outgrown Brian Epstein, had it not been for his premature death.

As the music industry grew to accommodate the new generation of 1970s supergroups so too did the role of accountants and lawyers. Someone now needed to collect the money and balance the books. The pioneers were left behind. Lambert and Stamp made bad deals and terrible mistakes, but without them The Who might never have made it out of the pubs and clubs of Shepherd's Bush. Their frontier spirit paved the way for the bureaucrats of the years that followed.

In the middle of the decade, during the dying days of Track Records, Malcolm McLaren, the former Harrow art student who'd watched The Who at the Railway Hotel, walked into Track's Old Compton Street

HQ and asked to see Chris Stamp. McLaren told him that he wanted to form a band that would be bigger than The Beatles. What the Sex Pistols' Svengali needed to know was how Stamp had first discovered The Who and made them what they were. Years later, Stamp shared the story with Townshend.

'Chris told Malcolm McLaren, "We went to a club and found the four ugliest guys we could find. They were idiots and they couldn't play. But we added our panache, gave them a decent name and dressed them up,"' recalled Townshend. 'And as soon as McLaren heard that he went, "Gotcha!"'

Soon after, McLaren had assembled his own 'four ugly guys' and had them playing 'Substitute'. The Who's 1960s legacy inspired the Sex Pistols and other punk rock groups, helping initiate a sweeping musical trend that threatened to render the 1960s vanguard obsolete, just as The Who had done to the first generation of British rock 'n' rollers twenty years earlier.

However, The Who's influence and legacy has withstood punk and any number of musical trends since. In 2014 the world is still partly populated by young men with guitars and an attitude, just as it was in 1964. Moreover, the musical and cultural distance between the two eras is far less than the distance between The Who and the post-war world of their youth.

In August 2012 The Who performed at the closing ceremony of the Olympic Games in London. 'At one point neither of us wanted to do it,' admitted Townshend. 'But the Olympics turned out to be a wonderful, poetic event.' On the night, Daltrey wore a jacket festooned with military insignia; similar to the one Townshend had sported in 1966. The Who's short set culminated with their once insurrectionary anthem 'My Generation', accompanied by a Union flag fluttering on a video screen behind them, and exploding fireworks where once there would have been exploding Marshall amps.

Like film director Danny Boyle's spectacular opening ceremony a fortnight earlier, it said much about Britain's cultural identity in the modern age. In the opening ceremony, the journey from the smouldering chimneys of the nineteenth century's industrial revolution to The Beatles on the cover of 1967's *Sgt. Pepper* seemed to pass in the blink of an eye. The Second World War that had so shaped The Beatles, The

Who and their contemporaries, had once been the starting point of modern history. Now it was as if the 1960s and The Who, a band whose very purpose had been to challenge the old order, had taken its place.

As the Olympics reiterated, two out of four of The Who never completely fulfilled their early promise to die before they got old. Moreover, these survivors grew old in public, where their mistakes, egotism and petty squabbles have been magnified and endlessly picked over.

Talking at the Questors Theatre, Townshend confessed to being 'in total shock' that he was still in a group with the boy who on their first meeting had 'wanted to knock my teeth out'. For Daltrey there is something indefinable about their relationship. 'I don't know what it is, but it works,' he once told the author. 'It doesn't matter what Pete says about me or I say about him. The truth is, we create together.'

Yet as Roger Daltrey and Pete Townshend, The Who's last men standing, undertake what might well be their victory lap, their extraordinary achievements are thrown into even sharper relief. The trail The Who blazed in the 1960s has lost none of its lustre. The music they made and the anxieties they addressed are still as pertinent today as they were then. The battles they fought and the music that came out of those battles suggest that, deep down, there will always be a part of The Who that needs to pretend they're in a war.

ACKNOWLEDGEMENTS

Pretend You're in a War would not have been possible without the help of friends and colleagues including my agent Rupert Heath, Phil Alexander, Johnny Black, Dave Brolan, Chris Catchpole, Niall Doherty, Danny Eccleston, Dave Everley, Pat Gilbert, Jo Kendall, Ted Kessler, Pete Makowski, Toby Manning, Matt Mason, Julian Stockton and Paul Trynka. Thanks to all at Aurum Press: Graham Coster for believing in the project from the start; my editor Sam Harrison for his patience, advice and invaluable support; Charlotte Coulthard for picture research, Emily Kearns for copy editing; Lucy Warburton for ushering the book to the finishing line; and Tony Lyons for his handsome jacket design.

This book draws on my own interviews with Chris Stamp, Roger Daltrey, John Entwistle and Pete Townshend conducted for *Q* and *Mojo* magazines between September 1997 and January 2014. Plus new interviews with and contributions from: Brian Adams, Mohammed Abdullah John Alder, Keith Altham, Peter K. Amott, Vic Arnold, Fery Asgari, Noel Baker, Richard Barnes, John Bonehill, Reg Bowen, Vernon Brewer, Tony Brind, Angela Brown, Arthur Brown, Geoff Brown, Richard Burdett, Peter 'Dougal' Butler, Brian Carroll, John Challis, Neville Chesters, June Clark, Richard Cole, Gabby Connolly, Tony Crane, Tony Dangerfield, Christine Day, Jeff Dexter, Chris Downing, Barry Fantoni, Robert Fearnley-Whittingstall, John Fenton, John Field (RIP), Chris Glass, Dave Golding, Dr John Hemming, Chris Huston, Colin Jones, Max Ker-Seymer, Dave Lambert, Roger Law, Harvey Lisberg, 'Irish' Jack Lyons, Terry Marshall, Mike McAvoy, Mike McInnerney,

David Montgomery, Chris Morphet, Simon Napier-Bell, Andy Newman, Andrew Loog Oldham, Tony Palmer, Alan Pittaway, Richard Newton Price, Mike Ross-Trevor, Doug Sandom, John Schollar, Matthew Scurfield, Chris Sherwin, Brian Southall, Roger Ruskin Spear, Richard Stanley, Ray Stock, Cleo Sylvestre, Shel Talmy, Storm Thorgerson (RIP), Philip Townsend, Fred Vermorel, Michael Weighell, Michael Wheeler and John 'Wiggy' Wolff. Thanks to everyone who took the time to talk to me.

Plus interviews and articles in the following publications: *Beat Instrumental*, *Boyfriend*, *Daily Express*, *Daily Mirror*, the *Economist*, *Fabulous*, the *Guardian*, *Goldmine*, *Guitar World*, the *Independent*, *International Times*, *Melody Maker*, *Mojo*, *New Musical Express*, the *New York Times*, the *Observer*, *Q*, *Rave*, *Record Collector*, *Rolling Stone*, *Sound International*, *Sounds*, the *Sun*, the *Sunday Times*, *The Times, Uncut*, *Zigzag* and the definitive Who fanzine *Naked Eye*. Special thanks also to Barry Ratcliffe, Ian Grant, Carrie Pratt at pete-townshend.net, and to Pat Gilbert, scriptwriter of the forthcoming biopic about the life and times of Kit Lambert, at patgilbert.co.uk

Any book about The Who written in the twenty-first century owes a special debt to these four impeccably researched titles from the days before the internet and mobile phones made private detective work much easier: Richard Barnes' *The Who: Maximum R&B*; Tony Fletcher's *Dear Boy: The Life of Keith Moon*; Dave Marsh's *Before I Get Old: The Story of The Who*, and Andy Neill and Matt Kent's *Anyway, Anyhow, Anywhere*.

Finally, many thanks to my wife Claire and my son Matthew for putting up with this book — and me.

BIBLIOGRAPHY

Richard Barnes, *Mods!*, Plexus, 1979

Richard Barnes & Pete Townshend, *The Story of Tommy*, Eel Pie, 1977

Richard Barnes, *The Who: Maximum R&B*, Eel Pie/Plexus, 1982

Johnny Black, *Eyewitness: The Who*, Carlton, 2001

Craig Bromberg, *The Wicked Ways of Malcolm McLaren*, Harper & Row, 1989

Dougal Butler, *Full Moon: The Amazing Rock and Roll Life of Keith Moon*, Faber & Faber, 1981

Chris Charlesworth, *The Complete Guide to the Music of The Who*, Omnibus, 1995

Chris Charlesworth, *The Who: The Illustrated Biography*, Omnibus, 1982

Nik Cohn, *Arfur: Teenage Pinball Queen*, Simon & Schuster, 1970

Nik Cohn, *Awopbopaloobop Alopbamboom: Pop From the Beginning*, Random House, 1969

Richard Davenport-Hines, *An English Affair: Sex, Class and Power in the Age of Profumo*, Harper Press, 2013

Tom Driberg, *Ruling Passions*, Jonathan Cape, 1977

Tony Fletcher, *Dear Boy: The Life of Keith Moon*, Omnibus, 1998

Simon Frith & Howard Horne, *Art into Pop*, Methuen, 1987

Jonathan Green, *Days in the Life: Voices from the English Underground 1961–71*, Pimlico, 1988

Ross Halfin, *Maximum Who: The Who in the Sixties*, Genesis Publications, 2003

John Hemming, *Die if You Must: Brazilian Indians in the Twentieth Century*, Macmillan, 2003

Rob Jovanovic, *God Save The Kinks: A Biography*, Aurum Press, 2013

Constant Lambert, *Music Ho! A Study of Music in Decline*, Faber & Faber, 1934

Bernard Levin, *The Pendulum Years: Britain in the Sixties*, Jonathan Cape, 1970

Dave Marsh, *Before I Get Old: The Story of The Who*, Plexus, 1983

Polly Marshall, *The God of Hellfire: The Crazy Life and Times of Arthur Brown*, SAF Publishing, 2005

John McDermott & Eddie Kramer, *Hendrix: Setting the Record Straight*, Time Warner, 1992

Joe McMichael & 'Irish Jack' Lyons, *The Who Concert File*, Omnibus, 1995

George Melly, *Revolt Into Style: The Pop Arts*, Oxford University Press, 1970

David Mercer, *The Generations*, Calder, 1964

Barry Miles, *London Calling: A Countercultural History of London Since 1945*, Atlantic, 2011

Andrew Motion, *The Lamberts*, Hogarth Press, 1987

Simon Napier-Bell, *Black Vinyl White Powder*, Ebury Press, 2001

Simon Napier-Bell, *You Don't Have to Say You Love Me*, Ebury Press, 1983

Philip Norman, *Mick Jagger*, HarperCollins, 2013

Jeff Nuttall, *Bomb Culture*, MacGibbon & Kee, 1968

Andrew Loog Oldham, *Stoned*, Vintage, 2001

Andrew Loog Oldham, *2Stoned*, Vintage, 2003

Andrew Loog Oldham, *Stone Free*, Because Entertainment, 2013

Andy Neill & Matt Kent, *Anyway, Anyhow, Anywhere: The Complete Chronicle of The Who 1958–1978*, Virgin, 2002

Tony Palmer, *All You Need is Love: The Story of Popular Music*, Futura, 1977

Tony Palmer & Ralph Steadman, *Born Under a Bad Sign*, William Kimber, 1970

John Perry, *The Who: Meaty, Beaty, Big and Bouncy*, Schirmer Books, 1998

C.B. Purdom, *The God-Man*, Crescent Beach, 1969

Keith Richards, *Life*, Phoenix, 2011

Andy Roberts, *Albion Dreaming: A Popular History of LSD in Britain*, Marshall Cavendish, 2008

Johnny Rogan, *Starmakers and Svengalis: The History of British Pop Management*, Futura Publications, 1989

David Roper, *Bart!*, Pavilion, 1994

Dominic Sandbrook, *Never Had It So Good: A History of Britain from Suez to The Beatles*, Abacus, 2010

Dominic Sandbrook, *White Heat: A History of Britain in the Swinging Sixties*, Abacus, 2009

Doug Sandom, *The Who Before The Who*, Christopher Hutchins, 2014

Jon Savage, *England's Dreaming: Sex Pistols and Punk Rock*, Faber & Faber, 1991

Mim Scala, *Diary of a Teddy Boy*, The Lilliput Press, 2000

Matthew Scurfield, *I Could Be Anyone*, Monticello, 2014

Terence Stamp, *Coming Attractions*, Grafton, 1988

Terence Stamp, *Double Feature*, Grafton, 1990

Terence Stamp, *Stamp Album*, Grafton, 1988

Pete Townshend, *Horse's Neck*, HarperCollins, 1985

Pete Townshend, *Who I Am*, HarperCollins, 2012

George Tremlett, *The Who*, Futura, 1975

Richie Unterberger, *Won't Get Fooled Again: The Who from Lifehouse to Quadrophenia*, Jawbone, 2011

Harriet Vyner, *Groovy Bob: The Life and Times of Robert Fraser*, Faber & Faber, 2001

Richard Weight, *Mod! A Very British Style*, Bodley Head, 2013

Richard Weight, *Patriots: National Identity In Britain 1940–2000*, Macmillan, 2002

Simon Wells, *Butterfly on a Wheel*, Omnibus, 2011

Francis Wheen, *Tom Driberg: His Life and Indiscretions*, Chatto & Windus, 1990

Mark Wilkerson, *Who Are You: The Life of Pete Townshend*, Omnibus, 2009

Tom Wright, *Raising Hell on the Rock 'n' Roll Highway*, Omnibus, 2009

RECOMMENDED WEBSITES

thewho.com

teenagecancertrust.org

petetownshend.co.uk

petetownshend.net

eelpie.com

thewho.net

rocksbackpages.com

markrblake.com

INDEX